✔ KU-170-282

BOMBS, BULLETS AND THE BORDER

WEXFORD
COUNTY
LIBRARY

Patrick Mulroe is a teacher in Monaghan with a PhD in Politics; living and working in the border area, he has an extensive knowledge of all aspects of border life.

'This is the most important study of how the conflict in the North impacted on the security of the southern Border counties. By trawling state archives, local newspapers and contemporary accounts, Mulroe has skilfully brought to life a period many would like to forget.'
Dr Brian Hanley, historian, lecturer and writer

'The role of the Irish state has become an issue of prime importance in current debates over the legacy of the Troubles. Patrick Mulroe provides us with a detailed, comprehensive and forensic analysis of the challenge posed by republican and loyalist terrorists to successive Irish governments during the worst years of the Troubles. He reveals the dilemma faced by successive Irish governments of responding to a direct challenge by the Provisional IRA without leaving themselves open to charges of "collaboration" with the British. This critical but sympathetic account will be indispensable for an understanding of the evolution of the IRA's "long war" and the spiky history of Anglo-Irish relations in this crucial period.'
Professor Henry Patterson, Emeritus Professor of Politics, University of Ulster, Jordanstown

'Patrick Mulroe's book shines a penetrating light on the under-studied role of the Irish government's security policy during the early years of the Troubles. This volume uncovers and illuminates the complexities that the Irish Republic faced in its vexed border relationship with Northern Ireland and the rest of the United Kingdom. The results might surprise even seasoned analysts of contemporary Irish history, revealing that even during the worst of times in the Northern crisis there was often, in fact, far more empathy and understanding of the mutual security dilemmas each state faced than hitherto might have been presupposed.'
M.L.R. Smith, Department of War Studies, King's College, University London

'This important book, based on extensive archival research in both London and Dublin, examines the contentious subject of security relations between the British and Irish governments in the first decade of the recent Troubles. Its great strength is the author's forensic examination of the delicate political line which Irish governments had to tread between popular nationalist sentiment and their responsibility to negate threats to the Republic's stability. Not only does Mulroe make an original contribution to our knowledge of the history and politics of this period, he also adds to our understanding of contemporary problems of border security.'
Professor Cathy Gormley-Heenan, Pro-Vice-Chancellor, Research & Impact, University of Ulster

BOMBS, BULLETS AND THE BORDER

Policing Ireland's Frontier:
Irish Security Policy, 1969–1978

PATRICK MULROE

IRISH ACADEMIC PRESS

WEXFORD
COUNTY
LIBRARY

First published in 2017 by
Irish Academic Press
10 George's Street
Newbridge
Co. Kildare
Ireland
www.iap.ie

© 2017, Patrick Mulroe

978-1-911024-49-1 (Paper)
978-1-911024-50-7 (Cloth)
978-1-911024-51-4 (Kindle)
978-1-911024-52-1 (Epub)
978-1-911024-61-3 (PDF)

British Library Cataloguing in Publication Data
An entry can be found on request

Library of Congress Cataloging in Publication Data
An entry can be found on request

All rights reserved. Without limiting the rights under copyright reserved
alone, no part of this publication may be reproduced, stored in or
introduced into a retrieval system, or transmitted, in any form or by any
means (electronic, mechanical, photocopying, recording or otherwise)
without the prior written permission of both the copyright owner and the
above publisher of this book.

Interior design by www.jminfotechindia.com
Typeset in ITC New Baskerville 11/14 pt
Cover/jacket design by edit+ www.stuartcoughlan.com
Front cover/jacket: © Photo by Derek Speirs.
Back cover/jacket: Courtesy of *An Phoblacht*.

Printed in Ireland by SPRINT-print Ltd

Contents

Acknowledgements

This book examines a deeply troubled time in Irish history. There have been excellent works written on the impact of the Troubles on the northern border counties but the focus of this work is on the southern border counties, and while events that take place in Northern Ireland are covered, these are not the primary focus.

I owe a sincere debt of gratitude to my supervisors Professors Henry Patterson, Arthur Aughey and Cillian McGrattan and my examiners Professor Cathy Gormley-Heenan and Professor Michael Rainsboroug. The support I was given at University of Ulster was second to none. Proofreaders Petrina Mulroe, Michelle Dowling, Michael Treanor and Sinead McDermott provided feedback at crucial times. Two fellow teachers, Finbarr Brohan and Joe Hanratty, did Trojan work further tidying up the text and are among the many outstanding colleagues at Our Lady's Secondary School who continually encouraged me to complete my studies. I also received invaluable feedback from Dr Brian Hanley. At Irish Academic Press, Conor Graham and Fiona Dunne have both been a pleasure to work with. Mark Dawson in *An Phoblacht* and Derek Speirs did great work helping me source pictures and the staff the Military Archives and the National Photographic Archive were extremely helpful.

I am particularly grateful to those who supported me on a personal level: my sisters Eibhlin, Teresa, Petrina and Jacinta; brother-in-law, Mark; and parents provided great support. Sincere thanks are also due to Margaret Gillespie, Fiona McManus, Niall Treanor, Barry McDonald, Darren McArdle and Niall McCarville. Other friends also helped at key times: Tom and Margaret Treanor, John Coggins, Colin Colleran, Marco Conte, Brian O'Neill, Gerard McArdle, Damian Lawlor, Micky Morgan, Mick Pierse, Declan McKenna, Mark Daffy, Fra Agnew, Patricia McDermott, and Paul and Aidan McDonald.

Finally, I would like to thank my students, who have been a constant source of inspiration. I like to think I have helped some of them through the years but they have given me much more: their friendship, good humour and respect speak volumes for them as individuals, their families and the wider community in Castleblayney, Co. Monaghan.

'The mystique of the unified nation-state': Introduction

Looking at newspaper coverage of the Troubles over a few random days in June 1974 is illuminating. *The Irish Times* reported on 26 June that British soldier Eugene Patton had managed to escape from his IRA kidnappers and was back at home with his family in St Johnson, Co. Donegal.[1] Patton was from south of the border but a member of the British Army. The same day the paper also reported that Dr Rose Dugdale had been sentenced to nine years in jail by the Special Criminal Court for her role in a republican robbery. Dugdale was described as the daughter of a millionaire head of an insurance syndicate in London who grew up on a 500-acre farm in Devon.[2]

The previous day, the *Irish Press* reported that two young IRA men had been killed when their own device exploded prematurely in Derry. One of the dead men was David Russell.[3] Unusually, Russell was a Protestant. The same issue of the *Irish Press* carried an account of how an IRA 'bomb expert' defused a loyalist bomb in Clones, Co. Monaghan.[4] It has been speculated that the bomb and subsequent 'bomb expert' appearance may have been an elaborate publicity stunt by the IRA in the town.[5] These news stories were not untypical of the times and they illustrate a range of points about the Irish border in the 1970s. Firstly, and quite obviously, it could be dangerous. Secondly, the situation was complex and simplistic assumptions about individuals and events should be avoided. Finally, the full truth of certain events may never be known.

The Northern Ireland conflict has received extensive academic and journalistic coverage dealing with almost every aspect of the situation, and the increased availability of archive material and first-hand accounts of combatants has added to this trend. One aspect of the conflict that has received little attention is the role played by southern security forces. Obviously, the Garda and Irish Army's response was not as high profile as that of the British Army and RUC, as the overwhelming majority of casualties took place on the northern side of the border. Nevertheless, there was constant discourse throughout the Troubles on the extent to which violent incidents emanated south of the border. In some respects, the security response of the Irish state is more interesting than that of the UK government: although there was a low-intensity war raging over the border, the Irish Republic was remarkably stable. This book explores the Irish state's security services' response to the violence that erupted in border areas. Others, notably Henry Patterson in *Ireland's Violent Frontier: The Border and Anglo-Irish Relations During the Troubles*,[6] have looked at the impact of violence on the Northern side of the border. This work aims to see how the southern state dealt with the threats, real and perceived, that it faced.

The official British Army report on the conflict, *Operation Banner*, noted that in the early years of the Troubles 'it was widely believed in the North that the Garda colluded or at least turned a blind eye; as long as IRA men did not break the law in the Republic'.[7] Indeed, related sentiments were made public in 1978. A UK Ministry of Defence document, *Northern Ireland: Future Terrorist Trends*, was found and leaked by the IRA, causing embarrassment for the British government. Among the points made in this document were: 'Republican sentiment and the IRA tradition emanate from the South'; 'the Gardaí, although cooperating with the RUC more than in the past, is still rather less than wholehearted in its pursuit of terrorists'; and 'the Republic provides many of the facilities of the classic safe haven so essential to any successful terrorist movement'.[8]

More general media reports painted a similar picture. The *Belfast Newsletter* carried a front-page article on 11 March 1978 headlined 'Dundalk is Murder HQ':

The current wave of Provisional IRA murder attacks on soldiers and police on patrol in Belfast is being masterminded from Dundalk ... Neighbouring towns like Castleblayney and Monaghan are also known to house wanted Provisionals – men whom the RUC are anxious to interview in connection with murders and explosions in the North.[9]

The Irish government strongly suspected that this and other similar reports were heavily influenced by off-the-record British Army security briefings to journalists, but to apportion the bulk of the blame for border violence to lax security on the Irish side is too simplistic an analysis, as we will see.

Significant security operations against the IRA took place throughout the Republic during the period under consideration. Often, the impetus for the more vigorous actions was a violent incident in the South rather than across the border. There was a period when some Gardaí may have 'turned a blind eye' to republican activities, but the phase during which the Irish authorities generally took an ambiguous approach to republicans was quite short. In fact, there was a significant level of antagonism between Gardaí and republicans from quite early on. The emphasis of Irish security policy was maintenance of domestic security, which required subtlety in dealings with republicans. To be seen to act at the behest of the British government could threaten internal security and in co-operating with counterparts over the border, the emphasis was on discretion. From 1972 until 1978, both Fianna Fáil- and Fine Gael-led governments emphasised the need for close but discreet security co-operation.

Other authors identified a similar emphasis on discreet security co-operation during the Second World War. A British official in the Foreign and Commonwealth Office in 1973 noted that 'Their [Irish] troops will sweep areas if we ask them to, but some at least prefer this to appear to be coincidental, and do not wish to be thanked in public. Good is thus done by stealth.'[10]

The 'discreet' aspect of security co-operation remains one of the unknown aspects of security policy. A Northern Ireland Office briefing in 1980 noted:

Cross border security cooperation has improved since Charles Haughey became Taoiseach on December 11, 1979. It is difficult to persuade the public of this without simultaneously publishing the methods of cooperation about which not only the Irish government but also the police forces remain understandably sensitive – and, by doing so, jeopardising the very process which we all want to see develop and flourish.[11]

While noting that cross-border co-operation did occur, it has also been found that considerable antagonism existed between the respective security forces on either side of the border. Suspicion of republican infiltration of the Garda and Army caused some disquiet on the British side. Meanwhile, allegations of collusion, illegal incursions and covert security operations heightened southern distrust of the British security services. Gardaí investigating loyalist attacks relied on RUC goodwill but this did not occur in some instances.

Material for the study has been gathered from a number of archival sources. Local newspapers have been reviewed to gather detailed accounts of day-to-day activities on the border. *The Irish Times* and periodicals such as *Magill* and *Hibernia* were examined to get a national perspective. To gain the views of the contending parties, the magazines of the Gardaí – *The Garda Review* and *Garda News* – were studied, as well as republican publications such as *An Phoblacht* and *The United Irishman*.

The most useful source has been official state archives in Dublin and London. Archival research gives a unique insight into what motivates states to behave in certain ways and the internal discussions taking place within parts of the state apparatus. For instance, access to the archives of former Eastern Bloc countries has enabled International Relations theorists to reconsider the motivations of the USSR at certain key junctures during the Cold War. New evidence from the archives in Moscow, for example, indicates that the Soviet crushing of Czechoslovakia in 1968 was not so much the behaviour of a ruthless superpower as the reaction of a nervous power fearing a loss of control in eastern and central Europe and pressurised into action.[12]

Much of the material quoted from the Irish and UK archives has not previously been referenced. It must be noted, however, that the archive material included is an incomplete record. Much of the bureaucratic material associated with the Troubles remains redacted or withheld.

Although the National Archives and Military Archives in Dublin contain useful information, the National Archive in London has more detail. One caveat to this latter point is that there are still significant files in the UK archive that are restricted. Freedom of Information requests were made for such files but they were denied. Therefore, while the archive material cited is useful, it is not the full picture from the respective bureaucracies and there may be an inadvertent reliance on the UK archive in places as it is the more comprehensive and user-friendly.

At this point it is worth making some brief comments on the concept of security itself. Most commentators agree that security is a 'contested concept'.[13] Several theses could be completed discussing the term 'security' conceptually. It is not the purpose here to digress significantly into this area. Rather it is intended to build an argument based on the theoretical ideas of security associated with Barry Buzan and others in what has become known as the 'Copenhagen School'.[14] Another recent political-science work on the subject, Michael Mulqueen's *Re-evaluating Irish National Security: Affordable Threats*,[15] adopted a similar approach. Buzan identifies three component parts to the state: its physical base, its institutional expression and the idea that establishes the legitimacy of the state in the eyes of its people.[16] It is argued that the 'idea of the state' is the most abstract component of the model but also the most central. Buzan argues that a state can be 'strong' or 'weak', not just in military terms but in terms of internal socio-political cohesion related to this 'idea'. A state can be as much threatened by the manipulation of ideas as by military powers.[17]

The IRA was as much a threat to the southern government on this level as it was militarily. Partition left the Dublin government especially vulnerable. Buzan categories some states as 'part nation states' whereby a nation is divided up among two or more states. For such states, he argues,

> The mystique of the unified nation-state frequently exercises a strong hold on part nation-states, and can easily become obsessive and overriding security issue. Rival part nation states like East and West Germany, and North and South Korea almost automatically undermine each other's legitimacy and the imperative for unification is widely assumed to be an immutable factor that will re-emerge whenever opportunity beckons ... Part nation states, then, can represent a severe source of insecurity both to themselves and to others. Their case offers the maximum level of contradiction in the idea of national security as applied to states, for it is precisely the nation that makes the idea of the state insecure.[18]

The Irish state was the classic 'part nation state' with the 'idea' of national unity central to official thinking – this was even stated explicitly in the constitution. There remained a danger for those in power in Dublin that republicans could emerge to challenge the state's record in this area, which created significant internal weakness.

Individual political decision-makers and security personnel genuinely feared that the institutions of state could be over-run if violence spread south. At times, there was an exaggerated perception of the internal threat. Such an obsession with internal threats is not unique. It is a characteristic of weak states generally:

> Whatever the reasons for the existence of weak states, their principal distinguishing feature is their high level of concern with domestically generated threats to the security of the government; in other words, weak states either do not have, or failed to create, a domestic political and societal consensus of sufficient strength to eliminate the large-scale use of force as a major and continuing element in the domestic political life of the nation. This indicator connects back to the internal security dimension of the relationship between the state and its citizens.[19]

Regardless of which Irish political party was in power in the 1970s, it will be shown that there was a primary emphasis on the domestic security threat. Of course, the issues that the Fine Gael–Labour coalition saw as security matters were not necessarily the same as those identified by Fianna Fáil. Therefore, for the coalition government, relatively minor issues, such as graffiti and parades, became a 'security' matter, whereas Fianna Fáil in office did not place the same emphasis on these matters. On the broader point of how to deal with the security threat, both parties had a remarkably similar approach. The binding 'idea' of the state had to be seen to be maintained while at the same time the domestic security threat had to be curtailed. Put simply, the IRA had to be defeated while the nationalist image of the state had to be maintained. Of course, there were occasions when these two aims conflicted. To avoid such divergence, successive Irish governments emphasised the necessity of discreet cross-border security co-operation. Dublin governments also made stances that were seen as very anti-British so as to ensure that they could be seen to have remained loyal to the state's nationalist heritage. Even rank-and-file security operatives grew attuned to this policy.

With the exception of Chapter 1, each chapter begins with a discussion of the political environment examining both domestic politics and Anglo-Irish relations, followed by an examination of the role of the Gardaí and the Army before a general discussion of the security situation along the border.

The book opens with a discussion of available existing material on Irish security policy. There is a general lack of academic work covering the topic and the reasons for this will be discussed. Existing literature highlights the high degree of political control exercised over the Gardaí and, by extension, security policy. This chapter provides background information on the Irish security debate and, significantly, observes that there was precedent for discreet security co-operation with British forces during the Second World War.

The third chapter considers the first two years of the Troubles, 1969–1970, a period dominated by the controversy associated with the 'Arms Trials'. There was speculation at the time and subsequently about possible Irish military intervention in Northern Ireland, but archive material shows that this was never a realistic option, not least because of the weakness of the Irish Army. The response to the outbreak of violence is considered and it is concluded that there was no overarching security policy, just a series of ad hoc responses to given events with an emphasis on containing the violence in Northern Ireland. The border itself was very quiet, with the focus of violence being in urban centres, particularly Belfast and Derry. However, there was a visible sign of the 'Troubles' in the form of the arrival of a significant number of 'refugees', as they were known, into border areas. The experience and treatment of these refugees between 1969 and 1972 provides an interesting insight into the official attitude towards northern nationalists.

The following chapter considers the period from 1971 until 1972, detailing how violence along the border went from being an occasional isolated incident to a daily occurrence. It was during this period that lawlessness along the border was at its most pronounced. Initially, the violence involved non-fatal shootings and stone-throwing often associated with 'cratering' operations on border roads but as time went on there were more fatalities and serious incidents. There were also significant street disturbances in border towns, particularly Monaghan, Ballyshannon and Dundalk. It is argued that the effect of the violence led the Irish government to begin to take greater steps to combat the IRA domestically. Evidence is also presented of some covert cross-border security co-operation. The response to 'Bloody Sunday' is also dealt with and it is revealed that public and political anger in the South dissipated remarkably quickly after the events in Derry. During this period the state's ambiguity in relation to the IRA waned with the setting-up of the Special Criminal Court in 1972 was a decisive action.

Chapter 4 looks at the Fine Gael–Labour coalition's first years in office. The possibility of a British withdrawal features heavily in the political discussion of the period. Again, evidence will be cited that illustrates covert cross-border security co-operation. The activities of loyalist paramilitaries and allegations of security-force collusion in incidents south of the border are all considered. Evidence will be presented that there was significant mutual distrust between the respective security forces. As co-operation became formalised, it will be noted that, from a British perspective, the Gardaí were not trusted with sensitive information due to fears of IRA infiltration. Meanwhile, there were significant problems from the Garda's viewpoint too. British covert operations south of the border, alleged links with loyalists and a perception that British forces still maintained a 'colonial'-style attitude all contributed to ill feeling. The emergence of South Armagh as the main trouble spot is evident at this stage but the reasons for the decline in violence in places like Lifford and Clones is also considered.

The penultimate chapter covers the period 1976–8. The Fine Gael–Labour coalition's last year's in office are examined, with particular attention paid to the allegations of a 'heavy gang' within the Gardaí. It is argued that the return to office of Fianna Fáil in 1977 did not significantly alter security policy but some of the anti-republican rhetoric was toned down. Particular attention is again given to the situation in South Armagh. Security co-operation appeared to be better in Donegal than elsewhere and potential reasons for this are offered. The growing animosity between Gardaí and republicans is discussed and the security implications assessed. More broadly, the general organisational malaise within the Irish security forces is considered further. It is again argued that steps taken to combat the IRA domestically did not equate to greater cross-border security co-operation. Meanwhile, the failure of the southern security forces to deal with the loyalist threat is highlighted and reasons why this threat was downplayed are presented. The general impact of the Troubles on day-to-day life along the border is also considered.

The final chapter concludes with key findings, notably that the Irish state took substantial action to deal with the IRA within the boundaries of the twenty-six counties. The IRA threat was perceived as the main danger to the long-term stability of the southern state so other threats, such as those from loyalists, were downplayed. Domestic security took precedence, so action against republicans was not necessarily accompanied by security co-operation with UK forces. The degree and intensity of violence along the border varied according to area and over time, and significant limitations in terms of resources and structures inhibited the Irish security forces.

CHAPTER 1

'Almost Like Talking Dirty': Interpretations of Irish Security Policy, 1969–1978

In a seminal work on Anglo-Irish relations in 1972, Conor Cruise O'Brien noted: 'Neither judges, nor the police, nor the army, nor the ordinary citizens who make up juries knew quite where they were expected to stand on this question [IRA activities] – and for anyone who did not know, the most prudent and convenient thing was not to annoy the IRA.'[1] Whether judges, the police or army did adopt such an approach to the IRA is debatable. A less controversial statement is that there has been a dearth of literature examining what exactly Irish security forces did do in response to the Troubles and what policy decisions informed such action/inaction. It could be argued that Irish security has become something of a taboo for discussion; one work on the subject was entitled 'Almost Like Talking Dirty: Irish Security Policy in Post-Cold War Europe'.[2] Meanwhile, a recent academic work on the topic began by stating 'Irish national security has been largely overlooked as a subject for scholarly attention.'[3]

The limited literature that does exist can loosely be divided into several categories. Firstly, there are the works that look at particular dimensions of Irish security policy in an academic context, such as O'Halpin's *Defending Ireland: The Irish State and its Enemies Since 1922*,[4] Mulqueen's *Re-evaluating Irish National Security: Affordable threats*,[5] and Vicky Conway's *Policing Twentieth Century Ireland: A History of an Garda Síochána*.[6] There are other academic works that touch on the subject indirectly as part of analysis of the Troubles generally. The most significant of these is Henry Patterson's *Ireland's Violent Frontier: The*

Border and Anglo-Irish Relations During the Troubles.[7] Other examples include *Talking to Terrorists: Making Peace in Northern Ireland and the Basque Country*[8] and Craig's *Crisis of Confidence: Anglo-Irish Relations in the Early Troubles 1966–1974.*[9] Although security is only a peripheral aspect to some of these works, they nonetheless merit mention as they provide a context for framing the discussion and understanding the nature of the Irish state. A further category of literature focuses directly on the functions of particular Irish security services. Brady's *Guardians of the Peace*[10] and *The Guarding of Ireland: The Garda Síochána and the Irish State 1960–2014,*[11] as well as Walshe's *The Irish Police,*[12] provide invaluable insights into the workings and history of the Gardaí.

A fourth source of material that merits mention is what could broadly be described as journalistic works dealing with Troubles-related issues. Examples include McArdle's *The Secret War: An Account of the Sinister Activities along the Border involving Gardaí, RUC, British Army and the SAS,*[13] which provides an interesting account of cross-border security co-operation. In a similar vein, Dunne and Kerrigan's *Round Up the Usual Suspects*[14] discusses allegations of a 'heavy gang' operating within the Gardaí. Before examining each of these categories, however, it is worth considering why there are so few works specifically focusing on Irish security.

There are several reasons for the lack of literature on the subject. A lack of access to appropriate archive material is cited by several authors, including O'Halpin.[15] More recently, Craig claimed 'historians have only seen a portion of what documentation was generated but this is enough to demonstrate that security co-operation remains the missing dimension'.[16]

The lack of archive material is compounded by the sensitive and sometimes informal nature of Anglo-Irish contact. In terms of contacts between North and South, for instance, it has been noted that 'These cross-border contacts were extremely sensitive and had the power to arouse hostility on both sides of the border. The use of secret channels allowed Dublin and Belfast to be kept informed of the progress of North-South contacts whilst keeping government ministers one step removed from the actual contacts.'[17]

An even more obvious reason for the lack of research on the subject is the fact that the southern security response was not as high profile, or indeed as interesting, to the outside observer. The bulk of casualties took place north of the border and that was obviously the main theatre of operations for paramilitary groups. More generally, there has been a tendency in studies of the northern conflict to concentrate on activities in the urban centres. Patterson notes:

> Most of the existing research on the IRA, like most research on the Troubles, is heavily dominated by studies that either focus on the main urban centres of Belfast and Derry, or treat Northern Ireland as a single unit for analysis. This has meant that the distinct experiences of rural and border areas, apart from the city of Derry, have been neglected.[18]

Obviously, the southern security forces have only limited relevance in the context of discussions focusing primarily on Belfast.

A further dimension has been a lack of public comment by those involved in security south of the border. This may in some respects be part of a broader phenomenon whereby the Troubles are dismissed as something that 'happened up there'. The British Army, RUC personnel and paramilitaries have been given various platforms to discuss their experiences of the Troubles. Crawford's *Inside the UDA: Volunteers and Violence*[19] and Alonso's *The IRA and Armed Struggle,*[20] for example, draw almost exclusively from the experiences of former loyalist and republican combatants respectively. A further indication of this trend has been accounts by former RUC/British Army personnel detailing their role in combating subversives. Examples of this genre include Barker's *Shadows: Inside Northern Ireland's Special Branch,*[21] *Phoenix: Policing the Shadows,*[22] Clarke's *Border Crossing: True Stories of the RUC Special Branch, the Garda Special Branch and IRA Moles*[23] and Holroyd and Burbridge's *War without Honour.*[24] With the exception of Courtney's *It Was Murder,*[25] there are few equivalents by either Garda or Irish Army personnel. With the changed political climate, there is some evidence that this trend may change: Mulqueen and Conway both based their work in part on interviews with individuals involved in the security sphere, while a recent oral history project, 'Green and Blue', included interviews with some Gardaí who served along the border.[26]

O'Halpin's *Defending Ireland: The Irish Free State and its Enemies since 1922* represents a good starting point for any discussion of Irish security. It provides an excellent historical account of the evolution of the Irish defence and security apparatus. The historian's influence is evident from the outset, where it is argued that 'the curious position occupied by the Irish Defence Forces can only be understood by reference to the state's perpetual internal security problem'.[27] There follows detailed historical discussions of the various aspects of the Irish security problem. Episodes that shaped defence and security policy are examined in detail, including the Army mutiny of 1924, the origins of the Gardaí, the civil war and the implications of the Second World War. Drawing extensively on archive material, there is a particularly interesting discussion of the Irish security response to the Second World War. It is noted that 'The generally effective liaison which evolved between MI5 and G2 [Irish military intelligence] naturally remained highly secret. Consequently, it could not be publicly adduced to counter the claims frequently aired in the British and American press that the IRA was running amok and that Dublin was a nest of axis spies.'[28]

This covert UK–Irish co-operation in the Second World War is dealt with in the most thorough manner and raises many questions about later periods. The discussion in subsequent chapters will show that the Irish security services similarly maintained an emphasis on covert co-operation as the Troubles developed.

In terms of policy formation, meanwhile, the mechanics of decision-making are discussed. It is noted that 'During the emergency security policy was made and decisions were taken almost entirely at administrative levels within the Garda, the Army, Justice, and External affairs. There is nothing to indicate that ministers played a decisive part in the implementation of security policy.'[29]

The issue of cross-border police co-operation is addressed but the discussion of the mechanics of its operation is typically vague: 'The RUC kept up its headquarters links [after the Second World War] with the Garda just as MI5 did with G2, individual officers maintained local understandings with their Garda counterparts in border counties and the force undoubtedly continued to attempt to penetrate the IRA and republican bodies on both sides of the border.'[30]

The post-1969 northern conflict is examined, but the discussion does not benefit from the extensive archive material available to support the investigation of the 'Emergency' period and is hence shorter and less detailed. That said, IRA activities south of the border, legislative and security developments, the role of the Gardaí and cross-border co-operation, particularly in relation to extradition, are all adequately discussed. More recent work from O'Halpin has benefited from archive material releases and examines aspects of security policy in more detail.[31]

While O'Halpin's work is very much written from the point of view of the historian and lacks any significant political theory foundation, Mulqueen's *Re-evaluating Irish National Security Policy: Affordable Threats* provides the fullest and most recent examination of Irish security policy. The focus is on the post-9/11 security situation and Ireland's role in combating global terror but the historical and theoretical discussion of Irish security policy is nonetheless highly relevant. For the historical overview, the work of O'Halpin is drawn upon heavily. Meanwhile, the ideas of international relations theorist Barry Buzan strongly influence the theoretical discussion.[32] Included is a fairly rare discussion on the operations of the Irish Special Branch.[33] Another significant aspect of the discussion relates to the unseen role of the Department of Finance in shaping security policy, particularly in relation to the Army. The discussion of the Irish security forces' role in the Troubles is well informed, if not particularly novel:

> Operationally, because the conflict was mostly played out within the borders of Northern Ireland, the primary task of policy implementation for the Irish security forces was to close off republican supply lines. Operationally this translated into duties such as the uncovering of arms dumps, watching safe houses, suspects and sympathisers and preventing easy access to cash through bank raids and extortion. A continuous watch was kept on the border for terrorists about to launch or escaping from an attack.[34]

Despite the lack of detail in relation to the Troubles, the thorough account of the bureaucratic functioning of the Irish security system is especially valuable.

Henry Patterson's *Ireland's Violent Frontier: The Border and Anglo-Irish Relations During the Troubles* is perhaps the most important work on border security to date. Patterson details the relationship between the two governments throughout the years of the Troubles and also documents many of the violent incidents that occurred. The description of the experience of Protestant communities in border areas is especially interesting. A compelling argument is presented that 'while successive Irish governments proclaimed their abhorrence of Provisional violence, their refusal, with the partial exception of the Fine Gael–Labour coalition of 1973–77, to take the issue of Provisional IRA exploitation of their territory seriously, objectively facilitated the organisation's ability to carry on its "long war" into the 1990s'.[35]

Patterson's conclusions are nuanced and do not imply that the Gardaí collectively colluded with the IRA. Nor does the study discount the steps taken within the twenty-six counties to deal with IRA. Nonetheless, Patterson's work focuses primarily on the experience on the northern side of the border. In contrast, this study focuses on south of the border and therefore utilises different valuable sources, notably material from official inquiries into the Dublin and Monaghan bombing.

Craig's *Crisis of Confidence: Anglo-Irish Relations in the Early Troubles 1966–1974* offers a similarly prescient insight, drawing heavily upon recently released archives. Dealing with the early years of the Troubles, Craig is very measured in approach, refuting evidence offered by O'Brien's *The Arms Trial*[36] of Taoiseach Jack Lynch's complicity in the illegal arms importation of 1969/1970.[37] Furthermore, he supports the view of O'Halpin[38] and FitzGerald[39] that the Irish government never seriously contemplated military action and had a deep-seated fear of British withdrawal.[40]

Another recent work that broadly examines Anglo-Irish relations is Bew, Frampton and Gurruchaga's study, entitled *Talking to Terrorists: making peace in Northern Ireland and the Basque Country*, which examines the various sets of talks that took place between the respective governments and paramilitary groups during the Troubles. Like Craig, recent archive releases help inform the discussion considerably. The work emphasises the dilemma IRA actions posed for the southern state and how deeply threatened the southern state felt. One Foreign Office memo, for instance, maintained that it was in UK's selfish interest to stay in Northern Ireland to avoid a left-wing takeover in the Republic: 'Herein lay an irreducible problem, which had often been ignored during [Harold] Wilson's periodic flirtation with the idea of withdrawal. The fact was the IRA was as much, if not more, of a danger to the integrity of the Irish state, than it was to British sovereignty.'[41]

The argument in the work is that 'it is not always good to talk to terrorists'. Certainly this view seems to be in line with the policies pursued by successive Irish governments which viewed poorly timed contacts as providing a stimulus for violence.[42]

Of works covering the security services directly, Conway (2014), Brady (2000) and Walshe (1998) are the most rigorous. Vicky Conway's *Policing Twentieth Century Ireland: A History of An Garda Síochána* builds on Conway's previous offering, *The Blue Wall of Silence: The Morris Tribunal and Police Accountability*, which examined the fallout of the investigation into Garda malpractice in Donegal. In *The Blue Wall of Silence*, the degree of freedom afforded the Gardaí as a result of their battle against subversives is dealt with in terms of discussions of the first Morris Tribunal report into fraudulent explosive finds in Donegal.[43] Significantly, Conway argues that 'when it came to policing the IRA, An Garda Síochána have been supported and ... were given a degree of leeway'.[44] The overriding view presented is that politics impinges on policing significantly in the Republic. What distinguishes Conway's more recent work is the incorporation of forty-two interviews with retired Gardaí.[45] These interviews provide a rare insight into grass-root thinking among Garda members, particularly those serving along the border. Conway emphasises that the development of the force has been heavily influenced by Ireland's colonial and post-colonial history. It is argued that Garda history has been idealised by a constructed narrative whereby the unarmed force represented a radical departure from the discredited RIC. Conway disputes this: 'Practically speaking, the Gardaí Síochána was not in any fundamental way different from the previous colonial force. Efforts to differentiate policing focused on image and rhetoric ... A myth was created at this time that the Gardaí were different from the RIC, while in reality many of the core problems with the RIC remained.'[46]

A range of important topics are addressed, including the experience of Gardaí serving along the border, the role of Special Branch, the impact of the ongoing violence on the attitude towards republicans, and allegations of a 'heavy gang' within the Gardaí.

Walshe's *The Irish Police* is a legalistic examination of the role of Gardaí, providing interesting views on democratic accountability, the role of the Gardaí as the state's secret service, and the connection between political institutions and the force. Significantly, Walshe views the promotion procedure as reflecting a strong government influence and desire to influence more specific operational activities.[47] In terms of explicit interference, it is stated:

> Neither the Minister nor any political authority possess a specific statutory power to direct the force on general or individual operational matters. However, powers to issue regulations on duties of several ranks of the force and to direct how the force shall be distributed and stationed throughout the state at least hold the potential for the Minister to influence contents of operational policies and practices.[48]

Some examples of direct political interference over a specified period are cited as evidence of political control. Indeed, Michael Noonan, former Minister for Justice, is quoted stating 'that during times of crisis the Minister of Justice in effect becomes CEO and he is asked for decisions'.[49] Compelling evidence is presented in support of the view that policing the Irish state is highly politicised.

Meanwhile, two works by former *Irish Times* and *Garda Review* editor Conor Brady further detail the history of the force. *Guardians of the Peace* covers the history of the force up until the early 1970s. An insight into the nature of political influence and the culture within the Gardaí is given in a discussion relating to the 1930s. It is noted that when Fianna Fáil came to power, Garda attitudes to the IRA changed: 'There were of course no official circulars to that effect, no orders, written or verbal, but the moral was drawn very swiftly from one or two instances in which the guards were either foolish or principled enough to try to continue their prosecutions against members of the movement.'[50]

It is argued that the politicised nature of policing seems to have stemmed naturally from the institutional setup, which mirrored that of the RIC. As is the case in Conway's work, the absence of an independent police authority is cited as being significant: 'what was to be really significant for the future development of the force and its relations with the various governments under which it was to serve was the recommendation of the committee that the Commissioner should be directly responsible to the government rather than to a police authority as was the case with British forces'.[51]

A more recent publication from Brady, *The Guarding of Ireland: The Garda Síochána and the Irish State 1960–2014*, discusses the more recent history of force. Drawing on content from Garda and political sources, a thorough discussion of the period is presented and many of the themes explored by Conway are addressed. The impact of the

Troubles is discussed, but the distinct experience of Gardaí policing the border is not dealt with as thoroughly as by Conway. Significantly, the autonomy of Gardaí in border areas during the Troubles is again cited as a contributory factor in the controversies that engulfed the force in Donegal in the 1990s.[52] Other significant works on the Gardaí include Gregory Allen's *The Garda Síochána: Policing Independent Ireland 1922–82*[53] and Liam McNiffe's *A History of the Garda Síochána: A Social History of the Force 1922–52 with an Overview of the Years 1952–1997.*[54] These provide more of a social history of the force and contain only limited political insights.

The Irish Army has received less attention from writers. Duggan's *The Irish Army*[55] is something of an exception, but the Defence Forces' role in the northern Troubles is somewhat glossed over. The Irish Army officer at the centre of the Arms Trial, Captain James Kelly, has also written on his role[56] but obviously these works represent a particular perspective on events.

Academics have not focused to a significant extent on security policy so it is worth noting some journalistic works that have addressed the topic. The range stretches from the well-informed and balanced contributions of O'Brien or Dunne and Kerrigan to the fringes of conspiracy theory, such as Ó Cuinneaghain's *Monaghan, County of Intrigue.*[57]

The Arms Trial by O'Brien looks at the events and implications of the conspiracy to import arms into the country in 1970. The work conveys the confusion inherent in Irish security policy responses to the eruption of violence in Northern Ireland. In particular, the conflicts within Fianna Fáil and the republican movement are comprehensively dealt with. The perceived threat to the southern state posed by the Goulding faction of the (later Official) IRA is emphasised: 'in the heat of the Belfast events of August 1969, it is clear now that those running Northern policies in Fianna Fáil viewed Goulding as perhaps the most serious threat.'[58]

Archive material and contemporaneous reports are used to detail how early security policy was confused in its design and application. The policies pursued by different factions of government were mirrored on the ground by different agencies of the state. O'Brien details the well-documented activities of the Haughey and Blaney Dáil sub-committee on Northern Ireland, but there is little discussion of mainstream security policy. Special Branch action/inaction and attitudes to republicans are not dealt with in sufficient detail, nor is there any discussion of how Gardaí and Army personnel interacted with republicans along the border in terms of arrests, seizures, checkpoints or other conflict. The work is quite critical of Jack Lynch. It concludes that 'the government papers for 1969 clearly reveal that [Jack] Lynch knew more about what was going on than previously stated'.[59] As noted earlier, this view is contested by others, including Craig.[60]

A similarly well-researched account comes from Dunne and Kerrigan's *Round Up the Usual Suspects*, which examines the highly controversial Garda investigation into the Sallins Train Robbery in 1976. McArdle's *The Secret War* discusses issues of border security from the perspective of a reputable local journalist. Although incidents where Gardaí reportedly 'looked the other way' to IRA activity are acknowledged, numerous examples are cited of confrontation between republicans and Gardaí.[61]

A Role for Academics

It is evident that the Irish security response to the outbreak of violence has not received sufficient academic attention. The reasons for the lack of literature were discussed at the outset and include a lack of archive material, the lower profile of Irish security forces and a lack of public comment by security force personnel. The position of the Irish state vis-à-vis Britain generally has received more academic attention. Works on this topic help significantly in understanding the threats felt by the Irish state and hence how it would frame its security response. Despite the rhetoric of Irish unity, the Irish state has obviously had reason to fear the IRA. The degree of uncertainty engendered in the Republic by the IRA post-1969 is well documented, particularly in recent works by Craig and Bew. This instability makes the southern state an intriguing subject for analysis.

Although works on Anglo-Irish relations discuss the security situation on the border, it is not the focus of such studies. In terms of Irish security forces, meanwhile, there are excellent accounts of the role of the Gardaí particularly. The politicised nature of policing in the state is addressed and the inadequacies in the policy-making infrastructure are examined. Discussions of past security responses show a nuanced Irish security response. These security responses have included a combination of ruthlessness, intrigue and conciliation depending on the prevailing political mood. In terms of cross-border co-operation, some works, notably O'Halpin (1999), have highlighted an emphasis on discretion in terms of dealing with the British Army/ RUC. Meanwhile, other works, specifically Brady (2014), have noted that, to an extent, individual Gardaí policing the Troubles were given a certain amount of autonomy in terms of national security matters.

The final section of this chapter included a discussion detailing just some of the journalistic works relevant to the topic. That journalists have written on this subject over the course of the Troubles is unsurprising. Experienced journalists have certain advantages over academics in dealing with security issues, including a network of sources and contacts built up over the course of a working life. However, such advantages should not preclude academic investigation. An academic writing in the years after the signing of the Good Friday Agreement cautioned colleagues against leaving the study of aspects of the conflict to journalists:

> Despite the large volume of literature on the Northern Ireland conflict, there is still little rigorous academic study either of a military and strategic nature or of the broader international relations implications. The barrier to scholarly interpretation is purely a mental hurdle that has grown up in the minds of academics, fortified by three decades of established methods of thinking about the conflict. The assertions that journalists are more capable, that there is an absence of information, or of reliable information, or that violence is so entrenched in the political landscape that it need not be examined, are simply rationalizations of the under-study of the military arena, and an excuse to avoid looking at the more unsavoury aspects of the conflict.[62]

More Cliché than Conspiracy: Security Policy from August 1969 until the Arms Trial

The British Army's official report into its operations in the North divided the conflict into different stages:

> The first period, from August 1969 until perhaps the summer of 1971, was largely characterised by widespread public disorder. Marches, protests, rioting and looting were the main issues. The next phase, from the summer of 1971 until the mid-1970s, is best described as a classic insurgency. Both the Official and Provisional wings of the Irish Republican Army (OIRA and PIRA) fought the security forces in more-or-less formed bodies. Both had a structure of companies, battalions and brigades, with a recognisable structure and headquarters staff. Protracted fire fights were common.[1]

Derry and Belfast were the epicentres of violence in the first years of the Troubles, whereas the southern border counties were more removed from the violence than was to be the case in subsequent years, but there were still significant issues to be dealt with in 1969/70, including an influx of refugees, threats from loyalist extremists and other domestic security threats. Although these were complex and challenging problems for communities and authorities in the respective areas, they were relatively minor compared to the wider breakdown of society in the urban areas of Northern Ireland. However, by 1971, and more so by 1972, the dynamics of the northern conflict had changed and the challenges facing the southern administration

WEXFORD
COUNTY
LIBRARY
2470126

became more severe. '[Operation] Motorman by driving the IRA out of urban "no-go" areas inside Derry and Belfast, made the borderlands the most crucial areas in the conflict for the British.'[2] By the end of 1971, there was a very real sense that the border counties could be dragged deeper into the conflict. The street disturbances that had previously been witnessed on TV screens were beginning to spread south, as evidenced by riots in Dundalk, Ballyshannon and Monaghan. In the year 1971 and subsequently, local papers and archives contain innumerable accounts of shooting incidents, arms finds and arrests along the border. The year 1969 and especially the earlier half of 1970 were different.

These early years shaped the future southern policy response. Focusing on the years 1969 and 1970, the discussion here will differ from later chapters. Activities that would become synonymous with border security later simply did not occur to the same extent in 1969 and 1970. There were virtually no shooting incidents at the frontier in the first year of the Troubles, nor were there extensive arrests, arms seizures or public displays of hostility between the southern security forces and republicans.

The initial response to the outbreak of violence by the Irish security apparatus was somewhat haphazard. During the period, the Irish Army played a more prominent domestic role than at later stages. The Army was ill equipped to serve any military role at the time and was confined primarily to care of refugees and displays for propaganda purposes. In particular, there was a lack of leadership in the military, as well as political interference in security affairs generally. In terms of the Gardaí, the situation in 1969/70 was complex. It is hard to discern what exactly their policy was upon the immediate outbreak of violence. The most frequent allegation is that Gardaí simply turned a blind eye to republican activities and there is little evidence to disprove this. The mixed signals emerging from higher echelons of government created difficulties in a force that was undermanned and under-resourced. The fallout from the general confusion came in May 1970 with the allegations of importation of arms into the country by a consortium of politicians, soldiers and paramilitaries. This affair, known as the Arms Crisis, had a massive effect in shaping government security policy in subsequent years.

It also informed those implementing security policies on the ground of the boundaries they should not cross. It is not intended to forensically re-evaluate the Arms Trial. Others have already done this with inconclusive findings. Nevertheless, it is an event of such significance that it cannot be ignored and, in fact, much of the material on security policy in this period emerged from the two Arms Trials and the later Public Accounts Committee inquiry.

The events of 1969 and 1970 demonstrated the fragility of the southern state and hence helped frame its security policy in subsequent years. During this dramatic period, a consensus emerged from the political, military and security elite that the southern state should not be destabilised by events over the border.

The Political Environment from August 1969 to the Arms Trial

In 2009, the Irish state broadcaster RTÉ aired a documentary entitled *If Lynch Had Invaded.*[3] The programme revisited the tumultuous mid-August period of 1969. The documentary centred on a series of cabinet meetings between 13 August and 15 August. The programme had as its premise that Irish ministers seriously considered incursions into Northern Ireland. The cabinet meetings in question took place after the outbreak of violence following the Apprentice Boys parade in Derry. In terms of drama, the story of government ministers seeking to send in troops is unparalleled. Whether, in fact, invasion was ever seriously considered is less than certain.

As a background to the cabinet meetings, it is worth noting that Taoiseach Jack Lynch had a divided front bench at this stage. As something of a compromise candidate for the leadership, Lynch's position was far from secure. Rumours had been circulating since spring 1969 that Lynch was unwell and would soon resign, with Charles Haughey and Neil Blaney the most obvious successors.[4] Blaney and fellow minister Kevin Boland voiced traditional republican views since 1968 and frequently expressed opinions contrary to official policy. Haughey, meanwhile, was not known for such views. The Troubles in the North had stirred deep emotions south of the border and Charles Haughey, who had strong anti-IRA credentials, 'was among those who behaved out of character that summer'.[5]

According to Seamus Brady's account in *Arms and the Men*, 'The first question at issue [at the cabinet meetings on 13–15 August] was the use of the Irish Army in crossing the border.'[6] However, this seems an exaggerated version of the truth at best. Two of those at the cabinet table from opposing standpoints paint a different picture. Kevin Boland stated that 'there was no suggestion at any time from any Minister that this opportunity should be taken by the use of force'.[7] Meanwhile, Minister for Education Pádraig Faulkner recalled that 'The possibility of incursions into the North was raised but quickly dismissed. As far as I can remember the matter was raised in a rather haphazard way and given little or no consideration.'[8]

Press reports of troop movements along the border accompanied by a TV address by Taoiseach Jack Lynch, in which he claimed that his government would not 'stand by', contributed to creating the myth that an invasion was not just being considered, but was quite likely. The creation of this myth helped contain republican sentiment at home but ominously it also meant that there was little clarity over what exactly policy was.

The immediate measures decided upon by the Irish cabinet were modest. These moves were ad hoc decisions and not part of a well-thought-out strategic policy, which meant that, considering the nature of Irish politics, individual political figures could have undue influence on how decisions were implemented. Among the steps taken were the creation of five field hospitals along the border, the expansion of intelligence services in the six counties and the setting-up of a subcommittee to advise the Taoiseach on Northern matters.[9] In particular, the relief fund established would have implications in subsequent months. It would later be alleged that money from this fund was used for illicit arms purchases. Likewise, the subcommittee that was established would create ambiguity and interfere with the Army's chain of command. The subcommittee met only once[10] but its two most powerful members, Blaney and Haughey, seem to unilaterally have taken over its functions. Along with these moves, an aggressive propaganda campaign was undertaken domestically and internationally that included an appearance by Foreign Affairs Minister Patrick Hillery at the UN Security Council.[11]

The very public creation of field hospitals was in some senses the most spectacular gesture. It was the sight of soldiers moving northward to set up the field hospitals that triggered media speculation and rumours. Within weeks, the movement of troops towards the border was criticised in the Dáil by the opposition as giving 'false hopes in the Bogside, to raise particularly false hopes in Belfast and to escalate a situation'.[12] Elsewhere, Fine Gael's Patrick Hogan claimed the manoeuvres 'with banner headlines beat the drums with all the abandon of a July Apprentice Boy'.[13] Indeed, it has been claimed that 'rumour of an impending invasion had certainly prompted the republican assault on Newry police station'.[14] Neil Blaney, seen as the most hawkish minister, attempted to portray the field hospitals as something much more substantial in a 1993 interview:

> It was the view of myself and others that we had to send our troops to protect the people and it was agreed to send the Army to the border, under the cover of field hospitals. But as it turned out the deviousness of certain minds thereafter utilised the 'good cover' as just that. But the field hospitals idea we went along with: I didn't give a damn how they went up as long as the Army went up and were there to go in.[15]

To test the veracity of this claim, it is necessary to consider the state of the Irish Army in 1969. Blaney's view massively overestimates the ability of Irish Defence Forces for subterfuge. There were just 8,500 poorly equipped Irish troops. By the Army's own estimate, the number capable of combat duty was just 2,300.[16] An assessment from the British embassy, some time later, was scathing:

> The efficiency of the Irish Army is thus limited considerably by a disorganised command structure at the highest level, an unwillingness to believe in its own usefulness, insufficient training, bad equipment except at personal level, and as promotion system that does not take fliers into account. Soldiers would probably acquit themselves well in fighting at platoon strength but could not organise or carry out a complicated tactical operation. They certainly present no threat to British forces in Northern Ireland.[17]

The Irish Defence Forces reported on the feasibility of incursions in September 1969 and similarly concluded that they had 'no capability of embarking on unilateral military operation of any kind (either conventional or unconventional), from a firm base at home'.[18] A later internal Irish Army assessment claimed that the experience of mid-August had borne out 'every defect of the present organisation referred to in correspondence over the last decade'. The assessment went on: 'No one unit from its own resources was capable of immediate response to the government's directive to place personnel at the strength required on the border in August. Personnel from different units had to be hastily assembled and formed into ad hoc groups.'[19]

In one respect, Blaney was right. There was more to the establishment of the hospitals than the humanitarian needs they fulfilled. The five field hospitals were of limited use in practical terms. The Rockhill and Dunree camps in Donegal treated thirty-one and eleven casualties respectively. Fourteen casualties were treated in Dundalk. Castleblayney and Finner camps both treated just one casualty while none were treated in Cavan.[20] To put these figures in context, it is estimated that about 750 people received injuries during the August period north of the border.[21] The field hospitals remained open for some months afterwards, treating just two new patients, one in Rockhill on 25 September and another on 27 September.[22] The real significance of the field hospitals was in the aesthetics of the operation: the sight of troops being moved towards the border helped assuage nationalist sentiment and reinforced the seriousness of the situation for the British government. Indeed, it has been argued that the subtext of the entire 'stand by' speech, in which the field hospitals were announced, was not that 'the Republic wished to invade Northern Ireland in defence of the minority, but that it wanted Britain, at least temporarily to take responsibility'.[23] A contemporaneous account cited Charles Haughey's support for this analysis: 'It seems Haughey calculated that unless the government acted strongly "irresponsible groups" in the Republic (the IRA) might attract substantial public support and take precipitous independent action. There was also a rather woolly hope that by escalating the situation, the British government would be forced to intervene directly.'[24]

In terms of what was to come later, August 1969 was a bit of a 'damp squib and life returned fairly quickly to near normal'.[25] However, the months that followed brought the political divisions in government to the fore, and the possibility of material support for northern groups, in particular, was to lead the state to the precipice.

When asked at the Arms Trial about requests for arms by northern groups in October 1969, Minister for Defence Gibbons denied any knowledge:

The only information conveyed to me in the matter of procurement of arms was that it appeared to be a rather regular occurrence for individual householders to present themselves at various army posts [along the border] asking the officers in charge if they could be given some type of weapon to defend themselves and their family.[26]

The veracity of Gibbons' claim that this was his only knowledge of arms demands is dubious, but the image of individuals demanding arms at barracks gates illustrates the atmosphere of the time. Gibbons' evidence to the Arms Trial was heavily criticised. Belfast republican John Kelly claimed that the visiting delegations left little room for ambiguity in their discussions.

I want to be very emphatic that we were coming from all parts of the six counties not to indulge in tea parties ... we did not ask for blankets or feeding bottles. We asked for guns and no one from the Taoiseach Lynch down refused that request or told us that it was contrary to government policy.[27]

That arms were being sought is not really in doubt. Even 'fairly respectable groups and politicians' sought weapons.[28] According to key Department of Foreign Affairs official Eamonn Gallagher, 'We kept saying no.'[29] Obviously, this contradicts both Gibbons' and Kelly's version. In private, perhaps, political figures, as opposed to diplomats such as Gallagher, may have found it necessary to be more ambiguous in their replies.

Irish Army officer Captain James Kelly had built up a range of contacts with groups demanding arms and he arranged a meeting on 4 October 1969 in Bailieborough, Co. Cavan, that would be 'the genesis' of the plan to import arms.[30] The degree to which some political figures engaged in duplicitous practices during the period can be gauged by the actions of Minister of Finance Charles Haughey during the weekend of the Bailieborough meeting. On 2 October, Haughey arranged for £500 to be paid to Kelly towards the costs of the Bailieborough meeting.[31] Secretary General of the Department of Justice Peter Berry, having learned of the meeting through Special Branch, was alarmed by reports linking it with subversive groups. Berry attempted to contact the Taoiseach on 4 October to report on the seemingly sinister development. The Taoiseach was unavailable, so Berry instead contacted Haughey, a former Minister for Justice as well as a member of the supposed four-man subcommittee on Northern Ireland. Haughey gave no indication to Berry that he knew of the Bailieborough meeting in advance or that he had funded it. Berry noted feeling 'reassured' after discussing the issue with Haughey.[32] While Captain Kelly was meeting with the northerners in Cavan, Haughey's weekend of intrigue continued when he called on the British Ambassador, Sir Anthony Gilchrist. Haughey discussed with Gilchrist the possibility of 'a secret long term commitment' between the British and Irish governments. With hindsight, Gilchrist's observation on such a deal is noteworthy:

> I said it was impossible for me to discuss such a question since I did not know what the Irish wanted (I doubted if they did) and had no idea what my own government would feel on the subject; but the conception seemed to me a very questionable one, since in modern political conditions I simply did not see how secrecy could be maintained. Haughey was puzzled by this but felt there ought to be a way around.[33]

The alternative diplomatic and security strategy pursued by Haughey directly undermined Lynch and left officials, including Berry, confused. Haughey was 'usurping the Taoiseach not simply in a matter of state security and on the Northern Ireland issue, but also in his diplomatic affairs including his relations with Britain'.[34]

The first objective outlined to Captain Kelly by the northern representatives in Bailieborough was procurement of arms, the next was training.[35] Some steps had already been taken with regard training. On the same weekend as the Bailieborough meeting, nationalists from Derry were due to undergo military training in Fort Dunree in Donegal under instruction from the Irish Army. This was to be the second such group. Already, ten men completed training, having been sworn into the reserve defence forces – the FCA. The background to this training, according to Captain Kelly, was that a group of nationalists from over the border approached Colonel Murt Buckley in Donegal after threats were made by local unionists. After a week, permission to begin the Dunree training was given by the Department of Defence.[36] The training for the second group was cancelled amidst some confusion. Army Director of Intelligence Colonel Heffernon claimed to have ended the training after media inquiries. Gibbons, meanwhile, said that he initiated the training but the Taoiseach ended it when he became aware of it.[37] Heffernon presented a clear chronology to the Dáil's Public Accounts Committee, citing numerous sources in support of his version.[38] Gibbons responded to this with a less convincing version and a strong attack on the 'the perfidy' of Heffernon.[39] Whether Lynch was directly responsible for ending the training or not, there is no evidence that he had any foreknowledge of it or that it was resumed in subsequent months.

As has been outlined, Lynch faced ongoing internal political dissension over policy on Northern Ireland. Blaney was the most vocal foe. For example, Lynch had spoken in Tralee on 20 September, categorically advocating peaceful means. Blaney directly contradicted this when he delivered a controversial speech in Letterkenny on 8 December.[40] Blaney was studiously building links with certain northern groups. *The United Irishman*, the official organ of the republican movement, alleged in its November 1969 issue that the Blaney/Haughey faction had attempted to take over the civil rights movement.[41] Even deep in the heart of Belfast, Blaney's perceived influence could apparently be felt. In a meeting with Irish government officials, nationalist MP Gerry Fitt claimed 'thugs and layabouts' received relief funds from the Irish government's account in Clones. Fitt claimed to have been squeezed out of influence over this account when he failed to back Blaney publicly and controversially alleged that street disturbances were orchestrated in Belfast to coincide with political speeches made in Dublin, presumably by Blaney.[42] Blaney had reason to choose his northern allies carefully. The southern government already felt threatened by leftist agitation to a certain extent. Peter Berry in the Department of Justice had prepared a memorandum for the new government in July 1969 on the seriousness of the subversive threat.[43] Jack Lynch met the editors of the national press and the Director General of RTÉ in early August 1969 to elicit their support against republicans. Part of what Lynch wanted was for the media to avoid using phrases or language that would glamorise republican actions.[44]

It has been argued that Blaney, fearing social unrest, agreed to only support republican elements which agreed to confine their campaign to the six counties, leading to the 'Official'/'Provisional' split. Those who would later take the 'Official' side in the republican movement split would argue that Blaney played a pivotal role in subverting the left wing at the time,[45] but the analysis that he split the IRA via his surrogate Captain Kelly is overly simplistic. Most importantly, it ignores the impact of events on the ground in accelerating the split. That said, no reliable source disputes that incentives in terms of material support were offered by Blaney/Kelly for those more inclined to traditional republican views. Certainly, 'the vigour and self confidence of Goulding's [leader of official wing] challengers was stimulated by the knowledge that they, and not the discredited "reds", had a prospect of material and ideological assistance'.[46] In the longer term, the net result was that a leftist campaign that the Cabinet had been warned about never materialised. The isolated incidents that did occur never developed into the wider social upheaval predicted. As military planners prophetically noted in September 1969, co-operation, real or perceived, with civil rights groups and northern republicans could 'have serious political implications on the national and international scene'.[47]

The crisis in the state's security came to a head on 3 April 1970 when a Garda, Richard Fallon, was shot dead during an armed robbery in Dublin. Fallon was the first Garda to be killed in the line of duty since 1942 and his death had significant political and security implications. A small republican splinter group called Saor Éire was blamed for the incident. Rumours spread almost instantly, alleging some sort of political involvement. Belfast republican John Kelly recalled leaving Leinster House on the night of the killing in the company of Neil Blaney and detecting 'a certain hostility from [assembled Special Branch detectives] against Neil Blaney'.[48] Later allegations were made of political interference in the investigation and even straightforward collusion with the killers.[49]

The impact of Fallon's death on the security services will be discussed later, but just weeks afterwards, another crisis erupted, which would rock the state to its foundations. Again, Peter Berry played a central role in the affair. Berry became aware of a plot involving government ministers, northern groups and at least one Army officer importing arms into the country via Dublin Airport on 17 April. On 18 April, Minister of Finance Charles Haughey phoned Berry to try and arrange clear passage for the weapons.[50] Berry claimed to have 'lingering doubts' about Lynch and feared that the arms importation may have been 'a secret government mission'.[51] That Berry, the man who 'more or less ran Garda Special Branch',[52] could have had such doubts about the Taoiseach indicates the highly unusual climate of the time. After calling on President de Valera for advice, Berry reported the details of the plot to Lynch on 20 April. On 6 May, Lynch announced to a stunned public that Haughey and Blaney had been sacked and Kevin Boland resigned in sympathy.

Eventually, the full details of the arms importation scheme were to filter out. The excited atmosphere on the day the news broke was captured by John Healy's *Irish Times* Dáil sketch. Among the masses of shocked TDs, Healy said, one question on everyone's mind that day related to Haughey: 'Blaney and Boland yes – but where did Haughey fit in? Blaney and Boland were old hands in the hawk business; together they had made no secret of their views on the North. But Haughey – this was a new one: nowhere on the files was there a wild speech by Haughey.'[53]

Captain Kelly, who had been pivotal in the Bailieborough meeting, was central to the affair. Having been the liaison with the northern groups, Kelly had become embroiled in the plot. He claimed that all his actions were in line with government policy and were known to Defence Minister Gibbons, Blaney and Haughey. The latter two ministers had been on the subcommittee on Northern Ireland, hence their role. Along with leading Provisional John Kelly, Captain Kelly had made a few cumbersome attempts to import arms. No arms ever seem to have materialised from Captain Kelly's escapades, although the government did over a period of several years attempt to recoup over £20,000 paid by Kelly to a German arms dealer.[54] Bulletproof vests were landed and these were reportedly commandeered from Kelly's house by IRA Chief of Staff Seán MacStíofáin.[55] A similar outcome would most likely have transpired had any actual arms landed.

Captain Kelly resigned from the Army but was charged in relation to the affair, along with Haughey, Blaney, John Kelly and Flemish businessman Albert Luyx. The charges against Blaney were dropped at an early stage and the others were eventually acquitted. Nevertheless, the murky details of the state's confused security policy over the preceding months were to be recounted in full public view at two trials and a Public Accounts Committee hearing over the next eighteen months.

There are disputed accounts about what happened both before and after Berry informed Lynch on 20 April, and the Taoiseach's role more generally. Some accounts claim that Lynch was aware of the plot much earlier and that the importation was in line with government policy. These accounts tend to rely in large part on the accuracy of the so-called 'Berry Diaries' and archive material related to Army planning.[56] On the opposing side, Keogh's biography of Lynch and Craig's account of Anglo-Irish relations look more favourably on Lynch and point out that Berry was ill during key periods upon which his account is based.[57] The full truth will perhaps never be known. Craig's conclusions on the events are worth noting, however:

> Unfortunately, there may never be a definitive account of the Arms Crisis, and with the death of Charles Haughey many questions remain unanswered, it is clear that the 1970s plots to import arms for the use of the IRA were simply the ultimate turn in a series of attempts by Haughey to run elements of a parallel Irish government behind Jack Lynch's back.[58]

The fact that, even after the release of archival material and numerous accounts from key principals, there remains such significant doubts about who knew what and when is highly illustrative of the broader confusion at the time. Desmond O'Malley, who would have had full access to Department of Justice files, has an interesting perspective on the Arms Crisis legacy:

> Crucial questions about the Arms Crisis were never answered. Which politicians conspired to subvert government policy through illegally importing arms? Did politicians conspire with members of illegal organisations? Did some politicians encourage the establishment of the Provisionals? What happened the bulk of money voted for relief of distress in Northern Ireland? The answers were unfortunately not always written down in files; some of what happened in 1969 and 1970 was never put down on paper.[59]

There was some hope on the British side that the airing of the arms debacle in public would lead to an immediate hardening of Irish government policy towards republicans. UK diplomat Kelvin White wrote somewhat optimistically at the end of May 1970 that there was 'an increasing volume of evidence to show that the Blaney/Haughey crisis, and its appointing of a new Minister of Justice [Des O'Malley], has decided the Irish government on a new tough line with the IRA'.[60] White's optimism was probably based on the intense activity surrounding the arrests and charges of the five involved in the Arms trial on 27/28 May. There was no wholesale roundup of republican suspects and the next batch of significant arrests did not take place for another six months. It was still not fully clear in the summer of 1970 that Lynch would retain control of Fianna Fáil. The depth of panic in government ranks can be gauged by the fact that a high-level meeting of security officials and available cabinet members was called on 5 July to discuss some 'vague' rumour of a coup.[61]

In the midst of this crisis, there was a real need for those loyal to Lynch to outflank the republican element in their own party. One such opportunity presented itself on 11 July when Minister for Foreign Affairs Patrick Hillery made a spontaneous visit to the Falls Road, Belfast. The British Army had placed a curfew on the Falls Road just days earlier during a door-to-door search operation for which their troops were widely criticised for mistreating residents. Four civilians were killed by the British Army in an episode that was seen as a landmark in relations between the British Army and the nationalist community in Belfast. Irish diplomat Eamonn Gallagher took the ad hoc decision to hire a car and take Hillery to Belfast to meet nationalist residents of the Falls. It was to prove a popular move with nationalists on both sides of the border, but it invoked the ire of unionist leaders and the British government. Ian Paisley described the visit as a 'disgrace' while Northern Premier James Chichester-Clark 'deplored' it. The Irish Ambassador was officially rebuked for the visit by the British government, but Sir Edward Peck at the Foreign and Commonwealth Office noted 'the Irish government's need to outflank, by some spectacular move, the Blaney faction'.[62]

As the North settled down, there was intense focus on the Arms Trial in autumn 1970. Newspapers carried extracts daily of the trial which revealed the strange goings-on of elements of the Irish security forces over the preceding months. The four defendants were acquitted on 23 October and again Lynch's position seemed vulnerable, but 'if Lynch had an unmerited reputation for weakness, over the following days he showed that his critics and enemies were mistaken'.[63] Buoyed by support from the Fianna Fáil old guard, Lynch won the support of his parliamentary party and a vote of confidence in the Dáil. The immediate political result of the Arms Trial verdict was that Boland and Blaney left the Fianna Fáil parliamentary party, while Haughey remained in the party fold but much chastened.

An Evaluation of Irish Security Policy: The Role of the Gardaí and the Army

Historically, there had been considerable political interference in the running of the Gardaí and Army. Therefore, the role of the relevant ministers in the two government departments is a good starting point for an evaluation of the Gardaí and Army in 1969/70. Justice was the primary department when it came to internal security matters and the minister in August 1969 was Mícheál Ó Móráin, who was 'dysfunctional as a consequence of his alcoholism'.[64] According to Peter Berry, Ó Móráin had not communicated information at vital times and was 'showing signs, increasingly as time went on, of illness on which he obviously needed medical help'.[65] Ó Móráin eventually resigned in April 1970, shortly after The Irish Times reported on an embarrassing outburst at an Irish Bar dinner.[66]

James Gibbons, the Minister for Defence, meanwhile, was inexperienced, having been appointed in June 1969. Reports suggested that a new Ministry of Physical Planning would be created and Neil Blaney was to move to this department, with Gibbons switching to Agriculture.[67] Hence, Gibbons may not have anticipated a long stay in Defence, traditionally seen as one of the least prestigious ministries. Had Lynch left the incumbent Michael Hilliard in Defence in June 1969, some of the subsequent difficulties may have been averted.[68]

Meanwhile, since June of 1969, concern had been expressed about the capabilities of the Gardaí. Republicans had been engaged in a campaign targeting foreign landowners, burning numerous houses. There was also agitation related to housing issues and armed robberies that alarmed the Dublin government to such an extent that it was, according to British sources, apparently on the verge of 'suspending the Habeas Corpus Act and locking up a hundred or two of the offenders'.[69] Berry's aforementioned memorandum left little doubt about the seriousness of the subversive threat.[70]

The Gardaí were not in a prepared state to combat this threat. Deficiencies in the Gardaí were dealt with in a series of articles in The

Irish Times in August 1969.[71] Issues identified included poor training, lack of selectivity in recruitment, poor morale, harsh discipline, inadequate crime statistics and the overarching role of the Department of Justice in decision-making. The series concluded:

> It will be difficult for the Garda themselves to bring about a situation where the force is granted autonomy and hence the professional integrity which so many of its members consider it needs. The structure of the force and the decision making process which governs it has no warning system, no mechanism which allows rank and file opinion to filter through to where power lies.[72]

Morale in the force was also low. The *Garda Review* explored the theme after a near mutiny over conditions in Crumlin Garda station in late 1969. The rank-and-file's magazine noted that 'Guards have many grievances from the big ones about pay and hours of work, to the lesser ones arising out of the effects that day-to-day duty arrangements have on their private lives and well being.'[73] Many of the shortcomings in terms of pay and conditions for the Gardaí were later addressed in the Conroy Commission on Garda Pay and Conditions. The commission's proposals were partially implemented from April 1970 but this created new headaches as the dramatic reduction in the working week, from forty-eight hours to forty, meant a massive loss of manpower.

The Fallon killing was a further blow to already-depleted Garda morale, and it has been suggested that those in the upper echelons of the Gardaí refused to sweep the Arms Crisis under the carpet as a result of unrest in the force over the Fallon case.[74] When a suspect in the Fallon murder was acquitted, British embassy correspondence claimed that Garda feelings had been 'brought to boiling point'.[75] The views of Fallon's colleagues indicate the impact of the killing: 'The death of Dick Fallon was a watershed. He was just a man in uniform … the incident shook the force to its roots'; 'When that word reached us, it stunned the place for days. Like I mean, never in our lifetime, the previous shooting of a guard had been in 1942 or something'; 'That brought the realisation to all of us at the time. A big shock and a big change.'[76]

Kieran Conway, then a republican activist, described the general tension:

On the Friday night of the killing I sat in a pub in Dun Laoghaire as the news came in and real working men at the bar were railing angrily against the IRA. I was wearing a Connolly badge on my then de rigueur combat jacket, a sure giveaway, and thought the men might have a go at me.[77]

A fortnight after the Fallon killing, *Hibernia* magazine called for an inquiry into the bank raid to be carried out 'if the confidence of the public, and particularly of rank and file Gardaí, is to be restored'.[78] The notion of conspiracy over Fallon's death continues to linger. However, the resultant Garda investigation also highlighted the substantial deficiencies in Garda Special Branch. Peter Berry had sought in October 1969 thirty extra Special Branch detectives to combat Saor Éire but a combination of a lack of resources and bureaucratic infighting meant this did not happen.[79] A *Hibernia* report referred to this removal of surveillance on the Saor Éire group and reported: 'As evidence of supposed high level interference in the investigations becomes thinner and thinner and less convincing, a number of Gardaí-uniformed and detective are beginning to wonder whether the vaunted surveillance being carried out by Special Branch was as effective or thorough as was believed.'[80]

    Conor Brady, a respected commentator on Garda affairs and future editor of the *Garda Review*, echoed this criticism of the investigation powers of the Special Branch, citing factors such as poor training, undermanning and bad management. He claimed that there had been a deterioration in Special Branch effectiveness due to a shift in focus during the sixties:

> Part of the reason for the debilitating condition of S.D.U. [Special Branch] is the silly season honeymoon of the mid-Sixties during which the threat of Republican militarism receded and the Branch justified its existence by watching left wing student groups. At the same time, strength fell and recruitment seemed to yield pride of place to brawn rather than brain at least in a few cases.[81]

A frequently overlooked aspect of Garda policy that is worth noting relates to the practice whereby Gardaí were not allowed to serve in their home district. British official Peck, commenting on the trend, noted that 'Gardaí are not accepted in Irish villages as are English policemen in their communities' and 'especially in outlying areas never achieve much rapport with locals'.[82] Because many Gardaí would soon be sent to rural villages along the border, this is a significant point. A further difficulty for the Gardaí related to a chronic shortage of equipment. Although Berry's July memorandum on security policy applauded the excellent 'calibre and morale' of the Gardaí, it pointed to the shortages of basic equipment 'in the form of radio networks and radio controlled cars which had been requisitioned and refused again and again by the Minister of Finance'.[83]

A final aspect worth considering is the degree of political interference in terms of promotions in the security services. Fine Gael's Gerry L'Estrange raised the issue in the Dáil when he alleged that 'for political reasons, certain friends of the ex-Minister for Agriculture and Fisheries [Blaney] have been promoted during the past few years over the heads of much more deserving colleagues'.[84] L'Estrange cited an individual case and, particularly in senior ranks, the problem seemed prevalent. Peter Berry alleged that Commissioner Wymes was appointed Assistant Commissioner in 1963 at the behest of Charles Haughey, despite being about twentieth in order of seniority. Wymes was granted the role of Commissioner 'largely due to Haughey'.[85] Similarly, when a new chief of staff of the Army was appointed in early 1971, it was viewed by a British Ministry of Defence advisor as 'a piece of blatant party political patronage'.[86]

It was necessary earlier in the chapter to highlight the inadequacies of the Army in the context of the fateful August 1969 cabinet meetings. At this stage, it is worth making a broader comment on Army planning subsequent to the initial crisis. Documents have been released by Military Archives which, on the face of it, indicate that the Irish government was contemplating military action along the border. Among these documents are the Planning Board Recommendations.[87] This document dealt with the state of Irish Defence Forces and its capabilities. It noted several immediate actions that needed to be taken to put the Defence Forces on a better footing should a doomsday situation arise. These steps included improved training, a new Special Forces unit, a motivation programme to indoctrinate troops and an intensification of the intelligence effort in Northern Ireland. A key recommendation was the establishment of 'a command structure to plan, organise, direct, coordinate and control operations in Northern

Ireland and that the structure be subject of a separate study'.[88] In terms of this recommendation, a difficulty was encountered which could be 'overcome by a broad written directive from the Minister'.[89] The report concluded that 'the Defence Forces have NO capability on embarking on unilateral operations of any kind (either conventional or unconventional) from a firm base at home'.

While co-operation with northern groups was mentioned by the report, so too were the dangers associated with such a course. As well as the ability to carry out small-scale operations up to company level, the report also claimed the Defence Forces were capable of providing arms training for nationalists living in Northern Ireland and supplying arms ammunition and equipment. As has already been stated, the report was quite clear that this course of action carried 'serious political implications'. The report of the Planning Board is viewed by some in quite benign terms:

> Some have argued that this planning paper showed the Irish government planned to invade Northern Ireland through the creation and sponsorship of a new – and specifically northern – IRA. And while this might sound like a green light for the later activities of Blaney and Haughey and the Arms Crisis, the reality was that the report was only ever the result of a planning scenario, and that inherent within these military papers is a realisation that such actions would never be sanctioned by government.[90]

Certainly, there is merit to this view, but the significance of the study should not be fully dismissed. Some of the conclusions and recommendations were acted upon. As has already been discussed, some arms training was provided. The intelligence function's activities in Northern Ireland continued, with Captain Kelly acting as principal point of contact. A recruitment campaign was also initiated and a highly controversial directive was issued by the Minister for Defence on 6 February 1970, informing the chief of staff and the Director of Intelligence to 'prepare and train the Army for incursions into Northern Ireland if and when such a course became necessary and to have respirators and arms and ammunition made ready in the event that it would be necessary for the minority to protect themselves'.[91] This directive was apparently issued after meetings with delegations from the North. 'At these meetings urgent demands were made for respirators, weapons and ammunition, the provision of which the government agreed as and when necessary.'[92]

As a result of the directive, 500 rifles, 200 Gustav machine guns, 3,000 respirators, 80,000 rounds of .303 ammunition and 99,000 rounds of 9mm ammunition were amassed in two barracks, in case the necessity to make use of them should arise.[93] Defence Minister Gibbons acknowledged at the Arms Trial that at one stage rifles were moved to the border town of Dundalk after a request from Neil Blaney. The request had come after an outbreak of rioting in Belfast. Gibbons denied that the arms were moved in anticipation of distribution, but this was an example of his evidence lacking credibility.

Again, the mechanics of the operation are worth considering. The decision to move the arms to the border seems to have been entirely political and left military personnel confused. On hearing the order, Chief of Staff Mac Eoin immediately approached the Director of Military Intelligence Heffernon and his understudy Colonel Delaney. It is an indication of the ad hoc nature of things in the Army that neither man knew anything about the operation or was able to assist the chief of staff, who must have been equally confused.[94] At the Arms Trial, Gibbons claimed he ordered the guns north when he was stopped 'in a crowded street in Naas by the Gardaí with an urgent request to contact Neil Blaney'. Upon contacting Blaney, Gibbons ordered the guns to Dundalk to placate his more senior colleague.[95] Gibbons justified his actions by saying that Blaney 'may do something rash himself' if no action were taken.[96] An even more sensational account of this event claims that the arms were being shipped to a monastery in Cavan for distribution and it was only the intervention of Lynch that got them diverted to Dundalk instead.[97]

That aspects of the Planning Board's recommendations were implemented means it was a document of some significance but it was not a policy document, nor was the February Directive, for that matter. State bureaucracies plan for all sorts of eventualities. That such plans existed says very little in itself. The February Directive was not issued at a time of particular panic and it could be argued that its issuance merely allowed the military to engage in planning of a sensitive nature. A military memorandum from the General Staff in April 1970, formulated in response to the directive, warned of the 'disastrous consequences that would follow if such operations were mounted'.[98] It further cautioned that any offensive move would require the closure of border posts and the removal of military guards from vital installations. Such a move 'in present circumstances would be a grave risk'.[99]

Guns were moved towards the border and military training was provided. Of this there is no doubt. However, the very mechanics of each of these decisions showed a lack of coherent policy and are indicative of a broader malaise within the Defence Forces. The Army lacked a defined purpose. There was no White Paper on defence or defence policy, as such. Chief of Staff Seán MacEoin wrote, in February 1971, that the most important implication of the lack of defence policy was that the Army had 'no sense of purpose'.[100] Indeed, the first item raised in a meeting with Jack Lynch by MacEoin in June 1970 was 'the lack of clear-cut Governmental policy on defence and indicated the urgency of this matter'.[101] That MacEoin raised this matter with the Taoiseach so early on the occasion of their first meeting since the Arms crisis revelations broke is significant.

In 1969/70, the planning papers indicated some of the policy options that were available. The existence of these planning papers in the absence of a broader policy framework caused confusion. The analysis presented seems to roughly correspond with the view from the British embassy but, as the following extract indicates, the embassy did not seem overly perturbed by the existence of Irish contingency plans:

> Contingency plans for rescue operations in the event of total breakdown of law and order in Northern Ireland involving an incursion into the North in aid of Northern Catholics and the distribution of arms to them during the worst of the 1969/70 troubles were pressed on the rest of the government by the Boland/Blaney faction before the Army had been given a proper opportunity to make an appreciation and express their views on the feasibility of the operation. During this period, also, we had a weak and ineffective Ministry of Defence (Gibbons) and the evidence of the Arms Trial has shown that the Chief of Staff did not have a grip on the situation that one would expect of the professional head of the Defence Forces.[102]

The Army and Garda inadequacies were obviously detrimental to an effective security response, and these difficulties were compounded by some inter-service rivalry. There seemed to be a particular breakdown in relations between Military Intelligence and the Garda Special Branch. This issue was raised by the defence in the Arms Trial;[103] indeed, Minister for Justice Ó Móráin said there had been 'a grave lack of cooperation between the two bodies'.[104] This rivalry may have had considerable depth, as 'relations between G2 and Justice had been difficult ever since the pugnacious Peter Berry had become his minister's main advisor on security issues in 1941'.[105]

The influence, real or perceived, of individual politicians along with a vacuum in terms of policy and personnel at the top of key departments were to prove significant factors in the confused circumstances of the time. The months prior to May 1970 had seen contradictory statements and actions coming from different government sources. Even the head of the Department of Justice, Peter Berry, was unsure of what government policy was and which political figures could be trusted.

The Security Situation in the Southern Border Counties

While newspaper headlines trumpeted the movement of troops to the border on the orders of their political masters, the atmosphere on the streets of border towns was more sedate, with newly arrived refugees being the focus of most attention. The *Donegal Democrat* of 22 August 1969 reported on its front page that collections were being organised in the county for the relief effort, with a countywide committee formed for the purpose by the Bishop of Raphoe.[106] In each of the border counties a similar pattern emerged, with collections being organised in aid of relief efforts and support coming from broad sections of the community. In Sligo, refugees received assistance from an eclectic mix that included the National Farmers Association, Leitrim's Men Association, Sligo Rotary Club and the women's section of the British Legion.[107] In Leitrim, the Red Cross described the £1,600 raised as 'colossal'.[108] Obviously concerned that public goodwill would be exploited by subversives, the Government Information Bureau issued a statement warning individuals not to subscribe to certain collections, notably by the Northern Defence Fund.[109] There are no reports of prosecutions for associated collections. In later years, local papers regularly noted the prosecution of republicans for such collections.

As well as the charitable outpourings, there were more militant responses to violence across the border. The *Donegal Democrat* noted prominently, on its front page, that rumours had circulated in Donegal that some local Protestants were active in the B-Specials. Threats were made to several individuals and there was a petrol-bomb attack on the home of one man.[110] More generally, allegations made by Ian Paisley of a boycott of Protestants in Donegal were described as mischievous by local Protestant councillor William Patterson.[111] Also in Donegal, a Sinn Féin statement condemned attacks on holidaymakers from Northern Ireland by 'Catholic Paisleys and creeps'. This condemnation followed an explosion at a caravan in Milford.[112] In Monaghan too, the B-Special rumour seemed to earn some credence and was discussed openly at a Castleblayney Urban District Council meeting.[113] A small number of physical attacks, mainly on property, took place in Monaghan. There was a sectarian petrol-bomb attack on a home in Newbliss,[114] an attempt to burn an Orange Hall on the Monaghan–Armagh Road[115] and slogans were painted on walls in Rockcorry.[116]

Further away from the border, there were other incidents, including intimidation of residents of an interdenominational holiday retreat in Greystones, Wicklow.[117] Meanwhile, a statement from Monaghan Sinn Féin condemned the 'verbal and physical intimidation of Protestants throughout the county and at Kingscourt'.[118] Sinn Féin was usually to the fore in condemning sectarian attacks; after Monaghan TD Billy Fox used his maiden speech in the Dáil to address issues of sectarianism directed against him during the general election, a local Sinn Féin councillor wrote to the local paper corroborating Fox's account and offered to act as a witness in any future proceedings.[119] Meanwhile, in Sligo town, the local newspaper colourfully described a public meeting where a Union Jack and an effigy of Northern Ireland Prime Minister James Chichester-Clark were burned. A section of the crowd at the meeting, however, took exception on the night to the flying of the Starry Plough as opposed to the Tricolour.[120] Dundalk had a unique response to the onset of violence over the border: 'thirty youths, some carrying blankets and haversacks and wearing crash helmets, marched to the military barracks in formation and demanded arms'.[121] In Dublin on 16 and 17 August, meanwhile, there was some violence: sixteen Garda and fifty civilians were injured and there were reports of petrol bombs and missiles thrown at Gardaí.[122] Marches had taken place in Dublin throughout the week, with a call from Tomás

MacGiolla, Sinn Féin, and Paddy Devlin, MP, later a founder of the SDLP, for arms to be made available.[123]

Considering the upheaval in Northern Ireland, the general response in communities along the border was moderate. None of the public meetings deteriorated into violence. Accounts from local newspapers indicate that those mobilised in support of refugees covered the full spectrum of society and included official state agencies, GAA figures and the Catholic Church. The fact that northern Catholics were getting support from the 'pillars of society' may have tempered some radicalism.

As well as street protests and collections, there is also evidence of significant movement of arms and men along the border in August 1969. Initially, IRA members fleeing from Northern Ireland and IRA reinforcements from the South 'more or less met in the border counties'.[124] Again, training camps were established first in the border areas before later being moved further south.[125] With the exception of an attack on Crossmaglen police station on the night of 17 August, the IRA took little military action on the border. The IRA received criticism after the Crossmaglen attack. A statement from IRA leader Cathal Goulding on 18 August claimed that the IRA were active in the North and demanded Irish Army intervention. Goulding received a public rebuke for this from Taoiseach Jack Lynch.[126] It was then decided at an IRA meeting in the Castle Hotel in Dublin that units would not take further direct action along the border.[127] The IRA seemed to have concentrated their efforts on gathering weapons and transporting them to border locations. IRA leader Seán MacStíofáin describes operating from a base along the South Armagh border and receiving four carloads of materials. MacStíofáin claimed: 'The Gardaí had not been interfering with us in any way in our area. Undoubtedly they were aware that any arms traffic through the South was one way, to the North and for defensive purposes.'[128]

MacStíofáin partially ascribed the Garda inaction to 'some fellow feeling for the sufferings of their own compatriots and the anguished condition of women and children'.[129] The IRA had some reason for their confidence in Garda inaction in 1969. According to a later intelligence report, a cabinet minister had a meeting with Cathal Goulding in August 1969, at which the IRA was promised a free hand in launching a cross-border campaign if activities in the twenty-six counties were ended.[130] In fact, the IRA Army Council was left perplexed by the Taoiseach's rebuke of Goulding on 19 August, having previously been assured of a free hand by a cabinet colleague.[131] Then Minister for Agriculture Neil Blaney later claimed that some twenty-five TDs and senators went even further and gave guns directly for use in the North. Blaney further said an order was given to Gardaí along the border that no one moving arms was to be interfered with from August 1969 to April 1970.[132] Separately, it was also alleged that a Cork TD had brought a boot load of guns to Leinster House and these were transferred north by a senator from the border counties.[133]

Evidence does suggest that the IRA were certainly freer to act than would later be the case. It was an open secret that units were present in certain border areas, with some men even seen drinking in McGirl's pub in Ballinamore in battledress.[134] Blaney's allegation was put to Minister for Justice Desmond O'Malley in the Dáil in April 1971. O'Malley pointed out that the allegation of a directive was denied by the Garda Commissioner:

> The Commissioner's reply, based on this comprehensive check, is that there was no such order, directive or suggestion. It may be relevant to mention that, at intervals throughout the period in question [August 1969–April 1970], various seizures of illegally-held arms were made by the gardaí and a number of people were prosecuted for illegal possession of arms or explosives.[135]

The arrests and seizures O'Malley mentions seem to have taken place well after August 1969. Again, local border newspapers, which in subsequent years would give prominence to Garda arms finds, mention no such seizures in August 1969. That a directive was issued, as Blaney suggests, seems unlikely and there is no archival evidence to support its existence. Indeed, when reports reached the government on 25 August of IRA overtures to Gardaí on the ground to 'turn a blind eye', Peter Berry noted that the Taoiseach had sent out the instruction that there be 'no fraternising'.[136]

With troops moving towards the border and mixed signals coming from political figures known to have powerful influence on the force, it would be unsurprising if some Gardaí did 'look the other way'. There was nothing new in this for the force. As previously discussed, when Fianna Fáil came to power in the 1930s, the Garda attitude to the IRA changed: 'There were of course no official circulars to that effect, no orders, written or verbal, but the moral was drawn very swiftly from one or two instances.'[137]

After the initial conflict of August 1969 had subsided, the emphasis shifted from the prospect of incursions into the six counties to the procurement of arms for northern nationalists.[138] This has already been discussed in the context of the Arms Trial and the Dunree training. There were also allegations of ongoing subversive training, which attracted public attention when arrests were made in December 1969. Again, Donegal, the closest border county to a main hub of violence, was the scene. The mechanics of the arrests are interesting as they reveal no pre-planning on behalf of the Gardaí. A vigilant neighbour noticed a stray vehicle at an isolated cottage and when the local sergeant went to investigate, he discovered seven young men and a quantity of firearms.[139] Obviously, the situation created a dilemma for the security chiefs. When Ó Móráin put the matter to Lynch, the Taoiseach instructed his Justice Minister to 'throw the book' at the defendants.[140] Twenty-four hours after charges were made, Peter Berry was contacted by Haughey, who was enquiring as to who made the 'stupid' decision to arrest the men.[141] Berry raised with Haughey the possibility of contempt-of-court charges complicating the case, if there was a refusal by the men to recognise the courts. Haughey seemingly intervened with the men to ensure there was no such issue.[142]

The occasion of the court appearances of the men was to present the state with an opportunity to deliver a clear message. The presence of 200 protestors and 50 Gardaí outside the courthouse indicated that this was not a normal case. In evidence, the defendants were described as 'cooperative', 'respectful' and 'seemed like decent men', according to the arresting officer.[143] The more serious charges of possession of firearms with intent to endanger life were withdrawn and the men were freed in January, having received the Probation Act. Their addresses were not read out in case that information was used by 'police officers of another jurisdiction'[144] and when they were remanded in Mountjoy after their initial appearance, they were not handcuffed or fingerprinted.[145] If the intention of Lynch's instruction to 'throw the book' at the men was to send out an unequivocal message, it was unsuccessful. Within a few years, such court cases would be the scenes of bitter confrontation but in this, the first such incidence, the state's case carried an almost apologetic air.

Two other issues that concerned security forces at this time were the threat posed by loyalists and the threat from left-leaning groups, including those that were later to become Official Sinn Féin/IRA. The threat from loyalists was a strain on Army manpower. Thirty installations received military guards, with another sixteen covered by motorised patrol. There were a further 100 installations identified as vital, but which were not being protected.[146] In total, 450 Army personnel were tied up in these protection duties, with a further 865 assigned to border posts.[147] Considering the small number of combat-ready troops at Army disposal, this was a considerable strain on resources. The prolonged periods of guard duty did nothing to improve Army morale or preparedness for more serious challenges. The threat level was emphasised when loyalist Thomas McDowell blew himself up while planting explosives at Ballyshannon power station on 19 October 1969.[148] Other bombs exploded at RTÉ headquarters in Dublin and the Wolfe Tone memorial in Kildare.[149] Whether these were the work of loyalists remains unclear, but the reports of such incidents added to concern. Early November seemed particularly tense, with reports that 'every by road approved or unapproved, leading across the border is manned by a Garda'.[150]

A report from a Sligo-based Garda gives an indication of the vague nature of the threat posed:

> Just now a lot of our comrades are being drafted to border areas to guard against intrusion from across the border by a self styled cleric in the 'Rasputin' mould and his blindly led henchmen. Being a border division ourselves we have our own troubles in this respect. Thank God, that none of our comrades was injured in the Ballyshannon raid. I earnestly hope that we will receive a lot less of those 'hazy' messages such as 'keep a look out,' 'be on the alert', etc. No one questions the veracity of most of these messages, but still some of the ones received of late border on the ridiculous.[151]

The loyalist threat was a relatively new challenge to Gardaí but left leaning republicanism was flagged by Berry's report earlier in 1969. Such activists were not confined to the main urban centres where the agitation campaign of the Dublin Housing Action Committee, for example, was receiving particular prominence. As early as March 1969, the organ of the republican movement, *The United Irishman*, led with the headline 'Civil Rights for South?'[152] Along the border, Sligo seems to have been a particular centre for agitation with young socialist republican Declan Bree a key figure. Sit-in protests on civil rights issues took place in the town.[153] Some of these incidents included councillors, protestors and Gardaí exchanging blows.[154] Campaigns not only related to housing but also other issues, including fishing rights. Protestors mainly from Louth and Monaghan occupied Slane Castle in July 1970. After a force of fifty Gardaí overpowered the protestors, thirteen of them were remanded on firearms charges, which were eventually dropped.[155]

Even in traditionally conservative Donegal, there was some left-wing agitation. In a similar manner as in Sligo, protests took place at council meetings, leading to raucous scenes.[156] While such incidents can be dismissed as the actions of a small number of committed activists, there is some evidence of broader support. For example, Bernadette Devlin brought over 1,200 onto the streets in Donegal in March 1970 to address civil rights issues in the county.[157] While speaking in Donegal, Devlin directed particular ire towards sitting TD Neil Blaney. The antipathy that existed between the leftist republicans and Blaney was even evident on the streets of Letterkenny on the night Blaney made his famous December speech calling for a more republican stance from government. About fifteen republican protestors picketed the event, with Fianna Fáil senator Bernard MacGlinchy among those involved in a physical confrontation.[158]

In contrast to 1971 and 1972, the border was remarkably quiet as the summer of 1970 ended. The IRA had engaged in a campaign of sabotage from 1970 and this had a minor effect as some customs huts were destroyed.[159] There was one notable exception to this trend in an incident that saw the first RUC men to be killed by republicans during the Troubles. The two officers, Robert Millar and Samuel Donaldson, were blown up when they went to examine a booby-trapped car near the border on the Crossmaglen–Dundalk Road on 11 August 1970. In view of the subsequent history of the area during the Troubles, it may seem unsurprising that the setting for this incident was the South Armagh border area but, as already noted, border areas were hitherto insulated from the violence. After the explosion, former Nationalist MP for the area Eddie Richardson stated that he knew 'for a fact that everyone in Crossmaglen is very depressed and annoyed about this whole incident'.[160] *Irish Times* reporter Henry Kelly noted that, unlike

Derry, Belfast or even nearby Armagh, Crossmaglen was peaceful and 'never a flashpoint'.[161] The editorial in the local paper, *The Dundalk Democrat*, expressed a similar theme, stating that 'their deaths were all the more unfortunate as the occurrence took place in an area where political and sectarian strife have been singularly absent'.[162] At the inquest into the men's death, the police asked for their appreciation for the support they received from people in Crossmaglen to be put on the record.[163]

Crossmaglen was later to become synonymous with militant republicanism and much of the discourse on cross-border security centred on this area along the Louth–Armagh–Monaghan border. Yet, in the years 1969 and 1970, the particular significance of border towns like Crossmaglen was not apparent. The border war had not yet begun.

In a pattern that would come to be frequently repeated, the RUC suspected that one of those involved in the bombing moved south after the attack. In 1971, the British contacted the Irish authorities, giving extensive details of the suspect's alleged criminal/paramilitary background.[164] The Gardaí, whether by luck or design, arrested the suspect on firearms charges shortly afterwards, but he did not receive jail time.

The death of the two RUC men raised unionist fears and increased pressure on the Northern Ireland government to be seen to do something. The decision was taken to 'spike' a few border roads in the South Armagh area. The road closures were a definitive failure. At Courtbane on the Armagh–Louth border, for example, the road was 'spiked' eleven times, having been re-opened by locals.[165] A Northern Ireland Office analysis was scathing:

> The scheme has failed. Not all unapproved roads were spiked and the spikes that were installed were not proof against the implements of an agrarian society – tractors and land rovers. As Major Chichester Clarke has said the performance in Crossmaglen was absurd. It has caused the Northern Ireland government to lose face: it has caused the Army more manpower problems than it saved because of the need to replace spikes daily: it has caused inconvenience to many people living along the border; and perhaps it has given unnecessary publicity to the border and its associated problems.[166]

The spiking of border roads was quietly dropped later in the year. In discussions with the Department of Foreign Affairs, the British Ambassador asked the Irish government to provide additional Garda patrols in the vicinity of the Crossmaglen border as part of the winding down of the 'spiking' operation. The Ambassador also emphasised that the discontinuance of the 'spiking' depended to a large extent on 'the absence of press and political comment' in the Republic.[167] Luckily for the Irish security forces, on this occasion the British Army avoided confrontation with those opening the roads, so there were no major public disturbances to deal with. It was apparent from the concerted effort of those removing spikes that road closures was an emotive issue.

Two final trends in security from the summer of 1970 are worth commenting on, as they were to become more commonplace as time progressed. Firstly, there was another arrest in Donegal on firearms charges. Derryman Thomas Carlin was charged with firearms offences in Donegal on 4 August 1970. As was the case with the arrests the previous year, there was a sizeable Garda presence at the courthouse, which was picketed beforehand. The courtroom was also packed with supporters of the defendant during the hearing.[168] As such cases became more common in the months ahead, the scene of protests, often accompanied with a set-piece confrontation, would become a common occurrence.

The second trend relates to British Army incursions. These were becoming more frequent as the summer of 1970 progressed. As the conflict became bitterer, incursions would become a matter of considerable divergence between the two governments and cause a headache for local security forces. In 1970, there were fifteen such incidents upon which representations by the Department of Foreign Affairs were made.[169] These incidents were a mixture of crossings by foot patrols and jeeps. Eight infringements occurred in Donegal, two in Monaghan, four in Louth and one in Cavan.[170] In contrast, in 1971, there were no infringements reported in Donegal, eleven in Monaghan, seven in Louth and four in Cavan.[171] This shows the changing nature of the conflict, with extra focus on the border areas in Armagh, Tyrone and Fermanagh. The British offered the explanation that their transgressions were due to 'lack of knowledge of localities by new units'.[172] The shooting war on the border had not begun in earnest so the Irish government did not protest with the same vigour it would over later territorial transgressions. Nevertheless, each incident was catalogued and reported by the Department of Foreign Affairs.

The Spillover into the South

An often-overlooked aspect of the 1969 crisis was the influx of refugees from the North. The *Dundalk Democrat* noted that it was 'hard to assess the exact number of refugees, as many from the North seem to have been put up by friends in the town, but it seems that about 500 refugees have been assisted'.[173] The earliest Military Situation Report with official figures on refugees housed by the Irish Army is from 22 August and appears in Table 1.[174]

The bulk of refugees arrived in the mid-August period, but there was considerable fluctuation in numbers, including on 9 September when ninety-six new arrivals came to Gormanston, amongst them the family of Samuel McLarnon, one of the first victims of the violence.[175] Most of the refugees were Catholic, but a report in Donegal contains an account of a Protestant family housed in Finner Camp.[176] Many refugees went home within a month but some stayed considerably longer. There were still 452 refugees in total between camps in Gormanston, Finner and Kildare at the start of October.[177] By the end of November, the numbers had dwindled further to just 129 concentrated in Gormanston.[178] The conditions in these camps were far from satisfactory as described by one refugee:

> Our living quarters were the army billets. To me they were huts bordering on the likeness of a garden shed. I clearly remember our hut, it was hut number 48. It was a long rectangular apex roofed hut. No kitchen, no bathroom, the toilets were public toilets as were the shower facilities on the campsite.[179]

Table 1. Refugees on 22 August 1969

Camp	Men	Women	Children
Gormanston camp	62	105	280
Gormanston College	1	9	10
Finner	44	22	81

This account goes on to describe an unhappy school experience where the new arrivals suffered 'the same inane prejudices targeted at the foreign nationals who [in recent times] are accused of getting benefits and jobs belonging to locals'.[180] The poor conditions in the camp were a worry to the camp medical officer, who warned that numbers in the camp should be limited to 200 in the interests of public health.[181] The dreadful circumstances that some families found themselves in can be gauged by one terse Situation Report from Gormanston, which, after relaying the end-of-day figures for refugees, curtly noted that 'a family of three refugees named Coleman which left Gormanston on 2 January 1970 were found dead in a caravan at Brownstown, Curragh'.[182]

The official attitude to the refugees does not seem overly sympathetic after the initial few weeks. This may have been due in part to the fact that the refugees continued to receive welfare entitlements they held in Northern Ireland.[183] Also, the refugees were a strain on Army resources, particularly after August. Individual volunteers and students helped significantly with refugees when the crisis first erupted, but as the weeks progressed and the holiday season ended, this support was no longer available. The Army did attempt to make use of the refugees as an intelligence source but most of those interviewed seem to have left before any violence had begun or had stayed indoors, so the intelligence gathered was 'already common knowledge'.[184] One official noted 'the standard of intelligence of some refugees who furnished evidence is not high, so that the dependability of their statements is doubtful'.[185] It seems that some official sources were very suspicious of the bona fides of many of those who sought refuge, seeing them as little more than holidaymakers.

An Irish Army report anticipated more refugees arriving in the summer of 1970 if the weather was good. It was further noted that 'one family in Belfast had expressed the wish to the Red Cross to book in for the first fortnight in July 1970'.[186] An Army memorandum also outlined problems with regard to maintaining discipline, complaining that the lack of a screening process meant that 'non refugees and undesirable persons may be and in fact have been admitted'.[187] Issues of refugees returning to the camp 'drunk and noisy or at unreasonably late hours' and teenagers failing to attend school or being non-co-operative also concerned the military, who were unaccustomed to performing the role of truant officer cum social worker.[188] There was

to be further experience of refugees in 1970 and to a greater extent
again in 1971. In 1975, a Garda Chief Superintendent reflected that:

> Refugees from Northern Ireland in the past, limited though their
> numbers were, showed that they were demanding, undisciplined
> and destructive, indicating that they felt entitled to the best
> treatment here while at the same time showing scant regard for
> the property placed at their disposal. This category alone while
> being more of a nuisance value than a serious threat, could make
> demands on Garda time and divert attention from more important
> serious work.[189]

An RTÉ report in 1969 explored a similar theme and concluded that:

> Refugees were taken into the camp without question. Some of
> them undoubtedly came mostly for the 'free holiday'. But they
> were of course the first to go home. Among those who remain are
> some who are hiding from other things as well as petrol bombs.
> Gormanston can also provide a refuge from marital problems or
> even just a comfortable retreat for the mildly neurotic or over
> nervous.[190]

This uneasy relationship worked both ways, as indicated by
these comments from northerners who settled:[191] 'People from the
North were not immediately welcomed into the Dundalk community
and tended to socialise together around a number of bars/pubs
frequented by northerners ... I would hear through my work this part
of the town being referred to as Provo Land'; 'Sometimes there were
tensions, people particularly in the early years were suspicious of any
northerners and often wild stories were spread and everybody was on
the Army Council ... but likewise I have seen Northerners not afraid
to misuse this fear and act in a bullying fashion.'

The experience of 1969 was only to be a prelude for things to
come. The largest holding of refugees in a single day in 1969 was
720. In 1971, 5,409 refugees were to be held in a single day, with
9,800 arriving in 1972 between 11 July and 22 September 1972.[192] The
arrival of the refugees in August saw a massive community response in
support in terms of collections and volunteerism. It seems, however,
that this welcome dissipated as time and events progressed.

Table 2. Refugees on 13 July 1970[193]

Camp	Men	Women	Children	Total
Gormanston (Meath)	54	140	276	470
Kilworth (Cork)	7	111	384	502
Finner (Donegal)	1	5	9	15
Coolmoney (Wicklow)	10	69	255	334
Kildare	12	52	173	237

Another influx of refugees came in the summer of 1970, with a predominance of women and children arriving. There seems to have been a more determined policy of shifting the refugees further south, away from the border, as Table 2 illustrates.

The numbers of refugees fluctuated considerably over the summer months. By 13 August, 272 remained in Gormanston, 266 in Kilworth and 84 in Finner.[194] The spike in Finner camp figures can be explained by Derry residents crossing the border in anticipation of violence during the Apprentice Boys parade. The *Donegal Democrat* of 14 August reported on tense scenes on the border and Garda fears of violence as Donegal-based Apprentice Boys returned home.[195] By 25 September, there were just 101 refugees left, all based in Gormanston.

The early experience with refugees had not been positive. Somewhat ominously, an *Irish Times* report on Kilworth Camp noted: 'For some this is almost a routine thing. Some mothers had left home at least four times since last August.'[196]

Heading Towards the Border War

The response to the outbreak of violence in the North was more cliché than conspiracy. One of the most thorough examinations of the period posits the question 'Just what was government policy and who was running it – Lynch, Ó Móráin or Blaney and Haughey?'[197] Considerable time and effort has been devoted to answering this question. In truth, however, there was no set policy. Ministers simply made ad hoc decisions as circumstances arose. Gibbons stopped his car in Naas and ordered guns north. Hillery hired a car at the last minute to take a tour of the Falls Road. Such was what passed for policy. There was no coherent strategy at play. Obviously, this implies a clear lack of leadership on the part of Lynch. The clichéd strategy of appointing a subcommittee is well worn in Irish political life when dealing with uncomfortable issues. The decision to give over the northern issue to a subcommittee proved disastrous. In this respect, some have argued that something positive came out of the Arms crisis:

> it forced the government and a political system to begin to face up to the Northern Ireland problem as something which had to be addressed with patient diplomacy and cautious statecraft rather than impetuous speeches and the nod-and-wink encouragement of irredentist militancy, and as a matter which required the constant attention of the serving Taoiseach and of a standing committee of appropriate ministers.[198]

Meanwhile, the decision to send troops to the border and deliver the 'stand (idly) by' speech raised expectations unrealistically for northern nationalists. A future scenario was set in the minds of northern nationalists whereby if things got bad the Irish Army would roll over the border to the rescue. This would never occur.

Nevertheless, in the circumstances, there was merit to having a security policy that was, to use modern parlance, 'fudged'. The mobilisation of the Irish Army in August 1969 calmed the situation south of the border. Likewise, a security clampdown on republicans would have been impossible in the context of the violence in Derry and Belfast. However, the clear discrepancies in government attitudes could not be reconciled forever. The policy espoused by Blaney in Letterkenny and Lynch in Tralee were so different that it was obvious that the ambiguity could not last. This is particularly true when the mixed signals in political circles coincided with a breakdown in the military chain of command.

For security personnel on the ground, the situation must have been particularly confusing. While Peter Berry had the luxury of receiving advice from President de Valera when he was in doubt about the correct course to pursue, there was no such luxury for those on checkpoint duty on a lonely border road. Moreover, the entire Arms Trial debacle had clearly demonstrated the price that would be paid by those who made the wrong call. Captain Kelly took on his function with too much republican vigour and lost his career and nearly his liberty as a result. Meanwhile, Peter Berry was identified as an arch-anti-republican. He too suffered as a consequence. Berry's home was picketed by Republican protestors[199] and he eventually retired, having been the subject of death and kidnap threats.[200] There was a stark, if not very well-defined message, for those involved in security. In this context, the views of the British Ambassador John Peck are interesting:

> 'Security authorities' do not seek out and arrest would-be trouble makers but expend many men and much money on permanently guarding fixed installations ... Not all Republican activity can be ignored. While the police can with little risk to public order look the other way when they come across illegal drilling in the hills or uniformed parades at some rural Republican commemoration, they take action against more dangerous activity.[201]

As the Troubles evolved, the Gardaí would come across activity of the 'dangerous' variety more and more frequently. Already, new Minister for Justice Des O'Malley was concerned by rising crime. Writing to the Taoiseach seeking extra numbers for the Gardaí, he decried the 'truly appalling' crime figures, made worse by the implementation of the Conroy Report.[202] Yet, things were to deteriorate further. In 1970, there were eleven armed robberies in the state,[203] which had caused much disquiet. In 1971, there were 56 such robberies and 143 in 1972 but, as we have observed, the border was remarkably quiet relative to what was to come.

The threats to the Irish state that festered along the border in 1969/70 were to explode in 1971/2, leaving the state in a position whereby it would have to definitively come down for or against the republicans. Already, experience with northern refugees had hardened the attitudes of some within the security services. This trend would continue over the coming years and contribute to conflict in border towns between republicans and the Gardaí. As we will see, by the end of 1972, the Irish state adjudged that it faced a greater threat if it did not act against the IRA, especially in light of the renewed loyalist threat that emerged in October/November 1969.

The strategy of keeping the conflict sealed in the six counties would not, however, be easy. Already, the experience of the first British soldiers showed that incursions were inevitable. As confrontations on the border became more commonplace in 1971/2, such transgressions would take on added significance. Those who would be at the frontline of implementing security policy – whether judges, Gardaí, or soldiers – were well attuned to the political sensitivities of their role post-Arms Trial. Within weeks of the Arms Trial verdicts, some observers discerned a shift in government security policy but the repercussions of the preceding period, along with a deteriorating situation over the border, meant that any shift in policy would prove difficult to implement.

CHAPTER 3

'There is a lot to be said for trying to hold refugees in the North': Security Policy, December 1970–December 1972

The years 1971 and 1972 saw the conflict reach the border in earnest. Just as in Northern Ireland, some places were more affected by violence than others. Towns like Dundalk, Clones, Ballyshannon and Lifford experienced particular difficulties. Dundalk was the most prominent town affected:

> For a brief time Dundalk took on a little of the tawdry glamour of a frontier town. IRA men on rest and recreation brawled and drank their way around the clock. On one celebrated occasion a disgruntled Provisional watching the racing on television at the Imperial Hotel shot up the screen when his horse trailed in last.[1]

The story of a gunman shooting up a pub TV may be apocryphal but it is nonetheless illustrative of the climate of the time. More generally, throughout the Republic, the realities and complexities of the northern conflict were becoming apparent. The more militant sentiment that surfaced after Bloody Sunday dissipated remarkably quickly. This was in part due to the spread of violence southward as well as the IRA bombing campaign. The governing Fianna Fáil party, which had been bitterly divided at the outset of the conflict, adapted to the changed circumstances. Those, such as Neil Blaney and Kevin Boland, who advocated a more traditional republican agenda, were marginalised. Nonetheless, nationalist sentiment in the country remained high. For example, in terms of popular culture, 'The Men Behind the Wire', which was a ballad in support of internees, topped the charts for six weeks.[2] Politicians, particularly of the Fianna Fáil hue, had to remain cognisant of the fact that latent republican sentiment remained a significant political cleavage that could re-emerge in certain circumstances. Reflecting on the period, former Minister for Justice Des O'Malley noted:

> It is relevant to say also that at the time there was enormous media opposition to any steps taken against subversive organisations. Of course, there was much political opposition too. The media opposition made matters very difficult because there was a great deal of ambivalence towards violence and subversion. I think perhaps people did not fully understand the significance of some of the things that were happening.[3]

It was therefore not a simple task to clamp down on the subversive elements. Additionally, there was traditional support for republican aims, especially along the border, and this was augmented by the arrival of republicans from Northern Ireland. However, simplistic assumptions about attitudes along the border should be cautioned against. It will be shown that the mounting death toll had a particular impact in the southern border counties where social and economic ties with the North were greater. As well as republican violence, there were significant loyalist attacks in the latter half of 1972. Therefore, somewhat paradoxically, while there may have been a significant republican element in the border counties, there was also a sizeable lobby advocating an increased security presence.

By the end of 1972, most of the ambiguity in the relationship between the state and republicans was gone. The IRA was, according to O'Malley, 'the greatest scourge in Ireland'.[4] The focus of both the Garda and Army was on containing this threat but they lacked the manpower, equipment and resources for the job and did not enjoy a functioning relationship with the RUC across the border. From a security perspective, British Ambassador John Peck noted 'the Irish government will only act in our interest where they coincide with theirs, not out of some ulterior motive but because to act on our behalf might in some cases cause an internal crisis'.[5] Therefore, co-operation took place on an ad hoc basis dependent on local factors. O'Malley recalled that 'Sometimes it [co-operation] was forthcoming but often it was not, or if it was, it was forthcoming long after the event – perhaps two or three months later – which was not very useful in investigating these matters which really needed instant co-operation.'[6]

To complicate matters further, after the fall of Stormont, the British Army rather than the RUC took the lead in border operations, making cross-border communication even more difficult.[7] That co-operation did take place between the security forces on both sides of the border is apparent. That much of the co-operation was discreet, even clandestine, seems likely. We will see that this form of co-operation was favoured by Irish politicians.

By the end of 1972, the Irish state had restructured its court system, introduced draconian legislation and pumped increased resources into its security services in the hope of preventing violence from spreading south. The state as an entity mobilised its resources to counter what it saw as the greatest threat to its existence: the IRA. It will be argued that this was a gradual process. When republicans by deed or word moved to undermine the southern state or its institutions, it was then that the state acted. Unlike 1969/1970, there was less ambiguity in security policy by the end of 1972, with one exception: co-operation with the British. This would remain an area of policy that was ill defined and would depend on the willingness of individuals to co-operate with the British forces. Therefore, in some areas, significant cross-border co-operation would be achieved, discreetly, whereas in other cases co-operation was negligible.

The chapter begins with a political discussion that provides an explanation for this discreet co-operation. The desire to be seen as being loyal to the binding 'idea' of the state remained central to government policy. Hence, public utterances and the actions of security personnel could not be seen as being pro-British but the increasing visibility and self-confidence of republicans at ground level highlighted the internal threat. Some republicans were cognisant of the dangers of flaunting their presence in the South but others were less circumspect. Typical of a Minister for Justice of a 'weak state', O'Malley emphasised the republican threat above all else. It will be shown that domestically this was a popular strategy. In the discussion of Garda/Army performance during the period, neither organisation was equipped to deal with the internal threat. The discussion in the latter half of the chapter highlights the significant degree of violence that occurred along the border. Of course, this violence in itself was significant but the great fear for security planners was that it was the precursor of even more large-scale upheaval. The potential for such violence to spread south and destabilise the entire state emerged as the central fear of policymakers in Dublin.

The Political Environment from December 1970 to the Offences Against the State Act

In the weeks following the Arms Trial verdict, there seemed to be a real prospect of a government crackdown on the IRA. In November, twenty-three republican suspects were arrested in Dundalk and Dublin at what appeared to be subversive training camps,[8] the circumstances of the arrests indicating a degree of pre-planning with some political direction.[9] The significance of these arrests should not, however, be overstated. In the Dundalk case, the charges were eventually dropped against all but one of the defendants.[10] Meanwhile, the group in Dublin were convicted and fined £20 or sentenced to one month in jail.[11] During meetings with the Irish Ambassador, Kelvin White of the Foreign and Commonwealth Office (FCO) applauded the arrests but pointed out that 'instances of light penalties could not but be helpful to people like Mr Paisley'.[12] Nevertheless, the signs were ominous for republicans, with the *An Phoblacht* front page for December displaying a clear message: 'Stop Collaboration.'[13]

Later in the month, there was indication that further pressure would be put on republicans. The Minister for Justice Desmond O'Malley publicly threatened the introduction of internment after the discovery of 'a secret armed conspiracy to kidnap Ministers and important persons'.[14] The details of the threat were never satisfactorily explained. What is clear is that the plot centred on Saor Éire. This was the group that had been behind a spate of robberies in the preceding years, as well as the Garda Fallon killing. A member of the group was killed in a premature explosion near an Army barracks in Dublin in October and a paramilitary display at the subsequent funeral had caused disquiet in political and security circles.[15] According to a later account from Desmond O'Malley, the threat to introduce internment was devised so as to encourage the IRA to 'exert pressure' on the smaller group.[16] Apparently, it worked as IRA leader Seán MacStíofáin got a message to Saor Éire that 'if your people are responsible for internment down here, you're all dead'.[17] The Department of Justice official Peter Berry would later voice suspicion that the internment threat was inspired by a desire to be seen as tough on the security issue and attract Protestant support in a forthcoming by-election in Donegal.[18] The veracity of this claim is dubious. Historian Brian Hanley noted:

> There was a substantial Protestant minority in the constituency (as many as 4,000 voters in some accounts) and it was presumed that they would react favourably to harsh measures aimed at republicans. Like many great Irish political yarns, Berry's theory doesn't stand up to close examination. The by-election (which Fianna Fáil won comfortably) took place on 2 December and the prospect of internment was not publicly aired until two days later.[19]

It is hard to see how the circumstances of December 1970 would have justified internment, even on the small scale envisaged. *The Irish Times* reported 'the cumulative opinions of the public, the press and other agencies like the British Embassy in Dublin, suggest that Mr Lynch has over reacted with his information'.[20]

Meanwhile, the threat to Lynch's leadership from within had not disappeared. British Ambassador John Peck, who was sympathetic to Lynch's predicament, noted in January 1971 that:

> His [Lynch's] internal position is paramount and however much he would like to be rid of the IRA he will not take such strong action against its members as we would like unless, as happened last month, he has evidence of a serious challenge to public order in the Republic.[21]

Peck's sympathy for Lynch was rooted in the belief that the alternative was a more republican Fianna Fáil alternative or 'a weak and implausible Fine Gael–Labour coalition'.[22] While the bulk of the parliamentary party backed Lynch, the views of the party's grass-roots membership were not so clear. The test for Lynch in this regard would come at the 1971 Ard Fheis. Those delegates opposed to his leadership were 'vocal, well organised and determined to attack the party establishment from the outset'.[23] The whole weekend was chaotic, with wild scenes in the main hall. It is best remembered for Patrick Hillery's impassioned speech in which he declared to dissidents, 'You can have [Kevin] Boland but you can't have Fianna Fáil.'[24] Lynch's presidential address, meanwhile, was drowned out by competing chants of 'we want Jack' and 'Union Jack'.[25] Crucially, the dissenters were numerically a minority and lost out in party elections for all key posts.[26]

After the Ard Fheis, the trio of Boland, Blaney and Haughey were to pursue different courses. It is worth noting that while the trio had similar political outlooks on the North, they did not get on very well personally, according to Desmond O'Malley.[27] Therefore, that their career paths diverged is unsurprising. Boland left Fianna Fáil shortly afterwards to found a new party, but despite ongoing speculation in the media, there were only limited defections. Blaney remained within the party but definitively estranged from the leadership. Haughey was on the long road to political rehabilitation, making a point of speaking to Minister for Foreign Affairs Patrick Hillery, and disassociating himself from the dissidents on the floor during the shambolic Ard Fheis.[28] With hindsight, the Ard Fheis can be seen as a pivotal moment in cementing Lynch's position. At the time, *The Irish Times* noted the 'weekend certainly was not only a personal triumph for the Taoiseach but the burial of some part of Fianna Fáil'.[29]

The relationship between the Dublin and London government 'paused almost completely in the early months of 1971 as Fianna Fáil spectacularly imploded'.[30] Speculation over the future of Northern Premier Chichester-Clark prompted Edward Heath to request Lynch to move against IRA training camps in the Republic and patrol the border more effectively.[31] Added to this there was increased IRA activity generally. An IRA landmine was responsible for the deaths of five BBC engineers in Tyrone in February. The UK government representative in Belfast advised the UK embassy in Dublin that a group from over the border were responsible. It was requested that the matter be raised with Foreign Affairs Minister Patrick Hillery but it was noted that 'it is unrealistic to think that the Irish authorities will take any positive action for a crime outside their jurisdiction but perhaps the Gardaí could harass [named republican] and his associates'.[32] Incidents like this with an explicit cross-border dimension were as yet the exception. Hence the diplomatic pressure was moderate.

The issue of the IRA using the South as a training and logistics base still irked the British considerably. Peck had written to Lynch in February complaining that those involved in such IRA activities in the Republic were being treated with 'a continuing, if not growing, tolerance in the courts'.[33] A prompt reply from Hillery cautioned Peck of the dangers of interference in the independence of the judiciary.[34] Interference in Irish courts' decisions was to be a constant theme in discourse between the governments over the coming decades.

The issue of IRA training in the Republic was to the fore again in early 1971, partly because it had featured prominently during the Arms Trial hearings. The Irish attitude was quite straightforward: 'any training and drilling are done quietly and privately behind closed doors and in small groups'.[35] Therefore, it was hard to detect. More attention was focused on the issue when a young IRA man was accidentally killed at a training camp in April 1971.[36] Politically, the training camp issue gave ammunition to opposition parties in the Dáil on the 'law and order' issue,[37] but also it was diplomatically embarrassing. For example, in May 1971, after Lynch made a speech critical of the British Army, British officials responded by raising the issue of training camps with the Irish Ambassador.[38]

Politically, it was beneficial for Lynch to be seen to be active on northern affairs, particularly at times of heightened tensions. Any suggestion that Lynch had abandoned the North left him open to criticism from the republican fringe within his own party. When in the House of Commons Under Secretary in the Foreign and Commonwealth Office Anthony Royle claimed that Dublin had only once made 'official representations' on northern affairs, this embarrassed the Dublin government, leading to awkward questions in Leinster House.[39] A month later, during an emotive Dáil debate, the Labour Party's Frank Cluskey equated Jack Lynch with Pontius Pilate.[40] Lynch's government was under pressure to be vocal in its defence of the nationalist cause in order to maintain republican credentials.

The fate of Lynch was therefore politically linked to what was happening in Northern Ireland. In March 1971, Chichester-Clark was replaced as Northern Premier by Brian Faulkner. Although questioned by some recent studies, the traditional view is that, on coming to power, Faulkner pushed for internment.[41] When the decision was eventually taken to introduce internment, Lynch was approached and encouraged to introduce similar measures.[42] Politically, this was impossible: there was as yet no major cross-border dimension to the violence and the threat to intern even the marginalised Saor Éire had led to considerable opposition. Additionally, Lynch needed to be seen to be acting in support of the northern minority, not against, if he wished to survive politically.

The immediate effect of internment was to bring refugees flooding over the border in unprecedented numbers, as well as an upsurge in border violence. Politically, Anglo-Irish relations reached a low ebb. Hillery was dispatched to London on 11 August to meet Home Secretary Reginald Maudling. The Foreign Affairs Minister warned that British government policies would lead to 'war in Ireland, not only the North'.[43] When asked to clamp down further on the IRA, Hillery replied:

> The Irish government has no control over the IRA; 'they hate us as much as they hate you'. It would be politically impossible for the Irish government to take action against the IRA which would appear to be for the benefit of Stormont. Internment in the South has not been absolutely ruled out but there is no intention of introducing it, unless it could be presented as part of a move towards a united Ireland.[44]

Maudling raised the bugbear of IRA training south of the border, but also highlighted two specific border incidents, including the shooting of UDR man Winston Donnell on the Tyrone–Donegal border. Hillery's reply on the issue was a vague claim that 'it was very difficult to ascertain the truth of these reports'.[45]

Against the backdrop of internment in Northern Ireland, focused almost exclusively against the nationalist population, relations between Dublin and London soured further in August when Heath and Lynch publicly exchanged telegrams that illustrated to all concerned the depth of mistrust between the two governments. Heath wrote, 'Your telegram today is unjustified in its content, unacceptable in its attempt to interfere in the affairs of the United Kingdom, and can in no way contribute to the solution of the problem in Northern Ireland.'[46]

Peck later wrote that 'it is hard to imagine the heads of state of any two other states brawling publicly in this fashion'.[47] A public spat with Heath did Lynch no harm domestically. In fact, public bickering with the UK prime minister strengthened the Taoiseach's position. Lynch was still concerned about securing grass-roots support in his own party. Boland's new party Aontacht Éireann launched in September with 1,100 delegates in attendance, including Sean Sherwin TD, Captain Kelly and Charles Haughey's brother Pádraig.[48] The sight of nationalists fleeing over the border had the potential to ignite republican sentiment so aggressive statements from Lynch and a public row with Heath were something of a necessity.

The situation on the ground in Northern Ireland, meanwhile, was getting more serious. In the latter three weeks of August 1971, thirty-six deaths took place – more than had taken place in 1970[49] and violence at or near the border was becoming more common. In this context, it was inevitable that some public meeting between Lynch and Heath would have to take place. Already, a two-day summit had been pencilled in for 20–1 October[50] but with the upsurge in border violence, the date for talks was moved forward to 6–7 September in Chequers. To compound the already difficult situation, the week before the summit, a controversial border incident on the Louth–Armagh border resulted in the death of a British soldier.[51] Increased security co-operation was therefore an imperative from a British perspective, but a pre-conference British briefing paper was not confident:

> It is not likely that this will prove a rewarding part of the discussion. The lamentable showing by Irish Police and Army at Crossmaglen [scene of the border incident] suggests co-operation in practical terms would be unlikely to amount to anything effective even if it were agreed. Mr Lynch may welcome informal co-operation, but he will not want his government openly to be associated with 'repression'.[52]

It has been argued that in the longer term the London talks represented a significant milestone, giving recognition to the Irish government's interest in a situation that threatened the security of both parts of the island.[53] The more immediate effect was further tripartite talks, to include Stormont Premier Faulkner, later in the month. This meeting achieved little. There were no major political or security outcomes as a result of the endeavour. Lynch claimed he would not be countenancing a return to London talks in 'present circumstances' for three reasons: the results of the Chequers talks had been 'almost entirely negative'; even if he felt he should return, his government and party 'would not let him'; and he 'may face a political crisis on his hands in the near future'.[54] Lynch did meet Heath on other occasions in subsequent months, but relations between Dublin and London 'had become a dialogue of the deaf'.[55] Nevertheless, the series of talks served a purpose, showing that Lynch was active on Northern Ireland and countering charges that he had abandoned the northern minority, but it was also apparent that the British government would require further moves against the IRA in exchange for Irish input into northern affairs.

With a political solution further away than ever, Lynch's immediate concern remained his own internal dissidents. A motion of no confidence in Minister Jim Gibbons was tabled for November but was won by the government. Blaney and fellow dissident Paudge Brennan abstained, while Seán Sherwin voted against the government.[56] The result was another milestone in Lynch's battle with internal dissent. A combination of resignations and expulsions meant that Boland and Blaney, as well as supporters Seán Sherwin, Des Foley and Paudge Brennan, were no longer within the parliamentary party.[57] Pressure on Lynch's leadership was definitively easing from the republican fringes.

Meanwhile, the northern Troubles were gradually beginning to spill over the border. The decision to renew the 'cratering' operation along border roads in October led to a further spike in border incidents.[58] Riots in Ballyshannon and Monaghan showed increasing lawlessness. Additionally, there were a few high-profile incidents, including the killing of Senator Barnhill in Strabane and an arms raid on the home of retired British Colonel C.R.P. Walker in Meath, during which he was killed.[59] The British response to the death of Senator Barnhill on 12 December and the killing of UDR soldiers Kenneth Smyth and Daniel McCormick on 10 December indicates the level of diplomatic pressure on Dublin:

The fact remains that Her Majesty's government regard it as intolerable that the Republic should provide a refuge from which the murderers can operate with impunity, whether the men are from the South or the North. The murders cannot in any way be regarded as a local reaction to road cratering, but are clearly acts of sheer terrorism designed to contribute to the breakdown of order in Northern Ireland. HMG therefore wish to press most strongly that the Irish government take more comprehensive and

more vigorous action against terrorists operating on the border ...
[namely] IRA units based in Dundalk, Monaghan, Ballyshannon,
and Ballybofey or Stranorlar.[60]

When challenged about security, Desmond O'Malley went on the
attack:

> The simple unchallengeable fact about trouble in border areas
> is that there was no trouble of any kind worth mentioning there
> until the Unionist administration, for their own political purposes,
> persuaded a credulous British government to send out the British
> Army to implement a policy of 'cratering' roads in border areas.[61]

Regardless of who was to blame for the upsurge in violence, the
institutions of the southern state were facing more direct challenges.
Two incidents illustrate this. Ten masked men stole rifles from
twenty FCA personnel training in Louth.[62] Louth had seen several
gun battles but this incident saw the Irish Army directly confronted.
Northern MP Paddy Kennedy was next to question the authority of
the southern state. Kennedy was speaking at a press conference held
by IRA escapees from Crumlin Road jail, in itself an embarrassing
occasion for the southern authorities. The northern representative
claimed the Republic's government would not move against the IRA
as republicans were too strong. Lynch's government would not, he
said, 'take any action against the IRA even if he wished to do so,
as it would be against the wishes of the majority of Irish people'.[63]
The Irish Times leader headline read 'Lynch Challenged on Security
by Britain and Provisionals'.[64] Apparently, the provocative nature of
Kennedy's statement was noted by an angry Provisional chief Seán
MacStíofáin and led to a cooling of the relationship between Kennedy
and MacStíofáin.[65]

Lynch responded strongly to the 'arrogant suggestion' that the
majority of people supported the IRA and notified the UN that he
might have to withdraw 800–900 troops from Cyprus.[66] A few days later,
a government spokesperson had to deny rumours that internment in
the Republic was imminent.[67] The combination of British pressure and
an increased domestic threat saw the government move incrementally
further against the IRA. Both Stewart Crawford at the Foreign and
Commonwealth Office and Peck in the British embassy agreed that it

was Kennedy's comment rather than British diplomatic pressure that had the greater effect on Irish security policy.[68]

At the start of January 1972, *Hibernia* magazine commented on the trend:

> After the bank raids, after Ballyshannon and Bundoran, after Drogheda, after the murder of Col Walker, after the graveside gun salutes and after the border skirmishes and after the seizing of FCA arms, it is only a question of time until some major confrontation will force the Taoiseach (reluctant to the last) to act against subversive organisations. His method of doing so will call for all the guile and subtlety of which he has shown himself so fully endowed during the past two years.[69]

The likelihood of immediate moves against the IRA quickly dissipated when news came through on 30 January that thirteen civilians had been killed by the British Army in Derry, in what was to become known as 'Bloody Sunday'. It was to prove a pivotal moment in the conflict. A fresh public inquiry into Bloody Sunday issued its report in 2010 and British Prime Minister David Cameron made an official apology. As part of this inquiry, transcripts of a late-night phone call between Lynch and Heath on the night of the atrocity were released. The transcripts display a worrying dynamic in relations between the two men. Lynch seems bullied by Heath, beginning the conversation by apologising for 'ringing at this hour'. Writing in *The Guardian*, Derry socialist Eamonn McCann observed:

> At a number of other points, it seems to be Lynch, not Heath, who is under reprimand. If Lynch had denounced the Derry march in advance, Heath suggests, the killings might never have happened. At no stage does Heath express personal regret for the deaths. The closest he comes is an acknowledgment that 'there will be ... feelings of regret' in Britain. This is conceded in the context of the 'very strong feeling' which, he says, is likely against the organisers of the march.[70]

Publicly, Lynch was more forceful. He withdrew the Ambassador to London and Patrick Hillery was dispatched on another fruitless appeal to the UN. A national day of mourning was held, with protests and masses organised across the country. Thomas McNulty, a republican active along the border, described his experience:

> The southern state turned a blind eye to us. The southern police and Army ignored us; some of them encouraged us. 'I hope you have one set up for those bastards'. That remark came from a patrol car of Irish police who met us at the border shortly after Bloody Sunday. There was an understanding between us and the southern Irish security forces. They wouldn't bother us and we didn't bother them.[71]

Most dramatically, the British embassy in Dublin was burned. Former Taoiseach Bertie Ahern was one of those who protested at the embassy on the night it was burned. He recalled 'the Gardaí hardly made an effort to stop *them* [those who burned the embassy]'.[72] While this is the most commonly repeated narrative of the event, the burning of the embassy was a complex affair, with significant Garda resistance on successive nights of protest at the embassy. Sixty-seven officers received injuries in defence of the property.[73] Desmond O'Malley claimed the decision to effectively let the crowd burn down the embassy was taken to prevent loss of life. The British Ambassador wrote to the Garda Commissioner to compliment the Gardai for their 'restraint and discipline'. For O'Malley, the burning of the embassy was a clear indication 'that the Provos had the ability to cause serious trouble in the Republic too'.[74]

The impact of Bloody Sunday politically south of the border was surprising. Peck wrote that 'Bloody Sunday and the resulting explosion of frustration and anger in the South brought many in the Republic up with a jolt. The dangers of Republican extremism sank in.'[75] Less than three weeks after Bloody Sunday, the Fianna Fáil Ard Fheis was again held. In contrast to a year earlier, the event was 'remarkable for moderation to Britain, [and] severity to IRA'.[76] Reflecting on Justice Minister Desmond O'Malley's contribution, *The Irish Times* noted 'thousands from rural Ireland cheered lustily "get tough" [with IRA] sentiments which the elected Fianna Fáil backbenchers in the Dáil did not support'.[77] The following weekend at the Labour party conference, Conor Cruise O'Brien's position as Labour spokesperson on the North was reaffirmed, despite his strong anti-IRA stance, with the 'pro Sinn Fein people' outnumbered five to one.[78]

A minority of Labour delegates at the conference still put forward
a traditional republican line. Christy Kinnehan, a delegate from
Tipperary, pointed out that he was not supporting violence but 'it had
worked before' and that the only language the British understood
'was the language of the gunboat'.[79] Fear of such violence spreading
southward had for some time been pushing the majority of Labour
more towards an accommodation with Fine Gael. O'Brien was central
to pushing the party in this direction and his victory at the 1972
conference was a decisive victory for those within the party who shared
this analysis. A study of the Labour Party during the period concluded
that

> the moving factor behind both the abandonment of anti-
> coalitionism in 1970 and traditional Irish nationalism during
> 1970–72 was the threat posed by the Northern Ireland conflict
> to the stability of the institutions of the Republic of Ireland state.
> [Labour's] Anti-coalitionism was scrapped in the aftermath of the
> Arms Crisis amid fears that parliamentary democracy had been
> jeopardised by Fianna Fáil, while the gap between a vague, ill-
> defined republicanism and loyalty to the Southern state – straddled
> by Labour for decades – opened up into an unbridgeable chasm.
> The result was the emergence of a party committed to coalitionism
> and one that viewed the Northern conflict through a revisionist
> prism.[80]

Republican atrocities post-Bloody Sunday contributed to the
changed climate and made it easier for the southern government
to act. For example, after an Official IRA bomb killed six civilians
at a British Army base in Aldershot, several leading figures in the
Official movement were arrested, including their chief of staff, Cathal
Goulding.[81] Moreover, the cabinet received an intelligence report that
warned that the IRA Army Council had discussed the possibility of
assassinating Minister for Justice Desmond O'Malley.[82] O'Malley would
spend much of his time in office under armed Garda protection, having
been issued a personal firearm. He changed his accommodation on a
week-to-week basis. Meanwhile, O'Malley's wife's family pub in Tyrone
was twice bombed by the IRA.[83]

Within Fianna Fáil, there were obviously differing opinions as
to the merits of coming down hard on the IRA. The British embassy

noted a discernible difference between strategies favoured by Minister for Foreign Affairs Patrick Hillery and Minister for Health Erskine Childers:

> Ever since the Ard Fheis Erskine Childers has been cock-a-hoop because he claims that Fianna Fáil at last adopted the policy that he has long been advocating, and the government is now prepared to take strong action against the IRA. Dr Hillery during his conversations with me twice went out of his way to say that Childers was quite wrong in his approach ... strong arm methods would only rally people behind the IRA and against the government.[84]

Peck's assessment on the depth of disagreement on this matter should be treated with a fair amount of caution as Lynch seemingly encouraged Hillery to take a more hawkish role in dealing with the British.[85]

A political row developed in March, the long-term significance of which did not immediately seem apparent. UK opposition leader Harold Wilson visited Dublin and secretly held talks with the IRA.[86] This move annoyed the leaders of all three political parties to an extent that they publicly did not vent.[87] A British leader willing to deal directly with the IRA obviously had the potential to undermine the Dublin government. The initial impact of the Wilson initiative was a three-day IRA ceasefire. Later in the summer, the IRA announced a further ceasefire on 22 June. This time, IRA leaders held face-to-face talks with Secretary of State for Northern Ireland William Whitelaw.[88] The negotiations yielded nothing except a two-week ceasefire, but did upset the Irish government as the negotiations were seen to undermine constitutional nationalists in the SDLP.[89] For the republican movement, the failure to engage in talks at this point showed a lack of strategic thinking.

> By refusing to play the kind of diplomatic game to which Whitelaw was alluding – that is, using the meeting with him to manoeuvre the British into substantive negotiations – the Provos undid much of the potential advantage created by their military efforts. Above all, by refusing to accept limited goals in a limited war scenario, the Provisionals had, thanks to the absolutist nature of republican

ideology, torpedoed their own strategy, thus providing a clear case of over-escalation in a low-intensity conflict.[90]

Among those negotiating with the British was IRA chief Seán MacStíofáin. Later in September, Heath put pressure on Lynch to arrest MacStíofáin, who had since gone to ground.[91] Lynch, affable as ever, avoided confrontation on the matter, but when questioned in a radio interview, the more combative Desmond O'Malley hinted at his government's displeasure, pointing out that the British 'had not only taken no action against him [MacStíofáin] but had met him and five other IRA leaders in London transported by the RAF at the expense of the British taxpayer'.[92]

During the IRA ceasefire, the British, via Ambassador Peck, had urged Lynch not to take action against some IRA members exiled south of the border. It was felt that if the southern authorities made life 'too hot' for republican suspects south of the border, they would flee north, which the British did not want.[93] The discussion on this subject was kept deliberately vague on the advice of British diplomats who did not want their government to appear to be blowing 'hot and cold' on security co-operation.[94]

It was ironic that it was as the IRA was discussing a ceasefire that the Dublin government made its strongest security moves. The courts had been the subject of British, as well as Irish, criticism for the leniency shown to republican defendants.[95] An IRA defendant described his experience of appearing before the courts before the establishment of the Special Criminal Court:

> The arrests of IRA men along the border were token arrests to show the British government that the Fianna Fáil government led by Jack Lynch was doing something ... So when this group of IRA men were taken from Mountjoy jail on this lovely spring morning it was a CIE coach that pulled up to the gates of the prison! Everyone was in high spirits, IRA men, Garda escorts and the bus driver ... There were about 15 or 16 IRA men on board and about 20 Gardaí, mostly young fellas with a couple of senior Gardaí who were in charge. They were a friendly bunch and we got on well ... No one was worried about today's court; it would be just a five minute appearance. None of the District Judges were handing out jail sentences to IRA men anyway so there wasn't much to worry about.

The above account continues to describe the remainder of the trip to court with Gardaí and IRA suspects apparently sharing significant quantities of alcohol on the bus journey back to jail until a fight broke out between the respective sides.[96]

Lynch acknowledged to Peck that there were 'two bad district judges and one weak judge but others were handing out tough sentences'.[97] A combination of factors left Lynch's government able to act on the courts issue. The collapse of Stormont eased republican sentiment somewhat while the ratification of the EEC accession referendum in May of 1972 was a massive political boost for Lynch. The issue had mobilised left/republican opposition but an overwhelming 83 per cent endorsed Lynch's position[98] and internal dissidents in Fianna Fáil had been routed at the Ard Fheis. When republicans rioted in Mountjoy jail on 18/19 May, the Prisons Act was passed, allowing prisoners to be transferred to military custody.[99] Then, at the end of the month, the court problem was tackled. Part V of the Offences Against the State Act was brought into operation, replacing ordinary jury trials with the Special Criminal Court, where three judges would rule.[100] On 2 June, the southern security forces made their preliminary moves against Provisional leaders, arresting Ruairí Ó Brádaigh and Joe Cahill, among others.[101] There was no mass roundup, however. These were just the latest in a series of moves against prominent republicans, often linked to speeches given at commemorations.

As well as the Special Criminal Court's introduction, there is some evidence that these moves were accompanied by increased security co-operation with the British. This will be explored later. The security clampdown in the months after the Ard Fheis moves cannot be seen as a complete volte face by Lynch's administration. Extradition remained shelved as a matter for the courts and a case was taken by the Dublin government to the European Court of Human Rights on behalf of some internees. The latter issue was raised when Heath and Lynch met in September and 1972, with Heath directly urging Lynch to drop the case.[102]

The year 1972 had started well for the IRA. Having contributed to the collapse of Stormont, they welcomed a flood of new recruits post-Bloody Sunday and entered negotiations with the British government. They had also improved their bomb-making capability,[103] but their support base north and south was to be considerably undermined by a range of incidents linked to this new capability. Most notoriously,

on 21 July, between nineteen and twenty-one bombs were left in
Belfast city centre, killing nine and injuring 131 in an event that
became known as 'Bloody Friday'.[104] There was widespread outrage.
In response, the British government launched 'Operation Motorman',
whereby it established control of the 'no-go' areas. This was its largest
troop movement in Europe since 1945.[105]

With the no-go areas occupied, more IRA personnel moved south,
adding to instability. This trend can be seen in a rise in the average
number of 'border incidents' recorded by the British in the months
after August 1972.[106] It was after 'Motorman' that O'Malley referred
to the IRA as 'the greatest scourge in Ireland'.[107] Four extra judges
were appointed to the Special Criminal Court,[108] 2,000 firearms with
calibre above .22 were recalled[109] and extra explosive controls were
put in place.[110] It was claimed that the recall of firearms certificates
gave the state the 'most restrictive laws in western Europe'.[111] Later,
O'Malley made a direct appeal to Irish-Americans to desist from giving
material support to the IRA.[112] At street level, there was added pressure
being put on republicans. Summons were issued to those selling
political papers on O'Connell Street,[113] whereas those taking street
collections had been clamped down some time ago, with 250 people
being prosecuted for making illegal collections.[114] Meanwhile, the
(Provisional) Sinn Féin Office in Dublin was closed down by Gardaí
on 7 October. By November, the Special Criminal Court had heard
130 cases and recorded 103 convictions.[115] The arrests figures under
Section 30 of the Offences Against the State Act shown in Table 3
illustrate how pressure on republicans increased. While it is dangerous
to read too much into just this one set of figures, they do support
the argument that there was an increased clampdown on republicans
in the months immediately after the Ard Fheis and 'Motorman'
respectively.

In the last two months of 1972, more draconian legislation was
passed and pressure was put on the media to toe the line with regard
to republicans. In November 1972, IRA chief of staff Seán MacStíofáin
was arrested after giving an interview with RTÉ. The broadcast of
details from the interview breached government directives under the
Broadcasting Act.[117] Showing a determination to tackle any vestige
of republicanism in RTÉ, the interviewer's home was raided and the
government took the unprecedented step of sacking the entire RTÉ
Authority.[118] MacStíofáin immediately went on a short-lived hunger

Table 3. Arrests under Section 30 Offences Against the State Act 1939 (1972–1973)[116]

Month 1972	Arrests under Section 30	Month 1973	Arrests under Section 30
April	24	January	17
May	27	February	5
June	3	March	11
July	7	April	16
August	8	May	23
September	22	June	5
October	16	July	27
November	23		
December	16		

and thirst strike. Marches in support were held across the country, notably in Dublin, where 4,000 protestors gathered.[119] A rescue attempt heightened tensions further, with a resultant gunfight between the IRA and Gardaí at the Mater Hospital.[120] Before MacStíofáin quit the strike, a near-fatal bomb in a Dublin cinema was believed to have been planted by his supporters.[121]

Surprising opposition from Fine Gael, historically the party of law and order, emerged at the next legislative stage in O'Malley's moves against the IRA. Amendments to the Offences Against the State Act were to go before the Dáil in early December, to include a range of coercive provisions, including one whereby a conviction for IRA membership could be secured on the word of a Chief Superintendent. Fine Gael had been in opposition for sixteen years and elements within the party saw the bill as Fianna Fáil's attempt to look for 'cover for perceived failure [in the area of security] rather than a genuine attempt to strengthen the existing law'.[122] Others would suggest that opposition to the bill was rooted in an internal leadership heave against Fine Gael leader Liam Cosgrave.[123] Without support from the Fianna Fail dissidents, it looked like the government would be defeated in the bill, leading to a general election. Fine Gael reversed their opposition when two Loyalist car bombs exploded in Dublin, killing two CIÉ staff. Speculation, from Jack Lynch, among others, linked British intelligence with these incidents.[124] The timing of the bombings and their political impact led many to suspect a high degree of political sophistication on the part of the culprits. That Lynch would later admit that he had 'suspicions'[125] of the involvement of British intelligence in the attacks illustrates the considerable mistrust between the two governments.

The activities of British intelligence would cause further friction in Dublin–London relations before the year ended. A dossier on IRA activities in the Republic was passed to Dublin by the British government. According to Patrick Hillery, British information on IRA activities 'had frequently been of low quality, but had suddenly shown a marked improvement'.[126] This alerted the Irish government to a leak, leading to the arrest of a Garda clerk and British agent. The clerk was suspected of handing over Garda intelligence over several months. Hillery was instructed by the cabinet to 'make the strongest possible protest'.[127] This incident would lead to much future speculation about the links between some Gardaí and British intelligence.

While there were ongoing disputes with the British over border incursions, IRA activities and British intelligence operations, the broad thrust of Dublin–London relations had improved by the end of 1972. The release of a Green paper on new political structures in Northern Ireland by the UK government had been warmly welcomed by Dublin, particularly as it contained an 'Irish dimension'.[128] The quid pro quo for Dublin having an input in northern affairs was for greater security pressure to be put on republicans, and the possibility of this had been made considerably easier by the fact that the republican element within Fianna Fáil had been outmanoeuvred by Lynch. 'Dead but not buried' was how *Hibernia* headlined a profile of the Fianna Fáil dissidents as the year closed. [129] Lynch had established full control of his party and the machinations within the opposition Fine Gael party over the Offences Against the State Act had given his party renewed credibility in terms of security policy. Peck's December dispatch to London commented on Lynch's total control of his party: 'If Fianna Fáil HQ said the moon was made of green cheese, 70 deputies would be on their feet asserting the fact.'[130]

While Peck's analysis of the period could be viewed as being overly sympathetic to Lynch,[131] his summation is nonetheless prescient:

Whatever Mr Lynch's obligations under international law, throughout 1970, 1971, and the early part of 1972 he could not act in such a way to appear to co-operate with the British and Unionists in the North against the IRA in defence of the old Stormont system. Since direct rule in March, there has been a slow but fundamental change of attitude as Mr Lynch, his cabinet, the majority of the population and, last of all, his own backbenchers have slowly become convinced that HMG intend to bring about a new deal in Northern Ireland.[132]

An Evaluation of Irish Security Policy: The Role of Gardaí and Army

As protestors gathered outside Leinster House to demonstrate for the release of Seán MacStíofáin in November 1972, the depth of the state's security crisis was evident. Over 1,000 Gardaí were on duty;[133] they were supported by 300 troops with orders to 'shoot to kill if necessary'.[134] The Army remained in a secondary role in terms of security but in the preceding twelve months it had used CS gas against a crowd in Dundalk, dealt with riots in Ballyshannon and Monaghan, and become involved in the prison dispute protests at Mountjoy.[135] With the rise in tension that accompanied MacStíofáin's hunger strike, once again the Gardaí called upon the Army for support. The burning of the British embassy after Bloody Sunday had embarrassed the security forces and they were anxious for there to be no repeat performance.

In the 1969–70 period, the discussion of the Army focused on its (in)ability to mount offensive operations over the border, but the optics of the demonstration outside Leinster House illustrated that the security forces' primary focus was now domestic security threats.

We have seen how ill prepared the security forces were for the outbreak of the Troubles. In terms of resources, equipment and personnel, both the Gardaí and Army were not in a fit state to cope with the internal security threat. Morale within the Gardaí remained low. Although the Conroy Report significantly improved conditions and wages of members, an authoritarian disciplinary system and constrained working environment stifled ambitious Gardaí,[136] and the overarching influence of the Department of Justice rather than a Police Authority, as in the UK, also affected decision-making.[137] Garda dissatisfaction was compounded by the perceived weakness of the courts in dealing with subversives. In October 1971, frustrations within the force came to a head when strike action was threatened by the Gardaí after four members were dismissed under the discipline code. A statement issued by the Garda Representative Body read:

> We are forced to work under grossly inefficient officers whose negative and obstructive policy, and servile attitude toward the Department of Justice, have helped to undermine the morale and well being of the entire Garda force ... As responsible members of the community, and the Gardaí, we deplore the situation where armed criminals, who are known to the Gardaí are permitted to rob at will, or when apprehended they are permitted by our legal system to hold the country to ransom.[138]

Shortly afterwards, Garda disaffection surfaced again. Shots had been fired at Gardaí during an armed robbery in Cork. The perpetrators were eventually convicted but two of them received suspended sentences. This led to a demand from 300 Gardaí at a meeting for the dismissal of the President of the High Court.[139] At the meeting, cases were cited in which 'political elements were obvious and industrious Gardaí were quietly told not to pursue the matter'.[140] In the end, neither incident resulted in industrial action, but the mood within the force was evident.

The biggest challenge along the border was a shortage of personnel. This meant that there was considerable pressure on the Army in particular. A report in November 1971 found that in three camps the average incidence of duty per week was 103 hours for officers, 93 hours for NCOs and 96 for men.[141] This report was based on visits to the Cavan, Cootehill and Castleblayney Army positions. It was noted that no post had more than three Land Rovers and there was no armoured car.[142] As well as a shortage of personnel, other border-specific issues affected the competency of the Army. The temporary nature of most deployments meant that 'men return to their home units just when they are most effective'.[143] Meanwhile, communication with Gardaí was somewhat inhibited by the fact that Gardaí were divided into four separate divisions along the border,[144] compounded by the 'historical weakness' of the military in border areas where they had no permanent posts prior to the outbreak of Troubles.[145]

Lack of the most basic resources was also a factor inhibiting the performance of Gardaí. Paddy Harte, TD for Donegal, alleged that the standard of patrol car used in Donegal was inadequate, citing the breakdown of two Garda cars involved in a chase of armed robbers.[146] An inspection of border stations in 1973 revealed that due to staff shortages some patrol cars were being left at stations unmanned or in other cases being undermanned, i.e. just the driver.[147] Meanwhile, even the basics of riot control were lacking. An *Irish Times* observer noted that Army personnel policing a protest at the Curragh camp lacked riot shields and resorted to 'fixed bayonets' for crowd control.[148] Again when a riot resulted in injuries to nine Gardaí in Lifford, it was reported that no riot shields were available.[149]

When the Army was called in to support the Gardaí during a riot in Monaghan, forty-four troops arrived from Castleblayney with just five riot shields and twenty-one helmets between them.[150] The Irish archives reveal that in August 1972 the lack of equipment led to 200 riot shields being manufactured at short notice by a Dublin supplier.[151] Whether related or not, a British supplier refused to supply riot shields to the Department of Defence. Previously, the firm had issued a prototype shield but it was rejected and returned by Dublin. Later, the UK supplier observed an exact replica of the shield in use in Dublin, presumably manufactured by a local firm.[152]

Other British suppliers were also reluctant to supply equipment to Irish security forces, but for different reasons. For example, a company selling night-vision equipment was prohibited by the Ministry of Defence from selling to the Irish Army for fear that it would fall into IRA hands.[153] Likewise, the latest bomb-disposal techniques were not shared by the UK military for fear that 'sooner or later something would leak [to the IRA]'.[154] Even in terms of uniforms, there was a noted deficiency in Defence Forces equipment. A British officer who encountered an Irish Army patrol described their attire: each member wore different forms of the uniform, some with berets of different colours and some without any headgear.[155]

In terms of facilities, both the Gardaí and Army's were basic. Forty-six Garda rural stations were closed in 1969/1970 but this process was stopped in order to curb the IRA.[156] The remaining stations were often, through a combination of neglect and weak public finances, 'such dismal places that public confidence in Garda work suffered rather than improved'.[157] Similarly, Army barracks were in poor condition. Before 1969, there were scarcely any troops near the border, with the exception of Finner Camp in Donegal, which was used as a summer training camp.[158] This meant that when troops were posted to the border, facilities were below par, sometimes with security implications. For example, the Army barracks in Dundalk had been unoccupied for years and part of the facility was being leased out to a shoe manufacturer.[159] Therefore, the facilities for the 1,058 troops on border duty were poor and combat efficiency of forces was 'extremely low'.[160]

Some steps were taken to improve the resources of the security force. Between 1971 and March 1973, the strength of the Gardaí was increased by 1,317, from 6,560 to 7,877.[161] This is not as dramatic an increase in manpower as it might seem, as the typical Garda working week was reduced from forty-eight hours to forty-two due to the implementation of the Conroy report. There was a similar rise in Defence Forces numbers, which jumped from 8,242 in 1970 to 10,466 in 1972.[162] Spending on defensive equipment also increased dramatically in 1971–2, as can be seen in Table 4 This additional investment was not enough to modernise long-neglected forces, but it does indicate the increasing importance of the army.

In terms of relations with the public, the Troubles posed a new challenge, particularly for the Gardaí in border areas. Minister for Justice Desmond O'Malley commented on public support, stating that 'though it is better than it was, it must be admitted that in other countries the amount of support given to the police in the way of assistance and information far outstrips what happens here'.[164] Reflecting on his period as Minister for Justice, O'Malley, lamenting the lack of public and media support he received, commented that 'a

Table 4. Purchase of defensive equipment 1968–72[163]

Year	Cost of Military Equipment
1968/69	£511,000
1969/70	£367,000
1970/71	£256,000
1971/72	£1,184,000
1972/73	£1,281,000

lot of reasonable people were not entirely unsympathetic [to the IRA] at the time'.[165]

In border areas, the influx of displaced persons had a broader effect on the Gardaí. One judge commented that '30 percent of the list at his court last week was taken up with assaults by young men from across the border'.[166] While the burning of the British embassy was the most visible affront to the Gardaí's authority, other incidents occurred at Garda stations along the border that equally undermined the force.

In December 1971, serious rioting in Ballyshannon included an attack on a Garda station. Rioters only retreated from the station after the intervention of republican leaders.[167] Again in Donegal in March 1972, forty youths from Strabane attacked Lifford Garda station, breaking all the windows. The Army and extra Gardaí arrived to restore order.[168] Later in the year, there were further violent incidents directed at the Gardaí in Milford and Buncrana.[169] Meanwhile, also in March 1972, petrol bombs were thrown at Monaghan Garda station during serious rioting following the arrest of three republicans.[170] A month later, 60 Gardaí baton-charged a group of 300 protestors outside Clones Garda station. Some windows in the station were broken and a Sinn Féin councillor who refused to become involved in the protest had windows and a door broken in his house.[171]

In a more personalised attack, the house of a uniformed Garda sergeant in Monaghan was blown up by the Official IRA. The Garda claimed that this attack took place in response to his prominent role in an arms seizure in the county some weeks after the shooting of Northern Minister John Taylor.[172] In Louth, petrol-bomb attacks were carried out on Louth and Castlebellingham Garda station. The Littlejohns, two brothers who worked for British intelligence, later took responsibility for these attacks.[173] The activities of these brothers, which included an armed robbery in Dublin, became something of a cause célèbre and, along with the case of the Garda clerk arrested for spying, further highlighted concerns about the activities of British intelligence south of the border.

In September 1972, the Garda barracks in Dundalk was set on fire and twenty cars parked in the yard were destroyed during a riot that attracted much media attention.[174] A Garda on duty that night described being besieged in the barracks:

A good friend of mine who is now dead God rest him, he was tough now. And below the stairs he was saying an act of contrition, and I said 'What are you at'; 'We're gone. We're never going to get out of here. I'm going to say some prayers.' I said 'I haven't time for that.' That really shook me … eventually the door burst open and I was just inside it. And these fellas stood there. He had a five gallon drum in his hand. And next thing all hell broke loose from the Guards gunfire. I didn't know where it was coming from. It was a friend of mine in the station, broke into the press, got the gun out, sitting on top of the stairs, and he opened up. Not on him, it was just, blew the fan light over the door. The boys they dropped the can and ran. There was a five gallon drum of petrol there. They were going to burn the place and us inside.[175]

At a more routine level, there was ongoing confrontation between the Gardaí and republicans at court proceedings. Arrest operations or court appearances sometimes resulted in riots, but lower-level antagonism in the form of 'scuffles' was commonly reported.[176] In terms of direct shooting incidents between republicans and Gardaí, these remained the exception, with one example being the exchange of gunfire during the rescue attempt of Seán MacStíofáin while he was being treated at the Mater Hospital.[177]

Two further aspects of the Irish security forces require some analysis: namely their level of co-operation with the British Army/ RUC and the IRA respectively. In terms of republicans, active co-operation seems to have been rare. One Garda after Bloody Sunday was convicted for inciting another member of the force to steal explosives.[178] Meanwhile, a Reserve Defence Forces officer, who was close to Kevin Boland, was arrested by the Gardaí in September 1971. The British authorities believed that the officer received injuries in a border engagement with the British.[179] The allegation levelled against the Irish security forces most often was inaction. Some accounts of the period include anecdotes of IRA members being stopped at checkpoints and Gardaí ignoring weapons found in the boot of the car.[180] In one incident recounted by Kieran Conway, a former IRA man, a republican was stopped near a checkpoint in Portlaoise with a Sten gun. The Garda offered to let the man go free if he gave up the weapon. The republican refused and after a discussion with a senior officer at the Garda station the man was allowed go free with his weapon.[181]

British authorities singled out one Garda in Clones for particular criticism, claiming that unlike most other border Gardaí 'there have been several instances when he could have apprehended the insurgents as a result of information passed to him by security forces but he has always failed to carry out any action'.[182] A more sympathetic assessment of the same Garda claimed that his inaction might be explained by long-established ties to friends in the community rather than ideological support for the IRA.[183] There was a separate allegation that Clones Gardaí had come to an arrangement with the IRA that there would be no harassment of republicans provided there was no IRA activity in the area.[184] A different British report made a similar allegation against Gardaí in Lifford.[185]

In Donegal, there were further allegations that personal relations were interfering with police work. In one instance, a known IRA man apparently babysat for a local Garda sergeant every Wednesday.[186] Additionally, many of the Gardaí transferred to the border stayed with local families, at least initially. A British account reported that some of those stationed in Lifford 'talked to civilians about their work'.[187] Apparently this had been a factor in the failure of a raid on an infamous caravan used as a headquarters by the IRA from September 1972 in the Cloughfinn area. According to British accounts, so established was the IRA headquarters that a wall had been built around the caravan to provide cover in the event of shoot-outs.[188] The Gardaí, according to a member stationed in the area at the time, adopted a strategy whereby Cloughfinn was treated as a 'sterile area', with traffic stopped on the main approaches. The lack of military backup made this the wisest decision from their perspective, it was claimed. When the Gardaí did later move on the caravan, there was a strong reaction from republicans, with a mini riot in Lifford. The Gardaí, lacking rudimentary riot equipment, armed themselves with hurling sticks to repel the would-be attackers.[189]

The general Garda performance in the area did not impress their counterparts across the border. An RUC report alleged that Gardaí in Lifford passed information about impending searches to the IRA. The case of initial searches of the Cloughfinn caravan was cited. The officer filling in the monthly report for the Strabane area controversially concluded that 'the Garda cannot be informed of intended operations close to the border by the British Army because there is more than an even chance that the information will be passed to terrorists, and thus compromise the operation'.[190] Intriguingly, a Foreign Office official handwrote below this point, 'does this mean that they are not using the special arrangement? Is this based on fact or opinion?'[191] This reference to 'special arrangement' may have related to some informal security co-operation.

Another allegation of collusion arose after a British Army soldier, Ian Caie, was killed at the Louth–Armagh border on 24 August 1972. A suspect car connected to the incident was seized by the Gardaí but it was subsequently destroyed by a malicious fire in the precincts of the Dundalk Garda station, raising suspicions amongst the British authorities. A British Army report noted 'perhaps Gardaí for reasons best known to themselves are still not prepared to assist wholeheartedly in matters involving subversion and politics'.[192] Of course, it is equally possible that subversives may just have destroyed the car due to lax security at the Garda barracks. Several vehicles were destroyed in the riots at the station and whether the vehicle in question was one of these is unclear.

The view that all occasions of Garda inaction represented collusion with the IRA should be cautioned against. At times, the broader problems of lack of resources, poor facilities and lack of manpower meant the Gardaí could not perform the tasks required of them on the border. Common sense dictates that personal experience would have influenced individual Gardaí's actions most. Gardaí came more and more into direct contact with republicans in the antagonistic settings of arrest operations, court protests and street disturbances from 1972 onwards. It seems unlikely that a wide level of republican sympathy would have persisted in such an environment.

The degree of co-operation between the Irish security forces and their equivalents over the border is a similarly complex subject. When pressured in the Dáil by Neil Blaney on the the issue, Desmond O'Malley was not completely clear in his response:

As far as co-operation with other police forces in general is concerned the Garda Síochána, like the police force of every civilised country in the world, co-operates with other police forces to the best of its ability to try to curb the activities of criminals. It is usual, where it is clear that a particular crime has a political motivation, to give special consideration to the degree of assistance that would be given as between any one police force and another in those circumstances but, as I pointed out already in the house on 17th February last, while as a general rule co-operation in matters that are obviously political might be refused the particular circumstances of each case must be looked into.[193]

Blaney had received a list of 'suspect' northern registration plates held by the Gardaí and was using this as evidence of cross-border 'collaboration'. He further cited Garda involvement in some arrests of republicans in Britain. As early as 1970, IRA prisoners in England were angered by the alleged collusion between Special Branch in London and Dublin. It was claimed that when prominent republican Jim Monaghan was arrested in London in August 1970 there was co-operation between Special Branch in Dublin and London within twelve hours of him being brought into custody.[194] However, the extent of cross-border co-operation remains a grey area. One reliable account claims that G2, military intelligence, co-operated with their British equivalents during the introduction of internment.[195] For obvious reasons, co-operation in such incidences remained something politicians chose not to discuss. There is evidence to suggest that Lynch and O'Malley preferred whatever co-operation took place to remain discreet and kept outside the confines of the Dáil. A policy of unofficial agreements with local security services was identified by a British discussion paper as the best interim solution from their perspective.[196]

Heath wrote to Lynch on 25 April 1972 requesting urgent moves toward co-operation on the border;[197] when questioned in the Dáil, Lynch denied that the matter was raised.[198] In private discussions with Peck, Lynch agreed with the analysis that 'discreet collaboration was clearly called for'.[199] Peck was then given by Lynch what the British Ambassador viewed as 'carte blanche' to follow up in establishing security co-operation directly with the departments of Defence and Justice.[200] The British Ambassador in a later telegram outlined how he envisaged co-operation working. It would be 'mutual and discreet, bearing in mind that it has to be deniable in the Dáil'.[201] As part of this co-operation, a meeting was held between the chief of staff of the Irish Defence Forces and the British military attaché.[202]

Peck discussed 'other forms of deniable contact with London not involving the RUC' with O'Malley .[203] Likewise, Lynch later accepted Army-to-Army contact, in theory at least, on the basis of 'an ingenious and completely deniable arrangement about communications that has been worked out with Lisburn [Army HQ]'.[204] Peck concluded that there existed 'a paradoxical situation in which contrary to normal form, deeds are more likely than words'.[205] Whether these series of concessions by Lynch/O'Malley ever led to the level of discreet but deniable co-operation envisaged by Peck is hard to gauge. Nevertheless, if Peck's account is believed, it illustrates the attitude towards co-operation among those in positions of power.

Sensing a political weak spot, republican propaganda of the time made much of southern 'collaboration'. Anecdotes about supposed cross-border collusion were regularly reported in republican periodicals. For example, *An Phoblacht* claimed in November 1971 that some RUC detectives were active south of the border – including in Cavan, where one received Garda protection.[206] Such incidents may not have been as farfetched as they might seem. For example, Desmond O'Malley discussed with Peck the case of Gardaí carrying out surveillance on a republican house on the southern side of the border who came across an RUC detective hiding in bushes, performing a similar task. According to Peck's version, the Gardaí had no particular objection to the RUC man's presence and O'Malley was not in any sense complaining. Gardaí were, however, concerned that the particular officer was 'wanted' by the IRA for allegedly shooting at civilians and they did not want an incident in the South.[207]

Informal co-operation certainly took place, according to one former RUC officer. Writing under the name George Clarke, the officer claimed to have made forty-seven trips south between September and December 1971.[208] Clarke's account cites Garda support during the period as 'immeasurable and essential'. It is pointed out that as IRA personnel were freer in their movements in the South, Garda Special Branch was in a better position to profile the organisation and its members.[209] Republicans south of the border did make gathering intelligence somewhat easier by adopting a less than low-key approach. Certain pubs were identified with Provisionals in each border town and it was easy for the security forces in the South to build up an accurate picture of the IRA.[210]

The degree and extent of co-operation seemed to depend on the circumstances and individuals involved locally as well as the political climate. The sensitivities involved can be seen from one such incident. A border clearing operation on the Monaghan border took place on 5 August 1972. There was 'excellent' co-operation from the Irish Army, according to the British forces commander, a Major Wright. This incident received some minor media comment and the good relations between the respective forces was commented upon. It seems the publicity may not have been welcomed on the southern side of the border, as an end-of-month security report by the British noted:

> Scotstown's [the Garda station nearest where co-operation was given] attitude seems to have changed somewhat. The Garda there appear at present not to be very helpful and very loathe to have any contact with us. This may be due to all the newspaper comment as a result of Major Wright's co-operation with Eire Army on 5 August.[211]

Even at local level, the lesson was being learned: co-operation had to be discreet and deniable.

One positive area of co-operation was in control of explosives. The car-bombing campaign of 1972 that culminated in Bloody Friday had led to pressure to find the source of the explosives and detonators. It was frequently alleged that a lot of the explosives came from the South. In August and September 1972, there were a series of meetings between the upper echelons of the Gardaí and RUC to deal with the explosives issue. Among those involved in these meetings were Chief Superintendent Wren and RUC Chief Inspector Drew. The meetings were amicable, with both sides anxious to gain greater control of explosives, and samples of explosives seized by the Gardaí in Louth were handed over to the RUC representatives for analysis.[212]

The Irish security forces had enough popular support to confront republicans on issues of domestic law and order but could not be seen to co-operate with the British. This meant that what co-operation did exist often came down to the willingness of individuals to engage in actions that were publicly shunned by their masters but secretly favoured.

The Security Situation in the Southern Border Counties, 1970–December 1972

There was some dispute as to exactly when the situation in the border counties began to deteriorate. As already noted, Desmond O'Malley claimed that it was an 'unchallengeable fact' that there was no trouble 'worth mentioning' prior to the British 'cratering' operation of October 1971.[213] The British analysis differed. They pointed to the introduction of internment in August 1971 as the catalyst as republicans fled south. In fact, both August and October represent times when the intensity of the conflict increased. Between 29 April 1971 and 25 July 1971, there were just nine border incidents. During the week of 9–14 August alone, there were ten incidents.[214] Peck noted that 'in August, September and the first half of October, there occurred two murders and one wounding in the course of 8 shooting incidents, 6 bombings, 4 armed robberies, 2 burnings. This is quite a lot to pass off as "not worth mentioning"'.[215]

For O'Malley, putting the entire blame for the violence on cratering was politically astute, as it played well with republican-minded Fianna Fáil voters. Nevertheless, if internment marked an upsurge in hostilities, the impact of cratering was to bring the border counties close to full-scale conflict. Irish Army figures shown in Table 5 illustrate how the changed circumstances impacted on them.

Prior to cratering and internment, the security situation along the border had been much the same as 1969/70. As already mentioned, a landmine blast killed five BBC technicians on Brougher Mountain near Omagh in February 1971.[217] There were of course other incidents that had a more specific border dimension. These incidents ranged in

Table 5. Border incidents recorded by Irish Army[216]

Month	Border incident
June	2
July	2
August	7
September	7
October	23
November	31

levels of seriousness. In April, one of the two border incidents cited was the suspicious movement of a tractor in Derry.[218] Taking June as a more typical month, meanwhile, there were four border incidents cited by the British. These were a car driving through a checkpoint without stopping, an explosion at Killeen near Newry, an explosion in Clady and a further shooting incident at Killeen.[219] While potentially serious, these were not the types of incidents that would threaten national security.

In the weeks after internment was introduced, *Hibernia* magazine observed a noticeable increase in Garda personnel along the border. It was stated that 'the Gardaí are there watching every move but, for the moment it would appear the policy is to stand idly by'.[220] This policy would be tested by the 106 border incidents that took place between internment and 23 November.[221] The British Ministry of Defence identified six main areas of IRA activity emanating from IRA units in neighbouring southern towns:

- Killeen Customs Post/Jonesborough (Dundalk Unit)
- Forkhill (Dundalk Unit)
- West of Keady and south of Middletown (Monaghan Unit)
- Roslea (Clones/Monaghan unit)
- Belleek (Ballyshannon unit)
- Clady/Strabane (Ballybofey/Stranorlar unit)[222]

Broadly speaking, these would remain problem areas in the months and years ahead. In a report on 'The Border War', *Hibernia* noted that the most surprising aspect of the series of shootings along the border was the low number of fatalities. A UDR member, Winston Donnell, was shot dead on 10 August in Clady, Co. Tyrone. The Gardaí found 'nothing to suggest' that the culprits subsequently crossed into the South.[223] The next fatal border incident occurred on the South Armagh border. Feelings in the area had been running high after a local man, Harry Thornton, was shot by the British Army after his lorry backfired outside a Belfast RUC station.[224] Two British Army Ferret armoured cars crossed the border at Courtbane in Louth on 29 August. A crowd of about 150 locals gathered and prevented the troop carriers retreating to the northern side. One of the troop carriers was abandoned and the other was eventually recovered and taken over the border, where the troops proceeded to change its wheel.[225]

Shots were then fired by a group of IRA personnel, resulting in the death of a British soldier, Ian Armstrong. There were differing accounts from the respective forces about whether the fatal shots emanated from the North or the South.[226] A statement made by the Taoiseach after the incident cited thirty prior British incursions and Lynch also countered accusations of Gardaí/Army inaction.[227] Reflecting the political climate, post-internment, the statement did not contain an expression of sympathy.

The next upsurge in violence came with the British cratering of cross-border roads, beginning on 13 October. Peck opposed the strategy and warned the Foreign Office that:

> Such action would exacerbate border communities. Few in the Republic, certainly not in government would discourage anyone who sought to remove or fill in obstacles. Relations between the RUC and the Gardaí would be damaged, and the Irish government made less able politically to cooperate with HMG even tacitly over security matters or to hinder the IRA at home.[228]

Cratering operations were to play a major role in radicalising elements of the wider border population and bringing about disturbances on the southern side of the border. Anything from a couple of dozen to upwards of 1,000 civilians would make attempts to reopen roads. Frequently successful, the road openers would often have agricultural machinery at hand, including JCB diggers, to aid their task.[229] One IRA activist described the positive impact of cratering on the organisation:

> IRA units just took to the lanes and fields and carried on as usual; switched cars on the southern side to a car on the northern side and continued on the journey north. But this British tactic opened up a whole new front for border IRA units; instead of having to go into the North in search of the Brits they were now coming to us. The local population on both sides of the border were infuriated as their farms straddled the border ... Road committees and action groups were set up to coordinate the effort and it became a real battle of wills as to who would win. IRA units became involved in all these action groups and became a real focus of resistance for local people.[230]

Before internment, there were on average four border incidents a month; after internment, there were sixteen; after cratering, there were thirty-three.[231] With such an upsurge, it was inevitable that more controversial incidents like Courtbane would occur. To the annoyance of the British Army, the Gardaí did not interfere with attempts to fill in craters. Meanwhile the presence of British troops at the border presented ideal targets for the IRA. Local papers contained numerous reports of shooting incidents along the border, as well as border infringements.[232] A pattern soon began to emerge. On the British side, there were complaints of Garda inaction.[233] Even when the Gardaí did act, the outcome was not positive from the British perspective. For example, Gardaí apprehended four gunmen at Dungooley in Louth after a gun battle with British troops. Having been convicted, the four received only fourteen-day prison sentences.[234]

On the Irish side, there were complaints of British incursions, firing shots into Irish territory and aggressive behaviour. During cratering operations such accusations were more frequent. A Garda car was shot by the British Army at Drumnart, Clontibret, Co. Monaghan.[235] On the Clogher–Tydavnet Road in Monaghan, forty-five CS canisters and forty-five rubber bullets were fired after 150 people filled a crater.[236] Forty CS gas canisters and rubber bullets were fired during a road-filling operation in Scotstown, Co. Monaghan.[237] In Donegal, County Council offices in Lifford had to be vacated due to British Army gunfire and there were complaints that CS gas came into Lifford, having been fired over the border.[238] In Kiltyclogher, Co. Leitrim, British Army taser rounds were fired 'indiscriminately' into the streets of the town. [239]

The management of the border protests was a delicate issue for the Gardaí.

> Our [Garda] general approach to the question was to assign two dependable members with a good local knowledge at the border points in question with instructions to endeavour to keep the peace on our side of the border, observe events, seek assistance should the need arise and be in a position to report fully and accurately for the information of our authorities.[240]

It was felt by the Gardaí that they did not want too many of the force 'at a border point as it might be interpreted by civilians as lending support to their operation and the northern authorities might view a large force of Gardaí as protecting their advancement close to the border, and thus possibly intensifying the violence of any confrontation'.[241] Initially, at least, the relatively passive role played by Gardaí meant that there was little overt antagonism with protestors. Three Gardaí who parked a patrol car on Munnilly Bridge near Clones, preventing a British Army unit placing explosives on the southern side of the border, were lauded by the local paper, *The Northern Standard,* for their 'courageous stand against the British Army'.[242]

It seems the British forces did not help their cause with Gardaí by displaying needless aggression on occasions. They drew the ire of Chief Superintendent McMahon, the senior Garda in Cavan–Monaghan Division, on one such occasion. McMahon was called out to a road protest where the protestors where 'obviously normal, respectable country people'.[243] As the protest ended, McMahon followed the last of the crowd away from the border, at which point two CS canisters were fired by British troops. The Chief Superintendent was no republican apologist and his opposite number in the RUC in Armagh found him 'very good to deal with'.[244] Incensed by the 'wanton assault on unarmed civilians and Garda', McMahon summoned the commanding officer of the troops to the border, where the two engaged in a robust discussion on the finer points of border security.[245]

The presence of Fine Gael TD Billy Fox, a Protestant himself, at many protests in Monaghan and his strong Dáil contributions on the subject could be seen as an indicator of the broad level of support for the road-opening campaign.[246] The borders of Monaghan and Louth were where the 'cratering' campaign was most keenly resisted. It was in Monaghan that the potential for such cross-border road openings to get out of control became evident on 19 March 1972. An aspect that may have added to the volatility of this situation was the arrival of busloads (approximately 250 individuals)[247] from Dublin in support of the road openers. The usual mix of stone throwing, road opening (at three locations), British Army incursions and IRA shots took place throughout the day. Three republicans were arrested, which led to an estimated 1,500 civilians besieging Monaghan Garda station.

In the melee that followed, the Gardaí drew batons and some petrol bombs were thrown. Two FN rifles were stolen from troops who arrived in support of Gardaí.[248] After the riots, republicans put the blame for the disturbances on the heavy-handedness of Gardaí.[249] When the Fianna Fáil chairman of the Urban District Council Lorcan

Ronaghan, who, like Fox, had previously attended border protests, placed the blame on an outside 'hooligan' element, a republican picket was held at his home.[250] The only person charged in connection with the riots was a local youth, sixteen-year-old Seamus (Jim) Lynagh, who was convicted of throwing a petrol bomb at Gardaí.[251] Lynagh would become a leading IRA figure along the border in subsequent years and his significant role will be touched upon in later chapters.

Some in the British establishment viewed 'cratering' as a success. Kelvin White, of the Foreign and Commonwealth Office (FCO), noted 'as a result of internment killings and shootings went up ... as a result of "cratering" cross border incidents went down'.[252] For the Irish government, 'cratering' created a security headache for at least six months. In the winter of 1971/2, a cat-and-mouse opening/ closing of roads game became a Sunday ritual in certain border areas. In the week prior to the Monaghan riots, *The Northern Standard* warned that some young people had begun to see the stone throwing on the border as 'a weekly entertainment matinee'.[253] Bordering Armagh, Tyrone, and Fermanagh, Monaghan had been pivotal to the road-opening campaign but judging by the lack of subsequent reports, the movement seemed to have dissipated for a few years after the riot.

During the second half of 1971, there were a number of fatalities affecting the southern border counties. A nineteen-year-old waitress from Donegal, Bridie Carr, was killed when she was caught in crossfire between the IRA and the British Army on the Lifford–Strabane border in November.[254] A brother of the victim, Father James Carr, was in later years critical of the Garda investigation into his sister's death and wondered 'whether the Gardaí had been instructed to go "soft" on the IRA'.[255] In testimony to a Dáil subcommittee, Fr Carr was also critical of Neil Blaney, who delivered a fiery speech on the bridge where his sister was killed just twenty-four hours after her death.[256] Three witnesses to Ms Carr's death identified well-known republicans as being involved in the shooting incident.[257] The Gardaí did not question the three suspects, as it was felt that it would be a futile exercise.[258]

In September, an RUC constable was kidnapped in Dungannon but released on the border unharmed.[259] At the end of November, a Dundalk man serving in the British Army, Robert Benner, was less fortunate. He was abducted and killed, apparently by the Official IRA. In a practice that was to become familiar in the year ahead, Benner's body was dumped at the side of a border road.[260] Reporting on the killing, *The Irish Times* noted that the IRA in Dundalk was having trouble controlling its men, citing a spokesman who said 'at least six local members were drummed out'.[261] Just a few days after Benner's death, a former British Army Colonel died in Co. Meath after an arms raid on his house, having suffered head and leg injuries.[262] Meanwhile, as was mentioned in the political section of the chapter, the killing of Senator Barnhill and another double killing on the Donegal–Tyrone border had led directly to diplomatic pressure on Dublin for a security clampdown.

Dramatic incidents in Donegal over the Christmas break would give the government further impetus to act against republicans. In the days prior to Christmas 1971, Gardaí searched a few houses in the Donegal area. After the Walker killing in Meath, there had been increased Garda activity.[263] The net result of the Donegal searches was three arrests. This prompted a riot in Ballyshannon town. Barricades went up at the bridge leading to the town and fighting continued until the early hours of the morning.[264] In a pattern that would be repeated in Monaghan in March, republicans blamed a heavy-handed Garda approach.[265] There were also recriminations afterwards, with a local priest receiving a public rebuke from republicans for delivering a sermon strongly critical of the IRA.[266] Charges were brought against thirty-two individuals for their part in the riot and some received heavy fines.[267]

Whether influenced by the Ballyshannon riot or not, an interesting ruling took place in a Donegal court the following week. A jury convicted Joseph Doherty of possession of ammunition. It was unusual for a border jury to return a guilty verdict in such circumstances but what was even more noteworthy were the judge's comments. In summation, Judge Ryan claimed that internment would be necessary if 'the jury system fails'. Meanwhile, in sentencing Doherty to the uncharacteristically long sentence of twelve months, Judge Ryan stated:

> Quite unwillingly I know on your part you might have started something that would not have stopped at the border. Nobody thinks of that these days. Unless people start thinking of it there will be serious trouble one of these days in close proximity to that border, which nobody likes in this jurisdiction.[268]

The riots in Ballyshannon, the upsurge in incidents on the border and the goading of the authorities by northern MP Paddy Kennedy had raised the temperature so that a security clampdown was looking more likely. Any number of events could have sparked a crackdown. The funeral of IRA leader Jack McCabe in Cavan, for instance, included an IRA firing party.[269] Even more seriously, on Thursday, 28 January 1972, a gun battle lasting two hours took place at Dungooley on the Louth–Armagh border. The British Army reported firing over 2,500 rounds during the engagement. The Gardaí and the Army were on the scene during the gun battle. They opted not to challenge the republicans but instead execute an arrest when the IRA retreated.[270] By the time the Gardaí/Army caught up with the IRA group, which was led by Martin Meehan and Anthony Holland, the republicans were unarmed, so there was no arrest made. Meehan subsequently boasted to journalists that the IRA had given the British 'a pasting' and 'you could hear them squeal in Belfast'.[271] This bravado seemed to have the same effect as Paddy Kennedy's statement. The following morning, Meehan and six others were arrested, but by the time the men made their court appearance, the political climate had shifted. Bloody Sunday occurred that weekend.

The reaction to Bloody Sunday along the border mirrored the rest of the South. Five thousand marched in Monaghan. *The Northern Standard* commented that 'it is doubtful if in the last half century any event has evoked such a reaction from the people of Monaghan'.[272] Another 5,000 marched in Dundalk;[273] 10,000 in Sligo,[274] and 1,000 students marched in Ballyshannon.[275] A religious dimension was noted in each of the border counties, with prayers offered at demonstrations and 'in practically every Catholic Church requiem mass was offered for the repose of the souls of victims'.[276] There was no equivalent of the burning of the British embassy along the border as demonstrations seemed peaceable. There were, however, allegations of intimidation in Clones, where two days of mourning were held. It was alleged that some Protestant members of the community were intimidated into observing the second day of mourning. This resulted in a heated debate at a meeting of the Urban District Council.[277] Fr Joe McVeigh, a republican-minded priest based in Monaghan at the time, recalled that a teacher in a school in the town who took pupils to a demonstration lost his job as a result.[278]

The number of British security force fatalities along the border continued to increase after Bloody Sunday, with a noticeable trend in kidnappings. In February, a British soldier from Dublin, Tommy

McCann, was kidnapped and his body found at the border.[279] Another ex-soldier based in the Republic, David Seaman, described as a 'Walter Mitty'-type character, was found shot dead on the Dundalk–Castleblayney road on 6 February 1972.[280] In March, a former UDR man, Marcus McCausland, was kidnapped and shot when he was returning from a night out in Donegal. The latter three killings are normally ascribed to the Official IRA. In March, a part-time UDR member, Joseph Jardine, was shot dead in Middletown, Co. Armagh, with the gunmen escaping the 100 yards over the border to Co. Monaghan.[281] The border, so porous for the previous fifty years, was becoming a more dangerous place for those connected with the British Army/RUC. Another UDR member, James Elliott, was driving a lorry from Kingscourt in Cavan when he was kidnapped. His body was found at the border.[282]

The number of incidents on the border decreased somewhat for April, May and June 1972, averaging just over twenty per month.[283] This was less than at the peak of 'cratering' activity but the increased frequency of dead bodies appearing along the border was ominous. Four other kidnappings and executions were also associated with the 'Disappeared' in 1972. Most likely the victims of those killings were interrogated and killed near the border.[284] It is only in recent years that details of these killings have emerged.

On 3 March, the Irish Ambassador in London was presented with a list that identified roughly the same border areas as troublesome.[285] Meanwhile, tension continued to grow between Irish security forces and republicans. One Garda who unofficially contacted his counterparts over the border claimed Gardaí were harassing 'known IRA members charging them with minor civil offences on every occasion possible'.[286] The same Garda noted the frustration of the force with the failure of courts to convict. Evidence for the increase in harassment can be seen in the rise in prosecutions for illegal collections and the like. Additionally, a directive had been issued to Gardaí to take detailed reports on republican commemorations in 1971.[287] It was noted earlier how the Gardaí were seen to 'stand idly by', listening and watching along the border as internment was introduced. Evidence gathered during this period was used to bring charges against leading republicans. Accounts of speeches monitored by the Gardaí at protests in September/October 1971 were used in 1972 to charge leading republicans, including Cathal Goulding,[288]

Joe Cahill,[289] John Joe McGirl,[290] Alphonous Hand[291] and Frank Morris.[292]

Throughout the first half of 1972 there were continuous arrests and prosecutions for subversive activity. The local papers in the border counties contain accounts of numerous such operations, including occasions where there were multiple arrests.[293] Securing convictions remained difficult: some effort was made to move hearings from the border to Dublin,[294] but prosecutions frequently failed in high-profile cases such as that involving Martin Meehan.[295] Additionally, court cases were becoming more difficult to police and protests were commonplace, as was the occasional escape attempt.[296] It was estimated that 200 Gardaí were on duty in Dundalk on the day of Meehan's case.[297] Therefore, the decision to introduce the Special Criminal Court, non-jury trial, not only made it theoretically easier to secure a conviction but also reduced the security headache associated with frequent court appearances in border towns.

As the violence in Northern Ireland escalated in the summer of 1972, there were further fatalities. Garda Inspector Sam Donegan was killed when he examined a landmine that was about 30 yards on the northern side of the border.[298] As the first Garda killed near the border, Donegan's death caused shock in the locality.[299] No one was ever convicted for the attack and no organisation admitted responsibility. Nationally, the attack was front-page news in the immediate aftermath but, considering the intensity of violence elsewhere, Sam Donegan's killing did not receive the same national coverage as other Garda fatalities. Media coverage of the blast 'was pitifully low' and limited mainly to follow-up reports of the funeral.[300]

July/August were particularly violent months, as evidenced by an upsurge in refugees. Frank McKeown from Rockcorry in Monaghan was among those killed in the Belfast disturbances – a civilian, he was shot by the British Army.[301] Philip Fay from Stradone in Cavan was killed by loyalists, also in Belfast.[302] Illustrating the complexities of the conflict, a British soldier from Carrick-on-Shannon, Martin Rooney, was killed in Belfast. Rooney's death was marked by Leitrim County Council with a vote of sympathy.[303] Although not in large numbers, others from the southern border counties were active in the British Army/RUC, some rising to prominence.[304] The killings of Private Benner and McCann have already been noted. A year earlier, Cecil Patterson, a RUC Special Branch detective originally from Belturbet,

Co. Cavan, was shot in Belfast.[305] Meanwhile, in October 1972 a young RUC man, Gordon Harron, from Donegal was killed in an incident with loyalists.[306] Previously, another RUC man from further south in Wicklow, Dermot Hurley, was killed by the IRA in Belfast.[307]

Just as internment and 'cratering' had brought upsurges in border violence, so too there was a further spike after 'Operation Motorman'. There were between thirty-one to thirty-four incidents per month for August, September and October.[308] The upsurge in violence led the British to deliver to Dublin the 'Border Dossier', which detailed IRA strength along the border as they saw it.[309] The 'Dossier' identified much the same hubs of IRA activity again: Dundalk, Monaghan, Bundoran, Lifford and Buncrana. Additionally, there were isolated groups operating in Inniskeen, Carrickmacross, Castleblayney, Redhills and Belcoo.

In terms of numbers, it was thought there were forty members of the Dundalk Active Service Unit (ASU), about a third of them locals. A second unit in the town made up exclusively of northerners was thought to contain a dozen or so members. Monaghan was seen as home to three of the five ASUs. The unit in Monaghan town was thought to have twenty-five members. Likewise, Clones unit had twenty-five members, with some from Coalisland and Dungannon. In Ballyshannon, fifteen to twenty members were identified, mostly southerners. The Pettigo unit of about ten members was judged 'small and inactive'. There were sixteen members in Lifford, drawn mainly from Strabane IRA members on the run. The Castlefinn unit had approximately twenty members and was led by a Cork man. It was thought that Buncrana was home to forty-five members of the Derry IRA, who lived mostly in caravans.

Of the smaller units, Carrickmacross was estimated to have twenty men from both sides of the border and engaged in daily shooting actions. The Castleblayney unit was based near Mullyash Mountain and drew its strength from those on the run from Coalisland and Lurgan. The Redhills/Belcoo area was seen as an area with fairly few IRA members, but occasionally 'visitors' from units in the South would arrive for a few days to engage the British Army/RUC.

The British obviously seemed to place credence on the material in the 'Border Dossier', as did the Irish authorities, considering they credited an internal leak as the source. The 'Dossier' gives an interesting perspective on the numbers and personalities involved along the border. There also seems to have been a certain amount of visibility about republicans' presence in border towns. In the 'Dossier' as well as court reports, there were frequent references to groups of young men living in caravans together at the edge of towns. For example, one of the most visible IRA units, according to the British, was that based in the infamous caravan in Cloughfinn, Co Donegal.[310]

There was certainly impetus for the British to put pressure on for greater security co-operation, as the rise in border incidents was now accompanied by a rise in fatalities among their personnel. In the last six months of 1972, twelve British Army/RUC personnel were killed in incidents at or close to the border.[311] Tensions were escalating along the Monaghan border, particularly. Included among the dead were several local UDR members.[312] In addition, the notorious 'pitchfork killings' of Catholic farmers Michael Naan and Andrew Murray took place near Newtownbutler, about a mile from the border.[313] The fear that these attacks would spark a fully-fledged inter-communal conflict was manifested in these latter deaths, which were initially blamed on local loyalists but years later ascribed to British soldiers.[314] In 1978, a former British soldier contacted a hotline set up in response to the Yorkshire Ripper case. The same individual also contacted the *Daily Mirror*. The former soldier believed that a former member of the Argyll and Sutherland Highlanders regiment involved in the Naan and Murray killings may have been linked to the Yorkshire Ripper case. No connection was found between the crimes but the investigation into the 1972 Fermanagh killings was reopened as a result of the soldier's tip-off. Four British soldiers were eventually convicted in connection with the killing.[315]

The Clones author Eugene McCabe wrote a trilogy of short stories that convey the degree of tension along the Fermanagh–Monaghan border at this time in 1972.[316] After the shooting of one UDR member, William Creighton, *The Northern Standard* described the greatest 'build up of tension' since the 1920s. It was noted that some families had moved away from the border as a result of the rise in tension, with one Protestant household being burned out.[317] Another local paper cited the rise in tension as the reason behind the cancellation of the annual Clones Show.[318]

In Dundalk, too, violence was escalating. On 22 August, lorry driver John McCann from Inniskeen was among eight killed by an IRA bomb that exploded prematurely at Killeen customs post. The lorry driver was killed as he awaited customs clearance. Another lorry driver was also killed, as were four Customs officials. Three IRA men from the Newry area were also killed.[319]

The Irish security forces, meanwhile, were coming under more pressure. The Irish Army used CS gas against a hostile group of rioters at Courtbane on 24 August.[320] On 21 September, Dundalk became the next border town to experience a riot on par with those that had already occurred in other border hotspots. In addition to the riots, two bombs were discovered in Dundalk.[321] The trouble arose amidst protests centred on an ongoing hunger strike among republican prisoners in the Curragh Camp. Seventeen were later remanded in custody in connection with the disturbances, many of whom had addresses in Northern Ireland.[322] The experience of a Garda in the barracks on the night has already been recounted. The local paper's editorial read:

> We, the people of Dundalk will have to foot the bill for the injuries and damages inflicted not the 'runners' from outside areas, who have duped a number of susceptible teenagers and hotheads into committing acts more likely associated with the less civilised tribes of Africa, and they disappear into the night when confronted by a few determined men.[323]

It was a recurring theme in border towns that outside elements would be blamed in the aftermath of violence. Minister for Justice Desmond O'Malley threatened 'extremely unpleasant measures' against subversives in a hard-hitting statement and almost doubled Garda strength in the town.[324] The riot came after a year during which the reputation of Dundalk was tarnished in the media. A BBC programme had highlighted increasing lawlessness and terms such as 'El Paso' and 'Gundalk' were used.[325] Compared to street disturbances that took place in the North, the violence in Dundalk was 'minimal'.[326] The incidents in other border towns could be described in a similar manner, as was acknowledged in a review of the year by the *Dundalk Democrat* in which it was noted that if the events had taken place in the North, they would have been treated as routine, not front-page news, but were seen as significant for what they might presage: 'the significance in each case was that it was happening in the Republic, and that each event was worse than that which went before'.[327]

To add to the instability along the border, a loyalist bombing campaign began. These attacks increased pressure for additional border security. In March 1972, there were two shooting incidents within four days in Emyvale, Monaghan, leading to the local development association putting pressure on the Gardaí for greater security.[328] Earlier the same month, a bomb was found in the nearby border village of Mullan.[329] However, it was after 'Motorman' that attacks became more frequent. In October, there were loyalist bombs in Carrigans, Donegal and Clones.[330] Like Emyvale, representatives of the local community called for greater security, with the Chamber of Commerce demanding more troops be brought into the area.[331]

There were other bomb attacks along the border[332] before loyalist bombs led to fatalities on 1 December in Dublin. Before the year ended, two teenagers, Geraldine O'Reilly and Paddy Stanley, were killed by a loyalist explosion in Belturbet, Co. Cavan.[333] Again, there was understandable pressure from local community leaders for greater border security.[334] The *Anglo Celt* called for no retaliation, stating 'there can no longer be our men of violence and their men of violence, there are only men of violence who are enemies of all and must be treated as such'.[335] The security services faced a particular difficulty in dealing with loyalists. Chief Superintendent McMahon wrote:

> Our main difficulty, however, is almost a complete absence of information on members of extreme Protestant organisations in Northern Ireland and the identity of vehicles used by them. A special effort is being made in this direction at present but I think the absence of members travelling into Northern Ireland and making determined effort to secure this information that much progress will not be made.[336]

At Dáil hearings into the bombings in recent years, there was some criticism of the Garda investigation into the Belturbet explosion. It was stated that the Gardaí inquiring into the Dublin bombings may have better used RUC contacts in contrast to the Belturbet investigators but there was a lack of documentary evidence to fully substantiate this claim.[337] Despite having good descriptions of the perpetrators and a prime suspect, a UDR member from Co. Fermanagh, no charges were ever proffered.[338] Given the ad hoc nature of cross-border co-operation, it is entirely plausible that the individual detectives investigating the Dublin blast simply had a better range of contacts over the border. In the case of the young Donegal couple, Brid Porter and Oliver Boyce, killed only a few days later, again by loyalists, the RUC were found to 'have cooperated fully',[339] although one of the investigating officers claimed that arrests were only made when he switched from his initial point of contact within the RUC to an officer he knew personally.[340] The loyalist attacks further incentivised southerners to disengage from the northern conflict but also gave impetus to the Irish security forces to deepen cross-border security co-operation. These effects of the bombing certainly suited the agenda of British intelligence and the debate still goes on as to whether collusion with loyalists took place.[341]

As well as the loyalist attacks, the arrest and hunger strike of MacStíofáin led to extra tension in border towns.[342] The number of incidents on the border continued to rise, with a new high of forty-eight such incidents occurring in November.[343] As 1972 ended, it seemed that the border counties were being dragged into the northern conflict. Albeit on a smaller scale, the counties of Monaghan, Louth and Donegal in particular had witnessed gun battles, street disturbances, bombings, kidnappings and violent deaths. More specifically, there seemed to be particular security problems in certain towns, notably Dundalk, Monaghan, Clones, Ballyshannon and Lifford. The introduction of the Special Criminal Court and the Offences Against the State Act were designed in part to empower the Gardaí to re-establish themselves in these areas. There was enough republican sentiment at a local and national level that it was not possible for the Gardaí to be seen to be joining wholeheartedly with the British in moves against the IRA.

However, standing back from the conflict was no longer an option. The government security policy had become avowedly anti-IRA. Arrests and harassment of republicans were commonplace. The courts had been reconstituted to make convictions more likely but one grey area remained. Full security co-operation with the British was still too politically contentious to contemplate. Therefore, there was no set policy on co-operation, just ad hoc responses. What seems to have occurred is different degrees of haphazard co-operation along the border, with some Gardaí/Army interpreting the ill-defined boundaries differently than others.

The Spillover into the South

The year 1972 would be the last year of the Troubles during which refugees would arrive from the North on a large scale. There were 5,409 refugees accommodated in one day in 1971, with a peak of 5400 in 1972. In comparison, only 300 arrived in 1973, with none recorded for 1974.[344]

The introduction of internment in 1971 seems to have seen one of the biggest influxes. Most refugees made their own way to the border, with *The Irish Times* reporting 'many cars and vans are carrying crude Red Cross signs or flags and in places residents are travelling in convoys marked with the Red Cross flag'.[345] On 11 August, there were 4,339 refugees spread between Gormanston Camp (2,827), Kilworth in Cork (222), Coolmoney, Wicklow (107), Kildare (308), Kilkenny (377), Waterford (228), Tralee (220) and Finner (50).[346] The strategy was to use Gormanston as a distribution centre, moving refugees further south where possible. Jack Lynch claimed at one stage that the pressure was so great that the Army had 'almost reached saturation point' in dealing with refugees.[347] The Minister for Defence was eventually required to call upon local authorities for assistance in providing accommodation, with the Army looking after 2,695 refugees and other agencies looking after a similar number.[348] In Dundalk on 14 August, 700 were fed at two hours' notice thanks to 'Dundalk housewives and daughters',[349] with the visitors spending the night on mattresses in local schools. Religious orders, schools and the Garda Training College in Templemore hosted many of those the Army could not accommodate.[350]

By 16 August, the crisis had dissipated and no camp was at that stage crowded.[351] In line with previous experience, facilities at the Army camps were described as 'primitive'.[352] The crisis did dissolve quite quickly but some refugees remained in camps for a considerable period afterwards. The reaction to some who stayed on was not altogether sympathetic: 'These are in the main people who, through ineffectuality of one sort or another find it difficult to cope on their own with the stresses and strains of life and are reluctant to leave any place in which there is free food and accommodation.'[353]

By October 1971 there were still 400 refugees being catered for, with 180 remaining at the turn of the year.[354] The ongoing presence of refugees in military camps was gauged 'unsatisfactory' in part due to the associated 'security risk'.[355] By 1972, responsibility for care of refugees was transferred to Civil Defence and local authorities. Between July and August 1972, 9,800 refugees were cared for. The operation was judged a success due to the 'thoroughness of the preplanning which had been carried out'.[356]

Particular issues arose with those who arrived in 1972 as they were considered to be largely holidaymakers. It seems at least some of those who arrived did not consider themselves refugees at all. There were reports that £3,000 had been collected from families in Belfast over the preceding year to pay for the 'holiday'.[357] While local media reports paint a picture of communities uniting in support of refugees,[358] the view in official files is different: 'Refugees are not always just frightened people who are thankful for the assistance being given them. Some of them can be very demanding and ungrateful, even obstreperous and fractious – as well as, particularly in the case of teenage boys, destructive.'[359]

A recent RTÉ radio documentary described the experience of refugees who were housed by the monks at Glenstal Abbey in Limerick in July 1972. The experience of the children in particular is interesting. Some of the kids were obviously deeply traumatised by their experience in Belfast and there were issues dealing with authority figures. With this in mind, the local Civil Defence made the decision not to wear a uniform as it was seen to be too militaristic. A local farmer in Crosshaven, Co. Cork, lacked this foresight and purchased a green military-style Land Rover. The farmer was spotted driving by a group of youths housed in Kilworth Camp and the vehicle was stoned. The monks in Glenstall adopted a unique approach to dealing with their visitors, opting for the only course available, as they saw it: having no rules. One monk reflected on the success of this approach, commenting that 'they were the best guests we ever had and not a day's trouble'.[360]

As well as civilians fleeing the conflict, there were also a large number of republican activists who moved south. As early as January 1972, northern MP John Taylor claimed that there were 110 individuals wanted for questioning residing in the Republic.[361] A further forty-five were wanted by May 1972.[362] There is some evidence to suggest that republicans from certain parts of the North gravitated to certain parts of the South. One republican noted:

Monaghan – that was a natural destination for members of the republican movement who were forced to leave home. East

Tyrone went to Monaghan, North Armagh to Castleblaney, South Armagh went to Dundalk or Carrickmacross, Belfast went to Dundalk, Derry and Fermanagh went to Buncrana or Bundoran.[363]

Broadly speaking, the evidence in the border 'Dossier' supports this view. There were some high-profile republicans who sought refuge in the Republic. Martin Meehan and Anthony Holland settled in Dundalk after escaping from Crumlin Road jail.[364] Meanwhile, seven prisoners who escaped from the Maidstone prison ship also made their way south.[365] The extradition of republicans back to the North was in its own right a massive political issue throughout the Troubles. Between January 1971 and October 1972, forty-eight extradition warrants were issued by the northern authorities but none were enforced.[366] The courts in the South generally ruled that extradition in cases deemed 'political' was not lawful. These judgements meant that Lynch and subsequent Taoisigh could plausibly plead to the British that extradition was 'a matter for the courts'.[367] The reluctance of the Irish authorities to grant extradition can be gauged by the response to warrants issued by the RUC for those who escaped to the Republic from the Crumlin Road jail. One of the grounds cited by a Garda Assistant Commissioner for not processing the warrant was that it was attached to affidavits with a pin rather than in 'a more formal fashion'.[368]

The presence of northern exiles in the Republic created a security headache. Subversive elements were a direct challenge to the state. Meanwhile, it was shown in 1971, in particular, that the Army simply could not handle large-scale arrivals. The potential for large-scale movements of tens of thousands in the future could not be ruled out. Examining this scenario with a view to past experience, a Department of Defence memo would later conclude that containing the problem within the six counties was perhaps the best solution:

There is a lot to be said for trying to hold refugees in the North. Their movement to the South would do nothing for either part of the country, but it would create another generation imbued with a hatred and desire for revenge. The refugees in question would be of the genuine article and not the holiday type we experienced previously.[369]

Towards the 'law-and-order' Coalition

Bomb attacks, inflows of refugees, killings, street disturbances and robberies all indicated that a security crisis existed in the Republic in 1972. In 1970, there were 11 armed robberies, which caused some disquiet, 57 in 1971 and 143 in 1972.[370] More worryingly, as has been documented in this chapter, at least thirty deaths in the conflict in 1972 had a border dimension. In response to Dáil critics of his record on security policy, Des O'Malley drew a distinction between 'criticism that says more should be done than has been done and criticism which says nothing is being done'.[371] In this regard, it is worthwhile considering some statistics. By 31 July 1973, 241 convictions were secured in the Special Criminal Court, with 97 acquittals.[372] This was a considerable number of charges, considering that the courts were operational for just over twelve months.

To give the figures some context, 531 were charged with equivalent type offences in the North in the last six months of 1972 alone.[373] In terms of arms seizures, in 1970 and 1971, 148 illegal firearms were seized and 1,156 pounds of explosives.[374] In Northern Ireland during the same period, there were 1,041 firearms seized and 3,546 pounds of explosives.[375] Of course, the levels of violence were much greater in Northern Ireland, so it is to be expected that the figures in the Republic for arrests and seizures are lower.

The state's response to the security crisis when it came was incremental. The threat to introduce internment in December 1970 could be seen as initial sabre-rattling. For most of 1971, meanwhile, Lynch did not have the necessary political support to move against republicans. By 1972, however, it was becoming apparent that republicans had overstepped the mark in the Republic too many times. The sight of a strengthened IRA negotiating directly with British political leaders further undermined Irish politicians. Incidents on the border, in the meantime, were rising and the authority of the Gardaí was being tested regularly. Republican leaders were aware that if violence spread south, Lynch would be forced to act. Hence IRA statements went out of their way to state that their actions took place on the northern side of the border in controversial cases.[376] MacStíofáin also cited a fear of violence spreading south as a rationale for ending his hunger strike,[377] but even if republicans genuinely wanted to avoid conflict in the Republic, the ongoing shooting and bombing activity at the frontier made this impossible. Prior to Bloody Sunday, republicans had tested the southern authorities. The burning of the embassy was a step further but it was the ongoing escalation of violence that led the state to act.

When Gardaí started arresting gunmen at the border, low-level confrontation with republicans became commonplace. Arrests and seizures led to significant prison sentences as the draconian legislation of 1972 took effect. Protests often accompanied arrests and on several occasions led to quite significant street disturbances. The combination of these factors, coupled with a more general level of violence along the border, meant that a certain amount of antagonism existed between Gardaí and republicans. That said, in some areas, there seems to have been a particular reluctance to combat the IRA. British documents point to Lifford and Clones specifically.

While security policy by 1972 was unambiguously anti-IRA, there may have been numerous reasons why areas of weakness existed. Firstly, the Gardaí/Army may simply not have had the resources. The RUC had virtually withdrawn from parts of the border[378] and the British Army, with its considerable resources, was struggling to police its side of the border. The Gardaí/Army were under-resourced, so, on occasion, they may simply not have been capable of doing what the British were equally incapable of doing. This would, in part, be the argument proffered by Irish governments in the years ahead.

A second reason for Garda inaction may have been due to the attitude on behalf of individuals. In areas where the IRA were particularly strong, this may have been a factor inhibiting action. Where the local community was strongly republican and mixed messages had emanated from the political establishment in the preceding years, the fact that some Gardaí adopted a lax approach to republican violence would not be surprising. Finally, bearing in mind the climate of the times, it is possible that some individual Gardaí/Army personnel held strong republican views. Even British accounts, however, only cite a small number of such cases.

The most intriguing aspect of security policy relates to co-operation with the British forces. The view of Peck on the matter in 1971 is worth quoting at length:

I do not believe anything short of a major security crisis would induce the Irish authorities to cooperate openly with the security authorities in the North. The Gardaí may be willing to cooperate, if mutual advantage is likely, with the RUC, but only if secrecy is maintained over the link. The government – perhaps even the Minister for Justice – would not want to know about such things. In short, a policy of increasing pressure on the IRA here does not necessarily involve the corollary of increased co-operation with the authorities in the North over a common enemy, however logical such a step may be. The political dangers are too great, and political habits too long seated.[379]

Peck's final point is worth emphasising. Irish security policy directed against the IRA would not necessarily involve co-operation with the British. To co-operate with Britain openly would have in fact created insecurity for the Irish state at the time. Therefore, such co-operation as did exist was kept discreet. From an operational point of view, this may not have been ideal; politically it was perfectly rational. One of the consequences of this strategy was that when co-operation was required from the RUC, clearly defined channels did not exist.

As 1972 ended, destruction had reached the border on an unprecedented scale. The government was facing ongoing demands for greater security in border areas[380] but despite the spillover from Northern Ireland, most of the South remained largely unaffected by the Troubles and understandably that is the way the bulk of the populace wanted to keep things. Going into the 1973 general election, Fianna Fáil ran general election broadcasts that contrasted bombings in the North with peace in the Republic,[381] the implication was that it was their party's effective security policy that maintained peace. In some border constituencies, Fianna Fáil successfully portrayed itself as the defenders of law and order, gaining seats at the expense of those seen as soft on security, notably Fine Gael's Billy Fox.[382] The outcome of the election saw a coalition government returned, which would be defined by its law-and-order strategy. One of the many legacies of the 1973–7 government is that due to its rigid approach to security, the role of its predecessor in clamping down on subversion is often forgotten.

CHAPTER 4

'There are times you may have to be rough with citizens': Coalition Clampdown on Republicans, 1973–1975

When an Irish Army patrol met British troops at Lackey Bridge near Clones on 5 October 1974, they exchanged pleasantries and cigarettes. A British soldier sought to mark the occasion by taking a photograph for his personal collection. So significant was the incident that an account of it reached the desk of the Irish Minister for Justice, who contacted the British embassy, fearing that the photograph would leak out.[1] The incident seems remarkably trivial to concern a senior politician, but it is nevertheless illustrative: the fear Irish politicians had of being seen to collaborate with British forces is evident. That details of the incident could reach the desk of the Minister for Justice is equally significant.

In 1969/1970, the average Garda on checkpoint duty may have been unsure of how to deal with republicans. In 1975, there was less ambiguity about how to deal with the IRA but dealings with counterparts over the border remained less straightforward.

British Ambassador Arthur Galsworthy's view of the coalition was of 'a heterogeneous Government without a long-term strategy, largely content to trundle along in power and to respond not without adroitness, to the stimuli produced by events as they happen'.[2] The events that happened ranged from mass murder on the streets of the capital to prison breaks, assassinations and kidnappings. The response to events was invariably a clampdown on republicans.

From petty misdemeanours to serious crimes, republicans were the focus of attention by security forces. In Cavan, the local Vocational Education Committee discussed the case of a fifteen-year-old school girl arrested and allegedly taken to Mountjoy for selling Easter lilies.[3] In Monaghan, a mother of two was given twenty-eight days in Mountjoy for possessing republican posters.[4] A Garda admitted to a government minister, Conor Cruise O'Brien, that he beat up a prisoner to obtain a confession.[5] Three prisoners escaped from prison in a helicopter and a song celebrating the jailbreakers topped the charts.[6] These were not normal times, although some aspects of policy remained unchanged. Even the new regime, with its bitter antipathy for republicans, was still not fully committed to openly co-operating with the British Army/RUC. If a Garda in a border barracks received a phone call from a neighbouring British Army/RUC location, how the matter was handled was very much dependent on the individual Garda's interpretation of his role. If the matter was handled in the wrong way, it could end up on the minister's desk. Hence, there was some understandable hesitancy in dealing with the British Army/RUC. It was still not politically prudent to be closely associated with the British Army or RUC, as evidenced by the Lackey Bridge photograph. This was particularly true as allegations of collusion between the RUC and loyalist paramilitaries persisted. Therefore, just as the previous administration had emphasised discretion in its co-operation, so too would the new coalition.

Despite some moves in the direction of institutional co-operation, it remained the case that the level of co-operation would depend on individuals. At ground level, the numbers involved in key security positions in the Republic were small. In the Cavan/Monaghan Division, for example, the Garda stations of Clones, Scotstown, Emyvale and Castleblayney were responsible for 112 miles of border between them – almost half the length of the entire border. Excluding those on temporary transfer, there were seven Garda sergeants stationed in these barracks in 1973.[7] With such small numbers, the disposition of individuals mattered considerably. The behaviour of British troops on occasion did not help matters. It was frequently reported that they adopted an arrogant attitude to Gardaí.

That relations between the respective security forces were not always smooth is almost self-evident but between 1973 and 1975, a host of factors combined to improve matters. That the coalition government was seen as being tough on the IRA helped, but so too did an increasing weariness of northern affairs in the Republic. Political factors, notably the prospect of a British withdrawal, gave Dublin added incentive to co-operate.

Along the border, the death toll continued to mount. Republicans, security force members, civilians, a politician and a loyalist were among those killed south of the border between 1973 and 1975. Bombs went off in border towns, military checkpoints became a common sight with some roads becaming no-go areas due to hijackings and shooting incidents. Antagonism between republicans and Gardaí persisted. The individual Gardaí and soldiers who arrived on temporary transfer were starting to settle in border areas. So too were the young republicans from Northern Ireland. The age and social profile of the two groups were not dissimilar. They generally lived in the same areas, socialised in the same communities, played the same sports and practised the same religion. They were, however, bitterly divided, with the tension between the two groups occasionally punctuated by violence.

In certain towns and areas, the tension related to northern affairs was greater than others. The previous chapter noted that several major trouble spots could be identified. In 1973–4, the border generally was problematic but, again, specific areas more so. As we will see, by 1975, one area, the border with South Armagh, would emerge as the predominant trouble spot.

Firstly, we will consider the build-up to the 1973 General Election. The resulting coalition government would define security in broader terms, covering a greater range of issues, but the fundamentals of security policy remained unchanged. The emphasis remained on containing the domestic threat while at the same time appearing loyal to the binding nationalist 'idea' of the state. Despite the strong hand taken against republicans, Articles 2 and 3 of the constitution, for instance, would remain sacrosanct. In this context, the political reaction to a possible British withdrawal is considered. Such a move was seen by the Irish government in the context of its own internal threat and the potential it had to destabilise the entire state. This fear incentivised the Irish side to deepen security co-operation.

There follows an analysis of the security forces during the period. The continued material weaknesses of the forces are again central to the discussion, as is the increased mutual hostility with republicans.

We will see that planning by the Army for an intervention in a 'doomsday scenario' was dismissed. Containing the IRA threat was the security forces' primary aim. The cabinet subcommittee on security regularly discussed the IRA but did not give any attention to the loyalist threat. The final section of the chapter, which examines the security situation along the border, illustrates the fallacy of this approach. Loyalist attacks were a central feature of rising violence, most notably the Dublin and Monaghan bombings of 1974. As already noted, another significant trend was the emergence of South Armagh as the main trouble spot. The response to violence generally along the border is interesting and the greater security response inevitably occurred when there was a threat to the southern state or its institutions.

The Political Environment from the 1973 General Election to 1975

The divisions on security matters that became apparent in Fine Gael with the regard to the Offences Against the State Act in December 1972 were noted in the last chapter. The party only adopted a unified stance in the aftermath of bombings in Dublin. With the opposition still reeling, Jack Lynch called a general election on 6 February 1973, anticipating that Fianna Fáil would capitalise on Fine Gael's disarray. Announcing the ballot, Lynch pointedly referred to the 'strong and effective government' of recent years, implicitly drawing a comparison with the weak and divided opposition.[8] As the campaign continued, security became a key issue, particularly in border areas. In Donegal, Fianna Fáil candidate Paddy Delap posited the question: 'when they cannot make up their minds about a simple measure like the Offences Against the State Act, when they have to have five meetings about law and order ... how in God's name could you expect them to run the affairs of the country'.[9]

The presence of significant Protestant populations in border areas may have given security a particular importance there. In Donegal North East, the Protestant Association's decision to back Fianna Fáil was cited as a deciding factor.[10] Similar sentiments were expressed by two defeated candidates in Monaghan who also lost out to Fianna Fáil.[11] Nationally, too, security was a key theme in Fianna Fáil's strategy. The party's political broadcast on television proved especially controversial. Images of bombs exploding in Northern

Ireland were contrasted with the peaceful South. Scenes from the December bombings were also shown, with the implication that more such incidents would accompany a coalition government. Opponents criticised the broadcast for seeking to 'crawl over the dead of the North' to get into office.[12] The strategy was not wholly unsuccessful. In border areas, particularly, Fianna Fáil's message seemed to get a sympathetic hearing as the party 'did proportionately better than they did nationally and gained two seats at the expense of Fine Gael'.[13] Fianna Fáil's vote actually increased nationally, but better vote management ensured that the Liam Cosgrave-led Fine Gael–Labour coalition emerged victorious from the campaign.[14]

It is worth noting that no traditional republican voting bloc emerged. One candidate bucking this trend was Fianna Fáil exile Neil Blaney, who topped the poll in Donegal North East.[15] Other republican candidates were less successful. Notably, Captain James Kelly stood for Kevin Boland's Aontacht Eireann, polling just over 2,000 first preferences in the border constituency of Cavan, losing his deposit.[16] At the ballot box, at least, there seemed to be little appetite in the South for militant republicanism.

The new coalition cabinet had a one-third to two-third balance, with the smaller share of ministers coming from the Labour Party. This gave the minority party a disproportionate say. Significantly, 'unlike Lynch, Cosgrave had fewer constitutional qualms regarding who in government dealt with Northern Ireland'.[17] Several ministers would have input on Northern/security matters. Taoiseach Liam Cosgrave was seen as a delegator, with critics suggesting 'any minister could talk on any subject and frequently did'.[18] This created the possibility of divisions emerging over policy.

Prior to taking office, Cosgrave and his Minister for Foreign Affairs, Garret FitzGerald, had divergent views on northern matters, but this apparently did not emerge as a factor in government.[19] On the other hand, the Labour Minister Conor Cruise O'Brien remained his party's northern spokesman and his presence at certain meetings alienated some nationalist representatives.[20] O'Brien feared that southern intervention was having a negative impact in stoking up loyalist fears. Therefore, he favoured greater disengagement, which was not popular with the SDLP. He was at the fore of criticism of the republican movement and would later in life become a Unionist representative.

The roles of ministers for Justice and Defence would prove to be key positions in the coalition. The Minister for Defence, Paddy Donegan, was a colourful political figure who was rewarded with a cabinet post for his loyalty to Cosgrave. Donegan came from a political dynasty that dated back to the Irish Parliamentary Party.[21] Hence, there was a political lineage that gave him a disdain for militant republicanism. The Minister for Justice, meanwhile, was Paddy Cooney, who was associated with previous moves against Cosgrave's leadership, opposing the Offences Against the State Act.[22] This record as opposition spokesman had led to some anticipation that he would prove something of a reformer in office.

Cosgrave, Cooney, O'Brien and Donegan sat with Labour leader Brendan Corish on a cabinet subcommittee on security. Despite the obvious potential for conflict between the respective figures, the cabinet was remarkably united on security matters. A combination of personal and ideological factors unified this core group. The experience in cabinet was particularly significant. The conflict became very personal, with ministers often facing protests at events, and they were under round-the-clock Garda protection. A bomb was left at Donegan's family business[23] and a device was found near a platform where Cooney was to speak.[24] Issues related to disturbances in Portlaoise jail, in particular, led to increased personal antagonism toward government ministers. Indeed, it was reported that a threat was made to assassinate two government ministers during an IRA hunger strike in February 1975.[25]

The personal impact of the killing by republicans of parliamentary colleague Senator Billy Fox cannot be underestimated. Fox was young and liberal in outlook. He had been prominent in highlighting issues associated with border roads and the plight of northern nationalists to an extent that may have cost him some support from Protestant constituents. Cooney, in particular, was close to Fox and was personally affected by his death.[26] The core group in the cabinet adopted a siege-like mentality and Cooney would increasingly see the battle with the IRA in absolute terms. Warning parents to be aware of republican-minded teachers, Cooney said,

> I repeat with greater urgency the calls I made in the past for full cooperation by each citizen with the Garda Siochana, in the work of defending our State and preserving our society. Any citizen who

refuses cooperation or fails to offer it to the authorities must carry some moral responsibility for the atrocities of the IRA.[27]

The new government received an early boost when a ship, the *Claudia*, containing five tonnes of IRA weapons sourced in Libya, was seized by the Irish Navy on 28 March 1973. Five republicans received convictions relating to this incident, including senior IRA leader Joe Cahill.[28] The captain and crew of the ship were freed at the request of British authorities. This was presumably done to protect the source of the intelligence on the arms importation and the request was made personally to Cosgrave. The Taoiseach 'did not reveal to any other person' why the ship was released.[29] Cosgrave took the ensuing political flack, presumably in the belief that this was for the benefit of national security.

This gives an interesting insight into what his expectations were in respect of those in public service. Obviously, letting the captain of a ship involved in gunrunning go free without charge caused some public anxiety. Opposition spokesman Desmond O'Malley accused the government of 'ineptitude and bungling'.[30] Nevertheless, the *Claudia* was a win-win situation for the government, increasing the prestige of security forces. In being so consciously secretive, the new government maintained the confidence of the British.[31] While co-operation with the British security services was widely suspected, it was not proven, so nationalist credentials were not harmed. It was a template for co-operation that the coalition sought to repeat.

Donegan seems to have especially revelled in the *Claudia* success.[32] Under Cosgrave's instruction, he arranged for samples of the shipment to be made available to the British on the understanding that it 'be done very discreetly, and on the basis that, if questioned, the Irish would deny [the handover]'.[33] Such was Donegan's initial enthusiasm upon taking office that he may have overstepped his boundaries somewhat. The new minister requested a senior British Army intelligence officer to visit Dublin discreetly for 'an uninhibited exchange of intelligence about terrorist activities on the border'.[34] As noted in earlier chapters, the long-term protocol was that security co-operation would be undertaken on a police-to-police basis. Donegan's proposal contravened this tenet of Irish diplomatic strategy and the permanent government intervened. The Department of the Taoiseach gave a clear instruction:

Contacts were to be between security forces, police to police and not army to army … He [Donegan] was told Foreign Affairs were the people to make contact with foreign governments … and if there are security questions they go to the police … There was a definite instruction from the Taoiseach to Donegan that these contacts were not to continue.[35]

Donegan's offer may have demonstrated a naivety on behalf of the minister but the fallout also showed a certain amount of confusion within the new government. Extraordinarily, the Minister for Defence was unaware of ongoing discussions between the two governments with regard to a proposed meeting of security experts.[36] A revised 'Border Dossier' had been presented to Cosgrave, as well as a proposal for a meeting of security figures.[37] It would be September 1974 before this initiative would lead to a summit in Baldonnell. In the meantime, the British did gain increased co-operation from these early exchanges. Army Director of Intelligence Colonel Quinlan was given the role of liaison with the British in order to share further intelligence.[38] From July 1973 until 1976, every three to four weeks, meetings would take place between the Director of Intelligence and, on the British side, the Assistant Director of MI5, the Director and Co-ordinator of Intelligence for Northern Ireland, and a representative of Army Intelligence in Northern Ireland.[39] The existence of these meetings was not made public until recently.

Donegan would continue to demonstrate maverick tendencies and he was not afraid to criticise cabinet colleagues. He once told the British that radio comments by FitzGerald on the subject of British Army behaviour were 'silly and ill advised'.[40] On another occasion, when FitzGerald was expressing opposition to border road closures,[41] Donegan expressed a contrary view to British officials.

Confused boundaries were perhaps understandable, considering the inexperience of the new cabinet in the early months of government, but the early experience is noteworthy for other reasons: significantly, the emphasis of the previous regime on discretion and confidentiality was maintained. Nonetheless, co-operation would go deeper and moves against the IRA would be more vigorous. On the ground, there was a conscious effort to re emphasise this point. Cooney, who visited Garda chiefs in border areas upon appointment, was aware that some Gardaí were 'unsure what their political master's attitude was to action against subversives'. He got the message out to the force via the Department of Justice that he expected 'the law to be enforced unequivocally and without question against the IRA'.[42]

Although the British view of the new government was generally positive, this was tinged with a significant dose of realism. Kelvin White in the Foreign and Commonwealth Office noted:

> We mean that Mr Cosgrave is prepared to cooperate, but only on terms which do not expose his flank to the opposition. He will encourage forceful action against the IRA, but this must be undertaken by the Irish and he will not permit, for example, Brigadier Bush to be seen meeting the Irish CO in Dundalk ... Their troops will sweep areas if we ask them to, but some at least prefer this to appear to be coincidental, and do not wish to be thanked in public. Good is thus done by stealth.[43]

Security co-operation remained a source of conflict between Dublin and London but it was by no means the only issue. In fact, heading into the 2 July 1973 meeting between Cosgrave and Heath, the British did not plan to push security as an issue. White in the Foreign and Commonwealth Office felt co-operation had been improving and there should be a greater focus at the meeting on putting pressure on the Irish government over its human rights case in the Court of Justice in Strasbourg. This was a constant sore as the Irish faced ongoing pressure to drop the case brought on behalf of nationalists in Northern Ireland, who alleged mistreatment by the British Army while in custody. White further felt it would be an inopportune time to discuss cross-border security after an embarrassing incursion by the British Army in Clones.[44] Garret FitzGerald similarly identified a range of issues that muddied relations with the British government in 1973. These included the activities of the Littlejohn brothers, the Strasbourg case, the behaviour of British troops in the North and the British White Paper on Northern Ireland.[45]

The Sunningdale Agreement, reached in December 1973, marked a significant development in Anglo-Irish relations. In essence, the deal involved a Council of Ireland containing ministers from Leinster House and the new executive that would deal with policing and cross-border co-operation on economic and infrastructural matters. The deal also attempted to address the issue of the Irish territorial claim.

A statement would be made by the Irish government declaring that the status of Northern Ireland would not change without the consent of the majority of the population.[46]

This final aspect requires some discussion as it gives an insight into the political pressures on the government. Removing the controversial Articles 2 and 3 of the Irish constitution would have been difficult. The Articles were, in essence, a claim for jurisdiction over the full island and their removal would have required a referendum. Given the bipartisan approach to northern affairs, some cognisance of Fianna Fáil's views had to be taken. Garret FitzGerald explains the rationale:

> A constitutional referendum in the aftermath of Sunningdale carried with it a risk of not alone destroying the agreement but of undermining the consensus within our democratic system, upon which at the time – less than two years after the embassy riots that accompanied and led to the burning of the British Embassy – the peace of our own state arguably depended.[47]

The traditional republican instincts in Fianna Fáil had not faded completely. As late as May 1973, a Fianna Fáil TD had in the Dáil called for 'more guns, bags of guns' for the North.[48] This was among the more extreme outbursts against the government but the republican wing of the main opposition party was still a significant factor. Repeated pressure was exerted on government parties by Fianna Fáil over issues such as incursions and the activities of British intelligence. Even after Sunningdale, Fianna Fáil's Desmond O'Malley, obviously not traditionally associated with the republican wing, questioned whether the coalition was guilty of collaborating too much with the Faulkner government after an initial clampdown on republicans.[49] Meanwhile, there were reports of Fianna Fáil TDs travelling the country, describing Sunningdale as a sellout.[50]

Therefore, the last thing the government wanted was a referendum campaign on the emotive Articles 2 and 3 that could unify the republican sentiment within Fianna Fáil against Jack Lynch.[51] It was in this context that the consent declaration was included in the Sunningdale Agreement as a compromise. The positive impact of the declaration for unionists was severely dissipated, however, when former Fianna Fáil Minister Kevin Boland made a challenge in the courts. The state was forced to defend the agreement on the grounds that declaration was compatible with Articles 2 and 3, thus neutralising the benefits of making the declaration.[52] Therefore, the compromise that was agreed to alleviate unionist fears was almost completely negated.

There were differing views on Sunningdale in Fianna Fáil, but the government was not fully united either. O'Brien disagreed with aspects of Council of Ireland proposals.[53] Giving such far-reaching powers to the council was too unpalatable for unionists and would jeopardise the entire deal, O'Brien argued. Meanwhile, Cooney was equally unenthusiastic regarding the Police Authority proposal, viewing it as an infringement on the Department of Justice's relationship with the Gardaí.[54] The Department of Justice continued to dominate the Gardaí and the accord threatened to dilute this control. The closer association with the RUC could also have created problems for the Gardaí. Such links could have undermined the legitimacy of the southern forces in the eyes of some, notably in border areas, and this was an issue Gardaí at ground level were acutely cognisant off.

Meeting Cosgrave in February, Stormont leader Brian Faulkner identified three areas where the Republic needed to act: the status of Northern Ireland, the common law enforcement commission and security co-operation.[55] As has already been noted, the Boland case hindered progress on the first area and, in terms of the second, Sunningdale did not deal with extradition. Southern representatives insisted that extradition was a matter solely for the courts. A law-enforcement commission was established to deal with the issue, which eventually resulted in legislation whereby a suspect could be tried in either jurisdiction for an offence committed in the other. There was no immediate value in this for Faulkner. Therefore, the third aspect, security co-operation, took on added significance.

By 1973, general violence levels in the North had reduced but border attacks had not. This is illustrated by the fact that in July 1972 there were 3,010 shooting and bombing incidents, but this dropped to 360 by August 1973; however, the number of border incidents had actually risen from twenty-three to thirty-one in the same period.[56] This trend continued as the year ended, with the number of border incidents rising from an average of thirty in the first six months of 1973 to fifty-two per month over the second six months.[57] On the southern side, there was also an impetus to improve security. Some towns, like Clones and Lifford, were becoming harder to police. Also, the memories of street disturbances in 1972, particularly the burning of the British embassy, remained fresh. Gardaí were not explicitly targeted by republicans but were increasingly being confronted by armed republicans. In addition, the increasing prison population was proving problematic: most spectacularly, three IRA leaders escaped from Mountjoy jail via helicopter in October 1973. This led to the establishment of a general security inquiry under Justice Finlay.[58] Typical of successive governments dealing with a security problem, the solution adopted was to increase the size of the security forces rather than restructure or reform its forces. January 1974 had seen the announcement of 500 extra Gardaí[59] and 3,000 soldiers.[60] Perhaps as a gesture of good faith after Sunningdale, high-profile arrests took place, with thirty held in one operation.[61]

Therefore, both North and South, security was a matter of massive significance. The topic was raised at a January 1974 meeting between Cosgrave and northern premier Brian Faulkner. The discussion followed a familiar pattern. The Taoiseach pointed out that all border superintendents had been called in to discuss the matter. Cosgrave argued that the black spots were those places where British Army/RUC presence on the northern side of the border was limited, specifically Crossmaglen and the Belcoo/Blacklion area.[62] The discourse was remarkably similar to that which regularly occurred between the British and previous Irish governments. In February, some members of the northern executive again accused the Republic of weakness in moves against the IRA. Cooney this time retorted in forthright terms. He blamed northern exiles and a lack of policing on the northern side. Faulkner was not impressed by Dublin's efforts:

> He [Faulkner] referred to cooperation between security forces on both sides of the border and said that this cooperation must be open and seen to be effective. He instanced a recent swoop in Lifford area where five or six men lifted had been subsequently released though it was well known that some of them were prominent in terrorist activity around Strabane. Two SDLP men had given him information which indicated that they shared his doubts about some of these releases.[63]

The SDLP's Ivan Cooper, voicing some support for Faulkner, suggested that 'it would seem better not to lift people at all if they are going to be released shortly thereafter'.[64] It seems that in the enthusiasm to demonstrate support for Sunningdale, arrests and prosecutions were made on grounds that were not particularly strong. Among those prosecuted by the Special Criminal Court, there was a noticeably high rate of acquittal in the early months of 1974.[65] In the last four months of 1973, there were ten acquittals from seventy-five cases (14 per cent). In the first four months of 1974, there were thirty acquittals from ninety-one cases (33 per cent). Garret FitzGerald claimed the short-sighted arrest operation launched 'backfired badly when the great majority had to be released shortly afterward'.[66] It is obviously a matter of conjecture as to why arrests did not lead to convictions but in light of the level of prosecutions, it does seem that there was a political will to take cases.

Secretary of State Merlyn Rees told Irish officials that actions on the border were 'effective and far reaching' but 'the great problem is that the public are not adequately informed'.[67] The coalition did not provide Faulkner with what he craved most: 'open' and 'effective' co-operation. Politically, this remained difficult in the Republic for much the same reasons that Articles 2 and 3 could not be binned. Meetings took place between top-level Garda officers and RUC officers, both before and after Sunningdale. While top-level military intelligence officers met regularly, publicity surrounding such meetings was avoided or kept low-key.

At ground level, meanwhile, it would take time for the benefits of co-operation to accrue. Additional manpower in the form of police and the Army was sent to problem areas. Perhaps more significantly, changes in personnel also took place. The previous chapter outlined British complaints of Garda inaction in Lifford and Clones. These two towns became emblematic of the problem as the British saw it. The issue in Lifford had been raised by the northern executive. At a meeting between Garvey and senior RUC officers, 'the weakness of the local outdoor sergeant [in Lifford] was acknowledged and [this] was being remedied by transfer'.[68] The Special Branch presence in the town was also increased. It is hard to know whether these changes in personnel were made as a result of diplomatic pressure or as a result of local concerns. There was considerable disquiet in the town after the killing of an RUC man locally. By 1978, Donegal was the area where cross-border security co-operation was best.

In Clones, another Garda officer was identified by the British as uncooperative and he too was transferred. While it is unclear whether this latter transfer came as a result of British complaints, official documents do not disguise their delight with the move.[69] Similar to the Lifford case, this transfer came after violence in the town.

The British government continued to push for greater structured co-operation, unsuccessfully requesting a security meeting in March 1974.[70] However, events in Northern Ireland outpaced progress on the matter, and a disastrous showing in the British general election highlighted Faulkner's weakness. In May, the Stormont executive collapsed after the Ulster Worker's Council (UWC) strike. The headline in *The Irish Times* left little doubt where Dublin stood: 'Angry Cosgrave blames Britain for N.I. crisis'.[71] In the midst of UWC strike, bombs exploded in Dublin and Monaghan, killing thirty-three and injuring one hundred.[72] The experience of preceding years had indicated that violence could spill over the border and this was the latest and most serious example. On a practical level, these attacks provided an added incentive to improve security co-operation in terms of the prevention of further attacks and investigation of the atrocities.

The Irish government also had to grapple with another threat. Noises were being made that suggested that the British were considering withdrawal. Irish planners and politicians concluded that the implications of such a course could only be negative. The failure of the British government to stand up to loyalist protests, the Dublin and Monaghan bombings, as well as memories of new Prime Minister Harold Wilson's talks with the IRA in 1972[73] left the Dublin establishment in an especially vulnerable position. Theoretically, nationalist politicians should have favoured a British withdrawal but the reality for those in office was different. Garret FitzGerald wrote that if the British government

> were at some point to abandon their responsibilities in Northern Ireland and to permit the emergence there of a fascist-type political entity run by extreme unionist politicians and loyalist paramilitaries, the peace of all Ireland could be threatened. Such a possibility had not previously entered our heads; now for a while we felt that we had to take it seriously especially in the view of the statement by NIO officials on a visit to Dublin on 5 June to the effect that withdrawal was not *at that time* being considered by British Ministers.[74]

Such was FitzGerald's concern about a potential withdrawal that he lobbied US Secretary of State Henry Kissinger for support in the case of such an eventuality.[75] For the subsequent twelve months, there was considerable concern over a possible doomsday scenario. This had implications for the ongoing dialogue on security. The Irish side had been procrastinating on the security meeting proposed in March. Kenneth Thom in the British embassy concluded that 'the Irish are so frightened at the thoughts of being seen to liaise with us on security matters that they are deliberately working themselves up into the state to ensure that the meetings do not take place'.[76]

There was some awareness on the part of the Department of Foreign Affairs that its criticisms and procrastination were adding to British weariness. Going into Cosgrave's September 1974 meeting with Prime Minister Harold Wilson, the Department of Foreign Affair's briefing advised ministers to avoid 'pinpricking criticism to the point where we will contribute to their desire to leave the North rapidly and hand us the bill'.[77] The prospect of a British withdrawal certainly added impetus to the Irish agreement to hold the frequently discussed security meeting.

The highly significant meeting was eventually held on 14 September 1974 in Baldonnel. A wide range of issues was covered, but the most important outcome was the emergence of four Garda/RUC panels to improve co-operation between the forces in the areas of communications, exchange of information, advance planning and the detection of arms, ammunitions and explosives.[78] As usual in security meetings, the Irish side emphasised the role of their Army acting as an 'aid to civil power'. Cooney significantly acknowledged that there were already unofficial contacts between the Gardaí and the British Army and said he was happy for these contacts to continue without 'official blessing'.[79] The Irish minister also pushed for increased sharing of intelligence. It was noted that Cooney had fewer qualms about involving the British Army than the permanent secretary of the Department of Justice.[80]

Although the Baldonnel panels were to prove a significant milestone, the practical results were mixed. Early progress was made in radio telephone links between police stations but the provision of direct telephone links via landlines was held up due to lack of available telephone lines.[81] The Irish telephone system was described by a later minister responsible for the area as 'primitive beyond belief'.[82] Some Goliath communication systems were provided to the Republic by the Northern security services. In terms of the intelligence panel, the system for passing information was 'very good', according to RUC Chief Constable Jamie Flanagan, but 'both the RUC and Garda would benefit by improved methods of gathering intelligence'.[83] Both sides agreed that the Baldonnel panels improved security, but by the end of 1975 a particularly significant problem area emerged that would require deeper co-operation: South Armagh.

More generally, what is striking about the 1974/5 period is the degree of political flux in both governments after the failure of Sunningdale. Neither government seemed to have a strategic plan as to how to proceed or even conduct relations with the other. The IRA had begun a ceasefire in December 1974 after talks involving clergy. This ceasefire was then extended in January and declared indefinite in February.[84] In parallel with this, Rees authorised talks with IRA representatives. Bew et al. (2009) points to a certain amount of confusion within the British system at the time:

> What becomes evident is the extent to which the British state was not the monolithic entity that republicans believed. Indeed, it might even be said that its lack of internal coherence on this issue presents a striking picture of 'amateurishness'. On the one hand, 'the machine' attempted to pull the government back from the brink [withdrawal]. On the other, intelligence officers – apparently acting independently from the 'machine' – seemed to predicate their communications with the IRA on the basis of the confused and reactive sentiment emanating from Downing Street.[85]

For the Irish side, the mixed signals were worrying. At the 28 May 1975 meeting involving Cooney, Rees and FitzGerald, both Irish ministers emphasised to Rees that the talks were bolstering IRA morale and argued for them to end. Rees, however, persisted, offering the flimsy excuse that the talks 'gave a bead on IRA thinking during what would be a long haul'.[86]

For the Irish government, Northern Ireland was becoming a problem from which it wanted to metaphorically withdraw. As one recent account put it, 'the collapse of Sunningdale had effectively left the Irish government without a strategy and it wanted to fold up its tent'.[87] Galsworthy, in his annual review of 1974, noted that the events of the year had 'caused the bulk of the Republic's population to push the aspirations of Irish unification right away from their minds as a practical goal'.[88] The rise in kidnappings and robberies in the state contributed to this feeling, as did high-profile incidents like the killing of Senator Billy Fox and loyalist bombings. Galsworthy cited the Birmingham bombings of November 1974 as the event that had the single biggest impact on opinion.[89]

The threat of British withdrawal and rising violence had given security co-operation a stimulus but political necessity prevented full and open co-operation. When explaining the difficulties associated with joint Garda–British Army operations, Cooney told Rees that the 'Garda was an unarmed force which had evolved from the Civic Guard and any association with the British Army as such would not only be resented by the Garda but would be counterproductive as far as the community in the South was concerned.'[90]

For both politicians and those implementing security policies, the dangers of deviating from established practice remained evident. When Paddy Cooney suggested dropping Articles 2 and 3, he faced strong opposition from a series of Fianna Fáil spokespersons, including Jack Lynch, as well as the SDLP.[91] The civil service seemed to have been particularly attuned to the dangers of overstepping traditional boundaries. For instance, when both Cooney and Donegan seemed to waiver when pushed on direct contact with the British Army, it was the permanent officials that reined them in.

Politically, the coalition faced something of a dilemma. Being seen as pro-British could cost it support but being seen as strong on 'law and order' was also a vote getter. A study of attitudes in Dublin, conducted in 1972–3, found strong levels of hostility to both the Provisional and Official IRA and support for jailing their members.[92] Therefore, a careful balance had to be maintained. Actions taken against the IRA had to be couched in a patriotic manner rather than being seen as at the instigation of the British. As Kelvin White noted, it was better for the coalition if support for the British appeared 'coincidental'.

Finally, the significance of Fianna Fáil policy in this period should not be underestimated. The party was shifting back towards a traditional republican posture and this had implications for government. Lynch restored Charles Haughey to the front bench.[93] Later in 1975, party policy shifted back to demanding a British withdrawal.[94] There were those in Fianna Fáil who wanted to 'exploit the ambivalence of the British Prime Minister on Northern Ireland'.[95] For a coalition anxious to maintain British involvement, this was not good news. Galsworthy was doubtful whether 'Fianna Fáil's change of front will be popular with the majority of the public, who have recently shown solid support for the government whenever "law and order" is invoked.'[96] Nevertheless, Fianna Fáil reinvigorated with a veneer of republicanism, coupled with a British government considering withdrawal, was a nightmare scenario for the coalition. Circumstances intervened in the government's favour.

By the end of 1975, the IRA ceasefire had effectively ended. Even more significantly, there was an end to speculation over British withdrawal, possibly due to some fortuitous diplomacy involving soon-to-be Prime Minister Jim Callaghan and Garret FitzGerald.[97] FitzGerald had met Callaghan while the pair were coincidentally holidaying in Cork. The Irish minister attached particular significance to this meeting in terms of influencing the British cabinet against withdrawal. Whether as a result of this behind-the-scenes diplomacy, or good fortune, the coalition's worst fears of a British withdrawal would not be realised.

An Evaluation of Irish Security Policy: The Role of the Gardaí and the Army

While the border was a key dimension to domestic security, it was obviously not the only aspect. Crime generally was rising. The number of indictable offences rose from 30,000 in 1970 to 63,000 in 1977. The number of armed robberies, meanwhile, rose from 11 to 298 in the same period.[98] This added to pressure for increased 'law and order'.

It is worth emphasising further that while the coalition's term did see increasing resources and attention directed to the security services, there was no significant change in the structure or management of either body. Increased numbers were central to the government's strategy. Donegan launched a high-profile campaign to boost Army numbers by 3,000, which included an extensive publicity campaign.[99] Overall spending on the Defence Forces rose from £14.4 million in 1969/70 to £49 million in 1975.[100] The manpower weakness on the border was generally acknowledged and this was to be a key area for the coalition. Edward Garvey, then Assistant Commissioner, reported on border divisions of the Garda in 1973. Garvey identified lack of manpower and weak intelligence gathering issues in both the Cavan/

Monaghan division and Donegal.[101] Steps were taken to address the situation. At the end of March 1974, there were 1,030 personnel in border stations, a rise of 50 per cent in five months.[102]

For the Irish Army, meanwhile, as noted in earlier chapters, there was very little presence along the border at the outset of the Troubles. Steps had already been taken to address this, with major barracks in Finner, Donegal and Dundalk and smaller posts in Letterkenny, Lifford, Manorhamilton, Ballyconnell, Cavan, Cootehill and Castleblayney. A key new facility in Monaghan was constructed in 1974/5.[103] In all, 1,500 troops were based in border areas by 1974.[104] There was strong negative reaction to the opening of the barracks in Monaghan. Reports in the local papers cited fears by local business people that the presence of significant number of soldiers would lower property values and lead to disorder in the town.[105]

There was a certain amount of old-fashioned snobbery associated with such views. There were reports that young soldiers were refused service in pubs.[106] Rural towns unaccustomed to the behaviour of groups of troops obviously found the experience challenging. At a meeting between the RUC and the Garda Commissioner, the problem was noted. Reference was made 'to Eire Army misbehaviour (drink and girls) in the Lifford area'.[107] There was also a political dimension to this. Kieran McCarthy, a Cork native who served in the Irish Army from 1976 and later became an active republican claimed:

> When we were off duty and went into either Monaghan Town or Cootehill to socialize, we soon discovered that there were only a few pubs where we could buy a drink. Dances were also out of bounds as they were guaranteed to end in a mini riot. The natives, or at least many of them, saw us as collaborators with the enemy.[108]

For Army personnel, just as in 1970–2, protection of government buildings as well as routine patrolling took up a significant portion of time but as the Army took a more visible role, checkpoint duty became a greater part of its function. Table 6 gives a breakdown of the total number of checkpoints per month for August 1973–August 1974 by Eastern and Western Command areas.

What is surprising about these figures is that there was no discernible rise in checkpoints in the months immediately after Sunningdale, but in the summer months of 1974, there was a sharp

Table 6. Army–Garda checkpoints manned by Eastern and Western Command, 1973/4[109]

Month	Total checkpoints manned
August 1973	1228
September 1973	1201
October 1973	1113
November 1973	1218
December 1973	1147
January 1974	1095
February 1974	1151
March 1974	1170
April 1974	720
May 1974	1531
June 1974	2454
July 1974	1639
August 1974	1753

rise due to increased domestic security concerns related to the Dublin/ Monaghan bombings and the Portlaoise escape. The figures give a context to an increasing role for the Army in domestic security. This is most strikingly illustrated by contrasting the figures with preceding years. There were just eleven such checkpoints in September 1972; this rose to 263 by December of that year.[110] This made the Army a much more common sight on the street and caused some concern. An editorial in *Hibernia* warned:

> Those who value their civil liberty in this country should take stock of what is happening: the Gardaí are handing more and more responsibility for the maintenance of civil order to the Armed Forces … The Northern experience has demonstrated the extreme danger of introducing the military into the civilian arena. But instead of learning that lesson we seem to be heading in exactly the same direction.[111]

With hindsight, *Hibernia*'s view may seem far-fetched but Donegan did nothing to allay fears. The minister warned Army personnel that 'in the months ahead I will ask the Army to perform tasks which they will not like'.[112] Shooting incidents involving northern youths and the Irish Army added to concerns.[113] In these incidents, young men were shot and injured by Army personnel at checkpoints. On one of these occasions, an ex-internee was shot at a checkpoint in Monaghan set up in the aftermath of the Portlaoise Prison escape in August 1974. On St Patrick's Day 1975, IRA prisioner Tom Smith was shot dead in Portlaoise prison by the Irish Army during an escape attempt. Kieran McCarthy, the former Irish Army recruit, describes in a recent book how the Smith killing was referred to during his Irish Army training in 1976. Different colleagues were erroneously pointed out to McCarthy as having fired the fatal shot. McCarthy saw this as part of a broader strategy.

> What I found most disturbing and sickening about these stories during my training, was that the individuals to whom they were attributed to, seemed to be enjoying the notoriety and did little to dispel them or put the record straight. Neither did the officers of our battalion do anything to stop such talk and rumours doing the rounds. I would later learn that it was all in fact, part of a pattern designed to motivate and condition upcoming recruits before they would take up such duties.[114]

The Gardaí were also facing serious questions about their methods. So prevalent were accusations of mistreatment of suspects that at one point Garret FitzGerald considered resigning from government.[115] The appointment of Edmund Garvey as Commissioner was indicative of the hard-line government approach. Garvey was known as a 'tough cop'[116] and on taking up the job was forthcoming in an interview with *The Irish Times*:

> I intend as Commissioner to keep in touch with the grass roots of the force. You hear people say at times, some people, that police are rough with citizens. Well I believe there are times you may have to be rough with citizens. Well I believe there are times you may have to be rough when it is put up to you. As for having black sheep in the force, we have 8,500 serving men sure there are bound to be a few odd balls.[117]

The use of force by Garda members was illustrated in the Tiede Herrema kidnapping case. Herrema, a Dutch industrialist, was kidnapped by a republican splinter group led by Eddie Gallagher. Gallagher's hideout was discovered and a two-week-long siege ensued. According to a version of the story related to Conor Cruise O'Brien by Gardaí on personal protection duties, detectives beat up a suspect until he divulged the location of the kidnap victim. O'Brien did not share this account with fellow minister FitzGerald, indicating the differing attitudes within cabinet.[118] It was O'Brien's implicit support of achieving the security of the state 'by any means' that was to be the hallmark of security policy. Another noteworthy aspect of the Herrema kidnapping was that Garvey apparently struck a deal with the kidnapper Gallagher for a reduced sentence in exchange for an end to the siege. Unsurprisingly, the deal was not honoured.[119]

Aside from Garda brutality allegations, other issues affecting the force included strict discipline and pay, particularly in relation to overtime.[120] Upon Garvey's appointment, oppressive discipline was a major factor. Garvey was an arch-disciplinarian, which made him unpopular in the ranks and led to rank-and-file members reportedly complaining frequently to politicians.[121] It was reported that Garvey expected uniformed Gardaí to serve four summonses a week. This was not always practical, particularly in rural areas.[122]

More generally, political influence remained a factor in promotions. Garvey himself was 'known to have Fine Gael sympathies'.[123] In discussing the Gardaí with the Northern Secretary of State, a border RUC commander noted that Garda promotions above inspector rank were politicised and hence 'the Gardaí were "good coppers" but were politically motivated'.[124] Meanwhile, proposed new regulations in the Army which would allow the Minister for Defence to promote officers without a recommendation from the chief of staff brought political influence to the fore in the military.[125] In Dáil debates on the issue, Donegan came in for particular personal criticism; he was accused of acting both as Minister for Defence and chief of staff, with the *Claudia* case in particular cited:

> One could be forgiven if one thought that the Army was the private plaything of the present Minister for Defence, Mr. Donegan. He is rarely photographed in the media but when he is, he is usually

bowler-hatted, inspecting or addressing soldiers or dressed up in an Army tunic with a machinegun in his hand.[126];

We all know what happened in the case of the *Claudia*. At that time the Minister took over complete command and he made a right 'cod' of the affair. People were allowed to go free out of the country while nationals who were on the same ship had to appear in court.[127]

Political patronage went beyond the Garda and Army to include the judiciary. Desmond O'Malley raised the issue in the Dáil and a British embassy assessment pointed to four judges appointed from a Fine Gael background to just one with a Fianna Fáil heritage.[128] Fine Gael's John Kelly, parliamentary secretary, in a related debate unapologetically claimed that 'For 16 years that phrase "the best men available" was interpreted to mean "the best men of the Fianna Fáil persuasion available". That situation must end and it has ended. I certainly will not complain if the men who were done an injustice now get a look in.'[129]

Political interference could be potentially disastrous for individuals and their livelihoods. Cooney's 'black-and-white' approach to security left those even moderately sympathetic to republicanism in a difficult position. Cooney warned business owners that if there was suspicion that their premises were used by the IRA, they could face closure orders. He told such individuals that they 'must now decide whether their loyalty is to their country and the community which supports them or to the IRA'.[130] Additionally, there were reports of a blacklist of individuals with subversive connections who were barred from state employment.[131]

Meanwhile, those convicted of republican offences were dismissed from employment in state jobs upon release. The most celebrated example of this was prominent Waterford school principal and GAA official Donal Whelan, who was not allowed to return to his teaching position.[132] In the media, section 31 of the Broadcasting Act continued to prohibit republican access to the media, sometimes causing difficulties for broadcasters and newspapers in terms of reporting events.[133] At street level too, there was a clampdown on republican propaganda. The editor of *An Phoblacht*, Éamonn MacThomáis, was imprisoned on IRA membership charges.[134] Other republican publications, such as *Freedom Struggle*, were banned and prosecutions were taken for possession of the booklet.[135]

Public demonstrations of republican sympathy were also targeted by the state. An area that had caused security issues in 1970–2 was pickets at court cases and prosecutions were now taken against individuals involved in such pickets.[136] Republican funerals were also policed more closely.[137] The round-the-clock guard being kept on the grave of republican Frank Stagg was perhaps the best example of this increased vigilance.[138] Stagg died on hunger strike in England. His family were very publicly divided as to whether he should be buried in the republican plot in Ballina. Stagg was eventually buried in a family plot, with a guard kept on the grave to prevent his reinterment in the republican plot.

In terms of organisational structure, the Sunningdale Agreement could have had serious implications for the Gardaí. In fact, there may have been some relief in the Department of Justice that the Policing Authority promised by Sunningdale never came to fruition. An Irish government briefing paper on the subject raised the point that 'identification of the Garda Siochana with the RUC would reduce to a dangerous degree the acceptability of the Garda'.[139] A *Garda Review* editorial reflecting rank-and-file opinion voiced an almost identical concern.[140] In the end, the Police Authority envisaged by Sunningdale never materialised and control of the Gardaí remained firmly with the Department of Justice.

During the period after the collapse of Sunningdale, attention among senior planners in the Garda and Army shifted to a potential doomsday scenario. The focus was on the consequences of a British withdrawal. Garda intelligence reported that 'the IRA ceasefire rests securely on some kind of undertaking by the British government that their troops will be withdrawn from Northern Ireland'.[141] Garvey foresaw a potential unilateral declaration of independence taking place in Northern Ireland, with IRA action leading to southern involvement. He therefore concluded that 'the progressive expansion and modernisation of the Armed Forces, whose first priority, no matter what the circumstances, will be the maintenance of the lawful government here'.[142] Army planners saw the situation differently, and envisaged a potentially different role for the military. In a submission to the Interdepartmental Unit dealing with a doomsday scenario, a senior military planner argued that

The situation is significantly different to 1969. The strength of the Army is at approx 11,500 as compared to 8,000 then. Approx

100 pieces of armour have been acquired. The Air Corp now has helicopters and light aircraft that can carry limited numbers of troops or arms and ammunition … The level of viability of units and their combat efficiency have improved over the five years because of the multiplicity of security tasks they have been performing … Finally the task postulated excludes opposition by the British Army which fundamentally changes the situation from what it was in 1969/70.[143]

The Army paper further argued that failure to intervene in a doomsday scenario would have 'a catastrophic affect on the Army' and consequently leave the IRA in a strong position in the South.[144] However, any Army planning in this regard was to remain a paper exercise, just as in 1970. The Interdepartmental Unit on Northern Ireland bitterly opposed the paper put forward by Defence Forces. Aspects of the plan for 'doomsday' were seen as 'patently beyond the capability of the Defence Forces' by Dermot Nally in Foreign Affairs.[145] The British did not seem overly concerned by Irish Army's 'doomsday' plans either. When the British Army was approached by their Irish counterparts for maps of Belfast with a religious breakdown of areas, they seemed unperturbed, if mildly curious.[146] The British Army view in 1976 was that their Irish counterparts had not taken part in any serious military movements since 1969 and the Irish Army's preparation focused mainly on 'training for its patrolling role on the border and other actions in aid of the civil power'.[147] An internal Irish Army report echoed this sentiment, emphasising that the heavy security commitment and shortage of staff meant training was 'not as thorough as is desirable'.[148]

The fear of a British withdrawal concerned senior planners and may have added to uncertainty at ground level but southern intervention was unlikely even in dire circumstances. As the Interdepartmental Unit correctly judged, the Army did not have the ability to intervene. More importantly, there was no political will, even at the wilder fringes of government. Unlike 1969/70, there was no Boland- or Blaney-type figure in cabinet to champion an interventionist line. Therefore, as Garvey predicted, the Army's key function would be in the maintenance of domestic stability.

In terms of domestic stability, the internal threat to the Irish security forces was becoming more apparent. By autumn 1973, an Irish Army intelligence report noted:

There has been increasing indication over the last two weeks that elements of the lower ranks of the Provisional IRA have become dissatisfied with their Army order forbidding armed action against the forces of the government of the Republic. They believe that in their present situation the order is meaningless and exposes their members to easy arrest. It is not known what proportion of the organisation are prepared to disobey the order which their higher echelons still adhere to. However, it may be that younger members who are active in border areas and particularly those on the run from Northern Ireland may in the future be prepared to resist arrest and use firearms against Gardaí or troops.[149]

The antagonism towards the Gardaí was often publicly vented in the pages of *An Phoblacht*.[150] On occasion, IRA actions deeply embarrassed the state's apparatus. The helicopter escape from Mountjoy by leading IRA figures and the escape from Portlaoise jail in 1974 both especially humiliated the southern security forces.[151] During this period, Garda Michael Reynolds became the third Garda to die since the Troubles began. He was killed in a botched armed robbery in September 1975. A couple, Noel and Marie Murray, from an ultra-left-wing faction were convicted.[152] While the IRA was not implicated, the couple were former members of Official Sinn Féin and the death highlighted the dangers faced by Gardaí when confronted by armed subversives.

On the republican side, as already mentioned, a serving IRA prisoner, Tom Smith, was fatally wounded by the Irish Army during an escape attempt in Portlaoise jail.[153] The occasion of Smith's funeral saw further violent confrontation between Gardaí and republicans. There were allegations of Garda brutality, with a small number of injuries reported, including by members of the press.[154] As we will see in the next chapter, IRA attacks on the security forces in the South became more common in 1976/1977, including on at least one occasion a pre-planned attack on a Garda search party.

Although there was evidence of security force–IRA hostility, there were also occasional examples of collusion. A Garda in Cork was convicted of passing information to a republican.[155] Meanwhile, soldiers were accused of stealing explosives from McGee Barracks in Kildare.[156] It seems the IRA directed at least some of its intelligence actions against southern forces. A telephone engineer was convicted of tapping Garda phones.[157] The security of the phone system remained a cause of concern for several years.[158] A high-level Garda report claimed that the Irish Army had been 'carefully infiltrated by the provos'.[159] The British likewise felt that the Irish Army had a security problem in Donegal 'as a proportion of their men come from Derry'.[160] Another British Army discussion paper in 1975 concluded that 'some members of the Irish Army may have sympathies with the Provisional IRA and therefore cooperation with them should not be considered further'.[161] It is hard to assess how successful the IRA was in its efforts to infiltrate the Army but, during 1976, there were thirty discharges from the Defence Forces on security grounds and more in the Army reserve.[162]

Fears of subversive influence within the Irish security forces was one of several factors limiting cross-border co-operation. This was demonstrated very visibly in one incident. A party of Gardaí travelling legitimately on a 'concession road' were halted by a British Army patrol. The Gardaí, including a superintendent, were wearing civilian attire over their uniforms. The Gardaí later claimed to have been subjected to 'humiliating treatment' when stopped and the incident caused 'intense resentment'. [163] According to the Garda account, one British soldier intervened on their behalf, telling his colleague, who was behaving aggressively, to 'cool it, don't act like a cowboy, they're alright'.[164] An apology was issued and the incident was passed off as an unfortunate case of mistaken identity but the car being driven by the Gardaí belonged to the Clones Garda suspected by the British of republican sympathies, hence the detailed interrogation.[165] At a more general level, there was reluctance by the British Army to notify the Irish security forces in advance of security operations. This was due to potential leaks on the Irish side. The British Army had 'always taken the line that disclosure of [surveillance] operations could put their men at risk and make no bones about the fact that they consider information is not secure in the hands of the Garda'.[166]

Some Gardaí and some stations were seen by the British as more open to co-operation than others. In Dundalk, Superintendent MacAtamney was seen by the British as 'cautious' but Superintendent Grant was 'better'. Some Army officers of captain rank in Louth, meanwhile, 'frowned on cooperation'. In Monaghan, Superintendent McMahon was seen as 'good' to deal with and the sergeants in Keady and Tynan had good relations with their opposite numbers. In Donegal, it was noted that Garda reaction was 'quick and improved

since the departure of Neil Blaney'.[167] The inquiry into the Dublin–
Monaghan bombing also noted the importance of personal relations.

> Detective Inspector Browne told the inquiry that 'there was full
> co-operation with the RUC. Anything we asked for we got. They
> were helpful in every way possible.' Detective Garda Heavin said:
> 'There were very good man-to-man relations ... you had your
> own contacts; you went to them or they came to you.' Detective
> Garda McCoy stated that RUC co-operation was 'very, very good'.
> All three officers confirmed that contact was usually personal or
> occasionally by phone; nothing was written down. It should be
> noted, however, that other officers with whom the inquiry has
> spoken were not as positive concerning Garda–RUC relations.
> Though the competence of the RUC was never questioned,
> some doubted whether they were being fully open with Gardaí in
> sharing information in their possession.[168]

An example of RUC co-operation being less than forthcoming
is the bombing of Dundalk in 1975, when Jack Rooney and Hugh
Watters were killed. Two detectives visited Belfast to speak to an RUC
officer about the theft of the bomb car. There had been a positive
personal relationship between the respective officers beforehand but
this was not enough to elicit co-operation. The RUC simply refused to
help, leading to speculation that the RUC Special Branch had vetoed
co-operation, possibly to protect a source or agent.[169]

The Irish Army remained more reluctant than Gardaí to deal
with the British in line with political protocol. After meeting the Irish
chief of staff General O'Carroll, a British Army officer speculated on
two reasons for this: 'They [Irish Army] want to avoid public criticism
for collaborating with the forces of occupation'; and 'They fear that
closer contact with us will lead them into sharper conflict with the
IRA and they are not confident of their ability to come out on top in
a shooting match.'[170]

In terms of Garda–RUC co-operation, meanwhile, the combination
of Sunningdale and the later Baldonnel panels improved the working
relationship between the forces. Even before Baldonnel, RUC Chief
Constable Jamie Flanagan agreed with Paddy Cooney's analysis that
there was 'good cooperation on police and security matters' generally.
Given the security problems in the North, Flanagan noted that the

British side 'must have some understanding of the task confronting security forces in the South and not expect too much too soon'.[171]

There is some evidence of the informal communication between the British Army and Gardaí. In his account of operating along the border, British Army intelligence officer Fred Holroyd describes repeated contacts with the Gardaí. Among his wilder allegations was an unauthorised exchange of intelligence involving Assistant Commissioner Garvey.[172] Whether Holroyd's specific allegations were accurate or not, Cooney acknowledged that there was some unofficial contact, as noted earlier. British files report that along the South Armagh border by 1975, the British Army 'often had direct contact with the Garda because in this area the RUC are not in evidence or are slow to respond'. Further north, the vehicle checkpoint at Middletown was useful for keeping in touch with Gardaí who were considered 'highly efficient'. It was noted in the same file that Gardaí in Castleblayney were less welcoming than those in Monaghan, again indicating the significance of individual relations.[173] As the South Armagh–Monaghan border increased in importance, these informal contacts became more significant, as we will see.

Obviously, there was significant co-operation but there is also evidence to suggest that there was also a certain amount of animosity present at local level between the respective forces. A series of relatively minor incidents led to the Irish Ambassador complaining of 'a lack of respect for the necessary basis of understanding for cooperation in matters of security'. Examples cited by the Ambassador included the aforementioned detention of a Garda patrol, arrests made by the British Army south of the border and cross-border firing that resulted in a Garda car being shot up.[174] Garret FitzGerald told the UN Secretary General that 'we were doing our best to cooperate with the British Army on manning the frontier but relations were not improved by their frequent hostile behaviour, including shooting across the border into the Republic'.[175] Instances when the Gardaí/Army were fired on by the British included near Emyvale and Ballyconnell in December 1974[176] and near Courtbane in Louth in August of the same year.[177] On other occasions, it was the pure aggression of British troops that was complained about. The Irish authorities reported 'frequently documented instances of arrogance' on the part of British Army.[178]

A typical incident that attracted media coverage occurred at a trouble spot near Killeen customs post on the Louth–Armagh border.

A party of British troops crossed the border by about 250 metres in 'hot pursuit'. When they caught the suspects, Gardaí arrived on the scene and informed the British party that they were in the South. It was alleged by the southern authorities that the British troops used foul language and pointed their rifles at Gardaí. Additionally, troops were accused of using excessive force against the suspects. These allegations were denied. In its complaint, the Department of Foreign Affairs noted that it was difficult to reconcile such behaviour with requests for more co-operation, noting that 'it was the threatening and unmannerly behaviour of troops which was at issue not the incursion'.[179]

One Irish official complained that

> incidents on the border are now so numerous and the disdain of the British Army for the Gardaí so marked that the Irish, while not retreating from their position of consenting in principle to the holding of security cooperation meetings at official level, are beginning to seriously to doubt whether anything is to be gained from doing so.[180]

At ground level, the average British soldier on a short tour of duty may not have appreciated the intricacies and diplomatic niceties associated with policing the border. Personal relations would prove vital, especially considering the small numbers in key positions south of the border: the same Garda insulted by a British patrol may have remained in situ for years, even decades.

It would take time for relationships on the border to improve. A Northern Ireland Office report in December 1974 summarised the reasons why dramatic results could not be expected:

> First they [the Gardaí] are just not used to moving fast. It goes against the grain of their whole way of life and whole way of conducting business. Second, in their heart they are scared. They have never yet been targets of the IRA and do not want to become them now. Thirdly, they just have not got enough men or enough money to provide a comprehensive police service, comparable to our own. For these reasons, especially the third, it is by no means easy to get Garda to deliver really dramatic improvements, whatever Irish Ministers may say and however honestly they may believe it.[181]

The Security Situation in the Southern Border Counties, 1973–5

The last weeks of 1972 had been difficult times along the border. Bombings in Dublin, Belturbet and Clones had heightened tension, along with the killings of Brid Porter and Oliver Boyce in Donegal. When local TD Erskine Childers visited Clones in the early days of 1973, suggestions from the local community included giving the Army power of arrest, the closure of border roads, increased Garda/Army presence and the formation of a vigilante force.[182] These were not the typical complaints a Fianna Fáil TD would expect to hear. While some of the local proposals were politically unlikely, they illustrate the tensions in the town. The threat of further loyalist attacks persisted in the months ahead. This was again illustrated in March 1973 when a UDA member was blown up by his own device in Donegal.[183]

Despite this apparent loyalist threat, the security focus remained on republican violence. Confirmation that republican subversives were generally believed to pose the greatest threat to national security can be found in the minutes of the meetings of the Cabinet Sub-Committee on National Security during 1974. Containment of the IRA and other subversive republican organisations was regularly discussed, but there is no record of any attention being given to the threat posed by loyalists.[184] Considering the political background and experience of the cabinet this is unsurprising: it was the republican threat that was visible to the Gardaí on a daily basis. British diplomatic efforts also played a role in highlighting republican violence. As has already been noted, the level of cross-border violence continued to increase in 1973. IRA efficiency along the border had improved. The British Army put the IRA's new effectiveness down to 'the use of multiphase explosive devices, large culvert mines detonated by wire or radio, mortars and rockets and a degree of ruthlessness which ensures the silence of the local population'.[185]

In 1971/2, South Armagh had been one of a number of trouble spots identified in the 'Border Dossier'. By the end of 1975, it would be the main problem area. In 1973, other areas remained troublesome. Visiting Clones during a by-election campaign in late 1973, Conor Cruise O'Brien noted similarities between two such areas: Lifford and Clones.

I have the strong impression that local people and the Gardaí
were turning a blind eye to the Provisionals provided that their
activities were confined to the other side of the border and that
the Provisionals found it convenient to abide by this provision. In
conversation with TDs from other border areas, I have learned
of similar situation in other border areas. Mr Paddy Freehill has
described to me conditions in Lifford which closely resemble what
I learned on the spot in Clones.[186]

After the killing of UDR member near the border in September
1973, which the British blamed on members of the Clones ASU, British
files similarly claimed that the IRA had 'an understanding with local
Gardaí in Clones which enables them to operate from a safe area in and
around Clones provided they do not undertake terrorist operations
in the immediate area'.[187] In May, Clones had been the scene of a
high-profile British Army incursion that caused diplomatic tension
and is given detailed treatment in Garret FitzGerald's autobiography.
FitzGerald claimed the incident illustrated 'the problem of patrolling
such a very eccentric border'.[188] The confrontation was fairly typical
of dozens of others that occurred through the years but it did lead to
awkward questions for FitzGerald in the Dáil. Galsworthy's reading of
the political stir caused by the incident is illuminating:

Although I am glad to say that co-operation along the border in
security matters has noticeably improved since the coalition came
to power, there are still some spots where it leaves a lot to be
desired. This invariably stems from the uncooperativeness of an
individual on the Irish side. The character who gets the Oscar
for uncooperativeness is [named Clones Garda subsequently
transferred]. He has pursued the matter relentlessly and Garret
FitzGerald told me that it is clear that the whole story has been
given to Fianna Fáil deputies from that part of the world.[189]

That the British troops in Clones were travelling in a civilian vehicle
and had attempted to make an arrest on the southern side of the
border adds context to the story. Known as a republican hotspot, there
was also a certain degree of local paranoia about British intelligence
operations. There may therefore have been a fair degree of support
for the recalcitrant Garda's actions.

Unusually for parish notes, which more typically dealt with issues like cake sales and births/deaths, the 'Clones News' frequently discussed security matters, illustrating the abnormality of the times.[190] The Garda view on the day of Ulster Final day 1973 in the town is further illustrative of the tension:

> It is understood that high ranking Garda officers are seriously concerned at the hostility directed towards members of the force in Clones on Sunday by northern visitors. It seemed to be a spontaneous reaction against the present role being played by Gardaí along the border and came close on the heels of the ominous death threat issued to the Gardaí on Saturday night by the Provisional IRA following Police activity on the Fermanagh–Monaghan border.[191]

The previous week, Gardaí had crossed the border by a matter of metres to investigate a suspect car and this resulted in the IRA issuing a threat against the southern security forces.[192] *The Irish Times* noted the largest security build-up in the town yet after these threats and a fatal armed robbery in Dublin.[193]

By the end of 1973, tension in the town was so great that the main 'concession road' between the two southern towns of Clones and Cavan had become 'almost devoid of traffic', so frequent were hijackings and other incidents.[194] The atmosphere was made even more tense when the house of a northern exile was attacked by an unknown group, presumably loyalists. Such incidents explain in part the local anxiety about British Army incursions. Afterwards, neighbouring MP Frank McManus said he was not surprised by the attack, as 'from information he had received, the British Army had been letting it be known in the last few weeks that Clones was in its opinion one of the centres of subversion thereby encouraging someone to do this sort of thing'.[195]

This incident had an epilogue in the Billy Fox killing. The IRA suspected that loyalists were receiving some support from south of the border.[196] A local Protestant family, the Coulsons, were erroneously identified due to personal spite.[197] When the IRA raided the Coulsons' house between Smithborough and Clones, Senator Fox arrived at the scene coincidentally. The Fine Gael representative was going out with Marjorie Coulson. Fox was shot by the intruders as he fled and the Coulson family home was burned. This incident was to have a transformative effect on the area. A survivor of the night, George Coulson, told an RTÉ documentary that 'It left a lot of the community afraid at the time. Some of them thought they were next. The reason I think [it was done] was to put a bit of fear into the Protestant community in the area.'[198]

The killing of Fox was a particularly senseless act from a republican perspective. The former TD was well thought of in nationalist circles. In fact, it is generally felt that Fox's criticism of the British Army actions along the border 'alienated him from his core [Protestant] constituency and lost him his Dáil seat'.[199] Five local men received life sentences for their role in the attack.[200] A few weeks after the killing, the local Easter commemoration in Monaghan attracted 1,000 marchers, 'the largest since its inception'.[201] It is therefore important not to overstate the effect of the killing on hard-core republican support.

However, there is some evidence that the IRA seemed concerned about its own position in the town. In June 1974, a man was forced to drive a proxy bomb, later claimed by loyalists, into Clones. With perfect timing, an IRA explosives expert appeared on the scene and dismantled the bomb. At a subsequent IRA press conference, the young 'hero' proclaimed that 'fear did not come into it – I wanted to save the town'.[202] Gardaí and many locals suspected the bomb was in fact left by the IRA 'to indicate to the people of Clones that the members of the Provisional IRA were their protectors and in this way boost their morale, which suffered considerably following the death of Senator Fox earlier in the year'.[203] By 1975, British sources noted the change in the town: '[Clones] was a well organised ASU until late 1974 when they suffered considerable attrition at the hands of the Garda.'[204]

Another factor affecting the Monaghan area was the Dublin–Monaghan bombing on 17 May 1974, during which thirty-three civilians were killed. The scale of the Dublin–Monaghan bombings against the backdrop of the Ulster Workers' Council (UWC) strike was unprecedented. Ongoing speculation over British intelligence involvement in the attacks led to the Barron/McEntee inquiries. The inquiries also investigated whether the informal co-operation between the British and Irish security forces in any way facilitated the atrocity. The discreet and informal co-operation that had become commonplace, but officially denied, led to serious allegations being levelled at some Gardaí in the years after the attack. Former British intelligence officer Fred Holroyd alleged that Irish security forces would 'freeze' areas to facilitate British intelligence operations within the twenty-six counties. These allegations were aired in TV documentaries in 1984 and 1987, on both occasions leading to internal Garda inquiries.

The allegations were again made in the *Hidden Hand* programme by Yorkshire TV in 1993. The Barron Inquiry report was sceptical of the 'freezing' allegation. Holroyd's evidence in relation to the aspect of contact with the Gardaí was adjudged 'flawed'[205] and the inquiry found no evidence to support the proposition that such informal exchanges in some way facilitated the passage of the Dublin and Monaghan bombers across the border.[206] On the substantive issue of whether collusion involving the British Army or RUC was a factor in the bombings, however, the conclusion was less certain:

> There are grounds for suspecting that the bombers may have had assistance from members of the security forces. The involvement of individual members in such an activity does not of itself mean the bombings were either officially or unofficially state-sanctioned. If one accepts that some people were involved, they may well have been acting on their own initiative. Ultimately, a finding that there was collusion between the perpetrators and the authorities in Northern Ireland is a matter of inference. On some occasions an inference is irresistible or can be drawn as a matter of probability. Here, it is the view of the Inquiry that this inference is not sufficiently strong. It does not follow even as a matter of probability. Unless further information comes to hand, such involvement must remain a suspicion.[207]

The coalition government and the Garda inquiry into the bombing were heavily criticised by the report. It was noted that 'the government of the day failed to show the concern expected of it'.[208] For a government that had focused its entire security effort on defeating the IRA, the possibility of any British involvement in the atrocity would have been hard to face. The 2003 report noted that 'a finding that members of the security forces in Northern Ireland could have been involved in the bombings is neither fanciful nor absurd'.[209] Had such a conclusion been made in 1974, the consequences for

Anglo-Irish relations would have been serious, particularly given the government's fear of a British withdrawal.

After the bombings, the national focus quickly switched back to republican violence. The kidnapping of the Earl and Countess Donoughmore in Tipperary in June attracted a lot of media attention. Meanwhile, in August there was a mass breakout from Portlaoise jail, which saw nineteen prisoners escape, including some of those convicted for the Fox killing.[210] That escapees could find shelter in such a 'small and intimate society' indicated a level of support for the IRA that worried Paddy Cooney.[211]

As strange and disturbing as it may seem, the bombings became something of a forgotten issue in light of the ongoing violence, but did create an incentive for greater security co-operation. At a national level, the decision to take part in what became known as the 'Baldonnel Panels' took place weeks later. Locally, there was an added incentive for security force personnel to co-operate. It was noted by a Garda Chief Superintendent investigating the bombings that 'There was reasonably good intelligence available on republican terrorists, but a dearth of information on loyalist terrorists. The latter weakness was recognised, and may have prompted some members of Detective Branch to cultivate RUC contacts in an effort to gather information.'[212]

Just as in Monaghan, northern violence was increasingly affecting life along the Donegal border. In notes to the revised 'Border Dossier', it was observed that 'Lifford/Clady/Cloughfin remains the most virulent of the border ASUs'.[213] Another analysis claimed that the Clady–Cloughfin area was seen as 'the most notorious trouble spot along the whole border'.[214] A detailed list of incidents in the Clady/ Strabane area in December 1973 illustrated the degree of the security problem, according to the British. The Gardaí received particular criticism. A Garda raid on IRA premises on 4 December was scuppered because the IRA was pre-warned. On 14 December, shots were fired by the IRA but no Garda response was noted. The next day a man was treated for injuries after a bomb he was carrying exploded but he was not questioned by Gardaí.[215]

Security on the Fermanagh–Donegal border was also problematic. The IRA used a wooded area adjoining the border as a firing point. This led to repeated requests for the Irish government to cut down the trees. When eventually action was taken on the southern side, it did little to enhance the reputation of the southern security

The border roads opening campaign was reinvigorated in the late 1980s. This photo was taken at Clones Free Rock Festival at Lackey Bridge/Clones. © Photo by Derek Speirs.

Moybridge customs post on the Monaghan–Tyrone border, 13 February 1981. This location was the scene of several cross border incidents. © Photo by Derek Speirs.

Road opening on the Monaghan–Tyrone border, 1990s. © Photo by Derek Speirs.

Road closure on the Leitrim–Fermanagh border, 1990s. © Photo by Derek Speirs.

Irish Defence Forces 27th Infantry Battallion, Eastern Command, on border patrol out of Dundalk barracks in 1979. © Photo by Derek Speirs.

GAA protest against the British Army occupation of the Crossmaglen GAA grounds, 15 July 1979. © Photo by Derek Speirs.

Funeral of Senior IRA figure Jack McCabe, 1971. Part of Colman Doyle collection, courtesy of the National Photographic Archive.

IRA activists in South Armagh prepare to launch an attack on the British Army, 1970s. Part of Colman Doyle collection, courtesy of the National Photographic Archive.

Michael Gaughan's funeral as it passed through Dublin, 8 June 1974. Part of Colman Doyle collection, courtesy of the National Photographic Archive.

The IRA near the border in Clady, Co. Tyrone, early 1970s. From *Patriot Graves* by P. Michael O'Sullivan (Follett, Chicago, 1972).

The IRA near the border in Clady, Co. Tyrone. British security papers identified this as a key trouble spot in the early 1970s. From *Patriot Graves* by P. Michael O'Sullivan (Follett, Chicago, 1972).

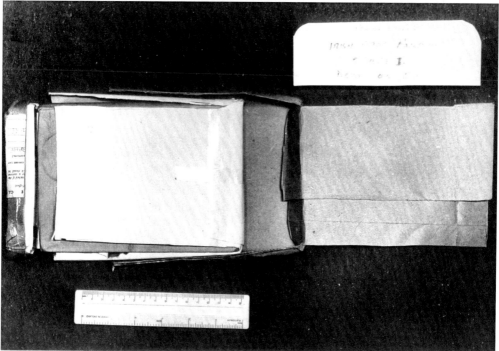

Parcel bomb sent to Irish Potato Marketing Company in Dublin, December 1973. Courtesy of the Military Archives, Dublin.

Irish Army undertaking public-order training. Courtesy of the Military Archives, Dublin.

Joint Army Garda patrols and checkpoints were a common sight along the border in the 1970s. The Gardaí favoured such mobile checkpoints rather than Permanent Vehicle Checkpoints. Courtesy of the Military Archives, Dublin.

An Irish Army patrol passes through the picturesque village of Glaslough, Co. Monaghan. Local community leaders made appeals to the Department of Justice to reopen the village's Garda station after an upsurge in violence in the late 1970s. Courtesy of the Military Archives, Dublin.

Grenades Hand (H.E.) (Arabic) 500
Diameter: 2" Height: $3\frac{1}{4}$"

Previous page, Joe Cahill (top) being escorted off the *Claudia* after IRA arms imported from Libya were seized in 1973. A sample of the weaponry is included (previous page, bottom; this page). Courtesy of the Military Archives, Dublin.

forces. Irish troops cleared some of the trees and 'neatly stacked [the timber] in piles that would give excellent cover for IRA snipers'.[216] In January 1974, the IRA used the cover of the woods to fire six rockets at the British Army/RUC.[217] From the British perspective this was another illustration of incompetence by the Irish security forces, but this localised issue was more complicated than it at first appeared. The trees were on private property and the owner had been warned of dire consequences by the IRA if he gave the authorities permission to clear the forestry.[218]

Violence in 1973/4 was spread the length of the border, with fatalities from varying backgrounds. When a large bomb was left in the village of Pettigo, the front-page headline in the *Donegal Democrat* read, 'Pettigo was Donegal's Claudy – massive bomb was meant to kill'.[219] A young Protestant from the county, meanwhile, Henry Cunningham, was killed by loyalists as he and a group of fellow tradesmen from Donegal travelled to work in Newtownabbey.[220] Earlier in the year, another young Donegal man, Michael Leonard, was shot dead by the RUC after a car chase near the border. Feelings 'ran high' in the area after the incident as Leonard's failure to stop was due to him being disqualified from driving.[221]

Locals linked to the British Army/RUC were also targets of republican violence. As was noted in earlier chapters, a number of southerners were members of the RUC. John Doherty from Lifford was one such member and he was shot dead a short distance from his home by the IRA. The local newspaper claimed that the attack 'horrified the people of Donegal'.[222] A year later, a British Army soldier from Donegal, Eugene Patton, was kidnapped when home on leave and was lucky to escape his captors.[223] There were other incidents of attacks on British Army/RUC personnel in the South. A party of six RUC men holidaying in Mayo was ambushed and a British Army Officer holidaying in Meath was also attacked but no fatalities occurred.[224] In Monaghan, part-time UDR member and school teacher Cormac McCabe was abducted while having a meal with his family and killed.[225] A month earlier, another former policeman, Ivan Johnston, was abducted and killed as he crossed the Monaghan–Armagh border.[226] There were other southerners killed in Northern Ireland at the time. Maurice Rolsten, a native of Longford, was killed by an IRA bomb in Down.[227] In February 1973, another Donegal native, William Wylie, was shot dead in Lurgan while serving with the RUC.[228]

There were republican casualties too. Seventeen-year-old Cork native Tony Ahern was killed by his own bombs while operating near the Fermanagh border.[229] A Tyrone IRA man, Dan McAnallen, living in Monaghan, was killed in an attack on Pomeroy Barracks.[230] Another border IRA activist, Michael McVerry, died on admission to Monaghan hospital after being brought there after an attack.[231] In Donegal, two IRA men, Seamus Harvey and Gerry McGlynn, were killed when the bomb they were transporting exploded.[232] The same year, another IRA man, Jim McGinn, was killed in Donegal transporting a device.[233] Meanwhile, some of those on hunger strike over conditions in the prisons had border connections. Patrick Ward from Donegal was a particularly high-profile prisoner. Some members of his family were strongly critical of the Provisional movement during the hunger strike, illustrating the divisions that existed within families over the northern conflict.[234]

Those suspected of informing were also casualties along the border, including Patrick Duffy from Derry.[235] The thirty-seven-year-old father of seven disappeared when out socialising with his wife in Buncrana. It seems as though there were initial attempts to 'disappear' Duffy but pressure from within the republican community led to his body being found in an abandoned car near the border.[236] Another example was a seventeen-year-old from Belfast, Terence Herdman, who was living with his grandparents in Belturbet.[237] Herdman, a father of a three-week-old child, was shot by the IRA and his body dumped on the Clogher–Monaghan road with a notice reading 'tout' around his neck. His family had sent him out of Belfast to get away from the violence. According to his former partner, republicans and the PSNI Historical Enquiries Team have in recent years confirmed that Terence Herdman did not knowingly give information to the RUC or British Army.[238]

Other civilians were also caught up in the violence near the border. These included farmer Patrick Duffy, who was killed near Belcoo in September 1973 when his tractor was blown up by an IRA landmine intended for the British Army/RUC.[239] Two men were also killed further south during armed robberies: Jeremiah O'Connor in Galway in August 1974[240] and James Farrell in Dublin in August 1973.[241] A Protestant man originally from Castleblayney, Samuel Martin, who had moved to Newtownhamilton was shot dead by the British Army on his way home from work in an incident described 'as a tragic accident' in March 1973.[242] In a particularly savage attack, a married couple, Frances and Bernadette Mullen, were shot and killed in an attack claimed by the UFF near Dungannon. The couple's two-year-old child was also shot and injured. Bernadette Mullen, née Carroll, was originally from Smithboro in Monaghan.[243]

Just as in 1972, violent deaths at or near the border simply could not be ignored. Nationally, incidents such as the helicopter escape from Mountjoy and assassination attempts added to public pressure for greater security action. More Gardaí and troops were moved to border towns. The effects were not immediately noticed. In Lifford, a new military post was established and a full-time vehicle checkpoint set up at Clady Bridge[244] but the effectiveness of Irish Army checkpoints was doubted by the British Army. A covert unit observing a border checkpoint in September 1974 noted:

> Morale, bearing and general competence: Bearing was poor, weapons slung on shoulders and hands were in pockets. Morale seemed low and soldiers bored. The static vehicle checkpoint appears to be more a show of presence than anything. No cars were stopped during the six hours that the operation was in position. Several times men were seen urinating outside the door of the hut that is used as a border post. Once it started to rain everyone disappeared into the hut.[245]

On 22 February 1974, the presence of troops did not deter the IRA when it fired twenty-five mortars and 300 rounds of ammunition from the roof of a hotel in the town in an operation that lasted twenty-five minutes. Gardaí who gave chase were stopped and warning shots were fired by the IRA.[246] The Irish security forces were chided by unionist politician John Laird, who claimed the incident took place 'too early in the morning for the Irish Army to intervene'.[247] This incident seems to have embarrassed the Irish government significantly. Donegan undertook to personally visit Lifford to find out why the Irish Army did not intervene. Both Donegan and his colleagues were 'taken aback' to discover that despite the presence of an Army barracks, there was no 'mobile military presence' in the town.[248] As Lifford had been singled out specifically as a cause of concern by the northern executive, this incident was particularly embarrassing. Speaking to the British Ambassador, Donegan was so enlivened by the incident that he undertook to raise again the issue of Army-to-Army communication at cabinet level,[249] presumably without success.

As was noted earlier, it was around this time that the Gardaí transferred a local officer who was deemed ineffectual and increased the Special Branch presence in the town. It would be a slow process, however, to curtail the IRA in the area. It is hard to know whether it was British pressure or incidents such as the killing of Constable Doherty that influenced moves to boost security in Lifford. A British Army report highlighted how attitudes in the area changed: 'As a result of recent bomb explosions in Castlederg and following the murder of Detective Constable Doherty in Lifford on October 27 there is considerable sympathy towards the problems of the Security Forces in this area.'[250]

Improvements in southern security played a role in reducing IRA activity in places like Lifford and Clones. Other factors were also significant: the imprisonment or death of one or two key individuals could be vital in border areas. If that individual or individuals ceased activity, it could lead to an area calming. In relation to Donegal, a British Army report argued that leadership in the republican movement was 'patchy ... but where there is a dynamic leader like [Jack] Brogan [in Donegal] ASU's are active and efficient'.[251] Brogan was himself a former UDR member who had been acquitted on IRA charges by the Special Criminal Court in early 1974. Brogan was targeted by the UVF and shot and seriously wounded at his house in Ballybofey on 21 February 1974.[252]

The most significant trend in border security in 1975 was the emergence of South Armagh as the principal trouble spot along the border. Journalist David McKittrick noted in 1975: 'Of the 50 violent deaths that Northern Ireland has seen since July 7, exactly half have taken place inside or close to the County of Armagh. This fact more than any other illustrates the drastic change that has recently taken place in a county which previously escaped quite lightly from the North's toll of civilian death.'[253] The truce had seen border violence drop[254] but the death toll in South Armagh was rising considerably. Seamus Mallon of the SDLP described South Armagh thus: 'The overall situation at that time was that law ceased to exist. There was no viable authority. Good senior police officers were vulnerable. The Government approach was to close your eyes and get on with worrying about winning the war.'[255]

Discussing the situation with Garret FitzGerald, Merlyn Rees similarly described the situation as 'almost uncontrollable'.[256] Rees continued:

The PIRA there had achieved a remarkable and highly dangerous level of sophistication in setting booby traps for security forces. There were too many British troops in the area, which was inherently impossible to control in view of the total intransigence and hostility of local people. The maintenance of such numbers of troops could only lead to further British casualties ... Normal patrolling could not be undertaken. The RUC presence was purely nominal.[257]

Several factors combined to make South Armagh different from other border areas. The degree of local sympathy, the comparative lack of a Protestant community and its proximity to the border have been cited as key factors.[258]

Some of the most notorious incidents of the Troubles took place near the South Armagh border during the period. Three members of the popular Miami Showband were killed by loyalists near the border on 31 July 1975, along with two UVF members involved in the attack.[259] In another random attack, two GAA supporters, Colm McCartney and Sean Farmer, were killed returning from a GAA match in Croke Park just after they crossed the border between Newtownhamilton and Keady. The two were stopped by an illegal loyalist checkpoint in circumstances that pointed to British Army/RUC collusion. Allegations from even moderate nationalists, such as Seamus Mallon, of loyalist paramilitary infiltration of the UDR followed this killing,[260] and the Irish Ambassador in London raised the issue of four RUC men in Portadown who were allegedly involved with the UVF.[261]

The IRA ceasefire saw a rise in attacks of a sectarian nature from the nationalist side, too. A month after the Miami Showband attack, five Protestants were killed in an indiscriminate attack on Tullyvallen Orange Hall.[262] In another incident in June 1975, three Protestant dog breeders returning from a dog show in the Republic were killed just after crossing the border.[263] There were numerous other fatalities in the area. A map in the British archives illustrating IRA attacks shows that the locally recruited UDR paid a particularly high price, including the deaths of Joseph Reid, William Meaklim and Bertie Frazer.[264] Regardless of the ceasefire, the British Army were also targeted. In its most audacious attack of that time, the IRA attacked a British Army outpost at Drumuckaval. During a sustained barrage lasting thirty minutes, three soldiers were killed. Indicating the vulnerability of troops on the ground, it was a further thirty minutes before Army reinforcements arrived.[265]

Some points regarding the upsurge in violence in South Armagh, while obvious, need emphasis. Firstly, most of the above incidents involved some cross-border dimension. In some cases, it was simply the targeting of cross-border commuters. Secondly, there was no corollary to this level of violence elsewhere along the border at the time. Finally, as evidenced by the material in the Barron Reports, allegations of British Army/RUC collusion was often a factor in loyalist attacks. This obviously had major implications for cross-border security co-operation. At its simplest, if the Irish side suspected collusion, they may have been reluctant to share intelligence. If collusion was taking place, the RUC were unlikely to properly investigate perpetrators of loyalist violence.

Inevitably, the violence spilled over the border into neighbouring County Monaghan. Loyalists/British forces also crossed the border. IRA man John Francis Green was shot in Castleblaney Co. Monaghan, on 10 January 1975. There have been persistent rumours of the involvement of SAS officer Robert Nairac in this killing, but the Barron Inquiry also cited allegations that the killing was a UVF revenge attack. Sightings of a British Army vehicle in the area days before the killing added to speculation of collusion but too much hard evidence is lacking in the case to definitively say that Nairac was involved, although circumstantial evidence does implicate him. At the very least, it has been suggested British forces had foreknowledge of the attack.[266]

Allegations of collusion did not just emerge years after these events but were widely cited at the time. The evening Green was killed, he had taken dinner with a local family in Castleblaney.[267] A year earlier, one member of the family had been the subject of a cross-border abduction attempt. On that occasion, a group of loyalists was hired, most likely by the British Army, to kidnap the man and another senior IRA man, Seamus Grew, from a house in Monaghan town.[268] The hapless kidnappers were, on that occasion, foiled by

Gardaí: two of the kidnappers were arrested at the scene, while a third was arrested when he called to Monaghan Garda station demanding the release of his colleagues. It seems the kidnappers felt they were on a legally sanctioned mission of some sort.

It was after Green's killing that the local newspaper, *The Northern Standard*, drew comparison between the kidnap attempt and the killing. It was claimed that one of the theories locally was 'that the murder was carried out by mercenaries, operating with British counter intelligence forces'.[269] Such precise targeting of active republicans in the Republic undoubtedly added to suspicions of British intelligence influence. The Brogan attack, the attempted kidnapping of Grew and the other local man, the shooting of Green and the attempted arrest in Clones were among incidents that deepened such suspicions. In this context, the discreet co-operation fostered by successive Dublin governments left security personnel on the ground vulnerable to serious allegations.

Aside from the assassination threat, loyalist bomb attacks continued. In December 1975, a bomb killed two customers, Hugh Watters and Jack Rooney, in Dundalk. Judge Barron concluded 'that without proof as to who was involved in the bombing, allegations of collusion were impossible to prove or disprove'.[270]

Aside from loyalist attacks, the violence also spilled over in other forms. It has already been noted that increased tensions existed between Gardaí and republicans. Garda surveillance and harassment of republicans was upped during the coalition even for relatively minor matters. Prosecutions of republicans were made for selling newspapers and taking up collections.[271] In one case, possession of a booklet, *Freedom Struggle*, was used as proof of membership of the IRA.[272] Protests over conditions in Portlaoise Prison proved particularly problematic. In Donegal, twenty-four defendants appeared before the courts as a result of protests.[273] The public relations officer of Sinn Féin in Monaghan complained that 'The Gardaí are also engaged in a campaign to get other republicans imprisoned by issuing large numbers of summonses, mostly in connection with demonstrations carried out at the time of the recent hunger strike in Portlaoise. Over two dozen summonses have been served on local Sinn Féin members in the last week alone.'[274]

Even issues as seemingly trivial as street graffiti supportive of the IRA attracted government attention. A circular was issued to all County

Councils to ensure political graffiti was removed after the Taoiseach took an interest in the issue.[275]

While street disturbances such as those in Ballyshannon, Dundalk and Monaghan in 1971/2 were not repeated, violence could erupt late at night, especially at weekends. As many new Gardaí and Army personnel were in their early twenties and attended some of the same social occasions as republicans, this is unsurprising. In October 1974, such violence led to a mini riot in Castleblayney. Thirty-seven people were detained during this incident; most of them had addresses in Crossmaglen or elsewhere in South Armagh.[276] This was a more extreme manifestation of a trend whereby 'hostilities between the Gardaí and hardline Republicans supporters grew to such a degree that weekend encounters between them were routine affairs in most border towns'.[277] A similar night of violence occurred in Ballybofey on St Patrick's night 1975 when a mob of 150 besieged the local Garda station.[278]

Sometimes trouble was avoided as republicans and Gardaí frequented different venues, but in small rural venues this was not always the case. Gardaí were often wary about where they socialised. A Garda stationed in the Manorhamilton area of Leitrim contributed to the recent 'Green and Blue' oral history project and reflected:

> The relationship that I would have had in the community down in Kerry, and even I had when I worked in England on the buildings for a while before I went in to the Guards, was always open and friendly, whereas now I was going into a situation where you were treated with suspicion by the people that you were interacting with, even the local people would have been wary of you. We got on well with them. You had to be careful where you went to because there were some pubs and things like that were what might be called republican strongholds and you stayed out of them.[279]

Other Gardaí contributing to the same project expressed a similar sense of unease about relations with the broader community in border areas:

> I didn't know anybody on the border from working on the border who said that they were relaxed, because they were not. Even the local Guards would find it difficult enough because they were

conscious as well that they had to take action against somebody they were living close to in the locality possibly. They had a family, you know, maybe some of their children going to school, so therefore you were looking over your shoulder all the time.[280]

There was always a reserve there from the locals they were not saying, you know 'you're welcome' and 'sure come on in and have a cup of tea or a cup of coffee' … There was always a bit of reserve there. In fairness to the locals, there were a lot of new Guards coming and going.[281]

Naturally, there were occasions when the young republicans and young Gardaí met socially. This account from republican Thomas Anthony McNulty gives a flavour of what could then happen:

[A Monaghan] Hotel was known as the IRA social club and groups of young Gardaí normally stayed away from it, but there were up to twenty of them there that night … Then all hell broke lose! The IRA men and the young border Garda got stuck into each other; it was like something you would see in a cowboy film! 20–30 young men making the dance floor into a battleground![282]

There was, of course, the danger that the hostility between republicans and Gardaí could go beyond bar-room brawls. The same republican noted the importance of refraining from taking military action against the Gardaí/Army:

There was a Standing Order within the IRA that under no circumstances were IRA weapons to be used against the southern security forces. Even if it meant arrest and loss of these weapons, so be it. For any IRA unit to have attacked members of the southern security forces and killed or injured them would have been an absolute disaster. It would undermine a southern support base.[283]

Not every republican may have followed this order diligently. As already noted, there were numerous incidents along the border where active IRA members confronted Gardaí. On several occasions, shots were fired or guns were pointed at Gardaí.[284] At an IRA funeral near Emyvale, there were disturbances in the graveyard when the Gardaí moved in to arrest members of an IRA colour party after a volley of shots were fired. *The Northern Standard*, generally sympathetic to republicans, warned 'by their ill advised interference at the funeral, the Gardaí have without doubt sown seeds for further and probably more violent confrontations'.[285]

Another trend was the disabling of a Garda car in pursuit, which sometimes resulted in Gardaí being stripped of their uniform.[286] On a few occasions, direct threats were made through the media, warning the government of the implications of Garda–RUC co-operation.[287] The degree of antagonism directed towards the Garda/Army by republicans seemed to vary. On one occasion, an armed republican resisting arrest was apparently told by a companion to 'cut out the nonsense'.[288] Other republicans, meanwhile, had a special disdain for the Gardaí/Army. After a Garda car was burned during street disturbances in Portlaoise, the Irish Army identified one republican speaker over others as being responsible for 'whipping up' the crowd.[289]

It was not just rank-and-file republicans who came into conflict with Gardaí. Senior republican Kevin Mallon received a conviction when he was charged with aiding another person to discharge a firearm at Gardaí as he was trying to evade capture.[290] Mallon also had an earlier conviction for assaulting two Gardaí on a social occasion in Monaghan town.[291] On another occasion in Cavan, leading republican, J.B. O'Hagan, was arrested at an IRA funeral. According to an Irish Army account, O'Hagan shouted to a colleague within earshot of the Gardaí/Army to 'get a Belfast unit in here – we have targets down here now'.[292] The net result of the antagonism between Gardaí and republicanism was that individual Gardaí were aware that their own lives could be made unpleasant if they were too enthusiastic in performing their duties. Republicans, meanwhile, realised that if they went too far in confronting Gardaí, they risked alienating their own support base. Emphasising this point, Paddy Cooney warned republicans to 'look back on the last 50 years and see that any confrontation between illegal organisations and the state invariably ended in favour of the state'.[293]

Finally, it is worth considering another aspect of border life that remained controversial: border road closures. Of the 187 unapproved roads, 97 were blocked.[294] In the aftermath of the Tullyvallen Orange Hall attack, when five members of the Orange Order were killed by

Republicans, there was pressure to close roads on the South Armagh border. Local opposition to closures was 'more concerted and vigorous than at any time in the past'[295] but it is possible to identify a new attitude to road closures/openings during the coalition's time in office.

As in the past, the Department of Foreign Affairs opposed the closures, viewing them as counterproductive. There was no law in the Republic forbidding the reopening of such roads, so the Gardaí could not intervene to prevent locals reopening roads. Cooney did not seem enthused about introducing new legislation on the matter.[296] The closure of a road involved significant security personnel from both sides of the border. Garret FitzGerald was critical that when roads were reopened it 'affected morale in border areas and gave the PIRA a great fillip'.[297] The closure of some roads was more controversial than others, and Gardaí in Dundalk were particularly concerned about the consequences of closing the Newry–Flagstaff road.[298] A march against the road closure was led by Fine Gael's Councillor Thomas Elmore in Omeath.[299]

However, there were those on the Irish side sympathetic to the arguments in favour of closing border roads. Paddy Donegan had told the British military attaché that he approved of closing the Omeath road.[300] In Castleblayney, local Gardaí claimed there was support for the closure of the Newtownhamilton–Castleblayney road in the area. There were fears, well founded as it turned out, that the town would suffer a reprisal attack after the Tullyvallen Orange Hall attack and it was thought the road closure would improve security.[301] When later representations were made to have the road reopened, the Department of Justice and Gardaí advised against it.[302]

Leitrim was particularly affected by border closures, particularly at Kiltyclogher. Again, though, the Irish view was more nuanced than is generally thought. The Department of Justice warned against intervening:

> Information available to the Department suggests that the existence of the barrier has not caused any serious inconvenience to those involved in legitimate trade. In fact it may be said that only smugglers and IRA activists are affected. Virtually half of those involved in the protest could be described as Sinn Féin/IRA and it is suspected agitation derives from that source.[303]

By early 1976, the Irish government had shifted its emphasis on the roads issue, agreeing to keep existing roads closed and trying to minimise disruption and inconvenience.[304] Considering the political climate of the time, those involved in border-road-opening campaigns undoubtedly contained republican elements, and knowing the 'black-and-white' views prevalent in the Department of Justice, it is unsurprising that the border-road campaign received only limited official support.

South Armagh Dominates

By the end of 1975 the IRA was in some disarray. The kidnapping of Tiede Herrema had caused considerable negative publicity for the organisation.[305] Feuding between republican groups had tarnished all organisations with some of the associated violence spilling over the border.[306] The years 1973–5 had seen the coalition continue the clampdown on republicans started by the previous government. The numbers brought before the Special Criminal Court by the coalition were not considerably higher than during the previous regime. In the last six months of 1972, 158 had been brought before the court. In 1973 and 1974, 286 and 288 appeared respectively. There was in fact a drop in 1975, with 198 appearing.[307] Therefore, the coalition was clamping down on republicans but it was not charging significantly more individuals and its methods were more all-encompassing. Republicans were challenged more frequently for holding illegal collections, distributing propaganda or more serious offences. The language used by government ministers was more openly hostile to republicans and conciliatory to the British, giving added emphasis to the clampdown.

Table 7 shows the figures for those arrested under Section 30 of the Offences Against the State Act. This was the catch-all legislation used frequently to detain republicans for periods of twenty-four or forty-eight hours.

The number of arrests made increased almost four-fold from 1973 to 1976, during which time the number of prosecutions was also dropping substantially. More than anything else, these figures illustrate how the coalition approached security. The implication of this data is that many individuals may have been detained primarily due to their political allegiance.[309] The relationship between Gardaí

Table 7. Numbers arrested under Section 30 Offences Against the State Act[308]

Year	Number arrested
1972	229
1973	271
1974	602
1975	607
1976	1,015

and republicans would continue to deteriorate in subsequent years. This incentivised further Garda co-operation with the British security services. It was not yet clear at this point whether full-scale conflict would occur between the IRA and Gardaí/Army. The next chapter will detail how such conflict grew increasingly likely after the IRA killed the British Ambassador in Dublin and a young Garda in Laois.

Another area for further examination is the emergence of South Armagh as the key trouble spot. By 1978, of the fifty-eight serious border incidents, forty-one would take place in South Armagh.[310] By the end of 1975, it was already obvious that this portion of the border was the most problematic and events in the first months of 1976, notably the Kingsmill massacre, emphasised this fact. Other border areas would, of course, still pose problems but often these were due to specific circumstances or the presence of certain individuals.

It has been argued in this chapter that a particular incident or an individual's presence could see Provisional support ebb in a locality. It could be argued that the loss of personnel and prestige by the IRA in the Clones area, for example, contributed to the lull in violence along the neighbouring Fermanagh border. The previous chapter outlined how attacks on off-duty UDR members in the area had increased tension. In 1973, the Clones unit was blamed for killing another UDR member, Matthew Lilley. In the mid 1970s, for apparently unexplained reasons, the number of such attacks decreased for several years.[311] The killing of Billy Fox significantly dented IRA morale and support in Clones and this surely affected its capacity to sustain cross-border attacks.

The Irish state's reaction to the deteriorating situation in border towns is especially interesting. Moves to improve security, whether by increasing personnel or transferring individuals, tended to occur when the Irish state felt threatened rather than as a result of British pressure. There was a dramatic rise in checkpoints after the Portlaoise prison break and the Dublin and Monaghan bombings but not after Sunningdale. Troublesome Gardaí were transferred after disturbances locally. The Baldonnel panels were instituted when fears of a British withdrawal were greatest. It is worth reiterating Kelvin White on this point: 'Their troops will sweep areas if we ask them to, but some at least prefer this to appear to be coincidental, and do not wish to be thanked in public. Good is thus done by stealth.'[312]

Even at grass-roots level, the pre-eminence of domestic security was noted. Commenting on co-operation with Irish security forces on the Derry–Donegal border, a British Army commander on the ground observed that 'the degree of cooperation depends on the effect the incident is likely to have on the Republic'.[313] The level of co-operation with the British Army/RUC continued to improve but was not comprehensive enough from the British perspective. A large part of the reason for this was that domestic political pressure in the South inhibited co-operation. Potential weaknesses in the internal security of the Garda/Army were also a factor, but these were not the only reasons. The behaviour of individual British troops/RUC along the border hindered co-operation. Negative attitudes towards the Irish forces created resentment and led to diplomatic complaints. More seriously, allegations of collusion with loyalist paramilitaries weakened trust between the respective security forces. Failure to give adequate co-operation to some investigations into loyalist attacks in the Republic accentuated this distrust and covert actions in the South, such as the activities of the Littlejohn brothers or the attempted kidnapping in Monaghan, left those who co-operated with the British in a difficult position.

Meanwhile, the Irish government reaction to loyalist violence and collusion is especially interesting. While complaints were made about relatively minor issues, such as the demeanour of individual troops on the border, the response to allegations of collusion in southern killings was somewhat muted. The Barron Inquiry noted: 'The Government of the day showed little interest in the bombings. When information was given to them suggesting that the British authorities had intelligence naming the bombers, this was not followed up. Any follow-up was limited to complaints by the Minister for Foreign Affairs that those involved had been released from internment.'[314]

IRA violence had been framed in black-and-white terms by the coalition and allegations of collusion did not fit comfortably within this narrative. Moreover, the government did not want to raise issues likely to contribute to British disengagement. Loyalist violence would continue to intermittently spill over the border and the state's security record in the area remained unimpressive.

CHAPTER 5

'They will hammer the IRA in their own way for their own reasons':[1] Border Security, 1976–1978

Members of the Boys Brigade from the small Northern Ireland border village of Tullyhommon near Pettigo went for a training run in December 1978. Unbeknownst to them, a party of six republicans were just ahead on the road, escaping on foot across the border after planting incendiary bombs in the town. It was initially unclear to the IRA who their pursuers were, but when the escaping party realised that it was boy scouts rather than the RUC giving 'chase', the republicans fired a warning shot into the air rather than at their 'pursuers'.[2] This incident ended more in farce than tragedy but it does highlight issues relevant to the time. Violence along the border persisted and uninvolved people could still easily get caught in the crossfire. The border itself remained an important escape route.

Removed from the border, rising crime, some of it associated with the Troubles, was impacting on life generally. Republicans were also becoming more willing to use violence south of the border. This increased existing tensions between republicans and the state. The preceding chapter established that the coalition government had framed the debate against the IRA in absolute terms. The new government under Jack Lynch in 1977 had previously shown itself in office determined to oppose the IRA domestically between 1970 and 1973. Lynch's new Minister for Foreign Affairs, Michael O'Kennedy, would describe the IRA as 'madmen' to the British, indicating that the new officeholders remained determined to confront militant republicans.[3] In public, the anti-republican tone of

Lynch's government would be more muted than that of the previous government, but there would be minimal difference in the actual implementation of policy.

Although the Irish security forces continued to tackle the IRA domestically, co-operation with the security forces across the border remained haphazard and based, to a large extent, on relations between individual policemen. Some institutional frameworks had been set up with the Baldonnel panels discussed in the previous chapter but much still depended on the willingness of low-ranking individuals to co-operate at ground level. Political pressure, the colonial legacy, allegations of RUC collusion with loyalists, as well as fears of IRA intimidation, inhibited co-operation in some incidences.

Between 1976 and 1978, there was increased media focus on the use of the border by the IRA. It was heavily suspected by Irish political figures that much of this publicity was driven by briefings from the British military. It was especially difficult for the Irish government to refute this criticism: if the government emphasised the extent of co-operation, it was politically admitting to having a closer relationship with the British than it wanted to portray. The Gardaí, meanwhile, continued to lack the necessary intelligence-gathering and technical resources necessary to deal with the upsurge in violence. The combination of political pressure to get results, growing hostility towards republicans and outdated policing practices led some within the Gardaí to begin using force in order to obtain confessions from suspects.

As the coalition continued with an all-encompassing approach to security, a related controversy emerged that would force the Irish president to resign. The coalition was to be increasingly defined by its approach to security but the analysis that it was voted out of office solely for this reason will be questioned. The continued difficulties associated with Anglo-Irish relations are included in the discussion and, in particular, the fallout from the assassination of British Ambassador Christopher Ewart Biggs is discussed. The return to office of Fianna Fáil is dealt with; despite initial apprehension on the British side, security policy continued much as before under the new Lynch regime. The IRA remained the state's primary enemy. The impact of the state's security strategy on the Gardaí is discussed in detail. It will be argued that the force was given something of a free hand to deal with the internal threat and this contributed to 'unofficial' security co-operation in some border divisions. In terms of border violence, the chapter identifies South Armagh as a key battleground again but the simplistic narrative that IRA forces simply hid across the border and raided into South Armagh is questioned. As in other chapters, it is attempted to portray the complexities of border life with individual cases, such as that of Seamus Ludlow, highlighting the legacy of violent incidents in border areas.

The Political Environment from Coalition to Fianna Fáil Majority

By 1976, the prospects of a British withdrawal had waned. The Irish government's Interdepartmental Unit on Northern Ireland concluded that 'the collapse of the political process was likely to follow the failure of the Convention'. It was anticipated that the place of politicians was likely to be taken by paramilitaries.[4]

The southern state's problems were not confined to the field of security. The state had the worst figures for inflation, unemployment, investment and public debt in the EEC. The British embassy's annual review for 1976 noted 'the Irish economy is in a worse state than any other in Western Europe and the Government had no real success in managing it'.[5] Economic realities meant that new initiatives on Northern Ireland were not high on any political agenda. For domestic security to be maintained, the dual strategy of clamping down hard on republicans while avoiding allegations of collaboration would persist. Both strategies remained popular. The British embassy annual review of Ireland in 1976 noted:

> Their [coalition's] policy on law and order, hard on terrorism but aloof from the British is a popular one. It is in tune with the average Irishman's growing weariness with the North, his fear that terrorism will become endemic in the South, his apprehension about the impact of violence on tourism and investment and his pathological dislike of feeling dominated by his British neighbour.[6]

There was also a notable downside to this dual strategy. The levels of antagonism between republicans and state institutions increased considerably. According to the British embassy, a range of factors contributed to the rise in hostility between the security forces and republicans:

One [reason for antagonism with republicans] is the fragmentation and lack of central direction on the republican paramilitary side. In addition, the 'live and let live' relationship, which has at various times existed between the security forces and the IRA, may have been undermined by the number of convictions secured in the last couple of years, mainly for membership of prescribed organisations and for bank robberies. More recently, the Criminal Law Act may have led more republicans to see the security forces in the South as a more direct threat than in the past. There is also evidence that the security forces, under the coalition, have been showing more toughness ... this is reflected in the more strident criticism of Garda brutality in the republican press.[7]

Older heads within the republican leadership seemed more cognisant of the dangers of the conflict spreading south. IRA policy explicitly prohibited military action in the Republic. Garda sources, for example, claimed older Provisionals, Dáithí Ó Connaill and Ruairí Ó Brádiagh, disapproved of the killing of British Ambassador Christopher Ewart Biggs.[8] Some actions by the IRA in the South were put down to 'rogue units' but Kieran Conway, an IRA man sent to investigate a 'rogue unit', strongly suspected that the cell had approval from higher-ranking officers within the IRA's GHQ staff.[9] Therefore, perhaps some within the IRA supported military action in the Republic. This may have stretched to include bomb attacks. A republican was convicted in connection with a series of firebomb attacks in Dublin in November 1976. The attacks occurred at cinemas and public houses.[10] Whether referring to these attacks or others, the IRA informer Sean O'Callaghan claimed that an IRA leader organised attacks in the Republic to be ascribed to the UFF to ferment anti unionist feeling.[11]

There were other IRA actions in the South with a different explanation. In Swanlinbar, Cavan, a bomb exploded on Main Street, causing damage to a local business on 14 February 1976. The context of this bomb was that the Gardaí had made several arrests and seizures in the vicinity. A local man accused of informing was tarred and feathered. Gardaí believed the IRA left the bomb to 'intimidate local people from giving any assistance to security forces and to demonstrate that the arrest of their leading members would be followed by violence'.[12]

By June 1976, relations between the IRA and state officials deteriorated further when the paramilitary group classified 'as legitimate targets any Free State civil servant, court official, solicitor, counsel, judge or police officer found in the occupied area in a prosecuting capacity against republican prisoners of war'.[13] This threat came as the prospect of Gardaí travelling north in Criminal Law Jurisdiction cases seemed likely.

The IRA hunger strike in Portlaoise in 1977 further heightened tensions. The failure of the hunger strike to attract mass support is particularly interesting. As part of its public relations strategy, government publicity highlighted the offences committed by the striking prisoners. That one of those on hunger strike was convicted of the killing of Senator Billy Fox was seen as especially significant.[14] It was noted in *Hibernia* that 'The protest methods employed by the organisers of the support groups outside also contributed to the failure. The use of what could be considered military tactics in marches and rallies only served to alienate the public in Portlaoise and Dublin and also convinced many outsiders that the marchers had provoked Garda reaction.'[15]

A further illustration of the disenchantment with violence was the emergence of the Peace People. A Garda estimate claimed 50,000 marched in support of peace in Dublin in August 1976.[16] In border towns, too, substantial numbers marched, including 3,000 in Monaghan town.[17] Electorally, those espousing the traditional republican message remained on the fringes. The exception was Paddy Keavney's victory on a 'Blaney ticket' in the Donegal by-election of June 1976.[18] Despite this success, Neil Blaney was more marginalised than ever. A motion at the February 1976 Fianna Fáil Ard Fheis proposing Blaney's return to the party fizzled out, with a strong message delivered by Donegal party officials opposing the former minister.[19]

It should be noted, however, that the attitude of Fianna Fáil voters may have been different to that of activists. Keavney's election was facilitated by 3,054 second-preference transfers from the official Fianna Fáil candidate, indicating that at some level support remained among party voters for a more republican analysis.[20] It was therefore hard for Lynch to fully jettison the party's republican heritage. Rhetorically, at least, the Fianna Fáil leadership remained committed to traditional aims. The demand for a British withdrawal remained official policy although the commitment of the front bench to this policy was questionable. When Northern Ireland Secretary of State Merlyn Rees met then opposition leader Jack Lynch in 1976, the demand for withdrawal was 'low key'.

Similarly, in a 'friendly and relaxed' way, Lynch and his Northern spokesman Ruairí Brugha expressed disquiet about SAS patrols along the border. Fianna Fáil representatives portrayed this as 'a strong protest' when speaking to the media after the meeting.[21]

In general terms, the British viewed security co-operation as improving, but it remained 'restricted, cautious and covert'.[22] Just as in previous years, the Irish government did not want to publicise its role in co-operation. The security situation in South Armagh would test relations between Dublin and London. There was particular outrage after six killings in one evening – three members of the Reavey and O'Dowd families were killed by loyalist paramilitaries. This was followed by the killing of ten Protestant workmen in what became known as the Kingsmill massacre in January 1976. Finding the Kingsmill getaway vehicle in Dundalk was a very public illustration of the cross-border dimension.[23]

In Anglo-Irish meetings in February 1976, Cooney agreed to discuss with the Garda Commissioner the possibility of pressing 'membership charges' against some of the sixty or so republicans based, at least some of the time, on the southern side of the South Armagh border.[24] The perennial issues of Army-to-Army communication and overflights were again pushed by the British. Cooney also resisted further pressure for direct communication with the British Army.[25] Overflights were once more brought up at a 28 May intergovernmental security meeting when Rees handed over a list of thirty-nine incidents in support of his case for greater access to Irish airspace. There was a considerable discrepancy between the British and Irish version of the thirty-nine incidents. The thrust of the Irish argument was that better use of existing procedures would be more effective than extending overflights. The tone of the Irish report is highly illustrative of the mindset within Irish government circles:

> The analysis of the incidents cited by the British in support of their request for hot pursuit flight suggests that there is room for improvement, particularly on the part of the RUC/British Army in their own internal communications and in notifying Gardaí of incidents near the border … The British request implies in some

unspecified way that our security forces are less well able [than theirs] to cope with the violence along the border.[26]

Whether real or imagined, it seems that there was a feeling in some parts of Irish government that the British authorities maintained a colonial attitude. As the dialogue between the two governments continued, so did media criticism of apparent Irish inaction. Even reports in liberal outlets like *The Guardian* were critical of Irish security.[27] The Irish authorities strongly suspected that briefings by British political and military figures influenced such articles.[28] Minister for Foreign Affairs Garret FitzGerald vented his disquiet publicly on the matter, stating 'some of the propaganda that has been issued on this subject from some British sources is incomprehensible to us when combined with public statements by politicians and private statements whenever we meet them, of congratulation on the closeness of cooperation'.[29]

The funeral of IRA hunger striker Frank Stagg in February 1976 was a very public test of wills between the coalition and republicans. Stagg's wife and some other family members wanted a private funeral whereas other relatives supported a traditional republican burial. Stagg was eventually buried in a private ceremony boycotted by most of his family, who attended a republican commemoration that took place in Ballina the same day. Over 1,000 Army and Garda personnel policed the crowd of 5,000 attending the commemoration and there were sporadic scuffles.[30] It was to be a divisive occasion. The coalition had very deliberately put in place a strategy whereby republican displays were to be marginalised.

The government again showed its resolve to isolate republicans some weeks later when it banned a 1916 commemoration in Dublin city centre.[31] Among the substantial crowd of up to 10,000 defying the ban was Labour TD Dr David Thornley. The Labour Parliamentary Party voted 22 to 3 to remove the whip from Thornley. The margin of the vote against Thornley indicated the surprising degree of support in the Labour party for the stance.[32] A clear message was being sent. Whatever personal ties or political convictions individuals had, they had to choose between the state and republicans.

British Army incursions continued to be politically sensitive and one such event caused a mini crisis in Anglo-Irish relations in May 1976. Two separate groups of SAS personnel in civilian attire, carrying an unorthodox array of weapons, including shotguns, were arrested at the same Garda checkpoint in Co. Louth. One group of SAS men had apparently accidentally crossed the border in search of their colleagues, who had also accidentally crossed it. The arrests created a 'mini propaganda war'.[33] While the British were working for the release of the soldiers, opposition TDs in the Dáil were demanding 'definite and firm action'.[34] The procedure for incursions in some cases seems to have been to quietly escort those involved back to the border but the circumstances and context on this occasion were perturbing. The rather implausible SAS explanation of the event was that it was a result of a map-reading error. The type of weapons carried, the demeanour of the men and the circumstances of the arrest make acceptance of that benign explanation difficult.[35]

Events locally added to suspicion. The previous week, a local man, Seamus Ludlow, was killed by a party of loyalists. The weapons of SAS troops were forensically examined to determine whether they were in any way connected with Seamus Ludlow's death. The *Sunday World* went so far as to claim that Ludlow was killed by the SAS in a case of mistaken identity.[36] It was not merely the tabloid media that alluded to SAS action south of the border. An interview by an indiscreet SAS officer in *The Guardian* in December 1976 gave the general impression of the SAS as 'a dirty tricks unit which does not draw the line at murder'.[37] The SAS officer in question was travelling on a train in Scotland and unwittingly gave an account of the unit's Irish operations to a grateful journalist, Simon Winchester, who just happened to be sharing a carriage with him. It seems that the officer spoke with little or no filter. Such was the consternation caused by the story that the Northern Ireland Office launched an investigation to determine whether the briefing had in fact been deliberately given to further a military agenda. As it transpired, the SAS officer had just been indiscreet and unwittingly gave an honest account of the unit's operations as he saw it.

There had been ongoing concern about British intelligence operatives kidnapping republicans in the South. Republicans persistently alleged that one of their members, Seán McKenna, was kidnapped from Louth by the SAS in March 1976.[38] Mention has already been made of the case of the attempted kidnapping in Monaghan of Seamus Grew and a local man that almost certainly had some British Army/RUC involvement. It is very hard to reach firm conclusions on the SAS incursion in Louth, but in the context of the time it can be seen to have raised fears and levels of distrust. There was great media interest in and comment on the affair. That much of the material related to the issue in the UK archives is either retained or redacted adds to suspicion.[39] Several Freedom of Information requests were put in by the author for material on the incursion but these were denied. For now, all that can be concluded is that the incident coloured Anglo-Irish dialogue for twelve months until the men were acquitted of more serious charges and released with a fine.

While the SAS incursion caused a local media frenzy, an event on 21 July 1976 would command global attention. The newly appointed British Ambassador Christopher Ewart Biggs and his private secretary, Judith Cooke, were killed in an IRA landmine attack on the outskirts of Dublin. The state's security services were already reeling from an IRA escape involving the use of explosives at the Special Criminal Court weeks earlier.[40] For a brief period, the assassination seemed set to be a watershed in Anglo-Irish relations. The *Irish Independent* described the ambush as the 'work of people whose moral sense has atrophied or never existed'. The usually more republican *Irish Press* likewise condemned strongly the 'terrible deed'.[41] All accounts reported the almost universal repugnance after the attack but the ease with which the perpetrators carried out their task and escaped raised questions over the efficiency of the security forces. The *Irish Independent*'s headline, 'Security Shambles', pointed to incompetence,[42] while the *Guardian* headline read 'Security flaws allowed the killers through'.[43] *The Sun* went a step further in alleging that 'an IRA agent highly placed in the Dublin administration may have put the finger of death on the British Ambassador'.[44]

Nothing subsequently emerged to substantiate allegations of collusion, but the Gardaí's reputation was damaged by the entire incident and subsequent investigation. Prior to the bomb, Ewart Biggs himself had felt the Garda's personal security was not reassuring, claiming the Gardaí 'do not seem to have given much thought to the scenario of attack'.[45] 'The Department of Fingers Crossed' was how the Ambassador humorously described his protectors.[46] Aspects of the investigation indicated the abnormality of political relations between the two states. The fact the British officials were later concerned about whether the briefcases of Ewart Biggs had been tampered with is highly illustrative.[47] Likewise, a police report presented by the Gardaí to the embassy lacked any real detail. The British suspected the report was left deliberately vague so that the Gardaí would avoid criticism.[48]

The British were circumspect in their statements about the Gardaí in the aftermath of the attack, realising that criticisms of the Irish security forces could potentially dilute public goodwill. They hoped that the public sympathy generated by the attack would be used to push the Irish side for security concessions.[49] Earlier in the year, Minister for Justice Paddy Cooney had signposted the introduction of a new bill with heavier penalties for IRA membership and related offences.[50] The Ambassador's assassination created an opportunity for this proposed emergency legislation to be introduced but this legislation was not the turning point the British hoped for. An embassy official observed that the package of security measures, including a declaration of a State of Emergency, was 'deliberately confined to dealing with an increase in terrorism in the Republic as a separate problem from terrorism in Northern Ireland'.[51] The Ambassador's 1976 annual report concluded that 'the best we are likely to get from the Irish is that they will hammer the IRA in their own way for their own reasons'.[52]

The measures adopted by the government were a failure from several points of view. Firstly, the political side was handled badly. The debate over the legislation took place two months after the assassination when the initial horror had waned and reports were beginning to emerge of Garda brutality. Rather than being credited with a swift response to an emergency situation, the coalition's public image was damaged by association with what were seen as draconian measures.[53] Fianna Fáil came out of the debate with enhanced credibility, appearing tough on law and order but more cognisant of concerns over human rights.[54] From a practical law enforcement point of view, the longer sentences for IRA membership coincided with an internal reorganisation within the republican movement. The longer sentences merely further encouraged republicans to begin contesting membership charges.[55] The conviction rate for IRA membership dropped dramatically, as did the number of prosecutions taken as illustrated in Table 8.

The day the Emergency Powers Bills were signed into law, an IRA booby-trap bomb killed Garda Michael Clerkin near Portlaoise. The attack intensified feelings within the cabinet. In the mind of at least some members of the coalition, anyone with concerns about

Table 8. Number of people charged and convicted of IRA membership, 1974–79[56]

Year	Number charged	Number convicted	Percentage convicted
1974	153	98	64%
1975	55	26	47%
1976	88	51	58%
1977	37	8	21%
1978	17	6	35%
1979	28	7	25%

the emergency legislation was suspect. Even the president, Cearbhall Ó Dálaigh, who had referred the bill to the Supreme Court to test its constitutionality, was not beyond reproach. This particularly irked Minister for Defence Paddy Donegan. In a speech at an Army barracks in Mullingar, Donegan launched an expletive-filled attack on Ó Dálaigh, labelling him, according to the politest accounts, 'a thundering disgrace'.[57] Given the position of the president, this created a constitutional crisis. A motion in the Dáil calling for Donegan's resignation was defeated by sixty-three votes to fifty-eight, amid heated criticism of the minister.[58] A half-hearted apology from Taoiseach Liam Cosgrave further compounded the crisis and Ó Dálaigh resigned.[59] A fair analysis of the incident published in recent years concluded that both Donegan and Cosgrave behaved disgracefully throughout.[60] In the context of Irish security, the Ó Dálaigh controversy illustrates how much the government's battle with the IRA had become a conflict between 'us' and 'them', with no room for nuance.

The sense that the government was behaving in an overly draconian manner, coupled with the fallout of the Ó Dálaigh affair, left the coalition damaged. This instability made the Irish government thorny partners for the British. On EEC affairs, the government had been 'increasingly difficult' and it was anticipated that this would extend to security matters.[61] When the new Secretary of State Roy Mason met FitzGerald in Dublin in September, it was clear from the exchange that public opinion was moving in a more nationalist direction, which had implications for any further development on security issues.[62] There were also public glimpses of British dissatisfaction with the

Irish government. The case of the SAS soldiers was ongoing, as was the European Court of Human Rights torture case. When the Irish government did not sign up to the European Convention against Terrorism, Prime Minister Jim Callaghan delivered a public rebuke.[63] While the coalition was 'hammering' the IRA at home, this was not leading to any significant advances in security co-operation in its final years in office.

Early in 1977, the coalition faced the issue that would define its term in many ways. Allegations of Garda brutality had been made for several years. Republican publications documented such incidents on a weekly basis.[64] It was easy for those in power to dismiss this as propaganda, but a series of articles produced in *The Irish Times* made the allegations harder to refute. The strongly worded editorial commented that 'The most important question to be answered in connection with the ill treatment of persons in Garda custody is to what extent if any it has been condoned or ignored by people in authority over the force.'[65]

In Chapter 4, it was noted that Conor Cruise O'Brien was aware of the use of force by Gardaí in at least one incident. In Garret FitzGerald's own account of the allegations, he notes that both Liam Cosgrave and Paddy Cooney were reluctant to tackle the matter. In Cosgrave's case, the unwillingness stemmed from his 'preoccupation with law and order and protectiveness vis-a-vis the Defence Forces'.[66] At the outset of the general election, Cosgrave pointedly fired a broadside at critics of the Gardaí, implicitly referring to *The Irish Times* and Amnesty International. '[Cosgrave] spoke of a malicious campaign of vilification against the Gardaí of "blow ins" who as far as he was concerned could "blow out or blow up" and of papers that had been associated in the past with the "ascendency of alien administrations".'[67]

For Cosgrave, criticism of state institutions was unacceptable, particularly from those outside traditional nationalist circles. As the election drew closer, the coalition's anti-republican thinking was further evidenced in its unwillingness to yield to republicans on the hunger strike in Portlaoise. Personal animosities were increased as TDs received threats.[68] Political grudges became personal grudges. The combination of the hunger strikes and the emerging story of a 'heavy gang' within the Gardaí came at an inopportune time for the coalition, but the general election was not fought over security policy, Garda brutality or Northern Ireland policy. Prices, unemployment and the economy were the key issues. In a survey in the run-up to polling day in June 1977, only 20 per cent of voters felt security or Northern Ireland were going to be important issues. In contrast, at least 75 per cent of voters believed that employment and inflation would be important issues.[69]

Hibernia magazine profiled each constituency and concluded that the coalition parties would return with seventy-eight seats versus sixty-eight for Fianna Fáil.[70] This view was reinforced by changes to the electoral boundaries that should have favoured their candidates in the capital, but Fianna Fáil ran a much slicker campaign, emphasising Lynch's personal popularity with the slogan 'Bring back Jack'.[71] Opinion polls showed that the financial package proposed by Fianna Fáil resonated with voters, especially plans to abolish rates and motor tax.[72] Those drafting the give-away Fianna Fáil manifesto were of the view that the party would not be elected, hence the extravagant election promises.[73] The coalition had been defined by security and Northern Ireland but this was not what voters were basing their decision on. Fianna Fáil achieved a landslide victory, returning with a twenty-seat majority. Ministers Conor Cruise O'Brien and Paddy Cooney lost their seats. That these two, who were so closely associated with the anti-republican agenda, lost their seats was certainly significant. A simple narrative could be constructed that the coalition was thrown out because of its harsh security policies:

> The brutality with which the electorate treated the coalition in the June 1977 general election and the loss of their seats by Patrick Cooney and Conor Cruise O'Brien, the toughest of the anti Sinn Féin ministers, clearly illustrated the enormity of the opposition generated among the public not only because of the Portlaoise situation, but as a result of their handling of issues and the Donegan–Ó Dálaigh affair and their general attitude towards nationalists.[74]

A more nuanced analysis would conclude that both ministers lost their seats more through neglect of their constituencies than for ideological reasons.[75] O'Brien himself quipped that if there had been a personal vote against him it was not because of his opposition to terrorism but because of the dire state of the Irish telephone system.[76] On the republican side, there was no breakthrough. In Donegal, Blaney had to content himself with finishing second in the poll. The wave of Blaney candidates in border constituencies, predicted in the months preceding the election, never materialised, nor did Blaney's hopes of holding the balance of power.[77] The border constituencies had gone from five three-seat constituencies to two five-seat constituencies and a four-seat constituency. Bucking the trend of the rest of the country, Fianna Fáil dropped a seat to eight, with the coalition winning five and Blaney the other.[78] In Donegal, Fianna Fáil had the endorsement of the Donegal Progressive Party, which claimed to represent the bulk of the county's Protestant voters.[79]

The transfer of power had a less dramatic impact on Anglo-Irish and security policy than imagined. Prior to the change of government, Sean Donlon conveyed to British officials his view that a Lynch-led government would not make changes to security policy.[80] After Lynch made a contentious comment on Northern Ireland, Fianna Fáil press officer Frank Dunlop assured Ambassador Haydon in June that 'Mr Lynch had not intended to give prominence to the Northern Ireland problem. He recognised that this was a dangerous area and he would move cautiously. In any case as far as Dunlop was aware, Mr Lynch had no ideas in mind for an initiative on Northern Ireland.'[81]

The early indications, according to British Ambassador Haydon, were good; procedures for handling contentious issues such as overflights and incursions remained the same as before. However, it was noted that officials were slightly more cautious about departing from the norm and felt the need to refer upwards before agreeing to changes in procedure. Presciently, Haydon concluded that 'there will be press skirmishes with this government as with the last'.[82] When Lynch first met UK Prime Minister Jim Callaghan in London in September 1977, the official communiqué stated that the British were satisfied with the continuing level of cross-border co-operation. It is hard to disagree with *Hibernia*'s caustic editorial on the Callaghan–Lynch meeting:

> Lynch overtly wants a 'British commitment to implement an ordered withdrawal from their involvement in the six counties', but he has shown no signs that he is ready, willing or able to face the consequences of that fundamental step. And so the leaders go their paces. The media report the minute details of their irrelevant routine, and of course, nothing of substance transpires.[83]

The Irish minutes of the meeting noted that Callaghan was 'extremely impressed by security cooperation',[84] but privately the prime minister recorded that he was not satisfied that Lynch was taking the need for cross-border security co-operation sufficiently seriously.[85]

On the political front, the size of Lynch's majority perversely proved an area of weakness. The cabinet appointed was somewhat stale, with *Hibernia* headlining a profile piece 'Little Cabinet talent'.[86] The British embassy's assessment of the cabinet is interesting. Gerry Collins got the sensitive Justice post. Seen as a Lynch loyalist, he had conducted extensive background research, travelling the country weeding out dissidents in the build-up to the 1971 Ard Fheis. Bobby Molloy got the other security portfolio in Defence. Despite some speculation about his republican tendencies, Fianna Fáil press secretary Frank Dunlop privately reassured the British about Molloy's loyalties. The new Minister for Foreign Affairs, Michael O'Kennedy, was seen as part-author of Fianna Fáil's unity policy of 1975 and was hence considered by the embassy 'a liability on Northern Ireland'.[87] Haughey returned as Minister for Health.

Haughey would succeed Lynch in 1979 after relentlessly politicking in the background. In opposition, Haughey had built up support at *cumman* level. As the new Dáil met, he worked on building a base at parliamentary party level. Frank Dunlop estimated prior to the election that of the sixty-five outgoing TDs only fifteen would support Haughey for the leadership.[88] The crop of 1977 TDs was to prove vital to Haughey's succession plans.[89] Future Taoiseach Bertie Ahern was one of the fresh intake of TDs. Ahern claimed Jack Lynch never spoke to him once after the election. In contrast, Haughey 'could not have been more different ... always careful to court the backbenchers'.[90] Haughey was reported to have quipped 'They're all mine!' when welcoming the new deputies.[91] It should be emphasised that the republicanism of the new TDs loyal to Haughey was of a different hue than the 1969 cabinet. Of the old-school republicans, only Dr Bill Loughnane and Frank Gallagher remained. [92]

The new government enjoyed an initial honeymoon period. The opposition, meanwhile, regrouped with new leaders in Fine Gael and Labour, Garret FitzGerald and Frank Cluskey, respectively. An opinion poll in October showed that 70 per cent of the electorate was generally happy with the new government. Significantly, the two areas where the coalition was seen as more popular were security and Northern Ireland.[93]

An area of potential weakness for the new government was therefore security and the opposition were keen to exploit this. Paddy Cooney, now a senator, set an early marker in this regard, alleging that the government was showing signs of going 'soft' on the IRA. Cooney advised that 'the only way to defeat terrorism is to let the terrorist and his fellow travellers know that they stand condemned totally'.[94] With allegations of Garda brutality, Fianna Fáil faced a difficult balancing act on the security front. This was compounded by the fact that it was widely believed that the votes of large numbers of Gardaí and their families had helped it return to power.[95] A Commission of Inquiry into Garda Brutality was set up, but the hearings of the commission would not be held in public and it would not have the standing of a full judicial inquiry.[96] It seems this was a victory for the Department of Justice, which feared the impact of public hearings on Garda morale.[97] The bulk of the commission's findings were not implemented. The decision to hold an inquiry at all went against the view of Garda Commissioner Garvey.[98]

The Commissioner and new government had been uneasy bedfellows. One Fianna Fáil TD had noted that TDs were 'fed up with Gardaí in their constituencies coming into their clinics every weekend complaining about Garvey and his modus operandi'.[99] Garvey was an arch-disciplinarian, seen as setting unrealistic targets. The Commissioner shared some of Cooney's concerns about the new government. He told the British Ambassador that prison conditions were too lenient, that Gardaí were not getting the support they deserved and that Fianna Fáil contained too many republican sympathisers.[100] Animosity between Garvey and Collins would eventually result in the government sacking the Commissioner. Problems in the fingerprint unit of the Gardaí, the ongoing allegations of ill treatment of prisoners and the attempted prosecution of the editors of *Garda Review* all contributed to Garvey's demise.[101]

The *Garda Review* prosecution was a particularly bizarre illustration of the draconian discipline in the force. The Commissioner had approached the Director of Public Prosecutions with a view to prosecuting the editorial board of *Garda Review* in 1976 after the publication of a controversial editorial.[102] The desire for uniformed Gardaí to issue 200 summonses a year was seen as a similarly impractical and counterproductive proposal.[103] The Garda Representative Body had given Collins a six-page document, offering reasons for dismissing the Commissioner in December 1977, which further illustrated the depth of Garvey's unpopularity.[104] The immediate cause of Garvey's dismissal, however, seems to have been a dispute over promotions. According to British Ambassador Haydon, who had a good relationship with Garvey, the Commissioner submitted names for promotion to Collins. The minister was not happy and requested Garvey to resubmit the list. Garvey obliged but made no changes to the list.[105] In light of the traditional role of party patronage in such promotions, it is easy to see it as a cause of conflict. That the Commissioner enjoyed such a close relationship with the British Ambassador that he would share such information is of itself interesting. The British were reassured by Seán Donlon in the Department of Foreign Affairs that the sacking would have 'absolutely no implications' for existing North/South security co-operation.[106]

The sacking of Garvey had a surprisingly limited political impact and was overshadowed by a diplomatic row that had erupted between the two governments over border security. A combination of factors made early 1978 a timely occasion for the British to increase pressure on the Irish government on the security front. The rise in armed robberies and attacks on Gardaí in Donegal made security a priority domestically, and,while violence in the North was declining generally, attacks in border areas accounted for a greater number of British Army/RUC casualties. The first public sign of discord came after Jack Lynch, in a lengthy radio interview, reiterated Fianna Fáil's policy, calling for a British withdrawal, and hinted at the possibility of an amnesty in the event of a IRA ceasefire.[107]

Both opposition parties seized on Lynch's amnesty remarks. Garret FitzGerald warned that statements of this kind could seem like 'a license to commit further crimes of armed robbery with impunity'. Labour leader Frank Cluskey claimed it was 'the biggest boost for the morale the IRA godfathers could have hoped for'.[108] With armed robberies at record levels, it was domestically a political faux pas, giving the opposition leverage in area where Fianna Fáil was weak. Northern Ireland Secretary of State Roy Mason issued a statement unusually strong in tone, saying he was 'surprised and disappointed by the unhelpful comments'.[109] Mason's rebuttal further implied weakness on security, which annoyed the Irish cabinet.[110] Lynch in turn replied by explicitly drawing attention to the joint communiqué following the summit with Callaghan, when satisfaction with security arrangements had been expressed.[111]

At the Fianna Fáil Ard Fheis, the dispute worsened when Jack Lynch cited a contentious figure that only 2 per cent of violent incidents in Northern Ireland had a border dimension.[112] Again Mason publicly rebuked the Taoiseach, claiming he disagreed 'absolutely and fundamentally' with this 'paltry figure'.[113] Mason's comments came in the aftermath of one of the worst atrocities of the Troubles, the La Mon hotel bombing that claimed twelve lives. Mason further alleged that La Mon bombers had probably escaped to the Republic.[114] The Gardaí had been informed that one of the La Mon suspects was in the South and they were also told to be on the lookout for another individual but not informed of the suspect's alleged association with the La Mon attack.[115]

A spate of stories also appeared in the media about the use of the border by the IRA. The *Belfast Newsletter* linked the South with the arrival of M60 machine guns. The British had intelligence but no evidence to support this claim.[116] Another story labelled 'Dundalk Murder HQ'.[117] The British embassy itself seemed displeased: 'We have no prospect of converting the Irish to our view while allegations appear in the press without reliable corroboration being offered in private. Conspicuous examples of how this can go wrong are the M60 reports and the implication the La Mon murderers took refuge in the Republic.'[118] The opposition, notably Garret FitzGerald, weighed in strongly – on the government's side this time.[119] For any southern politician, it was a political no-brainer. The British government was criticising the Irish security forces. Any rebuttal of this would involve praising the Irish security forces and attacking the British government, both of which were politically profitable for any aspiring Irish politician.

Behind the headlines, an exchange of documents between the two governments further contaminated the diplomatic landscape. A document entitled *The Use of the Border by the Provisional IRA* was presented to the Department of Foreign Affairs on 6 March 1978. According to Irish officials, this dossier 'made a number of sweeping assertions alleging large scale use of the border by those involved in violence in Northern Ireland'.[120] The document highlighted the South's role as a base for republican leaders, as well as short-range and long-range cross-border attacks. The cases of specific individuals were highlighted as examples of republicans using the South as a safe haven. The Department of Foreign Affairs replied with a strongly worded retort on 14 March, alleging that the British paper was based on 'isolated incidents' and was largely 'unsubstantiated'.[121] It was further claimed that much of the trouble was due to British forces effectively withdrawing from the border:

> There is a constant Garda/Army presence in and intensive patrolling of border areas, this unfortunately not matched by a corresponding presence on the Northern side. The border has two sides: if the RUC wish to interview certain suspected persons it is at least as easy to apprehend them on one side of the border as the other.[122]

The relationship was repaired, to an extent, when Lynch met Callaghan informally at an EEC summit in Copenhagen. Lynch voiced his disapproval of the media briefings given by British Army officers. The meeting ended on a positive note, with both sides agreeing to 'talk privately when things went wrong instead of shouting publicly'.[123] Further smoothing in relations took place when Mason visited Dublin in May, but the usual tetchy moments punctuated the meetings.[124]

The public bickering had a positive side effect from a British perspective. Fianna Fáil was still not fully trusted. The fear from the British perspective was that Gardaí/soldiers on border duty would sense equivocation on the part of their masters. Reports to this effect were coming from border RUC stations. The Northern Ireland Office had also identified that:

> Most members of the Garda appear to be genuinely keen both to cooperate with the RUC and to crack down on the IRA on their side of the border – though even those who are keen are fairly slow to adapt their techniques to accord with modern police methods. But their enthusiasm is easily dissipated by any suspicion that they are acting more vigorously than their government would really wish them to.[125]

Therefore, by putting pressure on the Irish side, Fianna Fáil ministers, particularly those with a security brief, had to come out in a very unambiguous way against the IRA. P.J. Goulden in the British embassy similarly explained to government press secretary Frank Dunlop the British strategy in criticising Irish security: 'many who knew the Garda and their history saw them as a politically sensitive force who might well look over their shoulder to make sure that they were in line with new Ministers'.[126]

British Ambassador Haydon's observations on the fallout of the bickering in the first half of 1978 are worth noting:

> We have to recognise that Messers O'Kennedy and Collins are not as cooperative or basically so able and understanding as Dr Fitzgerald and Mr Cooney were. We also have to recognise that Mr Mason is going through the same stage of unpopularity in the Republic as his predecessors at the same stage in their terms of office. It is doubly tempting, therefore, for Irish Ministers to promote the impression that they have defended Irish interests robustly and told Mr Mason a few home truths ... So far as practical North/South security cooperation on the ground is concerned the omens are mixed but on the whole satisfactory. In the public sphere, however, the best we can hope for in the remainder of 1978 is a low key relationship and a civilised agreement to differ on the issue of Irish unity.[127]

The British took a less confrontational approach in September 1978 when they submitted a new dossier entitled *Cross Border Security*, which was adjudged 'considerably less offensive'.[128] With this more conciliatory tone, the Irish side was willing to demonstrate more flexibility. The British continued to demand greater access to the Department of Justice for face-to-face meetings. While resisting such a move, Hugh Swift in Foreign Affairs pointed out that the cross-border Explosives Cooperation Group had previously contained Department of Justice officials. This group, he claimed, had on at least one other occasion gone beyond its remit into other areas of security and this flexibility could be shown again.[129] Haydon in the British embassy picked up on Swift's hint regarding the explosives committee and noted that he was 'more than ever convinced that we are unlikely to succeed in this [security co-operation] if we appear to press for something which could develop into a structural innovation'.[130]

As the two governments continued to wrangle over security, Machiavellian moves for the Fianna Fáil party leadership incentivised the Taoiseach to keep co-operation discreet and unstructured. This discreet aspect of co-operation partially contributed to Lynch's eventual exit from office. Controversies over permission given to British planes to overfly the border, coupled with unease among backbenchers over security co-operation, led to Lynch being replaced by Haughey in 1979.[131]

For the period under consideration, therefore, Lynch adopted security policy strategies that had served preceding governments well. Co-operation with security forces over the border was to take place, but an emphasis was put on discretion. The sensitivity of Irish political figures to overt co-operation with the British remained just as great as in 1971 while the British felt that the lingering colonial legacy meant any implied criticism from them had a disproportionate effect. The brief for the incoming Secretary of State for Northern Ireland in 1979 warned that 'Irish history, republican mythology, partition and economic weakness have left the Irish with something of a political inferiority complex – a sensitivity to slight, a readiness to take umbrage, a tendency to blame the British for everything.'[132] None of these factors, however, were to inhibit the Irish state from hammering the IRA in its own way for its own reasons. For a Garda on duty on the border, there would be political support for taking strong action against the IRA but not necessarily for being seen to help the British do likewise. As a wily political campaigner, the new Fianna Fáil leader Charles Haughey understood this better than most.

Garda and Army: An Evaluation

The years 1976–8 would be among the most controversial in the history of the Irish security forces. They became synonymous with allegations of a 'heavy gang' operating within the Gardaí. Crime of the non-subversive kind became more prevalent, with the number of indictable crimes increasing from 30,756 in 1970 to 63,000 in 1977. There were only 11 armed robberies in 1970 but 298 in 1977.[133] As much as 70 per cent of armed robberies had nothing to do with subversives, according to a senior Garda.[134] When the £220,000 was stolen from a train in Sallins, Co. Kildare, in the state's largest ever robbery, Fianna Fáil Justice spokesman Gerry Collins accused the government of 'gross negligence and total failure in the maintenance of law and order'.[135] There was serious pressure on the Gardaí politically to achieve results in this case particularly. The investigation would end with serious allegations of Garda malpractice and a miscarriage of justice.

Despite the rise in crime, the primary focus of the Gardaí remained tackling the IRA. In the highly controversial editorial mentioned earlier in the chapter, the *Garda Review* warned that

> The government, the Department of Justice and Garda authorities believe quite rightly that the defeat of subversion is today the primary task of the Garda. None of us quarrel with that. But it should not be the only task. And we say more in sorrow than in anger that the government has forgotten that there are other tasks. What will it profit the Irish people if having defeated the IRA we find that the masters of our towns and cities and countryside are a new generation of professional and brutal criminals.[136]

Commissioner Garvey attempted to prosecute the authors of the editorial. Yet the significance of the magazine of the rank and file of the force issuing such a statement cannot be understated. The war on the IRA by the state was being conducted to the detriment of normal policing, according to those at the cutting edge.

The mutual antipathy between Gardaí and republicans had continued to escalate as the Troubles progressed. Of course, individual exceptions to this did emerge. One Garda was suspended for attending a public demonstration after Frank Stagg's death.[137] Meanwhile, after an IRA informer, John Lawlor, was shot dead in a Dublin pub, a Garda was arrested. The Garda had passed internal circulars known as *Fogra Tora* to the dead republican but the Garda's motivation seems to have been more related to his own mental health problems rather than any republican sympathy.[138] A former IRA Director of Intelligence recently hinted at individual support for the republican cause at higher levels:

> I think that the [IRA] Army Council had particular contacts with those in the security area which weren't even shared with me. We had contacts in the law offices of the State and contacts in the upper echelons of the guards. Take something like Feakle [where IRA leaders engaged in peace talks with clergy avoided a Special Branch raid]; the place was raided and they [the IRA leadership] got away. Because a tip-off was received that the Special Branch were on their way to Feakle and that tip-off came from within the

Garda … It wasn't just in 1974 and it wasn't just concentrated in border areas like Dundalk, it was some individuals but it was more widespread. [139]

The possibility of leaks from the Garda side meant that at one of the first Joint Coordinating Committee meetings with the RUC, Garda representatives stated that they did not want to co-ordinate plans for operations beyond a daily basis as 'they expressed some concern about their own security and that possible ambushes could be set up if proposed plans became known to terrorist organisations'.[140] It was noted in the previous chapter that the British Army was similarly reluctant to have joint operations included on the agenda for the bi-monthly Joint Coordinating Committee meetings because of fears over the security of information in the hands of Gardaí.[141] Goulden in the British embassy downplayed any support for the republican cause among Gardaí:

A small minority may be republican sympathisers. Others who do not share the views may nonetheless feel the need for a modus vivendi with the PIRA in areas which are strongly republican. But our impression is that these too are a small minority. The bulk of the forces are in varying degrees hostile to PIRA, who after all killed some of their colleagues and are one of their priority targets.[142]

While there were certainly incidents of collusion with republicans, the broad thrust of relations between Gardaí and republicans continued to be antagonistic. This was particularly true when it came to Garda Special Branch as Kieran Conway, the former IRA Director of Intelligence, recounts:

The Branch were a tough bunch who had been unleashed by their political masters and hated us with a vengeance, and it was no surprise to me that when they started beating up prisoners. Mind you, there were two of us in it, and when having left the IRA later that year, I came back in 1981 to find my old intelligence files intact, I was horrified to see how much time we had spent tracking the Special Branch rather than simply keeping out of their way.[143]

When Garda Clerkin was killed in what seemed like a premeditated ambush in 1976, feelings in the Gardaí were especially raw. One investigating Garda recalled: 'The IRA issued a statement denying involvement but we knew they were only trying to worm out with weasel words ... This was a cold calculated murder and it was sanctioned at the very highest levels by the Provisional Army Council.'[144]

While the earlier killings of Gardas Dick Fallon and Michael Reynolds could be explained by republicans as tragic errors or the work of mavericks, Clerkin's killing was generally seen as a direct IRA attack on the force. Unlike in the North, however, such attacks on Gardaí never became normalised. One Garda in later years remembered

> a different situation, it was so common there [in the North] that people just expected it every week that there would be another one killed ... it was a different feeling here, we didn't in general, it wasn't, it didn't feel like it was going to happen that much, because we were an unarmed force and we didn't, we weren't a great threat to anyone. We just went out with two arms one as long as the other as you say.[145]

As well as fatal shootings, there were non-fatal shooting incidents involving Gardaí and republicans. While no figures exist to indicate the number of Gardaí injured or shot at by republicans, analysis of newspaper archives for 1976–9 indicates that these were a not infrequent occurrence.[146] Locally, the impact of a non-fatal attack on Gardaí could have significance unappreciated nationally. In Monaghan, *The Northern Standard* often editorialised endorsing republican views,[147] but the tone of its editorial changed after an attack on local Gardaí:

> But for divine providence two or more of the Gardaí so viciously attacked by gunmen in the Scotstown area on Friday night last might have been killed. There is no doubt that this was a potentially lethal attack on unarmed Gardaí nor is there any doubt that the attackers were in doubt that it was a Garda uniformed branch and therefore unarmed ... the seriousness of this reckless and dastardly action cannot be overemphasised and it has to be hoped that it doesn't represent a change of policy on the part of republican activists.[148]

Aside from shootings, there was also the ongoing conflict between Gardaí and republicans at checkpoints, protests and house searches. One Garda stationed along the border described his experience of policing protests: 'They came down from the North to Monaghan … they were quite nasty. Not the local people, but the northern element that came down were quite nasty. And they were just looking for trouble … And they were very abusive as well. They would call you all the names under the sun.'[149]

A fascinating article in the republican paper *An Phoblacht* dealt with relations between Gardaí and protestors. The piece encouraged republican protestors to avoid both verbal and physical attacks on Gardaí. Presciently, the article warned that the net outcome of 'sneers, catcalls, barrages of abuse, jeers' was to indoctrinate Gardaí in an anti-republican mentality:

> Being ordinary chaps, mostly, the police and troops will dislike this intensely and as they stand there not permitted to reply in kind they will begin to burn in anger towards republicans in general. They will long for the day when they can get their own back by sneering at Republicans, by crushing their skulls and tearing them limb from limb.[150]

It seems that on at least some occasions this is precisely what happened in Garda custody. Republican propaganda had for several years alleged Garda maltreatment of suspects. Articles in *An Phoblacht* repeatedly made serious allegations against Gardaí.[151] The source of complaints meant they were dismissed by Gardaí in the same way as government ministers had. One Garda reflected:

> There were lots of vindictive vexatious complaints that were just being used as a plea bargaining tool by criminals. We found in searches Provisional IRA circulars which instructed that every time someone was arrested they were not to leave without making a complaint. This would completely clog up the system but it was part of their duty. They would then turn around in court and bring it up arguing 'he saw fit to make a complaint'.[152]

Publications such as *Hibernia* raised the issue, but they too were similarly dismissed by *Garda Review* as having 'ideological bias'.[153] The political climate of the time, whereby the battle with the IRA was pitched in absolute moral terms, meant that those highlighting human rights abuses could be discounted. The *Irish Times* articles in February 1977 identified a 'heavy gang' comprising plain-clothes detectives in the Technical Bureau. It alleged 'the change from the more traditional methods of painstaking detective work to the use of brutal interrogation methods to secure convictions appears to have developed in response to political pressure to get results'.[154] Internally, there were many in the force concerned about the abuse of suspects. It does seem that the revelations of a 'heavy gang', initially at least, divided the force.[155] Thirteen retired Gardaí contributing to a recent study acknowledged the existence of a 'heavy gang' and most were uncomfortable with its existence. One retired member noted that 'There would have been a lot of fear I suppose and the need to get results but, I mean it is hard to justify anything like that. To my mind, you do something like that, you're no better than the "crim" [Criminal] … in fact you're worse than the criminal because you are supposed to know different.'[156]

Individual members did take steps to stop maltreatment[157] but the black-and-white approach to republican violence meant that those opposed to the 'heavy gang' were limited in what they could do. After a Garda was shot, for instance, one member of the force reported in court how he had heard screams from within the station where a suspect was being held.[158] Despite this evidence, the Special Criminal Court rejected allegations of brutality against Gardaí.[159] The Garda reporting the screams was apparently 'sent to Coventry' by his colleagues.[160] Similarly when a mistake was made in the investigation into the assassination of Ewart Biggs, the two Garda officers in the fingerprint division who were, in modern parlance, 'whistleblowers' were victimised while those responsible were promoted.[161]

The force emerged from the 'heavy gang' scandal remarkably united and public support remained high. Both politicians and to a certain extent the general populace were aware of the mistreatment of suspects and were to some degree willing to accept it in the context of the ongoing violence. Vicky Conway in *Policing Twentieth Century Ireland* suggests that

> The Gardaí escaped the demolition ball for one reason: the Northern Irish conflict. Just as other institutions were falling apart, Gardaí were being asked to defend the nation, all that had

been built up over the previous 50 years ... In the very moment when the nationalist image fell apart in general, the Gardaí were reasserting their nationalism, risking and losing their lives for the Irish state, thereby retaining the confidence and authority that had been based on such imagery.[162]

When the government changed and there was an opportunity to institutionally reform the Gardaí, the Fianna Fáil government did not implement the recommendations of the Ó Briain Commission, which investigated treatment of suspects.[163] The *Garda Review* had warned that the implementation of Ó Briain report would 'prove a boon for the well up criminal who plays the system in order to remain "innocent" in the eyes of the law'.[164] Notably, the right to have a solicitor present during questioning was not introduced. In terms of personnel, the 'heavy gang' allegations had no impact on the individuals allegedly involved. *Magill* magazine reported that of the nineteen Gardaí against whom high-profile allegations were made in respect of the Sallins train robbery investigation, eight had been promoted, some to senior positions.[165]

Nonetheless, the new minister did take some steps to address concerns about indiscipline. According to the British embassy in Dublin, Collins

suspended the provisions for Gardaí to hold suspects for seven days. He has installed a more sensitive Garda Commissioner, who has reorganised the technical bureau and disbanded the "heavy gang". Perhaps most important of all, he has passed the word to Garda that no grounds must be offered for complaints of physical ill treatment.[166]

These changes had an effect. Allegations of Garda brutality received less prominence but did not disappear.[167] That fresh allegations emerged is unsurprising as there were no changes in institutional practice or personnel. In Monaghan, a fresh controversy emerged in 1978 and gained some national prominence.[168] A local priest with republican tendencies, Father Joe McVeigh, claimed that prisoners were being assaulted in Garda custody. The investigation into Garda malpractice again led to no changes in personnel within the force.[169] An interesting aspect of McVeigh's account of the related events was his recollection of the reaction of at least a section of the community to his allegations:

> The response to the appeal for the Gardaí to stop beating those in custody was unbelievable. I suppose I could say what I liked about the north and about the RUC but I soon discovered that criticism of the Gardaí was not tolerated in this close knit community in the twenty six counties. A large number of Gardaí lived in Monaghan and many were married into Monaghan families. After mass I was verbally attacked by one woman who told me I was a disgrace for bringing such matters into the pulpit. ... the local Gardaí 'downed tools' and refused to direct traffic in Monaghan town after masses ... the Gardaí also refused to pay at church collections.[170]

The Ó Briain commission found that about 80 per cent of convictions for serious crimes were based on confessions.[171] Areas such as intelligence gathering and computerisation were especially weak so there was pressure on interrogators to get a confession. Conor Brady, writing in *The Irish Times*, noted that 'Many armed robberies are no longer investigated in any meaningful way. Unless a suspect can be named, most of the groundwork which is theoretically associated with serious crime will be dropped.'[172]

Frank Dunlop of Fianna Fáil told the British embassy that the Garda's response to crime is 'interrogatory rather than investigatory' and that there was no prospect that they will beat the present crime wave by 'forensic or kid glove methods'.[173] Just as in previous years, there was no effort to modernise or change Garda methods. One veteran detective inspector told *The Irish Times*:

> We have no planning of any kind for the future. We have no ideas at all for improving our performance ... Do you know that after nearly a thousand armed robberies in five years there are still no basic instructions to Gardaí about handling them. Do you race in and get yourself shot? Do you follow and call for assistance? Or if you happen to have a gun, do you shoot the f******?[174]

A Department of Finance Memorandum was critical of the approach whereby numbers in the force were continually increased without accompanying organisational change.[175] Cooney in the Department of Justice's reply to this memo illustrates the tensions that existed between the respective departments:

> [The Memorandum's] tone is offensive. Its content is an amalgam of lecture to the Department of Justice and a line of argument so tedious as to be unworthy of a government department. It is as if people responsible for its compilation feel themselves under such pressure to suggest savings in public expenditure that they resort to any kind of argument in order to show that they are doing something and that the blame lies elsewhere.[176]

The area of intelligence gathering was one organisational aspect of the Gardaí that required particular attention. The RUC Chief Constable had raised with the Garda Commissioner the necessity of having a dedicated group to collate intelligence, as well as a separate unit capable of carrying high-quality continuous surveillance as late as 1979.[177] These recommendations accompanied requests for a task force to be sent by the Gardaí to the border. It is perhaps unsurprising that in the context of Anglo-Irish relations changes to Garda practice were not initiated at the behest of the RUC, but the Finlay Commission in 1974 identified similar intelligence failings. The Garda's C3 (Intelligence) Branch, theoretically responsible for collating intelligence, had in 1970 opened 55 new files; in 1971 that number had risen to 89 new files; in 1972 the number of new files opened was 1,595; and in 1973 the number of new files was 1,575. The rise in workload did not lead to a corresponding rise in manpower. The Finlay Report stated that, as of February 1974, 'the manpower and resources available to the Garda Síochána for intelligence gathering were inadequate'.[178] Although the Finlay report was never made public, media accounts corroborate its findings. *The Irish Times* reported:

> Many Gardaí do pass on the information. But many do not. Some find that it is so difficult to get through on the couple of phone lines [to the Criminal Intelligence Department] that they give up in despair. Others, who find they cannot get information OUT of that unit when they want it, decide they won't cooperate anyway.[179]

Obviously, computerisation would have been central to any improvement in the area of intelligence collation, but a Dublin-based sergeant lamented in 1978:

I get a pain in my head listening to Gerry Collins [Minister for Justice] on RTE about the wonderful equipment and all the men we have ... I suppose he means the radios. But that's about all. We have none of the crime aids which computerisation has put at the disposal of police forces elsewhere. There isn't even the beginning of a decent system of communicating information through the force.[180]

Aside from technology, low levels of pay remained an issue for the force. On average, overtime amounted to £1,000 per officer per annum.[181] There was reliance within the force on this overtime to supplement basic pay and this created significant problems because it meant individual Garda's take-home pay was very much dependent on getting on with their superiors, i.e. those organising the lucrative overtime roster. 'For management overtime was a disaster. It made people mercenaries. It created jealousies.'[182]

In terms of cross-border co-operation, the procedures established under the Baldonnel panels continued to develop. The Chief Constable and Commissioner met at bi-monthly intervals. The Joint Coordinating Committee involving divisional commandeers similarly met bi-monthly. Meanwhile, a designated group of 'border superintendents' met at quarterly intervals. These border superintendents met more often informally too. Contact between other low-ranking officers took place on a daily basis.[183] A well-informed *Irish Times* article on the subject in 1979 reported that

Quite apart from Joint Coordinating Committee meetings, Garda and RUC men occasionally make personal contacts on the border, sometimes on the border, sometimes on concession roads, sometimes when the Gardaí give a covering presence to an RUC search just north of the border. Some individual officers have struck up cordial relations, especially in Special Branch though most Gardaí keep their distance to avoid any local accusations of collaboration. 'No one will give us an earful if they believe we are passing it all on to the RUC' said one Garda Superintendent.[184]

In terms of this day-to-day communications, the X-ray radio channel was used. The RUC had twenty-four fixed X-ray installations and the Gardaí nineteen. There was a greater disparity in mobile equipment. The RUC had 121 units for mobile patrol while the Garda had just 11 transportable sets.[185] Part of the reluctance on the part of Gardaí to use X-ray equipment was ascribed to a perceived weakness in the security of units. The X-ray sets were only useful in communicating with neighbouring stations, while for longer-range secure conversation the phone was used. In terms of secure phone lines, the Garda had thirteen Goliath speech security devices in border stations for use in cross-border communication. Two of these devices were in Garda headquarters and the rest scattered along the border.[186] In terms of communications generally, a Foreign Office assessment rated Irish communications 'generally poor'. The Gardaí were seen as being circumspect in their use of the telephone, as were the departments of Justice and Foreign Affairs, although it was felt that 'most government departments and the armed forces use the telephone with little discretion'.[187]

The RUC remained unimpressed with co-operation in certain geographic areas. The RUC Chief Constable was especially unimpressed with Dundalk Gardaí.[188] In the strategically important border station of Aughnacloy, senior RUC officers 'had a feeling since Fianna Fáil had been elected [in 1977] that there was less commitment among Garda to defeat terrorism'.[189] In part, this change was ascribed to the arrival of new senior officers in Monaghan after the sacking of Garvey. Therefore, it is possible that the cooling in co-operation may have been due to lack of familiarity with the workings of a border station rather than any political bias. The RUC officers in Aughnacloy also reported that some Garda officers did not trust the Irish Army as they perceived it to have a 'green streak'.[190] There were reports in the Monaghan and Donegal local media about conflict between the Gardaí and Army. This was in part a result of Garda investigations of public order offences being obstructed by Army authorities.[191] A *Magill* article similarly reported that the Army authorities had shown a worrying willingness to protect its own members, who sometimes appeared before district courts in the border towns of Ballyshannon and Manorhamilton.[192]

Part of an agreed strategy to improve cross-border co-operation was the appointment of 'Border Superintendents' to meet and communicate as frequently as was deemed necessary. These men were to be based in Letterkenny, Monaghan, Dundalk and Manorhamilton on the southern side and Derry, Omagh, Enniskillen, Bessbrook and Dungannon across the border.[193] The workings of this grouping suffered a significant early setback when *Irish Times* journalist Conor O'Clery outlined the extent of cross-border co-operation in a series of articles.[194] O'Clery named the officers from both jurisdictions partaking in Joint Coordinating Committee meetings. Adding to Garda disquiet, O'Clery revealed to the Commissioner that the RUC had disclosed further 'highly sensitive matters' to him.[195] Minister for Foreign Affairs Michael O'Kennedy told the British Ambassador that the leak was 'quite deplorable'.[196] So great was the angst felt by Deputy Commissioner Lawrence Wren that he considered abolishing the entire Joint Coordinating Committee structure before being dissuaded by his opposite number in the RUC.[197]

The views of individual Gardaí still determined to a large extent how much they were willing to co-operate with British forces. A transcript of a meeting between a Garda sergeant and a patrol commander at the border in 1978 is highly illustrative. The Garda met the British commander after reports of a gunman in the area. The sergeant was very helpful and the fact that he engaged with the British soldier is in itself significant. Nonetheless, the thrust of the conversation as recorded by the British commander is illuminating.

> Patrol commander: 'Were you patrolling in the area when I called for you?'
> Sergeant Newell: 'Yes we have two cars patrolling all the time, around Dromad and over the other side.'
> Patrol commander: 'Do you carry weapons?'
> Sergeant Newell: 'No, if we did we would be targets as well.'
> Patrol commander: 'If I came under fire and I needed assistance how long would it take you to arrive?'
> Sergeant Newell: 'If you were under fire we would not come anywhere near you until the firing had stopped.'[198]

The outlook of individual officers and their personal contacts mattered immensely. Between Strabane and Lifford, there were difficulties when RUC Chief Inspector Scully left the area,[199] but this seems to have been a temporary setback as by 1979 co-operation in Donegal was considered 'good and increasingly effective'.[200] On one occasion when Gardaí were searching in the Strabane–Clady area, Gardaí were given a radio by the British Army. This allowed for two-way communication on the scene.[201] Such communication was against official policy. Gardaí in Monaghan town also extended their co-operation to include the British Army. Going against protocol, there was phone co-operation with the British Army billeted in Middletown and battalion headquarters in Armagh.[202]

In 1976, 'all matters requiring cooperation' were completed directly by contact between the Gardaí and the Grenadier Guards posted in Middletown.[203] When detectives based in Monaghan were interviewed in the 1980s about alleged contacts with the British Army, they all denied knowledge. At this stage, the Troubles were ongoing and most of the officers were still serving. The Garda authorities had instigated an internal investigation after former British officer Fred Holroyd's public allegations of unofficial Garda co-operation. This put individual officers in a difficult position. Discreet co-operation had been encouraged, but when it became public after the airing of TV documentaries and newspaper articles, those at ground level had to deal with the fallout. One Garda hinted that if he was made accountable for unauthorised contacts, he would disclose similar transgressions by superiors:

> He [named Monaghan based Garda] said that every Garda officer was involved in the same level of intelligence gathering and anti-subversive activities. He went on to say that he was aware of meetings between British Army Intelligence and high-ranking Garda officers. He did not elaborate, but said that he would use that information if this matter was being pursued, blaming him for something in which he was not involved.[204]

Efforts to foster contact between Gardaí in Castleblayney and RUC in Newtownhamilton were less successful. The Castleblayney sergeant had no contact with the British Army, which was reported to 'contrast strongly with the helpful attitude of Monaghan Gardaí'.[205] It is worth emphasising that the British papers in no way suggested that the sergeant in Castleblayney was pro-republican; rather he was unwilling to bend the rules and engage in dialogue with the British Army. Among the RUC personnel at Newtownhamilton during the period was Sergeant John Weir, himself a native of Castleblayney. Weir would later be convicted of a loyalist murder and was centrally involved in allegations of collusion.[206] Weir claimed that his appointment to the

Newtownhamilton post was due to his links with loyalist paramilitaries. That the sergeant in Castleblayney was circumspect in his contacts in this context is understandable.

The British forces also tried to foster social contact with Gardaí. One senior Garda told a British officer that he would be delighted to come to the barracks for a drink, although the British report wryly observed 'on the three occasions in which the company commander rang, he [the Garda] was out'.[207] Contact with the Irish Army, according to British reports, was minimal and much of it seems to have been less than friendly. That said, it was noted in the previous chapter that in the upper echelons of the military there was more contact, with the Director of Military Intelligence regularly meeting with British intelligence agencies.[208]

There are other reports of Army-to-Army/RUC informal co-operation, including one spectacular account that emerged in the media in recent years of an Irish Army officer joining in a fire fight with the RUC against the IRA deep inside northern territory.[209] On at least one occasion, Irish troops invited British Army personnel over the border to view an IRA firing position and on another occasion Irish security forces requested specialised equipment, known as 'Nitesun' (a powerful searchlight), mounted on a helicopter to cross the border. The British authorities opted not to discuss such occurrences with Irish government officials, presumably because they did not want to highlight unauthorised contact.[210]

The bulk of the evidence in the border reports for the latter half of the 1970s indicates that, at ground level at least, the Irish Army adopted a much stricter approach in dealings with their counterparts over the border. The Army's coldness towards British counterparts did go further on occasion. When a cross-border operation was taking place near the village of Clady, Irish soldiers were described as 'verbally abusive' and tried to entice British troops over the border. Irish officers were reported as being 'rude to the point where it was impossible to hold a useful conversation'.[211]

A covert British observation report of the Irish Army presence at Moybridge on the Monaghan–Tyrone border paints a picture of Irish troops as somewhat dishevelled and undisciplined. It was noted that the Army only stopped cars entering the Republic. The soldiers were described as 'scruffy and unshaven' and 'dislike their tasks and take little interest in them'.[212] It was further noted that there was mutual antagonism with the Gardaí. That the Irish Army was generally less forthcoming in dealings with their British counterparts could create awkward situations for Gardaí. A Department of Foreign Affairs analysis noted that the number of illegal incursions reported by the Irish Army was greater than the number reported by the Gardaí. Concern was expressed that 'a tendency seems to be developing for the Gardaí to regard some incursions as not as serious and hence not bothering to report them'.[213] For the Gardaí, the fact that Army officers reported back on incidents at the border separately, through their own chain of command, may have created distrust.

As noted in previous chapters, the Department of Justice adopted a domineering role when it came to national security. The fact that Foreign Affairs was not kept fully in the loop about incursions is evidence of this.[214] The complexities of interdepartmental difficulties created practical problems for Gardaí in terms of co-operation. Gardaí co-operated directly with the RUC through the Joint Coordinating Committee mechanism, which the Department of Foreign Affairs was excluded from. Meanwhile, the Department of Foreign Affairs was dealing with the Northern Ireland Office and Foreign Office often without full knowledge of the exact details of Garda–RUC co-operation and Joint Coordinating Committee meetings. The complexity of these arrangements caused difficulties.

On one occasion, the Department of Foreign Affairs complained to the British embassy about shots being fired by a British gunboat on Carlingford Lough on 13 July 1976. The incident, which received much local publicity, was also discussed at the Joint Coordinating Committee panel involving the security services at which British minutes recorded Gardaí saying 'there was nothing in it'. When the British chargé d'affaires met the secretary of the Department of Foreign Affairs, he quoted the Garda comment in defence of his case. The reference to the minutes of the Joint Coordinating Committee meeting was seen by Irish officials as a very worrying development. Undoubtedly, such incidents would have made Gardaí circumspect in their disclosures at future meetings with the RUC.[215] Gardaí had to be aware that anything they said to the RUC could end up being used in diplomatic exchanges. For a force that was controlled so centrally politically, the implications of saying the wrong thing at a Joint Coordinating Committee meeting were potentially serious. This may have made it hard for some senior Gardaí to engage with the

RUC frankly. One Garda remembered that even as a young member of the force he was aware of a guarded culture associated with official dealings with the RUC:

> There was professionalism about it, maybe it was because I was young or whatever, but you knew that you were in a delicate place. Even though you might not have known the political implications of it, you knew 'look, I better do this right, if I am talking to some other police force, I had better get it right'. You felt, without being told about it. You know you felt it within yourself, where it came from I don't know. Maybe it was listening to the other lads in the station, but when you were on to the RUC, everything was formal.[216]

The significant role of the Department of Justice in security did not go unnoticed by the British, who tried to foster more direct contacts. As noted earlier, the British continued to push for meetings between security officials from the Department of Justice. Following a meeting with Commissioner Garvey, head of the RUC Kenneth Newman concluded that if 'the Ministry tells Garvey "to jump" he will do so'.[217] The power of Justice officials was brought home to the RUC on another occasion. At a meeting about the Criminal Law Jurisdiction Act, a Garda Chief Superintendent welcomed the notion that RUC officers could interview suspects in Garda custody but a Justice official intervened to rein in the Chief Superintendent and scupper the plan.[218] Whether the Department of Justice opposed this move for political or legal reasons is unclear, but when the issue was raised again some years later, Justice officials noted that statements made in the presence of RUC officers could be ruled inadmissible in Irish courts.[219]

Another aspect of Garda–RUC relations worth considering is the strength of the respective forces along the border. This had emerged as a bone of contention at several political summits during the period.[220] An Irish diplomatic paper had caustically noted 'there is constant Garda/Army presence in and patrolling of border areas; this is unfortunately not matched by a corresponding presence on the Northern side'.[221] A British dossier explained that the British strategy in parts of Fermanagh and Armagh had been 'hold back some distance from the border so that ASUs have to come further into the open to find them'.[222]

The Garda strength along the border between 1975 and 1977 generally ranged between 1,030 and 1,050. Significantly, the strength dipped to 960 by June 1978, despite the overall size of the force increasing by almost 600 nationally in the same period.[223] Therefore, it seems that the new government reduced the Garda's border strength somewhat in its first year. In part, this may have been due to rising crime levels in urban areas.[224] On paper, the British Army/RUC were much greater in number. There were 2,436 full-time British troops within 5km of the border, as well as 1,043 RUC members and 408 part-time UDR members.[225]

A more localised breakdown of these figures highlights a weakness in the British security presence. Table 9 compares the relative strength of Garda versus RUC in terms of numbers at corresponding points along the border. There were slightly more stations on the southern side of the border and the RUC obviously relied on the support of the British Army. A British report concluded that numerical comparisons were misleading due to the 'greater organisational sophistication of the RUC'[226] but, nonetheless, the figures are revealing. Along the South Armagh border, in particular, the stations of Keady, Newtownhamilton, Forkhill and Crossmaglen seemed to be especially lacking in RUC manpower. A similar trend can be seen in other more republican border areas of Fermanagh, notably Roslea and Newtownbutler. In the places where security co-operation was weakest, the RUC presence was most thinly spread. As security co-operation was officially based on Garda–RUC dialogue, it was difficult to establish relations when the RUC presence was so minimal.

As in previous years, any publicity associated with security co-operation was actively discouraged. Even in localised situations, Gardaí were 'more cooperative in their dealings with the RUC when not in public'.[228] The Gardaí on occasion even wanted to keep the Irish Army out of the loop. A British report noted 'RUC/Gardaí relations are cooler when the Irish Army is involved.'[229]

While co-operation was often cited as being 'good' in many border reports, the significance of this should not be overstated. A 1979 Foreign Office review of security is worth quoting at length as it summarises the situation well:

[Gardaí] can nearly always be relied on to respond with vigour in the wake of a murder, but the response is more varied where

Table 9. Garda and RUC manpower in corresponding border stations circa 1977[227]

Town	Garda	Town	RUC
Dundalk	81	Newry	86
Lifford	33	Strabane	52
Carrickmacross	39	Crossmaglen	8
Clontibret	7	Keady	11
Castleblayney	32	Newtownhamilton	13
Hackballscross	21	Forkhill	9
Scotstown	33	Roslea	12
Emyvale	22	Aughnacloy	13
Blacklion	37	Belcoo	10
Pettigo	29	Belleek	13
Clones	38	Newtownbutler	11
Swanlinbar	32	Kinawley	11
Castlefinn	25	Castlederg	27
Dowra	23	Derrygonnelly	4

the request for assistance does not stem from such dramatic circumstances. The greatest variation occurs when no specific cooperation has been requested by the RUC, and when it is entirely up to the Garda how zealous they are in identifying terrorist activity, or taking action against it. In this last case, the extremes are again best illustrated by current experience in Donegal, where the Garda have several times recently shown great determination to obstruct and apprehend terrorists, while in county Monaghan their determination has been far less evident.[230]

There were other factors aside from obvious legal and political obstacles to co-operation. The colonial legacy still had an impact. In the midst of a heated discussion, Sean O'Higgins from the Department of Foreign Affairs told P.J. Goulden from the British embassy that the British regarded 'the Garda and the Irish Army as "lesser breeds"'.[231] If a senior diplomat voiced such views in 1978, it is likely that those operating at ground level felt similarly.

Donegal seems to have been the area where co-operation was at its best. Donegal was traditionally a good recruiting ground for Gardaí. As a Garda from Kerry, who served in Donegal, reflected in an interview with the 'Green and Blue' project on this aspect of policing,

> I discovered very quickly that there were an awful lot of parents in the Burnfoot, Buncrana and Muff area who had sons in the Guards, in different parts of the country themselves. Once you got to know those, they were kind of a rung on the ladder to get to know the locality a little bit better.[232]

The combination of families with Garda connections coupled with a significant Protestant population in areas may have meant greater general levels of support for Gardaí. In electoral terms, the Protestant vote was important in Donegal, making security an added political priority. An increased level of republican activity in Donegal in 1977 would also have given security co-operation an added impetus. The IRA presence was also stronger and better organised in Monaghan and Louth than in Donegal and there was awareness among Gardaí of the allegations of collusion associated with members of the RUC in South Armagh, particularly those associated with the Special Patrol Group. A senior Garda investigating the bombing of Dundalk in 1975 told an Oireachtas hearing that he was aware of collusion involving a group of RUC/UDR, known as the Glenanne gang and that this information was provided to Garda intelligence C3. Garda Commissioner Noel Conroy would further state that the names of members of the Glenanne gang would have been known to members of the Garda in border areas at the time.[233] Therefore, that a local Garda in somewhere like Castleblayney or Dundalk was reluctant to co-operate with his opposite number over the border is unsurprising in the context of such allegations.

The Security Situation in the Southern Border Counties, 1976–8

Levels of violence generally in Northern Ireland had declined considerably by 1978. There were 88 Troubles-related deaths in 1978 compared to 220 in 1976.[234] Nonetheless, many of the issues identified in earlier chapters persisted along the border. There were numerous shooting incidents involving Gardaí and republicans.[235] There was also, as in previous years, violence between Gardaí and republicans at political gatherings.[236] Loyalist attacks in the Republic continued to pose a threat. Border incursions also continued to cause controversy. Meanwhile, the experience of the Protestant community south of the border continued to be complex. Although 1978 saw the return of an Orange parade to Rossnowlagh in Donegal,[237] the Orange Order presence was still contentious, with reports of minor attacks on Orangemen returning from parades.[238] Therefore, there remained a series of significant fissures in border communities based on religious and political cleavages.

The IRA was in something of a flux during the period and this contributed to its increasing willingness to engage in military actions south of the border, such as the dramatic escape from the Special Criminal Court[239] and Ewart Biggs' assassination.[240] It has also been noted that Garda/Army officers were to be classified as 'legitimate targets' if they were active in Northern Ireland.[241] An Irish Army intelligence briefing in 1977 noted:

> We are convinced now that the IRA prohibition on attacks against institutions of the Republic no longer has any force. Indeed, it is to be expected that Army and Gardaí will be singled out for attack. There is clear evidence of PIRA gathering information on military posts-strengths, dispositions, procedures etc and attempts to subvert soldiers and to get PIRA men recruited into the forces.[242]

In the second half of 1976, there were several shooting incidents and hijackings of Garda cars along the length of the border.[243] The threat to state forces became more real on 16 October 1976 when a young Garda, Michael Clerkin, was killed in a booby trap bombing that injured four of his colleagues in Mountmellick, Co. Laois. The Gardaí were lured to the scene in the type of ambush scenario that was common in Northern Ireland. The killing caused widespread revulsion. The premeditated nature of the attack impacted on Garda colleagues particularly. A Garda stationed in the same area who also knew the victim told the 'Green and Blue' oral history project that

> this was another, another indication of just how callous those who said they were fighting for Irish freedom were, because, and this is one of the incidents where hands cannot be washed as to an

accidental killing that just happened because someone was in the wrong place at the wrong time. That cannot be put in this case because the information was given to lure the Guards to that location and the bomb was put in place so that it would explode in a very particular way. So in fact the miracle of that was that there was only one member killed, even though there were a number of members seriously injured, but it could easily have resulted in every member who went to that house being killed.[244]

Clerkin was from the border town of Monaghan: there was almost universal outrage. A local Sinn Féin councillor was among those condemning the action: 'I wish to unreservedly condemn this stupid act, no matter to what organisation the perpetrators belong or what motives they think they have.'[245] In an attempt to distance the republican movement from the attack and capitalise on public suspicion of the SAS, a fellow Sinn Féin councillor said that the attack had 'all the hallmarks of an SAS job'.[246] Few seemed to have accepted this explanation, but that it was publicly voiced offers a significant insight. It seems a combination of factors associated with conditions in Portlaoise jail and ongoing local tensions led an IRA unit to carry out the attack on Garda Clerkin.[247] According to one investigating Garda, resultant searches indicated further republican targeting:

> We searched the premises of known Provisional IRA men, seized ammunition, made arrests and discovered well advanced plans to assassinate a High Court judge and a Portlaoise prison officer. I was among five detectives called to Garda headquarters in the late hours one night to be told that we had been placed on a death list by the Provisional IRA.[248]

The *Irish Press*, the Irish daily traditionally more nationalist in its ethos, editorialised in the days after the killing, highlighting the effect on general public opinion:

> If the Mountmellick explosion was the work of any republican grouping, then, apart from being bad, the deed was mad also. Do the people who act in such a brutal fashion not realise that the average person in the South has become so sickened by the

horrors from Northern Ireland that, far from being inclined to work actively for unity, they will be much more likely to subscribe to having a great high wall built around the North to partition it off from the rest of the country, in the wake of such a happening?[249]

Violence along the border generally began to decline in the latter half of 1976, as illustrated by Table 10. Incidents within 2 miles of the border accounted for just 5.58 per cent of shooting incidents and 9 per cent of explosions within Northern Ireland. However, almost 20 per cent of British Army/RUC fatalities occurred in this area:[250] it was the lethality of attacks along the border that distinguished them.

Between March 1976 and May 1977, the IRA mounted 164 attacks against targets within 2 miles of the border. The British claimed that there was a clear cross-border connection in one-third of these cases and a strong indication in other incidents,[252] although the cross-border component was disputed by the Irish authorities in many cases. The Foreign Office presented a dossier to the Irish government detailing a series of cross-border incidents during which, they argued, permission for helicopters to overfly the border in hot pursuit would have been of benefit. Table 11 contrasts the Irish and British version of some of the incidents, illustrating the complexity of even minor border happenings.

South Armagh would continue to be the most active IRA area during the period. The IRA was reinvigorated in other areas in large part due to the presence of a small number of highly motivated

Table 10. Incidents along the border, April 1976–September 1977[251]

Period	Shootings	Explosions	BA/RUC fatality	Civilian fatality
April–June 1976	29	13	6	1
July–September 1976	12	16	1	1
October–December 1976	16	17	0	
January–March 1977	28	11	4	1
April–June 1977	23	11	2	2
July–September 1977	19	7	1	1

Table 11. Comparison of British and Irish versions of cross-border incidents, 1976

Date/Location	British version[253]	Irish version[254]
7 January 1976, Aughnacloy Vehicle Checkpoint (VCP)	100 rounds fired at VCP. Fire was not returned but 20 minutes later more shots fired. Garda discovered empty cases in Republic afterwards	Gardaí cordoned off the area having been notified by RUC 5 minutes after shots fired. A firing position was discovered but security forces, North and South, could not identify anyone to chase so helicopter usefulness questioned.
24 January, Middletown VCP	60–70 shots fired at VCP from Republic.	Garda were informed of incident by Irish Customs. RUC only notified Gardaí after 30 minutes. Gardaí searching came under fire from VCP. A firing position was found but Garda cautious about connecting it with incident.
29 February, Lisnaskea	15–20 shots fired at a mobile RUC patrol from Republic of Ireland.	Gardaí say firing position definitely in North. Garda/Army on scene within 15 minutes.
6 April, Clogher	A mine detonated from Republic. When Army patrol debussed a high velocity shot fired from South.	RUC did not notify Gardaí until 25 minutes after incident. Mine detonation point found in South. Usefulness of helicopter overflight in incident questioned.
11 April, Jonesborough	80 high-velocity shots fired at Army patrol. Gunmen seen crossing in South. Gardaí apprehended one suspect but he was released without charge.	Gardaí certain all shooting in North. Roadblocks set up as soon as notified. Gardaí publicly denied they had arrested fleeing gunman.
18 April, Lisnaskea	60–70 high velocity shots fired at UDR from two firing positions in South.	Irish forces on scene promptly but confused IRA members in full battle dress for UDR patrol. IRA members made their escape due to this confusion.

individuals. In north Monaghan, the Tyrone–Armagh border became the scene of a series of cross-border killings. Meanwhile, Donegal saw a significant escalation of republican violence which caused considerable local disquiet.

Unlike, other border areas, South Armagh would remain problematic for the British Army/RUC, regardless of the arrest or death of individual operators. Of the fifty-eight border incidents recorded by the Irish government in 1978, forty-one of these incidents were in South Armagh.[255] One IRA veteran noted that 'This area [South Armagh], and East Tyrone to a lesser extent, remained absolutely solid in the years that followed, while other rural areas were variously strong or weak depending on the presence there of perhaps just one or two strong personalities who would galvanise the rest.'[256] A Joint RUC–Garda report found that between 1 January 1975 and 31 January 1976 the fatalities in South Armagh included nine British soldiers, four UDR members, twenty Protestant civilians, fifteen Catholic civilians, two IRA casualties from premature explosions, two loyalists killed in premature explosions and two IRA members shot dead.[257]

The exact numbers involved in republican activity in the area are hard to determine. According to a 1977 Irish intelligence briefing, there were about 250 IRA activists in the Republic with just 10 in north Louth and 6 in Castleblayney.[258] These figures seem very conservative but presumably they refer to hard-core Active Service Unit members rather than those on the fringe. The British Army claimed that the number of 'hard-core' activists in South Armagh as a whole was 'probably at the most 30'.[259] The British figures indicated a wider number of activists beyond the core group and the breakdown of these activists is interesting. In total, there were 131 activists identified. One-third of this number had not been mentioned in intelligence briefs for twelve months, so they may have drifted away. Ninety-three were from South Armagh, while thirty-eight had home addresses in the Republic.

The bulk of activists were therefore South Armagh natives. Fifty-one suspects were living at their home address in South Armagh, whereas ten were at their home address in the Republic. In other words, the respective police forces should have had ready access to almost half the suspects. Sixty-two individuals were wanted for questioning, with thirty-seven of these from Northern Ireland and twenty-five from the Republic. Of the sixty-two, the British suspected the bulk were in the South. These were the individuals Minister for Justice Cooney targeted for membership charges. There were no warrants issued for the arrest of these individuals, so there was nothing actionable for the southern authorities to do if they encountered them. There were just eight republicans on the run who were facing charges.[260]

It is a matter of conjecture whether there was sufficient evidence for the RUC to charge the bulk of these republican activists wanted for questioning. In some instances, the Gardaí were notified by the RUC of the presence of a suspect. But this was not always the case. For instance, a high-profile female republican in February 1978 received injuries apparently handling incendiaries and was treated in Dundalk Hospital but the RUC did not ask the Gardaí to institute proceedings nor was any evidence against her handed over.[261] The case was cited by the British government in their dossier *Use of the Border by the Provisional IRA* as an example of the use of Dundalk as a safe haven. The Irish reply noted that no actionable information had been forwarded to them.

From the perspective of the Dublin government, there was little more the Gardaí could do in such cases. There was, of course, the prospect of questioning being carried out in the Republic under the Criminal Law Jurisdiction Act. However, the Department of Justice had objected to RUC officers questioning suspects in the Republic. The Gardaí did, upon request, question suspects about offences that took place over the border and the RUC could be available to consult in the interview process, but the practical usefulness of such an exercise was limited as interrogating officers would have lacked full insight into the case, and the line of questioning pursued may therefore have lacked rigour.

The difficulties involved with the RUC questioning suspects were evident in one of the very few cases where someone 'wanted for questioning' was actually interrogated in Garda custody. A Belfast man was arrested in connection with an assault on a Garda in Dundalk in December 1975. The man also happened to be wanted for questioning by the RUC in connection with a murder in Belfast.[262] Perhaps incensed by the assault on a member of the force, the Gardaí took the unusual step of contacting the RUC and allowed them interview the suspect. The man, who was subsequently detained by the RUC on a visit to Newry, was later convicted in a Belfast court based on evidence given in Dundalk Garda station. He served seventeen years in jail before being freed, with allegations of RUC brutality being central to a successful appeal.[263]

That the IRA had a strong foothold on both sides of the South Armagh border seems self-evident, but this was not universally accepted by those policing at ground level. From the perspective of the British, an internal briefing concluded that most of the violence in South Armagh emanated from the South: 'Dundalk acts as a base HQ for the South Armagh PIRA and the majority of PIRA engaged in terrorism in South Armagh return to Dundalk after specific operations.'[264] Garda Chief Superintendent Richard Cotterell held the polar opposite view, arguing just months earlier that;

> The plain fact of the matter is that both the Army and RUC have lost complete control in that area and are unable to supervise any subversives or their activities. The vast majority, if not all, attacks on the Northern Ireland security forces are carried out by persons who are natives of and who continue to reside in that area.[265]

Neither argument was completely fanciful or without substance, but in media discourse the British analysis seems to have gained most traction. As noted earlier, Irish politicians argued that this was due to concerted briefing of journalists by the British military.

The tension in the South Armagh–Monaghan border area was further heightened in March 1976 when loyalists detonated a bomb in the town of Castleblayney, killing one, Patrick Mohan, and injuring seventeen.[266] There was strong criticism of the lack of security in the town by local councillors, who called for greater resources for the Gardaí, more powers for the Army and the setting-up of a local security force.[267] Sinn Féin representatives contrasted the round-the-clock surveillance on republicans with the scant security presence in the town. There had been considerable apprehension in the area after the Tullyvallen Orange Hall shootings in 1975 and an attack was anticipated. Local Garda Chief Superintendent McMahon had felt that the closure of border roads and a general tightening of security had 'saved' the town in 1975.[268]

In the aftermath of the bomb, more questions about security were asked. In acrimonious exchanges at a Monaghan Town Council meeting, the local Sinn Féin representative pointed out that there had been eight loyalist bombs in Cavan–Monaghan in three years and no charges proffered. He further criticised Gardaí who, he claimed, 'spend more time out in the mountains hunting for and harassing republicans, neglecting areas where there are centres of population'.[269] The council wrote to the Minister for Justice for the third time in twelve months with regard to security, specifically complaining that there was no foot patrol in the town between 1 p.m. and 6 p.m. on the day of the bomb.[270]

The political reaction in Castleblayney mirrored that in other towns affected by bombings. The immediate concern for increased security, however, dissipated. After the Belturbet bomb in December 1972, there were similar calls for a Local Defence Force type organisation. This idea was resurrected after the Castleblayney bombing but when Assistant Commissioner Lawrence Wren went to Belturbet to explore the idea in March 1976, he was amazed to find that the locals 'showed no interest in setting up such a corp'. It seems much of the interest in the scheme waned in the weeks immediately after the bomb and there was a fear that a local defence force could develop into a UDA-type organisation.[271]

Within twelve months, local Fianna Fáil TD Jimmy Leonard lobbied the Department of Justice for the reopening of the Castleblayney–Newtownhamilton road. The area had quietened down a lot at this stage but the Department of Justice opposed the reopening largely because of the loyalist threat from the nearby Newtownhamilton area. The Department of Justice did not want the fear of loyalist attacks being cited to Jimmy Leonard and other community representatives seeking the reopening of the road.[272] Presumably, the government did not want to receive the blame politically for keeping roads closed and wanted to underplay the loyalist threat.

Among the first steps taken by Gardaí investigating the Castleblayney bombing was the searching of homes of local loyalists. The loyalist suspects had previously been observed gathering information on republicans and the southern security forces.[273] That the Gardaí suspected southern-based loyalists of involvement is both interesting and noteworthy. On a broader note, there is evidence of collusion between the bombers and the RUC/British Army. According to evidence quoted to the Barron Inquiry, former RUC Sergeant John Weir, a native of Castleblayney, claimed to have information that the bombing was carried out by a fellow RUC officer, Laurence McClure, and a UDR officer, Robert McConnell. [274]

There was a further loyalist killing in proximity to the South Armagh border shortly afterwards. Again, there were allegations of British Army/RUC collusion. In May 1976, forestry worker Seamus Ludlow was killed near Dundalk. The victim was by all accounts an inoffensive man killed in a random sectarian attack. He had little interest in politics, except a general political preference for the governing Fine Gael party. Given the climate of the time, it was not instantly clear who was responsible for the death with speculation linking the SAS to the incident. A *Sunday World* journalist erroneously reported: 'I learned from inquiries that the popular sawmill worker, who had no involvement in politics, was the "double" of a top Provisional IRA man who is on the wanted list of both the SAS and the outlawed Ulster Volunteer Force.'[275]

For some time, this killing was the subject of much local speculation, with sources variously ascribing blame to the IRA, loyalists and the SAS. It was 1979 before Garda Chief Superintendent Courtney received key intelligence from the RUC identifying four loyalist suspects – including two members of the UDR. It was at this point that the local murder investigation seems to have become entangled in the mire of Anglo-Irish political relations. The RUC had this key intelligence for eigtheen months. The timing of the passing of the intelligence was significant. When the lead Garda investigator Courtney raised the new intelligence with a Detective Sergeant at C3 (Special Branch) Headquarters, Courtney claimed that

[Boyle: Officer at C3 HQ] told me that he had discussed the case with Mr Larry Wren who was then either a Chief Superintendent or Assistant Commissioner in charge of C3. Mr Wren had advised Mr Boyle [HQ officer] that there was to be no further action taken in the case. I asked him why and he [Mr Boyle] said that Mr Wren had said that if the four suspects were to be extradited to the Republic of Ireland a similar number of extraditions of IRA suspects would be sought by the RUC and he didn't want this to happen.[276]

At the time the intelligence was shared, the Irish government was under pressure to allow the RUC interview suspects in Garda custody. According to then Minister of Justice Gerry Collins, the timely release of the intelligence may have been part of a British strategy to highlight the benefits of closer co-operation, forcing Irish concessions on the issue.[277] An official inquiry in the Republic concluded that suspects were not pursued,

in order to avoid a situation where Gardaí might feel obliged to reciprocate by allowing RUC officers to attend interviews of suspects in the State. Whether such a reciprocal obligation would in fact have arisen is beside the point: it is sufficient that senior Gardaí and / or officials from the Department of Justice held a perception that this was so.[278]

It was clear by 1979 that loyalists had killed Seamus Ludlow. This message was not conveyed to the victim's family. Instead, some of the family were led to believe that he was killed by republicans, possibly with some of Ludlow's own relations involved.[279] Obviously, this caused divisions within the family. That the Gardaí considered the IRA suspects in the context of the time and location is unsurprising. That the family and general public were not made aware that it was in fact loyalists responsible could be seen as an indication of a broader trend whereby the IRA was portrayed as the state's main enemy and the prime focus of security resources.

The same day the *Dundalk Democrat* reported on the death of Seamus Ludlow, it also recorded the arrest of the eight SAS men in Co. Louth.[280] It has been noted that this incident was to cause considerable diplomatic problems between Dublin and London in the year ahead. However, there were other similar incidents. In July, the SAS were blamed for illegally crossing the border and taking two men into custody at Dromad.[281] The Department of Foreign Affairs complained about the incident. There was also evidence that the men were assaulted in custody. The incident did give rise to significant local media comment and the UK Foreign Office alleged that this may have 'been stimulated by a Garda source in Dundalk, who in the past has not been helpful (e.g. over the SAS incursion)'.[282] There may have been lingering disappointment that the eight SAS men were not quietly escorted across the border, as happened in other cases. Significantly, one of the men arrested by the SAS in Dromad later received compensation for the incident, having taken a case for unlawful arrest to the High Court in Belfast.[283] Garda/RUC relations cooled for some days after the incident before returning to normal. Locally, in Dromad, relations remained strained for longer.[284]

In terms of incursions, a lot depended on the attitude of individual Gardaí. In June 1976, two British soldiers in an unmarked vehicle and civilian clothing were discovered on the Cavan–Fermanagh border; they were taken to Blacklion Garda station. Rather than being charged, as in the Louth case, the soldiers were simply escorted back to the border. The local Superintendent, Crutchley, had taken his own initiative in this case. It was emphasised to the FCO by the British military that nothing should be said to Irish diplomats about the incident in order to protect the Superintendent from domestic recriminations.[285] Tosh Lavery, a champion amateur cyclist and founder member of the Garda Sub-Aqua Unit, also details in his autobiography an incident when he quietly escorted a stray group of British soldiers back across the border. Despite Lavery's efforts to keep the incursion low-key, the media got wind of the story and the young Garda was made to account for his actions to a panel of senior officers the next morning.

> I was asked why I had not made an arrest [of the British soldiers]. I replied that I thought it was better to tell them to go back into the North as we would never have been able to secure them at the station. Tom Hughes, the local Inspector and a gentleman, winked at me and that was the end of it.[286]

Republican publications and the media generally highlighted the alleged role of the SAS operating in the Republic.[287] This added to a certain amount of paranoia about the SAS. In one incident, a visitor from Dublin attending a dance outside Dundalk was assaulted by an armed IRA man. The visitor was accused of being an SAS member. The IRA member received a three-year sentence in connection with the incident.[288] One SAS officer, Robert Nairac, achieved particular notoriety.

Several books have been written speculating extensively on Nairac's time in Northern Ireland and his links with loyalist paramilitaries.[289] Allegations of Nairac's involvement with these loyalists, including the killing of John Francis Greene near Castleblayney, featured heavily in the Barron Inquiry.[290] The original *Hidden Hand* documentary had alleged Nairac was linked to loyalist paramilitaries involved in the Dublin and Monaghan bombing and the Miami Showband attack,[291] but it is difficult at this remove to make any definitive judgement on his complicity in loyalist attacks. Nairac was abducted by republicans in South Armagh and killed in Louth in May 1977.[292] Although his body was never found, local republicans were convicted of the killing in southern courts. The full story of the controversial captain remains something of a mystery.

South Armagh would remain problematic for the British Army/ RUC for the remainder of the period, with several high-profile killings.[293] Of the thirty-four British Army/RUC casualties in 1978, ten were in that general area.[294] Aside from South Armagh, the East Tyrone area was the IRA's next most effective border unit. According to British reports, there were approximately sixty activists in East Tyrone, with Monaghan town acting as a base in the same way Dundalk did for South Armagh. British intelligence alleged that some IRA activists would spend a few days on 'active service' in Tyrone, resting up afterwards in Monaghan. Other activists would only spend a matter of hours over the border before returning to Monaghan.[295] Irish military intelligence reckoned there were ten IRA ASU members in Monaghan.[296] Again it is presumed that there were more members engaged in logistical support. The presence of highly motivated IRA activists in the area led to some republican attacks taking place in the South.

The experience of the Monaghan border village of Glaslough is illustrative. An off-duty UDR man, John Reid, was shot dead by the IRA when he was feeding cattle near the village in March 1977.[297] On 23 December 1979, an RUC reservist, Stanley Hazelton, was killed while he was collecting a Christmas turkey.[298] On 4 September 1980 a Protestant farmer, Ross Hearst, was abducted and killed by the IRA near the Armagh village of Middletown after attending a religious service in Glaslough.[299] The IRA alleged that the victim had given information to the security forces. A man was convicted under the Criminal Law Jurisdiction Act in a Dublin court in connection with the killing.[300]

As an indication of how out of context these three killings were for the environs, there were just nine recorded crimes in Glaslough in the four years from 1975 to 1979[301] and other incidents also affected the area in the early 1980s.[302] In 1976, RUC man William Turbitt was kidnapped after an ambush in South Armagh. The case received widespread publicity. The RUC man was from Tyholland in Monaghan, the next village to Glaslough.[303] After the kidnapping of a member of his own staff, local businessman Desmond Leslie wrote to the Minister for Justice complaining about the absence of a Garda presence in the village. Leslie argued that the area was becoming a 'criminal's paradise', complaining that since the local Garda station was shut in 1968 'the wide boys, smugglers, cattle rustlers and Provos moved in'.[304] While not agreeing with Leslie's analysis of the situation,

Garda Chief Superintendent Broderick concurred that there was considerable anxiety in the area.[305]

We have seen that the Fermanagh border had been noticeably quieter in 1975, but violence was to increase in that area too. A bomb disposal officer was killed at the start of 1977 in Newtownbutler. A Justice of the Peace, Douglas Deering, was killed in Roslea in May 1977. Deering's death had a significant effect in crystallising unionist opinion in the area and the local newspaper *The Impartial Reporter* pleaded with the Irish government to 'end this ghastly carnage'.[306] British security briefs on the Fermanagh border consistently identified IRA ASUs based in Ballyshannon, Swanlinbar/Ballyconnell and Clones.[307] The numbers involved were again small, with an estimate of twenty members. In contrast to the South Armagh border area, the units operating along the Fermanagh border were not as highly rated in terms of capability or planning.[308]

A common feature of the attacks identified in the Glaslough/Armagh area and the Fermanagh area was the role of IRA activists based in Monaghan. A group of relatives of victims of IRA attacks would later meet Prime Minister Margaret Thatcher in July 1980. The victims highlighted the role played by IRA units south of the border, with the Republic portrayed as a 'safe haven'. The families claimed 'they knew of members of the Garda who openly admitted to drinking with the IRA in public houses and to not being able to arrest them because they did not have the authority from Dublin'.[309] Although not agreeing with this analysis, the Gardaí confirmed the role of southern activists:

> The Gardaí have confirmed to the Department of Justice that there has been a considerable input from this side of the border in the case of most if not all these killings. There is also evidence to suggest that the same personnel are implicated in many of these murders. The security situation on our side of the border is also of concern to the people of Cavan and Monaghan. Recently the Minister for Justice received a deputation from Glaslough, Monaghan urging that a Garda station be opened in the area.[310]

One of the individuals the Department of Justice memo was referring to was probably Seamus McElwaine. According to a commemorative DVD made by republicans, McElwaine had been involved in reorganising the IRA in the South Fermanagh/Monaghan area from 1977 and had joined the IRA aged sixteen.[311] Henry Patterson, in *Ireland's Violent Frontier*, noted a decline in IRA activity in the Fermanagh/Monaghan border area after McElwaine's arrest in 1981 by the British Army.[312]

Another high-profile individual was Jim Lynagh, who was seen by the RUC as the most dangerous IRA activist in the Monaghan area.[313] Lynagh and the Gardaí had a mutually antagonistic relationship. As a teenager, Lynagh was convicted of throwing a petrol bomb at a Garda. According to republicans, Lynagh's movements would have been constantly monitored by Gardaí, with his home under visible, round-the-clock surveillance.[314] A brother of Lynagh, who was not an active republican, committed suicide in Mountjoy jail. There were repeated allegations of Garda harassment of the wider Lynagh family, including his deceased brother.[315]

Lynagh served a sentence in Northern Ireland between 1973 and October 1978. Upon release, his presence re-energised the IRA in the Monaghan area, according to local republicans.[316] However, Lynagh was not given a free run by Gardaí: he was charged with IRA membership in April 1980 but acquitted by the Special Criminal Court. Later that year, he became one of the first people charged by the Gardaí under the Criminal Law Jurisdiction Act but he was again acquitted. The use of the politically sensitive Criminal Law Jurisdiction Act to pursue Lynagh illustrates that there was a determination to get to grips with his unit. Twelve months later, IRA membership charges were again proffered and Lynagh jumped bail. Finally, a conviction was obtained when he was caught in possession of ammunition in Newbliss in April 1982.[317]

Donegal also was to prove problematic for the Irish security forces at this time. Members of the South Derry IRA were thought to have used Donegal as a base for operations from March/April 1977.[318] The catalyst for some of the South Derry men heading south was the killing of two RUC members in April 1977.[319] Perhaps being less cognisant of the necessity of keeping a low profile south of the border, the South Derry men were blamed for a range of attacks, including an attack on Carrigans Garda barracks.[320] Ten armed men raided the Garda station in August 1977, taking uniforms, files and confidential station records.[321] A week later, Ballybofey Garda station was showered with gunfire. Meanwhile, three Gardaí giving chase to a vanload of suspects were badly beaten on the Glenties to Ballybofey road. According to reports, older members of the fugitive group dissuaded younger members from killing the Gardaí.[322] There were similar incidents and a series of robberies in the neighbouring counties Sligo and Leitrim.[323] The media speculated as to whether the incidents were IRA-sanctioned or the work of maverick individuals and labelled the group the 'Donegal desperadoes'.[324]

In response, increased firearms training was given to local Gardaí.[325] There were allegations from Sinn Féin of heavy-handedness on the part of Gardaí investigating the violent upsurge.[326] The local newspapers in Donegal indicated that there was growing anxiety among the public generally. Six months after *The Irish Times* editorialised against Garda brutality and amid similar allegations locally, the *Donegal Democrat* implored the Gardaí and government to take firm action. The editorial was headlined 'time the kid gloves were off'.[327]

One of the South Derry men wanted for questioning by the RUC was high-profile republican Dominic McGlinchey. The legal view in Northern Ireland was that there was not sufficient evidence to charge McGlinchey under the Criminal Law Jurisdiction Act in connection with the Derry attacks.[328] McGlinchey and another South Derry man involved in Donegal incidents were eventually arrested in Monaghan in September 1977. In attempting to escape, the pair pulled a gun on Gardaí.[329] McGlinchey received a five-year sentence in Portlaoise in connection with the incident.[330]

The violence in Donegal continued into 1978. A shopkeeper, Bernard Browne, was killed in a robbery at Killygordon in January.[331] In the subsequent court case, two young men were convicted. One of the accused successfully argued that he was acting under duress during the robbery.[332] Court reports of the incident reflected poorly on republicans, not alone for the death of the shopkeeper but also in terms of exploiting and pressurising young people to join the IRA. To compound the tragedy, another Donegal man, Patrick Sills, named in court in connection with the offence, was shot in both kneecaps, presumably by the IRA, and bled to death. [333]

The Donegal grouping suffered a further blow when another of its members, Danny McErlain, was killed by the IRA. It was claimed that McErlain had used IRA weapons for 'unofficial operations'.[334] A further seven Donegal republicans were arrested at an RUC checkpoint and charged with serious offences when crossing the border to take part in an Easter commemoration.[335]

The increased activity in Donegal had seen a more visible Garda presence and the checkpoint arrests were just one of a number of significant security successes on both sides of the border. The Gardaí also recovered an M60 machine gun, which represented a significant blow to the local IRA.[336] Nonetheless, IRA attacks continued. In June, another M60 was fired from the southern side of the border in an attack that killed UDR member Alan Ferguson.[337] After this attack, the British Army would only patrol within 2km of the Fermanagh border in groups of twelve or more.[338] An RUC officer and soldier were injured in an IRA attack in August 1978. The vehicle used in the attack was hijacked in Lifford. In the same week, seven council workers were injured and one, Patrick Fee, was killed in an IRA attack near the border.

There had been moves to normalise border security somewhat in the weeks beforehand but these attacks renewed the security focus on the area.[339] By October 1978, the combination of security force pressure, arrests and internal troubles had seen the Donegal ASUs adopt a lower profile but it remained sporadically dangerous.[340] From the British perspective, cross-border security co-operation seemed to be greater in Donegal than other problem areas.[341] A FCO briefing paper contrasted the co-operation:

> The overall effectiveness and friendliness of contacts varies. There is a strong feeling in South Armagh and around the Monaghan salient, for instance, that the Garda are anxious to give the RUC comparatively minor titbits of information, and in addition often supply information after the event, but give very little hard intelligence on the basis on which security forces in Northern Ireland could undertake pre-emptive action. On the borders of Donegal, however, the flow of information is much stronger and there are few doubts about Garda's willingness to pass on all valuable information which comes into their possession.[342]

The increased violence in Donegal in 1977/78 coupled with public disquiet about such incidents may have had a significant role in explaining the more extensive co-operation in Donegal.

Aside from major incidents, daily life along the border was affected in other ways. Obviously, there was the ongoing hostility between Gardaí and republicans. A certain amount of tension was created during public protests about conditions at Portlaoise Prison.[343] Numbers attending republican protests were often small. Irish intelligence noted that few of the public protests in 1977 managed to attract any more than fifty

protestors, despite attempts at mass mobilisation.[344] Gardaí continued
to pay particular attention to those attending protests. It was alleged
that after one protest in Monaghan, a republican was given a severe
beating by Gardaí.[345] Ongoing republican poster campaigns and
graffiti led to further low-level conflict, and the 'Brits Out' slogan was
frequently painted on roads and public spaces by Sinn Féin members
and supporters. Particularly in areas relying on the tourism trade,
this caused much controversy.[346] Sinn Féin representatives sometimes
accepted responsibility for such sloganeering.[347] In Donegal, Sinn Féin
claimed members were harassed putting up 'Brits Out' posters.[348] On
other occasions fines were imposed.[349]

More seriously, in Monaghan, prison sentences ranging from
three to six months were imposed for graffiti painting.[350] As in
previous years, there were occasional incidents of violence between
Gardaí/Army and republicans in social settings.[351] From a republican
perspective, any time a major incident happened, they could expect
their house to be raided. Donegal-based republican Peter Pringle
claimed that 'Quite often, when incidents happened in the west of
Ireland the Gardaí would as they say "round up the usual suspects."
And if there was any political or subversive element in it they would
often arrest or detain me for up to 48 hours.'[352] A Tyrone republican
based in Meath, Thomas McNulty, shared a similar experience: 'It
became a long standing joke that the Irish Special Branch would raid
old reliables and bring in the usual suspects. I think it was like clocking
in to their superiors.'[353]

Republican funerals were sources of particular tension. Eleven men
were sent to face charges in the Special Criminal Court after violence
flared between Gardaí and republicans at the funeral of republican
Sean McKenna in Emyvale.[354] In Dundalk, while no violence erupted,
there were 150–200 Gardaí present at the funeral of republican Noel
Worthington.[355] The tension was even higher at the funeral of Patrick
Cannon in Dublin. He was killed along with another IRA man from
Donegal, Peter Elchar, when the bomb they were transporting exploded
prematurely on the Tyrone–Donegal border. When shots were fired
over Cannon's coffin, Special Branch officers moved forward to make
arrests and there was a confrontation with mourners.[356]

The abnormality of the times can be gauged by two incidents that
occurred at weddings near the border. Among the party at a Cavan
wedding in June 1976, was a police clerk from England. A party of

gunmen entered a pub where family of the bridal party were socialising. Three people were shot and injured, including two women and the London-based police clerk. One of those convicted in connection with this incident was an escaped IRA prisoner.[357] In follow-up operations, shots were fired at Gardaí. Those convicted in connection with this incident received sentences ranging between twelve and twenty years, indicating the seriousness with which the offences were viewed. The circumstances of the shooting in the midst of wedding celebrations caused widespread concern. A letter from Bishop McKiernan in Cavan was read at every mass in the county: 'Everyone who gave information to secret organisations or helped such a group was equally guilty of the foul deed that resulted. They must make it clear that they wanted rid of this thing from their town.'[358]

The attack seemed to prompt a significant security response, with allegations of Garda brutality in the county.[359] Meanwhile, at a society wedding in Meath in August 1978, the groom, a British soldier, was shot and wounded when leaving the church immediately after the ceremony. Again, there was widespread outcry. Two men, one of whom would become a prominent republican, Dessie O'Hare, were acquitted in connection with this attack.[360]

O'Hare's case is in itself interesting as he became one of the most high-profile paramilitaries to emerge from the Troubles and played a significant role along the border in the late 1970s. Like McGlinchey and Lynagh, the Gardaí did not turn a blind eye to his activity. As a seventeen-year-old, O'Hare had received a suspended sentence in the Special Criminal Court for firearms possession in December 1977.[361] The Keady man's defence argued that he was armed because he feared an SAS abduction attempt. In sentencing, the judge took a 'calculated risk' in suspending the sentence so O'Hare would not be exposed to the 'University of Subversion' in Portlaoise.[362] Perhaps the authorities regretted the leniency of the sentence.

O'Hare was involved in several other incidents in subsequent months. In 1979 two republican activists died in Monaghan Hospital in separate incidents. On one occasion, an IRA member, Peadar McElvanna, died having suffered injuries in an attack on Keady RUC station. O'Hare was also injured in the attack. As the incident occurred over the border in Keady, the Gardaí prepared a case against O'Hare under the Criminal Law Jurisdiction Act,[363] but the Director of Public Prosecutions felt there was insufficient evidence for a prosecution.[364]

In another incident, a travelling companion of O'Hare's, Tony McClelland, was killed after a Garda chase in Monaghan.[365] O'Hare received a lengthy prison sentence for firearms possession after this incident. As was the case with Lynagh, it took considerable Garda time and several prosecutions before O'Hare served significant jail time. The cases under the Criminal Law Jurisdiction Act involving both Lynagh and O'Hare were specifically raised by Margaret Thatcher at a bilateral meeting with the Taoiseach in June 1980.[366]

A general feature of the security response on both sides of the border was increased security patrols and checkpoints. There was of course the inconvenience associated with checkpoints and this had a significant impact on the day-to-day lives of those living near the border. Certain locations were particularly problematic. At some checkpoints, there was a feeling that British troops unnecessarily delayed traffic. The delay at Aughnacloy Vehicle Checkpoint (VCP) was frequently cited by Irish politicians.[367] Garret FitzGerald claimed that 'the Aughnacloy crossing gave rise to disproportionate complaints, not only from the likes of Neil Blaney, but from ordinary decent folk'.[368] Aughnacloy was one of seven vehicle checkpoints manned by British Army/RUC, including others at Middletown and Omeath. The checkpoints were described by the British Army's General Officer Commanding as 'operational nonsense'.[369] This view was shared by Gardaí who felt that such checkpoints 'soon became known and easily avoided'. The post in Aughnacloy and others were eventually removed in the latter half of 1976, significantly reducing the number of complaints the Irish government received.[370]

The checkpoints were politically popular with the unionist community. British Army reports noted that there had been little significant terrorist activity in the areas around the PVCP after their removal.[371] The main exception was the shooting and injuring of an RUC reserve officer in Aughnacloy in January 1977.[372] Six months earlier, IRA attackers used an alternate route for their escape after killing an RUC officer, David Morrow. On that occasion, the presence of the British Army did not deter attackers. British troops did not open fire on the culprits as they crossed the border and instead took pictures of the suspect van as it sped across the border much to the chagrin of local unionist politicians.[373]

Aside from the delays at checkpoints, there were relatively frequent hijackings in border areas and for civilians there remained the possibility of being caught up in a cross-border incident.[374] A female passenger, Marjorie Lockington, was killed in a hijacking incident just after crossing the border when she was returning from a rugby international in 1976.[375] Just weeks earlier, a bus driver, David McDowell, was shot dead while stopped at the VCP at Middletown after a soldier accidentally discharged his weapon.[376] In December 1976, Josephine McGeown was killed on a concession road linking Dundalk and Castleblayney when her vehicle hit a hijacked lorry.[377]A meat-factory worker from Clones, Larry Potter, was killed in an explosion months later when travelling for work in Belfast.[378] Meanwhile, the train network linking Dublin and Belfast was also a target for attack. A Dublin woman, Letitia McGrory, was killed when the Enterprise train was bombed by republicans in October 1978.[379]

By 1978, a pattern of violence had emerged along the border. IRA units, smaller in size than in 1972, were based in border towns and they engaged in military actions on a sporadic basis. Loyalist groups also showed themselves capable of attacking southern targets. Although the intensity of conflict was at a lower level than north of the border, life for many in border communities was not operating normally. A series of killings in a small country village, the massive police presences at rural funerals, the delays at checkpoints, as well as the occasional bomb or gun attack were all indicators of this abnormality. However, to the early 1970s, when refugee centres were in place and newspapers trumpeted talk of invasion, the prospect of civil war in the twenty-six counties had waned.

A Strategy of Containment

In September 1978, the EEC heads of mission from the respective embassies paid a visit to Monaghan for a briefing on border security. Those attending were struck by the sense of normality in the town. Additionally, it was noted that there was considerable sympathy among Irish security officials for their security force counterparts on the other side of the border.[380] In a sense, these findings were a vindication of the government's security policy. Violence was to a large extent contained across the border and, despite occasional incidents, life continued relatively peacefully in border towns like Monaghan, Dundalk and Lifford. The prospects of large-scale violence erupting had waned considerably: after Operation Motorman in 1972, there were between thirty-one and thirty-four border incidents per month.[381] By 1978, the Irish government recorded fifty-eight incidents in the entire year, with only seventeen of these incidents outside South Armagh.[382] Violence, therefore, had declined massively and was much more focused in one area, South Armagh. The death toll from the Troubles had also declined significantly but, as has been noted, the proportion of deaths of British Army/RUC personnel remained high along the border.

Successive governments had pursued a strategy whereby domestic security was given high priority. For the coalition, being strong on security became its defining feature. The coalition had framed the fight against the IRA in black-and-white terms. Minister for Justice Paddy Cooney compared the IRA threat to the rise of the Nazi party in Germany. Cooney posited the question: 'Do we want to share the same fate of the German people where a whole race and innocent generations have to bear the obloquy of the actions of a small number?'[383] The rhetoric of Fianna Fáil was less vitriolic but there was little evidence of a decline in Garda rigour in dealing with the republican threat on Fianna Fáil's return to power. Although the reports of Garda brutality were less frequent, Gardaí seen as taking a heavy hand against the IRA were not disciplined – some were promoted by the Fianna Fáil government. There was a slight decline in Garda numbers along the border, but this was in the context of worsening crime elsewhere and an overall decline in border violence. Meanwhile, the Joint Coordinating Committee and other frameworks for security co-operation continued to operate as before and further discreet co-operation was encouraged.

As in previous years, violence within the state attracted a more significant response as evidenced by the Ewart Biggs assassination and the incidents in Donegal in 1977. The exception to this trend was loyalist attacks. The Ludlow case, in particular, illustrated a lack of the requisite vigour in the security response. In common with the Ludlow case, it seems that the investigation into the Dublin and Monaghan bombings of 1974 was also wound down prematurely. Due to a lack of documentary evidence, an independent inquiry was unable to determine exactly when the bombing investigation ended or why.[384] Nonetheless, investigations into loyalist attacks followed a trend.

Politically, it continued to be popular for any Dublin government to be seen to clamp down on the IRA but it remained imprudent to be seen to be overly supportive of the British. A Northern Ireland Office briefing paper described the Irish security policy as 'correct rather than enthusiastic', explaining the Irish need to 'knock the Brits':

> When an Irish government are faced with pressures to say or do something to do with Northern Ireland, there is always a temptation to lash out at the British. To some extent this is a function of the Northern Ireland temperature; but there are other elements e.g. British unwillingness to treat Dublin as a principal in Northern Ireland constitutional matters, and the feeling of irritation at having to deal with the British at all in thinking about the future of Ireland.[385]

The security situation along the border was more complex than portrayed in the media at the time. We have seen that there was a view presented that towns like Dundalk or Monaghan were 'murder HQ' and all, or certainly most, republican violence emanated from south of the border. This view discounted the significance of the RUC's inadequate presence in key border areas. Cross-border police co-operation was extremely difficult when there was minimal RUC presence in key areas. The leeway afforded republicans by the Gardaí was also exaggerated in media reports but IRA members certainly lived, operated and planned in border towns.

However, these individuals were not ignored by the Gardaí. Measures, not always successful, were taken to deal with leading republican figures. It had been hoped in 1976 that this process would continue with the introduction of extra-territorial security legislation that would allow suspects in the South to be charged with offences committed across the border but it became increasingly hard to secure convictions using this mechanism.[386] Those policing the Irish border in the Republic were therefore left in a situation whereby they had to deal with a significant number of IRA activists who were 'wanted for questioning' by the RUC but against whom there was little evidence.

The increased difficulty in securing convictions for IRA membership compounded the situation and it seems likely that the Gardaí did not have the organisational or technological sophistication necessary to obtain convictions in some circumstances. In the case of some senior Republicans, the Gardaí mounted crude round-the-clock surveillance but this could not be sustained for all suspects. More generally, the RUC felt that the Gardaí needed to adopt new surveillance methods, with highly trained personnel dedicated to long-term sustained covert surveillance.[387] Given the significant number of IRA personnel living at home in South Armagh, it seems likely that the British may have had difficulty organising surveillance in thinly populated rural areas themselves. Republicans generally were becoming more refined in their counter-interrogation techniques, so it was becoming harder to obtain convictions, especially for offences taking place in another jurisdiction.

That there were differences in the willingness of individual officers to deal with the IRA is also not disputed. In some cases, Gardaí simply did not want to get involved if there was a chance of a gunfight. There is a range of possible explanations as to why co-operation was greater in other circumstances. Perhaps it was simply a matter of a senior officer pushing an agenda. The presence of a significant Protestant vote in Donegal may have meant officers had more political protection if they engaged in cross-border co-operation there. Other potential explanations include the traditional ties between the Gardaí and Donegal, while in counties Monaghan and Louth, there were factors that may have inhibited co-operation. Again, the role of individuals and their own disposition was significant.

There were other influences, such as the strength of the IRA in the area, and allegations of collusion against some security force personnel over the border were known to Gardaí in the area. Additionally, there were reports of high-profile, covert British security services operations in the Louth/Monaghan area that added to distrust. This is of course not to discount the possibility that there may also have been individual officers who sympathised with the IRA cause. Goulden in the British embassy provided quite a balanced summary of Garda motivation:

While deploring the PIRA and their methods, many Gardaí share the hope of a united Ireland and are therefore uneasy about our continuing presence in the North. This mixture of anti-Republican nationalism and ambivalence about the British involvement is, of course, typical not only of Gardaí but of 95 per cent of Irishmen who vote for the three major parties. It helps to explain why the Irish government and their security forces, even when fully committed to rooting out subversives prefer to do so in their own way rather than in visible cooperation with us.[388]

CHAPTER 6

'The state might not be able to hold the line': Conclusion

The debate about the cross-border dimension to violence would continue for the remainder of the Troubles. According to the British Army, as late as 1988, ten of the sixteen IRA Active Service Units were operating south of the border.[1] The issue of cross-border violence achieved particular notoriety in 1979. On 27 August 1979, an IRA bomb killed Lord Louis Mountbatten and three companions, including two teenage boys, in an attack in Mullaghmore, Co. Sligo. The same day, eighteen British soldiers were killed in a cross-border IRA attack at Narrow Water on the Louth–Down border. A civilian was killed by British Army gunfire after the incident.[2] The Garda response to Narrow Water was criticised. Many of the issues raised in the preceding chapters were evident in the Narrow Water attack, illustrating the ongoing difficulties with cross-border violence. The Smithwick Inquiry, which investigated allegations of Garda collusion in the 1980s, heard evidence that

> The detonation point [for Narow Water bombing] was across the river in County Louth. I [Smithwick] heard evidence, including from retired Assistant Chief Constable of the RUC Raymond White, that there was frustration among the CID Officers who had investigated the Narrow Water bombing in that they felt that the detonation site had been seriously trampled before a proper forensic investigation could be carried out. He added that there was a suggestion from one officer that the grass had been cut, the inference being that this had been deliberately done to destroy any evidence.[3]

The Narrow Water attack was outside the terms of the Smithwick Inquiry but Gardaí refuted the suggestion of laxity or collusion on their part:

> The Tribunal has heard evidence that a proper investigation was carried out on the Southern side, the site had been forensically examined and two suspects had been arrested. The site had not been destroyed as alleged by Witness 72 Dr Hall. Detective Sergeant Patrick Ennis gave evidence of an extensive list of exhibits collected by him and forwarded to the forensic Laboratory. On Day 77, Dr Hall agreed that he had not been told of the extent of the Garda investigation.[4]

Like many border incidents discussed already, it is hard to reach definitive conclusions. It has been seen in this study that official records and individual testimony often describe the same event in contradictory terms. Therefore, in presenting conclusions a certain caution will be applied. Thus, this study and its findings must be read in the context of incomplete records.

Political Environment Policy: Conclusions on Anglo-Irish Relations, Domestic Politics and Security

In terms of political influence on border security, successive Dublin governments took firm action to deal with the IRA in the twenty-six counties. The exception to this was in the years 1969/70, when there was greater ambiguity. As violence spread southwards, with incidents in border towns like Dundalk, Ballyshannon and Monaghan, official laxity towards republicanism waned. The contrast between the Fianna Fáil Ard Fheis in 1971 and 1972 perhaps best illustrates the changing political situation. The 1971 Ard Fheis saw scuffles on the floor and a split looking likely within the governing party.[5] By 1972, Minister for Justice Des O'Malley was being roundly applauded from the floor for his 'get tough' message.[6] The impetus for the early moves against the IRA came as a result of republican actions in the South rather than diplomatic pressure. Inflammatory statements by republican leaders also visibly challenged the Dublin government, prompting a response.[7] In later years, other IRA actions in the Republic seem to have triggered immediate localised security shake-ups. Examples include the killings of Constable Doherty in Donegal and Senator Billy Fox.

The political response to loyalist attacks is interesting in that there seems to have been an effort to downplay the threat. The investigations into the Dublin and Monaghan bombings were de-escalated or closed down quite quickly while the killing of Seamus Ludlow was erroneously ascribed to republicans. Politically, the loyalist threat sat uneasily with the official narrative that the major threat to the Irish state was the IRA. Even in the 'doomsday scenario' of an abrupt British withdrawal, Garda intelligence envisaged the IRA being the main threat:

> from usually reliable sources, the Provisionals would initially react [to a British withdrawal] with 'token resistance' giving the appearance of weakness and irresolution, but sufficient to provoke the Protestants to overreaction. The PIRA then plans to 'stage' border incidents involving the Irish Army, part of which has been carefully infiltrated by the Provisionals to this end.[8]

The threat of an abrupt withdrawal loomed large in the mid-1970s. It was a nightmare scenario for the Dublin government, as it was difficult for them to publicly oppose, considering the state's nationalist ethos. However, as the Troubles developed, there was an increasing desire by the Irish state and its institutions to disengage from northern affairs. The experience of Gardaí and officials dealing with the influx of refugees had not been positive. This added to distrust of northern nationalists. It is hard to disagree with the following analysis.

> It is evident by reading papers of the period that many officials viewed the ordinary people of Northern Ireland that they came across with disdain if not disgust. This was because they were now suspicious of all sides in the Northern Ireland conflict and had lost much of the affinity they had had with them back in 1969. By the summer of 1975 the alienation was complete. No government (British or Irish) wanted to aid or assist the basket case that was the six counties ... Public opinion in the Republic also became so disenchanted with Northern Ireland that even Fianna Fáil never again faced the Northern Ireland issue so divided as it had been through Lynch's first term in office.[9]

The focus, therefore, was on sealing the conflict within the six counties but it was still not politically possible to co-operate with British forces in this regard or to improve security at the behest of the UK government. The Irish state was weak militarily and economically. It was also weak in terms of internal cohesion. The state had a nationalist ethos at its core and therefore felt threatened by those with a greater claim to represent this ethos. The dominant nationalist party was overtaken by a more militant rival in the case of Sinn Féin in 1918 and Fianna Fáil in 1932, which would still have been in living memory in the 1970s. A violent civil war involving militant republicans also occurred between these two events.

In matters of national security internationally, historical experience can have an important role in giving prominence to certain threats. For example, attitudes towards German unification during the early 1990s were still strongly affected by memories of previous German bids for power, regardless of whether those memories had any relevance for contemporary developments.[10] An additional feature of national security policy is the propensity of those responsible for national security to hedge their bets, thinking in worst-case terms.[11] Put simply, fears of a rise in republican sentiment in the South were foremost in the mind of those formulating security policies. The IRA may not have had the support, manpower or organisational sophistication to overthrow the southern state but historical experience made the potential threat seem more potent. A senior Garda briefed the government in the early 1980s that 'if the state were to accede to the British demand for enhanced security cooperation and, in particular, if extradition procedures were to be implemented, there would be outright conflict with the Provisionals. The state might not be able to hold the line.'[12]

As bizarre as it may seem, even the most aggressive and apparently anti-British security decision, i.e. sending troops to the border in 1969, was carried out to counter the IRA threat domestically. The decision to move troops was in large part designed to undermine support for the republican cause. If the Irish state were to co-operate in areas like 'hot pursuit', extradition, RUC questioning suspects in Garda custody, and overflights, it would very publicly have been aligning itself with the British. In the context of a situation in which nationalist sentiment was on the rise, this would be a significant threat not only to an individual party but also to the state.

Those in the permanent government seemed to have fixated on this threat. Civil servants intervened when Minister of Defence Paddy Donegan agreed to Army-to-Army co-operation[13] and when senior Gardaí agreed to RUC interviewing suspects.[14] While it has been suggested that the Irish government had used security co-operation as a 'bargaining chip' from the earliest years of the Troubles, this is somewhat unfair.[15] Rather than withholding security co-operation as a 'trump card' to play at a later date, the Irish state was operating from a position of internal weakness. British diplomats in the Dublin embassy frequently acknowledged this Irish weakness and emphasised the necessity to keep co-operation discreet.[16]

The difficulty for the Irish state was not so much in co-operating with the British but being seen to co-operate. This raises the question of how much unseen co-operation there was. While this study has speculated on the significance of covert co-operation, this is an area that remains vague.

In 1979, Charles Haughey became Taoiseach, with the ambiguity over Lynch's security policy being central to Haughey's accession. Perhaps somewhat surprisingly, border reports indicated no significant change in levels of cross-border security co-operation when Haughey took office. One reliable account claims that the Gardaí were 'particularly helpful' at an operational level under the new Taoiseach.[17] This view is not shared by all. It is alleged that in a later meeting of senior officials and security personnel, Haughey instructed them to no longer co-operate in the prosecution of cases under the Criminal Law Jurisdiction Act. There are, however, disputed versions of this meeting.[18] When the full archive of the 1980s is released, it will be interesting to see whether discreet co-operation continued or even improved during Haughey's time in office, as initial indicators suggest.

Gardaí and Irish Army: The Effectiveness of Security Forces

The state's security strategy to deal with the IRA was to combine a tough legislative response with an increase in security force numbers. Between 1972 and 1980, 1,500 people were prosecuted in the Special Criminal Court, with two-thirds convicted. [19] One Garda noted the significance of the Special Criminal Court in this regard: 'There is no way they could have convicted any of them without the Special Criminal Court ... There was no jury. Their evidence would not have got past a jury. All the Judges wanted was sufficient evidence to convict.'[20]

As was noted in Chapter 3, before the introduction of the Special Criminal Court, the Irish judicial system was not seen as a threat by republicans. In later chapters we observed that significant sentences were imposed when the Special Criminal Court came into operation. Another legal mechanism introduced less successfully was the Criminal Law Jurisdiction Act. The practicalities of operating the Criminal Law Jurisdiction Act proved difficult in a climate in which relations between the RUC and Gardaí were not at a normal level.

Aside from legal mechanisms, Garda investigation techniques and intelligence gathering methods during the period seem to have been significantly weak. Organisationally, too, the lack of specialised units in the force was problematic. Failings in the force were identified by the Finlay Commission and implicitly by the RUC in terms of advice given with regard to specialised units and intelligence gathering. The Department of Finance was critical of increasing expenditure on the force without significant organisational change so it is difficult to disagree with Vicky Conway's conclusion that the Gardaí were not sufficiently trained or equipped to deal with many of the crimes that the Troubles brought their way.[21]

Meanwhile, political pressure on the Gardaí was a significant factor. In the first years of the Troubles, the political climate encouraged Gardaí to 'look the other way' when it came to IRA actions. Later, pressure to solve major crimes, such as the Sallins robbery or the Herrema kidnapping, led to an increasing tolerance of Garda misconduct, particularly in terms of how suspects were treated and the extra leeway officers were afforded in national security matters meant that supervision may at times have been lax. It has been pointed out that some of the subsequent scandals affecting the Gardaí occurred in border jurisdictions and this may not be coincidental.

In light of revelations from the Smithwick Tribunal, it seems that at least some individual Gardaí colluded with republicans. Some of the principal characters named in that Tribunal were serving along the border during the period of this study but the 1970s official papers viewed do not provide evidence of any significant support for the republican cause within the Gardaí. In fact, it has been noted that there was considerable antipathy towards republicans. Some Gardaí, however, were more pro-active than others in combating the IRA. One retired member noted:

> Well again the ones [Gardaí] who were threatened were the ones who were good. There were a few that were very active all the time or talking [about] the provos, others [Gardaí] were, if it happens we'll deal with it but we're not going looking for trouble. Others [Gardaí] were, they couldn't be content but they had to be searching, rooting around, and they were perceived [by the IRA] as a threat, more than a threat. And they would have been the ones that would maybe have got threatening phone calls.[22]

Although the reasons for a lack of cross-border security co-operation at a political level can be guessed at, different factors were at play at a local level. Personality clashes were a factor. Local feeling also played a role. Likewise, political interference may have been significant. Speculation about loyalist associations with the RUC was also important.

This study has identified that the Army had a highly visible but mostly ancillary role during the Troubles. There has also been evidence presented that there was some republican feeling within the armed forces and we have seen that as late as 1975 at least some Army officers envisaged a thirty-two-county role for the force in certain circumstances.[23] This 'green tinge' to Army thinking should not be exaggerated, however. It does seem that the experience of the force during the 'arms trial' was a defining one. One commandant speaking in 1977 commented:

> Jim Kelly [the officer at the centre of the Arms Crisis] was a bloody fool. That's what most of us think now anyway. If you're an Army man you don't go around mixing with the politicians because you're sure to get into some kind of trouble. Everybody is sorry for him but he was playing with fire.[24]

The Security Situation in the Southern Border Counties

The impact of the northern Troubles on the southern border counties was significant. Each chapter has documented a significant number of southern fatalities associated with border areas during the years 1969–78, including security force members, paramilitaries and civilians. The day-to-day impact of violence on individuals has been highlighted in addition to issues related to checkpoints and border roads. A recent oral history project has conducted interviews with those living near the border, which further emphasised the impact of such issues on daily lives.[25]

The development of violence along the border saw particular areas emerge as trouble spots, with Clones, Lifford and Dundalk frequently cited in the early years of the Troubles. As time progressed, South Armagh would be the focus of most border violence. The presence of individual figures could affect the security situation in an area. The case of the South Derry men in Donegal in 1977 provides one example. Similarly, the emergence of young republican leaders in Monaghan in the latter part of the 1970s seems to have been significant.

It was noted in the last chapter how victims' groups from Fermanagh had told Margaret Thatcher that Gardaí drank with IRA members across the border. Undoubtedly, there would have been occasions when this happened but this is an overly simplistic analysis of the dynamic that existed in border areas. The Gardaí's modus operandi in the mid-1970s lacked subtlety. Therefore, the constant arrest operations, surveillance and harassment of republicans were certain to cause tensions. Likewise, republicans frequently goaded Gardaí at protests. There is also evidence of ongoing hostilities at various social occasions, never mind when the Gardaí encountered republicans on active service. That said, it was something of a 'phoney war'. There was an awareness on the part of republicans that conflict with the southern forces would not favour them. When dealing with a Sinn Féin figure in negotiations over conditions in Portlaoise Jail, Fine Gael TD Paddy Harte was told 'we don't like you bastards but we don't want to fight with you'.[26] While Irish officials had a genuine fear of the republican threat to the state, republicans too realised that historical experience indicated that if they overstepped the mark they risked a serious clampdown. At one point, Paddy Cooney warned republicans to 'look back on the last 50 years and see that any confrontation between illegal organisations and the state invariably ended in favour of the state'.[27] A republican activist along the border, Thomas McNulty, summarised the situation as he saw it:

The way we looked at it, was, as long as we didn't get too much hassle from the southern security forces, and the Dublin government didn't bring in internment without trial in the South, we could still carry on our fight in the North, we'd be happy enough, let sleeping dogs lie. We didn't need an old civil war to fight, we already had a war in the North.[28]

The presence of such IRA personnel in southern border towns caused several problems for the Irish security forces. To the British, the republican presence was a very visible sign of Irish state complicity in IRA violence. However, most of those republicans based south of the border in the late 1970s were 'wanted for questioning' and it is unclear if there would have been sufficient evidence to merit charges in many cases. Therefore, the significance of the failure to extradite suspects should not be over emphasised. O'Halpin concluded:

At times during the 1970s and 1980s the British government gave the impression that they believed that the IRA could easily be beaten if only Ireland would stop playing semantic games and make extradition work. But the removal of the political exception, and the success of the majority of extradition applications after 1987, while it may have put dangerous people behind bars did not bring republican violence to a grinding halt.[29]

The area adjoining South Armagh was often cited as having a significant number of republicans 'on the run'. It was undoubtedly the most difficult border area to police, but for the period under consideration it seems unfair to ascribe the greater culpability to the Irish security forces. The South Armagh area lacked a significant RUC presence and there was unwillingness from British troops to come close to the border except in force and there was also inter-force rivalry on the northern side of the border between the RUC and British Army. Further belying the myth that all violence emanated from republicans based south of the border, there was a significant number of IRA suspects permanently resident in the South Armagh area not 'on the run'.

'The terrier and the rottweiler'

It would be easy to come to a simplistic conclusion and dismiss the effectiveness of the Irish security response. There is ample evidence to show that the Gardaí and Army were poorly equipped, lacking training, poorly organised, and heavily influenced by political and local considerations. The Tyrone republican Thomas McNulty claimed that 'The Gardaí were like a little terrier dog, always snapping at our [IRA] heals but doing very little harm, more annoying than anything else. The Rottweiler was in the North.'[30] An RUC detective in 1992 was similarly dismissive, noting that 'while the Gardaí were good fellows to drink with, his force was far ahead in the collection and management of intelligence'.[31] From the IRA perspective, the British Army/RUC was certainly a deadlier adversary. From the RUC viewpoint, criticism of the Gardaí is understandable. Nonetheless, although the Gardaí's methods belonged to a different era, the sometimes 'folksy' nature of their approach should not be entirely dismissed. The observations of another IRA activist, Kieran Conway, are noteworthy:

> I came to see a significant difference in security culture between the Gardaí on the one hand and RUC/British Army on the other; in the North they were fixated on their records, so if you had a clean car, clean driver or plausible fake identity papers yourself, you were fine. In the South, though, the Gardaí, particularly in border areas would hardly trouble you for your papers, instead questioning you closely on your reasons for being on a particular road at a particular time, an approach that was far more intrusive and effective.[32]

Rightly or wrongly, the entire thrust of Irish security policy was on ensuring stability in the Republic, which meant that the Gardaí were not necessarily always fighting the same battle as the RUC/British Army. It is in this context that security policy's effectiveness should be measured. In 1970, republicans were given suspended sentences for weapons offences. By 1978, people were going to jail for writing 'Up the IRA' on walls. Republican suspects were being beaten in custody. There was only limited and somewhat marginalised public outcry. In 1969, cabinet ministers conspired with republicans. By 1978, politicians were competing to outdo each other in their condemnation of IRA violence. The IRA threat to the twenty-six-county state had been weakened considerably.

Aside from documenting the border experience, the central contribution of this book is in explaining why the Irish state behaved

the way it did. In particular, it is the identification of the Irish state as a
'weak' state obsessed with the internal threat. It was 'weak' in material
and sociopolitical terms. Materially, the security forces lacked many
of the basic requirements. In sociopolitical terms, the binding 'idea'
behind the state was especially vulnerable. The state was constantly
vulnerable to threats from republicans who had a contrary claim to the
nationalist 'idea' behind the state. In this context, it was important for
the Irish security forces to be seen to hammer the IRA domestically, to
deal with the internal threat but not to be seen as pro-British. It has
been shown throughout the work that, from the Garda on checkpoint
duty at the border to the highest-ranked government minister, there
was an understanding that security policy had to be conducted within
these parameters. Overt security co-operation, extradition, removal of
Articles 2 and 3, etc., were all seen as steps too far in this regard.

Regardless of which party was in charge, there was a real fear,
whether justified or not, that an upsurge in nationalist sentiment could
destabilise the state. Security policy during the era was not deployed
as a means of developing this nationalist 'idea'; rather, the boundaries
for what the Irish state could do to deal with the internal threat were
curtailed by this 'idea'. The Irish state was not withholding security
co-operation from a position of strength, hoping to gain concessions
from the British in negotiations over the future of Northern Ireland;
rather, it was operating from a position of weakness, obsessed with an
internal threat.

Endnotes

Introduction

1 'Soldier gets away from kidnappers', *The Irish Times*, 26 June 1974.
2 'Dr Dugdale jailed for 9 years; Soldier gets away from kidnappers', *The Irish Times*, 26 June 1974.
3 'Provo bombers blown up', *Irish Press*, 25 June 1974.
4 'IRA bomb expert sought', *Irish Press*, 25 June 1974.
5 Oireachtas Report into the Bombing of Kay's Tavern, Dundalk, p. 186, http://www.dublinmonaghanbombings.org/KaysInterim.pdf.
6 Henry Patterson, *Ireland's Violent Frontier: The Border and Anglo-Irish Relations During the Troubles* (London: Palgrave, 2013).
7 Ministry of Defence, *Operation Banner: An Analysis of Military Operations in Northern Ireland* (2006), p. 33, http://www.vilaweb.cat/media/attach/vwedts/docs/op_banner_analysis_released.pdf.
8 NA (UK) FCO 87/976 'Northern Ireland future terrorist trends', 1978.
9 NA (IRL), 'Media briefings by British authorities', circa 1978.
10 NA (UK) FCO 87/248, 'Letter from Kelvin White to RC Cox', 25 June 1973.
11 NA (UK) CJ4/3084, 'Security in Fermanagh', circa September 1980.
12 Caroline Pike-Kennedy, 'International history and International Relations theory: a dialogue beyond the Cold War', *International Affairs*, vol. 76, no. 4 (2000), p. 743.
13 John Baylis and Steve Smith, *The Globalization of World Politics* (Oxford: Oxford University Press, 2005), p. 300.
14 See Barry Buzan, Ole Waever and Jaap de Wilde, *Security: A new framework for analysis* (London: Lynne Riennar Publishers, 1998) and Barry Buzan, *People, States and Fear: An Agenda for International Security Studies in the Post-Cold War Era* (Colchester: ECPR Classics, 2009).
15 Michael Mulqueen, *Re-evaluating Irish National Security: Affordable threats* (Manchester: Manchester University Press, 2009)
16 Buzan, *People, States and Fear*, p. 91.
17 Ibid., p. 93.
18 Ibid., pp. 77–8
19 Ibid., p. 94.

Chapter 1

1 Conor Cruise O'Brien, *States of Ireland* (London: Panther, 1972), p. 278.
2 Roger Mac Ginty 'Almost Like Talking Dirty: Irish Security Policy in Post-Cold War Europe', *Irish Studies in International Affairs*, Vol. 6 (1995).

3   Michael Mulqueen, *Re-evaluating Irish National Security: Affordable threats* (Manchester: Manchester University Press, 2009), p. 3.

4   Eunan O'Halpin, *Defending Ireland: The Irish State and its Enemies Since 1922* (Oxford: Oxford University Press, 1999).

5   Michael Mulqueen, *Re-evaluating Irish National Security: Affordable threats* (Manchester: Manchester University Press, 2009).

6   Vicky Conway, *Policing Twentieth Century Ireland: A History of An Garda Síochána* (London: Routledge, 2014).

7   Henry Patterson *Ireland's Violent Frontier: The Border and Anglo-Irish Relations During the Troubles* (London: Palgrave, 2013).

8   John Bew, Martyn Frampton and Inigo Gurruchaga, *Talking to Terrorists: Making Peace in Northern Ireland and the Basque Country* (London: Hurst & Company, 2009).

9   Anthony Craig, *Crisis of Confidence: Anglo-Irish Relations in the Early Troubles 1966– 1974* (Dublin: Irish Academic Press, 2010).

10 Conor Brady, *Guardians of the Peace* (Dublin: Prenderville, 2000).

11 Conor Brady, *The Guarding of Ireland: The Garda Síochána and the Irish State 1960– 2014* (Dublin: Gill and Macmillan, 2014), pp. 253–6.

12 Dermot J. Walshe, *The Irish Police* (Dublin: Roundhall, 1998).

13 Patsy McArdle, *The Secret War: An Account of the Sinister Activities along the Border involving Gardaí, RUC, British Army and the SAS* (Dublin: Mercier, 1984).

14 Derek Dunne and Gene Kerrigan, *Round Up the Usual Suspects* (Dublin: Magill, 1984).

15 Eunan O'Halpin, *Defending Ireland: The Irish State and its Enemies Since 1922* (Oxford: Oxford University Press, 1999). p. 351.

16 Craig, *Crisis of Confidence* (2010), p. 193.

17 Michael Kennedy, *Divisions and Consensus: The Politics of Cross-Border Relations in Ireland 1925–1969* (Dublin: IPA, 2000), p. 3.

18 Henry Patterson, 'Sectarianism Revisited: The Provisional IRA campaign in a border region of Northern Ireland', *Terrorism and Political Violence*, vol. 22, no. 3, 2010, p. 340.

19 Colin Crawford, *Inside the UDA: Volunteers and Violence* (London: Pluto, 2003).

20 Rogelio Alonso, *The IRA and Armed Struggle* (London: Routledge, 2007).

21 Alan Barker, *Shadows: Inside Northern Ireland's Special Branch* (London: Mainstream, 2004).

22 Jack Holland and Susan Phoenix, *Phoenix: Policing the Shadows* (London: Hodder and Stoughton, 1997).

23 George Clarke, *Border Crossing: True Stories of the RUC Special Branch, the Garda Special Branch and IRA Moles* (Dublin: Gill and Macmillan, 2009).

24 Nick Burbridge and Fred Holroyd, *War without Honour* (Hull: Medium, 1989).

25 John Courtney, *It Was Murder* (Dublin: Blackwater Press, 1996).

26 http://www.green-and-blue.org/ (2014).

27 Eunan O'Halpin, *Defending Ireland* (1999), p. 351.

28 Ibid., p. 229.

29 Ibid., p. 253.

30 Ibid., p. 291.

31 Eunan O'Halpin, '"A Greek Authoritarian Phase"? The Irish Army and the Irish Crisis 1969–1970', *Irish Political Studies*, vol. 23, no. 4, December 2008.

32 Barry Buzan, *People, States and Fear* (Colchester: ECPR, 2009).

33   Mulqueen, *Re-evaluating Irish National Security*, p. 16.
34   Ibid., p. 30.
35   Patterson, 'Sectarianism Revisited', p. 199.
36   Justin O'Brien, *The Arms Trial* (Dublin: Newleaf, 2000).
37   Craig, *Crisis of Confidence* (2010), pp. 66–8.
38   Eunan O'Halpin, '"A Greek Authoritarian phase"? The Irish Army and the Irish Crisis 1969–1970', *Irish Political Studies*, vol. 23, no. 4, December 2008.
39   Garret FitzGerald, 'The 1974–75 Threat of a British Withdrawal from Northern Ireland' in *Irish Studies in International Affairs*, vol. 17 (2006).
40   Ibid., p. 186.
41   John Bew et al., *Talking to Terrorists*, p. 60.
42   Ibid., p. 255.
43   Vicky Conway, *The Blue Wall of Silence: The Morris Tribunal and Police Accountability in Ireland* (Dublin: Irish Academic Press, 2010), pp. 51–5.
44   Ibid., p. 90.
45   Conway, *Policing Twentieth Century Ireland*, p. 4.
46   Ibid., p. 45.
47   Dermot J. Walshe, *The Irish Police*, p. 20.
48   Ibid., p. 86.
49   Ibid., p. 118.
50   Brady, *Guardians of the Peace*, p. 163.
51   Ibid., p. 44.
52   Brady, *The Guarding of Ireland*, p. 253–6.
53   Gregory Allen, *The Garda Síochána: Policing Independent Ireland 1922–82* (Dublin: Gill and MacMillan, 1999).
54   Liam McNiffe, *A History of the Garda Síochána: A Social History of the Force 1922–52 with an Overview of the Years 1952–1997* (Dublin: Wolfhound, 1997).
55   John Duggan, *The Irish Army* (Dublin: Gill and Macmillan, 1991).
56   James Kelly, *Orders for the Captain* (Dublin: Kelly Kane, 1971); James Kelly *Thimbleriggers: The Dublin Arms Trials of 1970* (Dublin: James Kelly, 1999).
57   Mícheál Ó Cuinneaghain, *Monaghan, County of Intrigue: An Insight into the Political, Legal, and Religious Intrigues in this Border Area During the Period 1968–1979* (Monaghan: unknown publisher, 1979).
58   O'Brien, *The Arms Trial*, p. 57.
59   Ibid., p. 216.
60   Craig, *Crisis of Confidence*, p. 70.
61   McArdle, *The Secret War*, p. 24–7.
62   M.L.R. Smith, 'The Intellectual Internment of a Conflict: The Forgotten War in Northern Ireland' in *International Affairs*, volume 1, issue 75, 1999, p. 94.

Chapter 2

1   *Operation Banner: An Analysis of Military Operations in Northern Ireland July* (2006), http://w1.publicaddress.net/assets/upload/224146/-1650345631/opbanner.pdf.
2   Anthony Craig, *Crisis of Confidence* (Dublin: Irish Academic Press, 2010), p. 130.
3   http://www.rte.ie/tv/programmes/if_lynch_had_invaded.html.
4   Craig, *Crisis of Confidence*, p. 67.
5   Dermot Keogh, *Jack Lynch: A Biography* (Dublin: Gill and Macmillan, 2008), p. 195.

6   Donnacha Ó Beacháin, *Destiny of the Soldiers: Fianna Fáil, Irish Republicanism and the IRA 1926–1973* (Dublin: Gill and Macmillan, 2010), p. 28.
7   Kevin Boland, *We Won't Stand Idly By* (Dublin: Kelly Kane, 1973), p. 49.
8   Pádraig Faulkner, *As I Saw It* (Dublin: Wolfhound, 2005), p. 90.
9   Craig, *Crisis of Confidence*, p. 51.
10 Faulkner, *As I Saw It*, p. 93.
11 Keogh, *Jack Lynch*, p. 191.
12 Dáil Debates, Barry Desmond, 23 October 1969.
13 'Taoiseach sent Army shadow boxing to border', *The Sligo Champion*, 2 November 1969.
14 Patrick Bishop and Eamonn Mallie, *The Provisional IRA* (London: Corgi, 1987), p. 128.
15 Donnacha Ó Beacháin, *Destiny of the Soldiers*, p. 286.
16 'Effectiveness of Defence forces', 1971 Release, Military Archives, Cathal Brugha Barracks.
17 NA (UK) FCO 33/1616, 'Defence forces of Irish Republic', p. 14.
18 'Interim report of planning board on Northern Ireland operations', 1970 Release, Military Archives (Dublin), p. 2.
19 'Brief for Gerry Cronin Minister of Defence Jan 1971' in file 'Brief for Minister of Defence January 1971', 1971 Release, Military Archives.
20 Release C/S 111/8, 'Refugees', 1969, Military Archives (Dublin).
21 Bishop and Mallie, *The Provisional IRA*, p. 117.
22 Ibid.
23 Craig, *Crisis of Confidence* (2010), p. 50.
24 'Crisis in North', *Nusnight*, October 1969.
25 Craig, *Crisis of Confidence* (2010), p. 58.
26 'Former minister for defence in witness box', *The Irish Times*, 10 October 1970.
27 'Kelly says guns were not refused', *The Irish Times*, 15 October 1970.
28 Craig, *Crisis of Confidence* (2010), p. 69.
29 Ibid.
30 Kelly, *Orders for the Captain*, p. 17.
31 Ó Beacháin, *Destiny of the Soldiers*, p. 292.
32 'Peter Berry Diaries', *Magill*, June 1980, p. 54–62.
33 NA (UK) CJ3/100, 'Note on Gilchrest meeting with Haughey Relations with Irish Republic'.
34 Craig, *Crisis of Confidence* (2010), p. 68.
35 O'Brien, *The Arms Trial*, p. 70.
36 James Kelly, *Thimbleriggers: The Dublin Arms Trials of 1970* (Dublin: Kelly Kane, 1999), p. 15.
37 'Haughey Concludes Arms Trial Evidence', *The Irish Times*, 20 October 1970.
38 Public Accounts Committee evidence, 30 November 1971.
39 Dáil Debates, 9 November 1971.
40 Dermot Keogh, *Jack Lynch*, p. 205–21.
41 'Takeover of civil rights movement planned', *The United Irishman*, November 1969.
42 NA (IRL) 2001/6/519, 'Partition and govt policy 30/11/70-1/3/71'. Conversation with Gerry Fitt 13/12/70.
43 'Berry Papers', *Magill*, June 1980, p. 50.
44 Robert Savage, *A Loss of Innocence? Television and Irish Society 1960–72* (Manchester University Press: Manchester, 2015), p. 367.

45 *Fianna Fáil and the IRA*, Official Sinn Féin Publication (1972).

46 Henry Patterson, *The Politics of Illusion: A Political History of the IRA* (London: Serif, 1989), p. 124.

47 'Recommendations of planning board', 1970 Release, Military Archives (Dublin), p. 5.

48 Sean Boyne, *Gunrunners: The Covert Arms Trail to Ireland* (Dublin: O'Brien Press, 2006), p. 29.

49 Ibid., p. 32.

50 'Berry Papers', *Magill*, June 1980, p. 60.

51 Ibid., p. 60–2.

52 'Haughey knew Captain Kelly had special role', *The Irish Times*, 20 October 1970.

53 'Review of events in politics longest day', *The Irish Times*, 7 May 1970.

54 Boyne, *Gunrunners*, p. 85.

55 'The Arms trial', *Magill*, May 1980, p. 46.

56 See O'Brien, *The Arms Trial* and Ó Beacháin, *Destiny of the Soldiers*.

57 Craig, *Crisis of Confidence* and Keogh, *Jack Lynch*.

58 Craig, *Crisis of Confidence*, p. 71.

59 Desmond O'Malley, *Conduct Unbecoming: A Memoir* (Dublin: Gill and Macmillan, 2014), p. 74.

60 NA (UK) FCO 33/1206, 'Briefing note on Parliamentary Question from Mr Chichestor Clarke by Kelvin White'.

61 'Berry Papers', *Magill*, June 1980, p. 70.

62 Craig, *Crisis of Confidence*, p. 87.

63 Keogh, *Jack Lynch*, p. 270.

64 Ibid., p. 233.

65 NA (IRL) 2001/61/12, 'Berry statement to Arms trial investigators'.

66 'Ó Móráin in walk out at law dinner', *The Irish Times*, 24 April 1970.

67 'The Army', *Hibernia*, 6 November 1969, p. 3.

68 Keogh, *Jack Lynch*, p. 215.

69 NA(UK) CJ4/100 UK Embassy Report, 'Ireland Seen from Dublin October 1969', in Relations with Irish Republic (point 40).

70 'Berry Papers', *Magill*, June 1980, p. 50.

71 Conor Brady, 'The Policeman's lot', *The Irish Times*, 19–21 August 1969.

72 Ibid.

73 John Merriman, 'Crumlin and After', *Garda Review*, September 1969.

74 'Arms crisis 1970: This inside story', *Magill*, May 1980, p. 56.

75 NA (UK) FCO 33/1619, Letter dated 7 October 1971, 'Disaffection in the Garda'.

76 Conway, *Policing Twentieth Century Ireland*, p. 113.

77 Kieran Conway, *Southside Provisional: From Freedom Fighter to Four Courts* (Dublin: Orpen Press, 2014), p. 20.

78 'The bank robberies: Why an inquiry is called for', *Hibernia*, 17 April 1970.

79 'Berry Papers', *Magill*, June 1980, p. 53.

80 'Special Branch', *Hibernia*, 17 July 1970.

81 Conor Brady, 'The Man from SDU', *The Irish Times*, 23 December 1970.

82 NA (UK) FCO 33/1594 Peck John, 'Safe Haven: Facts and Prospects', 21 December, 1971.

83 'Berry Papers', *Magill*, June 1980.

84 Dáil Debates, 21 May 1970.

85 'Berry Papers', *Magill*, June 1980, p. 55.
86 NA (UK) FCO 33/1616 Lt Col. A.H. Henderson Report from March 1971.
87 'Recommendations of planning board', 13 September 1969, Military Archives (Dublin), 1970, p. 5.
88 Ibid., p. 6.
89 'Recommendations of planning board', Military Archives (Dublin), 1970, and accompanying document entitled 'Response to Recommendations of planning board', dated 13 October 1969.
90 Craig, *Crisis of Confidence* (2010), p. 54.
91 'Brief for Ceann Forrinne: Interview with Taoiseach June 1970', Military Archives (Dublin), 1970.
92 Ibid.
93 Ibid.
94 'Release Memo Army Intelligence October 5, 1970' in 'Military Intelligence File 4', Military Archives (Dublin), 1970.
95 'Accuracy of Minister's statement questioned', *The Irish Times*, 26 September 1970.
96 'Gibbons authorised rifles', *The Irish Times*, 25 September 1970.
97 Keogh, *Jack Lynch*, p. 238.
98 'Memorandum Military commitments and requirements 6 April 1970', 1970 Release, Military Archives (Dublin), p. 4.
99 Ibid., p. 4.
100 'Memorandum for Government Military matters', Defence Policy letter 23 February 1971, 1971 Release, Military Archives (Dublin).
101 'Minutes of June 9 1970 meeting between Taoiseach Lynch and Chief of Staff McEoin', 1970 Release, Military Archives (Dublin).
102 NA (UK) FCO 33/1616, Note to Ministry of Defence from British Embassy, 6 January 1971, 'Role of Defence Forces of Republic of Ireland'.
103 'Jury sent out 4 times in Arms hearing', *The Irish Times*, 13 October 1970.
104 'Garda and Army intelligence', *The Irish Times*, 29 September 1970, p. 8.
105 O'Halpin, *Defending Ireland*, p. 275.
106 'Collections organised', *Donegal Democrat*, 22 August 1969.
107 'Support pledged for refugee relief', *The Sligo Champion*, 29 August 1969.
108 'Leitrim collected £1600 for northern relief', *Leitrim Observer*, 6 December 1969.
109 'Illegal collections', *The Sligo Champion*, 29 August 1969.
110 'Allegations of Donegal B men inflames tension near border', *Donegal Democrat*, 22 August 1969.
111 'No boycott of Protestants in Donegal', *The Irish Times*, 16 September 1969.
112 'Catholic Paisleys responsible for ugly incidents', *Donegal Democrat*, 5 September 1969.
113 'Castleblayney UDC', *Dundalk Democrat*, 30 August 1969.
114 'Attack in Newbliss', *Northern Standard*, 22 August 1969.
115 'Attempt to burn Orange Hall', *The Irish Times*, 3 September 1969.
116 'Slogans painted in Rockcorry', *The Irish Times*, 4 September 1969.
117 'Northern guests at Greystone threatened', *The Irish Times*, 7 October 1969. This incident was made public some weeks after the August violence.
118 'Kingscourt Intimidation', *The Irish Times*, 10 September 1969.
119 'Councillor supports Mr Fox', *Northern Standard*, 14 November 1969.
120 'They fought with words over flags', *The Sligo Champion*, 29 August 1969.

121 *Dundalk Democrat*, 23 August 1969.
122 'Gardaí use batons on demonstrators', *The Irish Times*, 18 August 1969.
123 Brian Hanley and Scott Millar, *The Lost Revolution: The Story of the Official IRA and Workers Party* (Dublin: Penguin, 2009), p. 131.
124 'Summary of situation in Northern Ireland Aug 31', 1970 Release, Military Archives (Dublin) in Intelligence File 4, 1970 Release, Military Archives (Dublin).
125 Ibid.
126 Dermot Keogh, *Jack Lynch*, p. 193.
127 Brian Hanley and Scott Millar, *The Lost Revolution*, p. 130.
128 Seán Mac Stíofáin, *Revolutionary in Ireland* (Edinburgh: Cremonesi, 1975), p. 126.
129 Ibid.
130 'Berry papers', *Magill*, June 1980, p. 51.
131 Dermot Keogh, *Jack Lynch*, p. 196.
132 *The Irish Times*, 19 April 1971.
133 'The Arms Crisis', *Magill*, May 1980, p. 40.
134 Hanley and Millar, *The Lost Revolution*, p. 130.
135 'Garda Border Patrols', Dáil Debates, 28 April 1971.
136 'Berry Papers', *Magill*, June 1980, p. 52.
137 Brady, *Guardians of the Peace* (1999), p. 163.
138 Ó Beacháin, *Destiny of the Soldiers*, p. 302.
139 *Donegal Democrat*, 23 January 1970.
140 'Berry Papers', *Magill*, June 1980, p. 55.
141 Ibid.
142 Ibid.
143 *Donegal Democrat*, 23 January 1970.
144 Ibid.
145 'Sam Dowling: Pre Trial treatment', *Hibernia*, 19 March 1971.
146 'Release Brief for Cean Forrinne: Memorandum Military Commitments and Requirements 6/4/70', 1970 Release, Military Archives (Dublin).
147 Ibid.
148 'Full Story of attempt to blow up UVF transformer', *Donegal Democrat*, 31 October 1969.
149 *The Irish Times*, 31 October 1969 and 1 October 1969.
150 'Army and Garda on full alert', *The Irish Times*, 3 November 1969.
151 'Sligo notes', *Garda Review*, December 1969, p. 51.
152 *United Irishman*, March 1969.
153 *The Sligo Champion*, 10 July 1970, 29 May 1970, 1 May 1970 and 11 June 1970.
154 'Gardaí halted Demonstration', *The Sligo Champion*, 1 May 1970.
155 'Protestors took over Slane Castle', *Meath Chronicle*, 11 July 1970.
156 *The Irish Times*, 7 April 1970; 'Councillors, Gardaí recapture Lifford board room', *The Irish Times*, 24 March 1970.
157 'Miss Devlin prevails in Donegal', *The Irish Times*, 23 March 1970.
158 'Blaney draws fire on force', *Donegal Democrat*, 12 December 1969.
159 'Customs post on fire', *The Irish Times*, 17 October 1970; 'Customs Station blast wreckage', *The Irish Times*, 3 August 1970.
160 *The Irish Times*, 13 August 1970.
161 'Silent Anger sweeps Armagh Town', *The Irish Times*, 13 August 1970.

162 'Another force at work', *Dundalk Democrat*, 15 August 1970.

163 'RUC Men's death in "Cowardly plot"', *The Irish Times* 15 December 1970.

164 NA (UK) FCO 33/1482, UK Representative in Belfast memo to FCO and Home Office, dated 16 October 1971, in 'Incidents on Border of Northern Ireland and Republic'.

165 'Border Road Spikes at Courtbane', *Dundalk Democrat*, 10 October 1970.

166 NA (UK) CJ4/809, 'Note on Border Roads' in NIO file 'Blocking Roads in Northern Ireland Security/Transport'.

167 NA (IRL) Taois 2001/6/550, Confidential briefing note by Sean Ronan to Department of Taoiseach.

168 'Further remand in Donegal Arms charge', *Donegal Democrat*, 7 August 1970.

169 NA (IRL) 2010/19/1705 Border Infringements reported to Department of Foreign Affairs.

170 Ibid.

171 Ibid. These figures relate to the end of October 1971.

172 NA (IRL) Taois 2001/6/550, 'Confidential briefing note by Sean Ronan to Department of Taoiseach'.

173 *Dundalk Democrat*, 23 August 1969.

174 File C/S 111/8, 'Refugees', 1969 Release, Military Archives (Dublin).

175 '96 more refugees arrive', *The Irish Times*, 9 September 1969.

176 'Refugees at Finner Camp', *Donegal Democrat*, 22 August 1969.

177 OPS/11 'Sitereps viacomcen', 1969 Release, Military Archives (Dublin).

178 Ibid.

179 *Dispelling the Myths* (Drogheda: Drogheda Community Forum, 2004), p. 12.

180 Ibid.

181 C/S 111/8 Refugees letter dated 20/5/70 from Commandant S. O'Sullivan, 1970 Release, Military Archives (Dublin).

182 'Site report Gormanston', File number :0ps 10 covering 19/10/69–31/12/69 Jan 8 siterep, 1969, Military Archives (Dublin).

183 Gerry Boland, Dáil Debates, 26 November 1969, in response to a question from Noël Browne.

184 NA (IRL) 2000/6/661, Department of Defence letter to Taoiseach, 27 October 1969.

185 Ibid.

186 C/S 111/8, 'Refugees', 1970, Military Archives (Dublin).

187 CS 111/8, 'Memorandum on refugees from Northern Ireland', 1970, Military Archives (Dublin), p. 2.

188 Ibid.

189 NA (IRL) 2005/155/6, 'Assessment of security problems consequent of an influx of refugees', in 'Refugees from Northern Ireland Letter', dated 1 August 1975.

190 *Dispelling the Myths* (Drogheda: Drogheda Community Forum 2004), p. 17.

191 Pobal Research Report, *All Over the Place: People Displaced to and from the Southern Border Counties as a Result of the Conflict 1969–1994* (2005).

192 NA (IRL) 2005/7/1966, 'Inter Departmental Unit', May 1970, report, p. 3.

193 'SiteReps 1970 duty officer brief', 1970, Military Archives (Dublin).

194 Ibid.

195 'Tense situation on Donegal–Derry Border', *Donegal Democrat*, 14 August 1970.

196 'Kilworth Camp at Capacity with Falls refugees', *The Irish Times*, 14 July 1970.

197 Justin O'Brien, *The Arms Trial* (Dublin: Newleaf, 2000), p. 117.
198 Eunan O'Halpin, *Defending Ireland* (1999), p. 311.
199 '15 arrested in picket of official's home', *The Irish Times*, 8 July 1970.
200 'Berry Papers', *Magill*, June 1980, p. 42.
201 NA (UK) FCO 33/1618, Peck, John, 'The Administration of Justice in Republic of Ireland' (point 10), 12 January 1971.
202 NA (IRL) 2001/6/42, 'Letter from Des O'Malley', 15 October 1970.
203 NA (IRL) DFA 2010/53/889, Report from Department of Justice on Armed Robberies.

Chapter 3

1 Patrick Bishop and Eamonn Mallie, *The Provisional IRA* (London: Corgi, 1987), p. 201.
2 Anthony Craig, *Crisis of Confidence* (Dublin: Irish Academic Press, 2010), p. 106.
3 Dáil Debates Public Hearing on Barron Inquiry, 1 February 2005, http://debates.oireachtas.ie/JUB/2005/02/01/00003.asp.
4 'Special Criminal Court Panel Raised to 7 Judges', *The Irish Times*, 5 August 1972.
5 NA (UK) FCO 87/11, 'Republic of Ireland-A crowded fortnight', 12 December 1972, in 'Policy of Fianna Fáil Party'.
6 Dáil Debates Public Hearing on Barron Inquiry, 1 February 2005, http://debates.oireachtas.ie/JUB/2005/02/01/00003.asp.
7 Craig, *Crisis of Confidence*, p. 126.
8 '23 Remanded on Arms Charges', *The Irish Times*, 10 November 1970.
9 'Dundalk Roundup', *Hibernia*, 20 November 1970.
10 '14 Freed on Arms charges', *The Irish Times*, 26 November 1970.
11 'North men fined on Gun charges', *The Irish Times*, 17 November 1970.
12 NA (IRL) 2000/6/82, 'Minutes of meeting of December 4, 1970 between FCO officials and Irish Ambassador'.
13 'Stop collaboration', *An Phoblacht*, December 1970.
14 'Threat to reopen Internment Camps', *The Irish Times*, 5 December 1970
15 'Scepticism by Gardaí at inaction over shots', *The Irish Times*, 20 October 1970.
16 Dick Walsh, *Des O'Malley: A Political Profile* (Kerry: Brandon, 1986), p. 36.
17 Donnacha Ó Beacháin, *Destiny of the Soldiers: Fianna Fáil, Irish Republicanism and the IRA 1926–1973* (Dublin: Gill and Macmillan, 2010), p. 310.
18 'Berry Papers', *Magill*, 1980, p. 73.
19 Brian Hanley, 'Internment 1970', *The Cedar Lounge Revolution* [website], 1 July 1970, https://cedarlounge.wordpress.com/2015/07/01/internment-1970/#comments.
20 'Dáil Statement by Lynch on Wednesday', *The Irish Times*, 7 December 1970.
21 NA (UK) FCO 33/1618, 'The Administration of Justice in the Republic of Ireland', 12 January 1971.
22 Ó Beacháin, *Destiny of the Soldiers*, p. 318.
23 John Walsh, *Patrick Hillery: The Official Biography* (Dublin: New Island, 2008), p. 243.
24 Ibid., p. 247.
25 Ó Beacháin, *Destiny of the Soldiers*, p. 313.

26 Walsh, *Patrick Hillery*, p. 248.
27 O'Malley, *Conduct Unbecoming: A Memoir*, p. 57.
28 Walsh, *Patrick Hillery*, p. 248.
29 Dermot Keogh, *Jack Lynch: A Biography* (Dublin: Gill and Macmillan, 2008), p. 284.
30 Craig, *Crisis of Confidence*, p. 93.
31 Keogh, *Jack Lynch*, p. 300.
32 NA (UK) FCO 33/1618, 'Telegram no 4 March 11, 1971'.
33 NA (UK) FCO 33/1618, 'Peck to Lynch February 11 1971'.
34 NA (UK)FCO 33/1618, 'Telegram 54 19 February 1971'.
35 NA (IRL) 2000/6/159, 'Memorandum for the Taoiseach on Current Security Situation'.
36 'IRA Bases endanger Lynch Line', *The Irish Times*, 6 April 1971.
37 'Illegal Organisations Camp', Dáil Debates, 15 December 1971, http://debates. oireachtas.ie/Dáil/1971/12/15/00021.asp.
38 NA (IRL) DFA 2002/8/78, 'Meeting at Foreign and Commonwealth Office on May 24, 1971'.
39 NA (IRL) DFA 2002/8/78, 'Briefing note June 16, 1971'; Dáil Debates, Volume 254, 16 June 1971.
40 'Labour's taunt of inaction after Derry men's death', *The Irish Times*, 14 July 1971.
41 John Bew et al., *Talking to Terrorists: Making Peace in the Basque Country and Northern Ireland* (London: Hurst and Company, 2009), p. 33.
42 Craig, *Crisis of Confidence*, p. 97.
43 NA (UK) CJ4/183, 'Northern Ireland: Dr Hillery's discussion with Home Secretary August 11, 1971'.
44 Ibid.
45 NA (UK) CJ4/183, 'UK Representative in Belfast Telegram number 23 August 23, 1971'.
46 NA (IRL) 2002/8/481, 'British Embassy Telegram 19 August, 1971'.
47 Keogh, *Jack Lynch*, p. 316.
48 '1,100 attend launching of Boland's new party', *The Irish Times*, 20 September 1971.
49 David McKittrick et al., *Lost Lives* (London: Mainstream Publishing, 1999), p. 78–96.
50 'Wide Agenda for Lynch–Heath Talks', *The Irish Times*, 30 July 1971.
51 'British version differs in detail', *The Irish Times*, 1 September 1971.
52 NA (UK) FC0 33/1612, 'Visit of Mr Lynch 6/7 September', p. 5.
53 Garret FitzGerald, *All in a Life* (London: Gill and Macmillan, 1991), p. 99.
54 Ó Beacháin, *Destiny of the Soldiers*, p. 326.
55 Craig, *Crisis of Confidence* , p. 108.
56 Ó Beacháin, *Destiny of the Soldiers*, p. 328.
57 Ibid.
58 Craig, *Crisis of Confidence* (2010), p. 102.
59 'Ex British Officer Shot in Hold Up', *The Irish Times*, 3 December 1971.
60 NA (IRL) 2002/252, 'Telegram dated December 15, 1971'.
61 NA (IRL) 2002/8/484, 'News Release December 15, 1971'.
62 'Ten gunmen steal 15 FCA Rifles, 2 Machine Guns', *The Irish Times*, 8 December 1971.

63 'Lynch Challenged on Security by Britain and Provisionals', *The Irish Times*, 15 December 1971.
64 Ibid.
65 Maria McGuire, *To Take Up Arms: My Year with the IRA Provisionals* (New York: Viking, 1973), p. 84.
66 'Lynch rejects IRA's "arrogant suggestion"', *The Irish Times*, 18 December 1971.
67 'Internment rumours denied', *The Irish Times*, 21 December 1971.
68 NA (UK) FCO 87/42, 'Letter from Dublin Embassy to Stewart Crawford', 10 January 1972, p. 3.
69 'State of the parties-Fianna Fáil', *Hibernia*, 7 January 1972, p. 3.
70 Eamonn McCann, 'Bloody Sunday: The truth was known 25 years ago', *The Observer*, 19 September 1999.
71 Thomas McNulty, *Exiled: 40 Years an Exile* (Dublin: TMN Publications, 2013), p. 75.
72 Bertie Ahern, *Bertie Ahern: The Autobiography* (London: Cornerstone, 2009), p. 31.
73 NA (IRL) 2003/26/6, 'Garda Report on burning of Embassy', p. 19.
74 O'Malley, *Conduct Unbecoming: A Memoir*, p. 92.
75 NA (UK) FCO 87/11, 'The Irish Political scene since the burning of the embassy', 27 June 1972.
76 'O'Malley supported in tough line against IRA', *The Irish Times*, 21 February 1972.
77 'O'Malley supported in tough line against IRA', *The Irish Times*, 21 February 1972.
78 Conor Cruise O'Brien, *States of Ireland* (London: Panther, 1972), p. 285.
79 Charles McGuire, 'Defenders of the State: The Irish Labour Party, Coalitionism and Revisionism, 1969–77' in *Irish Studies Review*, DOI: 10.1080/09670882.2015.1054123 (2015), p. 12.
80 Ibid.
81 'Goulding, three others held in Garda swoop', *The Irish Times*, 23 February 1972.
82 Keogh, *Jack Lynch*, p. 337.
83 O'Malley, *Conduct Unbecoming: A Memoir*, p. 82–3.
84 NA (UK) FCO 87/42, 'John Peck to Kelvin White', 2 March 1972.
85 John Walsh, *Patrick Hillery: The Official Biography* (Dublin: New Island, 2008), p. 274.
86 'Political Row over Wilson-IRA talks', *The Irish Times*, 22 March 1972.
87 Garret FitzGerald, 'The 1974–75 Threat of a British Withdrawal from Northern Ireland' in *Irish Studies in International Affairs*, vol. 17 (2006), p. 142.
88 Bishop and Mallie, *The Provisional IRA*, p. 227.
89 Craig, *Crisis of Confidence*, p. 123.
90 M.L.R. Smith, *Fighting for Ireland? The Military Strategy of the Irish Republican Movement* (London: Routledge, 1995), p. 111.
91 NA (IRL) 2003/17/304, 'Meeting between Heath and Lynch', 4 September 1972, p. 4.
92 NA (UK) FCO 87/121, 'FCO Telegram 679', 6 November 1972.
93 NA (UK) CJ4/251, Letter to Stewart Crawford 7 July 1972; Draft letter from Stewart Crawford circa July 1972.
94 NA (UK) CJ4/251, Draft letter from Stewart Crawford circa July 1972.
95 NA (UK) FCO 33/1619, 'Appendix Comparison of Court cases in England,

Northern Ireland and Republic'. Examples include Eight men received £20 fines for firearms possession in Dublin (November 1970); Fourteen men had firearms charges dismissed in Dundalk (November 1970); Sam Dowling of Newry Civil Rights Association had explosive charges dismissed in Dundalk (January 1971); Official IRA chief Cathal Goulding received a £400 fine for stealing a lorry (February 1971); An IRA member fired a shot into a Dundalk pub received a £5 fine (March 1971); Four men engaged in gun battle at border were given fourteen days imprisonment (November 1971).

96   McNulty, *Exiled*, pp. 91–4.
97   NA (UK) FCO 87/42, 'Telegraph from Peck to FCO April 25, 1972 Telegraph number 301'.
98   Ó Beacháin, *Destiny of the Soldiers*, p. 344.
99   'Not Detention Without Trial', *The Irish Times*, 20 May 1972.
100   NA (IRL) 2007/116/775, 'Security Measures 1969–73'.
101   'Ó Brádaigh, Cahill Held on remand', *The Irish Times*, 2 June 1972.
102   NA (IRL) 2003/17/304, 'Meeting of Taoiseach with Prime Minister Heath on September 4, 1972', p. 6.
103   Ed Maloney, *A Secret History of the IRA* (London: WW Norton, 2002), p. 116.
104   Ed Maloney, *Voices from the Grave* (London: Public Affairs, 2010), p. 103.
105   *Operation Banner: An Analysis of Military Operations in Northern Ireland*, Ministry of Defence (2007), p. 29, http://www.vilaweb.cat/media/attach/vwedts/docs/op_banner_analysis_released.pdf.
106   NA (UK) FCO 87/121, 'Letter from Kelvin White to KC Thom', 13 December 1972.
107   'Special Criminal Court Panel Raised to 7 Judges', *The Irish Times*, 5 August 1972.
108   Ibid.
109   'O'Malley calls in 2,000 guns', *The Irish Times*, 3 August 1972.
110   'O'Malley orders new controls on explosive materials', *The Irish Times*, 10 August 1972.
111   NA (IRL) 2010/19/1703, 'Exceptional Legislation measures taken by Ireland in period 1969–1979'.
112   'O'Malley hits at US funds for IRA', *The Irish Times*, 25 October 1972.
113   'Summons for Sinn Féin Groups', *The Irish Times*, 9 August 1972.
114   Desmond O'Malley in response to Gerard L'Estrange, Dáil Debates, 4 November 1971.
115   Keogh, *Jack Lynch*, p. 365.
116   NA 2004/7/2675, 'Border Security'.
117   Ó Beacháin, *Destiny of the Soldiers*, p. 357.
118   Ibid.
119   '4000 protestors march to Dáil', *The Irish Times*, 29 November 1972.
120   'MacStíofáin airlifted to Curragh Camp', *The Irish Times*, 28 November 1972.
121   Houses of Oireachtas sub-committee, *Interim Report on the Report of the Independent Commission of Inquiry into the Dublin Bombings of 1972 and 1973* (2004), p. 87, http://www.dublinmonaghanbombings.org/DubInterim.pdf.
122   Garret FitzGerald, *All in a Life* (London: Gill and Macmillan, 1991), p. 108.
123   Derek Dunne and Gene Kerrigan, *Round Up the Usual Suspects* (Dublin: Magill, 1984), p. 76.
124   Ó Beacháin, *Destiny of the Soldiers*, p. 365.

125 Ibid.

126 NA (UK) FCO 87/48, 'Telegram number 781', 21 December 1972.

127 Ibid.

128 Ó Beacháin, *Destiny of the Soldiers*, p. 355.

129 'Dead but not buried', *Hibernia*, 15 December 1972.

130 NA (UK) FCO 87/11, 'Republic of Ireland-A crowded Fortnight', 12 December 1972, p. 16.

131 Craig, *Crisis of Confidence*, p. 94.

132 NA (UK) FCO 87/11, 'Republic of Ireland-A crowded Fortnight', 12 December 1972, p. 12.

133 'A question of role: Defence forces', *Hibernia*, 15 December 1972.

134 Ó Beacháin, *Destiny of the Soldiers*, p. 363.

135 'A question of role: Defence forces', *Hibernia*, 15 December 1972.

136 'Half of Conroy's Loaf', *Hibernia*, 1 February 1971.

137 Ibid.

138 'Chance of Garda Strike Increases', *The Irish Times*, 5 October 1971.

139 'Munster Gardaí Frustrated', *The Irish Times*, 8 December 1971.

140 NA (UK) FCO 33/1619, 'Disaffection among the Gardaí', letter dated 8 December 1971 in 'Administration of Justice in Republic of Ireland'.

141 NA 2003/15/13, 'Border Posts-November 25, 1971', in 'Border Operations', Military Archives (Dublin).

142 NA 2003/15/13, 'Border Posts-November 25, 1971' in 'Border Operations', Military Archives (Dublin).

143 Ibid.

144 Ibid.

145 NA 2003/15/13, 'Establishment of two border Battalions' in 'Border Operations', Military Archives (Dublin).

146 'Garda patrol cars broke down in chase deputy alleges', *Donegal Democrat*, 4 June 1971.

147 NA (IRL) 2005/147/310, 'Report from Asst Commissioner Edward Garvey on visits to Cavan Monaghan (25/7/73) and Donegal (18-19/7/73)'.

148 'Curragh camp genuine "no-go" area warns Cronin', *The Irish Times*, 7 July 1972.

149 'Nine Gardaí injured in Night of rioting', *Donegal Democrat*, 10 November 1972.

150 NA 2003/15/96, 'Report on Patrol to Monaghan from Castleblaney' in 'Border Incident: Monaghan Garda station', Military Archive (Dublin).

151 NA (IRL) DFA 2006/132/225, 'Garda Riot Control Equipment', Letter from Assistant Commissioner P. McLaughlin to Barrack Master in Phoenix Park, dated 17 April 1973.

152 NA (UK) FCO 87/197, 'Letter to foreign office from supplier dated January 1, 1972'.

153 NA (UK) FCO 87/40, 'Letter dated November 30, 1972 to RB Bone in FCO' in folder 'Export of military equipment from UK to ROI'.

154 NA (UK) FC0 87/130, 'Letter to Kelvin White dated 13 January 1972' in 'Co-operation between governments on control of explosives and firearms'.

155 NA (UK) FCO 87/372, 'Irish Army contact report', 12 October 1972.

156 NA 2007/116/47, 'Memorandum on Proposed Garda Siochana Order', 20 December 1976, p. 9.

157 'Jack Marrinan, General Secretary of Garda Representative Body', *The Irish Times*, 29 August 1972.

158   NA 2004/7/2675, 'Border Security', 14 September 1973.
159   'The Border War', *Hibernia*, 18 February 1972, p. 17.
160   'Effectivity of Defence Forces Military Considerations', 1971 Release, Military Archives (Dublin), August 1971.
161   NA (IRL) 2007/116/775, 'Security Measure 1969–73'.
162   NA (IRL) 2007/116/768, 'Security', Summer (1977).
163   Ibid.
164   'Arming of Gardaí only as last resort-O'Malley', *The Irish Times*, 14 June 1972.
165   Walsh, *Des O'Malley: A Political Profile*, p. 34.
166   'Smugglers Paradise', *Hibernia*, 22 September 1972.
167   'Tensions grow throughout the day', *Donegal Democrat*, 31 December 1972.
168   'Lifford Garda Station Attacked', *Donegal Democrat*, 17 March 1972, p. 1.
169   'Garda barracks under siege', *Donegal Democrat*, 15 September 1972, p. 1 – September 1972: Milford Barracks in Donegal 'was under siege for a time', following a court appearance by republicans. Again stones were thrown, with windows broken; 'Bid to blow up Garda Station', *Donegal Democrat*, 13 October 1972, p. 1 – October 1972: An attempt was made to blow up Buncrana Garda station using 35 pounds of explosives by parties unknown.
170   'Crowds fight Army, Gardaí in Monaghan', *The Irish Times*, 20 March 1972.
171   '60 Gardaí clash with civilian', *Anglo Celt*, 21 April 1972, p. 9.
172   NA 2005/147/41, 'Application for compensation by named Garda', 1 January 1974.
173   Houses of Oireachtas sub-committee, *Interim Report on the Report of the Independent Commission of Inquiry into the Dublin Bombings of 1972 and 1973* (2004), p. 13, http://www.dublinmonaghanbombings.org/DubInterim.pdf.
174   'Dundalk Garda Barracks Fired by Rioters', *The Irish Times*, 22 September 1972.
175   Conway, *Policing Twentieth Century Ireland*, p. 129.
176   Examples include 'Gardaí attacked as McGuigan remanded', *The Irish Times*, 14 September 1972; 'Picketers, Gardaí in Courthouses scuffles', *The Irish Times*, 16 November 1972; 'Fistfights as IRA men oppose Garda at Drogheda', 30 December 1971, *The Irish Times*; 'Prisoners, Gardaí and public in courtroom brawl', *Donegal Democrat*, 22 September 1972.
177   'MacStíofáin Rescue Bid Fails', *The Irish Times*, 27 November 1972
178   Dunne and Kerrigan, *Round Up the Usual Suspects*, p. 67.
179   NA (UK) FC0 33/1616, 'Telegram from Peck Irish Army officer's arrest', 21 September 1971, in 'Role of Defence forces of ROI'.
180   For example, Hanley and Millar, *The Lost Revolution: The Story of the Official IRA and the Workers Party*, p. 169; Boyne, *Gunrunners: The Covert Arms Trail to Ireland*, p. 135; McArdle *The Secret War*, p. 24.
181   Conway, *Southside Provisional: From Freedom Fighter to Four Courts*, p. 65.
182   NA (UK) FCO 87/248, 'Note on named Garda' in 'Co-operation between defence forces of UK and ROI includes Border dossier'.
183   NA (UK) FCO 87/248, 'Letter to Kelvin White', 21 November 1973, in 'Co-operation between defence forces of UK and ROI includes Border dossier'.
184   NA (UK) FCO 87/245, 'Report on murder of Pte Lilley September 7 1973', dated 11 September 1973.
185   NA (UK) FCO 87/247, 'Terrorist activity in Clady/Cloughfin area March 29, 1973' in 'Co-operation on border security'.
186   Craig, *Crisis of Confidence*, p. 143.

187 NA (UK) FCO 87/247, 'Terrorist activity in Clady/Cloughfin area March 29, 1973' in 'Co-operation on border security'.
188 Patterson, *Ireland's Violent Frontier*, p. 45.
189 Interview with Jim Gallagher, 'Green and Blue' Project, http://accounts.ulster.ac.uk/repo24/files/original/f7fd515b0e8f9f709591be43894a9d39.pdf.
190 NA (UK) FCO 87/122, 'Report on Strabane RUC subdivision for August 1972'.
191 Ibid.
192 NA (UK) FCO 87/122, 'Monthly border report September 13, 1972', p. 16.
193 Line 1106, Dáil Debates, 26 April 1972.
194 Ruan O'Donnell, *Special Category: The IRA in English Prisons 1968–1978* (Dublin: Irish Academic Press 2012), p. 46.
195 Eunan O'Halpin, *Defending Ireland* (Oxford: Oxford University Press, 1999), p. 330.
196 NA (UK) FCO 87/119, 'Future Border Policy', April 1972.
197 NA (UK) FCO 87/121, 'Cross border incidents', in folder 'Border', p. 3.
198 Lynch in reply to Dr O'Connell, Dáil Debates, 2 May 1972.
199 NA (UK) FCO 87/42, 'Telegram 301', 25 April 1972.
200 Ibid.
201 NA (UK) FCO 87/42, 'Telegram no 306', 28 April 1972.
202 NA (UK) FCO 87/130, 'Telegram no 389', 30 May 1972, in 'Co-operation on control of explosives'.
203 NA (UK) FCO 87/42, 'Telegram no 306', 28 April 1972.
204 NA (UK) FCO 87/130, 'Telegram no 389', 30 May 1972, in 'Co-operation on control of explosives'.
205 NA (UK) FCO 87/42, 'Telegram no 316', 28 April 1972.
206 'IRPB 14/10/71', *An Phoblacht*, Samhain 1971, p. 2.
207 NA (UK) FCO 87/119, 'Telegram from Peck', 28 April 1972.
208 George Clarke, *Border Crossing: True Stories of the RUC Special Branch, the Garda Special Branch and IRA Moles* (Dublin: Gill and Macmillan, 2009), p. 124.
209 Ibid., p. 124.
210 Patsy McArdle, *The Secret War* (Dublin: Mercier, 1984), p. 23.
211 NA (UK) FCO 87/122, 'Border Report August 1972', dated 12 September 1972, p. 5.
212 NA (UK) FCO 87/130, 'Minutes of meetings held on September 5, 1972 and August 15, 1972' in 'Co-operation on control of explosives'.
213 NA 2002/8/484, 'News Item December 15, 1971'.
214 NA (UK) FCO 33/1481, 'Letter to Stewart Crawford MOD dated August 20, 1971' in 'Incidents on border of NI and ROI'.
215 NA (UK) FCO 33/1607, 'Peck note dated December 21, 1971' in 'Political Relations between ROI and NI'.
216 NA (IRL) 2003/15/13, 'Border Posts', 25 November 1971, in 'Border Operations'
217 'Five men killed in booby trap blast', *The Irish Times*, 10 February 1971.
218 NA (UK) FCO 33/1481, 'Use of border by terrorists April 1971' in 'Incidents on border of NI and ROI'.
219 NA (UK) FCO 33/1481, 'Use of border by terrorists June 1971' in 'Incidents on border of NI and ROI'.
220 'Along the border', *Hibernia*, 27 August 1971.
221 FCO 33/1483, 'Border Incidents', dated 7 December 1971, in 'Incidents on border of NI and ROI'.

222 NA (UK) FCO 33/1483, 'Ministry of Defence letter to Kelvin White in FCO November 1971' in 'Incidents on border of NI and ROI'.
223 NA (IRL) 2003/17/345, 'Incidents involving the border as reported by British', p. 2.
224 Bishop and Mallie, *The Provisional IRA*, p. 202.
225 'The battle of Courtbane', *Dundalk Democrat*, 4 September 1971.
226 'British version differs in detail', *The Irish Times*, 1 September 1971.
227 NA (IRL) 2002/8/481, 'Lynch statement 31 August 1971'.
228 NA (UK) FCO 33/1482, 'Telegram to FCO October 5, 1971' in 'Incidents on border of NI and ROI'.
229 'Border Folly goes on', *Northern Standard*, 3 December 1971.
230 McNulty, *Exiled*, p. 70.
231 NA (UK) FCO 33/1483, 'Border Incidents', 7 December 1971, in 'Incidents on border of NI and ROI'.
232 'Violence spreads along the border', *Donegal Democrat*, 26 November 1971; 'British Army reign of terror in border village', *Donegal Democrat*, 10 December 1971; 'Gardaí threatened by British troops', *The Sligo Champion*, 5 November 1971; 'Gas firing investigated at border', *Donegal Democrat*, 25 November 1971.
233 NA (IRL) 2001/43/1314, 'Note handed to Eamonn Gallagher by John Williams', November 1971. Examples cited include: November 11: After a gun attack in Belleek, Gardaí arrived but searched the wrong area; November 17: Shots fired by gunmen at British forces, Gardaí at Manorhamilton contacted but when they arrived the gunmen were allowed to drive away; November 18: Four gunmen after major gunbattle with British were arrested by Gardaí but later released; November 20: British troops fired shots at gunmen near Drumbilla. Those they hit were treated for gunshot wounds in Dundalk hospital but not arrested by southern authorities.
234 'Local men on arms charges', *Dundalk Democrat*, 20 October 1971.
235 NA (IRL) 2001/43/1314, 'Supt Cotterill report'.
236 NA (IRL) 2001/43/1314, 'Supt J Shea December 4, 1971'.
237 NA(IRL) 2001/43/1314, 'Report from Sgt Edward Kelly'.
238 NA(IRL) 2001/43/1314, 'Draft', 26 November 1971.
239 NA (IRL) 2001/43/1314, 'Sgt TJ Lang report', dated 12 December 1971.
240 NA (IRL) 2003/17/346, 'Border Incident in Cavan-Monaghan Division March 19, 1972', in 'Border-Incursions and Incidents 1972'.
241 Ibid.
242 'Border Folly goes on', *Northern Standard*, 3 December 1971.
243 NA (IRL) 2003/17/346, 'McMahon report on incident at Aghafin Co Monaghan January 23, 1972', in 'Border-Incursions and Incidents 1972'.
244 NA (UK) FCO 87/248, 'Links between security forces in Northern Ireland and Eire as of June 4, 1973', in 'Co-operation between defence forces of UK and ROI'.
245 NA (IRL) 2003/17/346, 'McMahon report on incident at Aghafin Co Monaghan', 23 January 1972, in 'Border-Incursions and Incidents 1972'.
246 'Monaghan Deputy averts border clash', *The Irish Times*, 6 December 1971; 'Rubber bullets and CS Canister from border help Fox's expulsion', *The Irish Times*, 10 December 1971.
247 NA (IRL) 2003/17/346, 'Border Incident in Cavan-Monaghan Division', 19 March 1972, in 'Border-Incursions and Incidents 1972'.

248 NA (IRL) 2003/17/346, 'Border Incident in Cavan-Monaghan Division March 19, 1972', in 'Border-Incursions and Incidents 1972'.

249 'Gardaí blamed', *Northern Standard*, 24 March 1972.

250 'UDC Chairmen's house picketed', *Northern Standard*, 24 March 1972.

251 'Monaghan Youth at Special Criminal Court', *Anglo Celt*, 3 November 1972.

252 Craig, *Crisis of Confidence*, reference no. 92, p. 117.

253 'Clones/Roslea Road protest', *Northern Standard*, 3 March 1972.

254 'Hotel Employee dies after shooting incident', *Donegal Democrat*, 26 November 1971.

255 *Final Report on the Report of the Independent Commission of Inquiry into the Dublin Bombings of 1972 and 1973* (2005), p. 26, http://cain.ulst.ac.uk/events/dublin/barron160205.pdf.

256 Dáil hearing on Barron report, 26 January 2005, http://debates.oireachtas.ie/JUB/2005/01/26/00003.asp#N64.

257 *Final Report on the Report of the Independent Commission of Inquiry into the Dublin Bombings of 1972 and 1973* (2005), p. 28, http://cain.ulst.ac.uk/events/dublin/barron160205.pdf.

258 Justice Barron in subcommittee hearing on Barron report, 27 January 2005, http://debates.oireachtas.ie/JUB/2005/01/27/printall.asp.

259 'Kidnapped constable walks home', *The Irish Times*, 16 September 1971.

260 'Man Found murdered near Crossmaglen', *Dundalk Democrat*, 4 December 1971.

261 'Soldier had been warned', *The Irish Times*, 2 December 1971.

262 'IRA denies colonel's murder', *The Irish Times*, 4 December 1971.

263 'Many homes searched at weekend by Garda', *The Irish Times*, 6 December 1971.

264 'Serious Rioting Followed Arrests', *The Sligo Champion*, 31 December 1972; 'Ballyshannon's day and Night of rioting', *Donegal Democrat*, 31 December 1972.

265 'Nearest thing to Duke Street', *Donegal Democrat*, 31 December 1971, p. 12.

266 'Priest challenged by Sinn Féin', *The Sligo Champion*, 31 December 1971.

267 'Heavy fines in Ballyshannon riot', *Donegal Democrat*, 23 June 1972.

268 'Twelve months gaol on ammo charge', *Donegal Democrat*, 14 January 1972.

269 Maria McGuire, *To Take Up Arms: My Year with the IRA Provisionals* (New York: Viking, 1973), p. 86.

270 NA 2003/15/15, 'Incident at Dungooley', report dated 29 January 1971.

271 'Protests likely over border battle', *Irish Press*, 28 January 1972.

272 'Monaghan's remarkable expression of grief', *The Northern Standard*, 4 February 1972.

273 'Dundalk Workers show solidarity', *Dundalk Democrat*, 5 February 1972.

274 'Sligo mourns Derry Dead', *The Sligo Champion*, 4 February 1972.

275 'Derry's Dead mourned', *Donegal Democrat*, 4 February 1972.

276 Ibid.

277 'Gardaí to investigate thuggery, intimidation', *Anglo Celt*, 25 February 1972.

278 Joe McVeigh, *Taking a Stand: Memoir of an Irish Priest* (Dublin: Mercier, 2008), p. 111.

279 'Shot British Soldier buried in Dublin', *The Irish Times*, 18 February 1972.

280 'Man found claimed to be a spy', *The Irish Times*, 9 February 1972.

281 'Callous Middletown killing', *Northern Standard*, 10 March 1972.

282 'UDR man's body found linked to explosives', *The Irish Times*, 20 April 1972.

283 NA (UK) FCO 87/121, 'Ireland Cross Border incidents', November 1972, in 'Border'.

284 Moloney, *Voices from the Grave*: victims Joe Lynskey, p. 114 (see also http://sluggerotoole.com/2010/02/09/he-was-subsequently-executed-and-buried-in-an-unmarked-grave/), Seamus Wright and Kevin McKee, p. 124; and Jean McConville, p. 126–7).

285 NA (UK) FCO 87/121, 'Cross border incidents' in 'Border'.

286 NA (UK) FCO 87/119, 'Report of contact with Gardaí', 24 March 1972.

287 Patsy McArdle, *The Secret War* (Dublin: Mercier, 1984), p. 34.

288 'Goulding on two incitement charges after Cork Oration', *The Irish Times*, 14 March 1972.

289 'Joe Cahill freed by special court', *The Irish Times*, 21 June 1971.

290 'Former Leitrim TD acquitted', *Anglo Celt*, 14 April 1972.

291 'Jail for inciting soldiers to steal arms', *The Irish Times*, 15 June 1972.

292 'Frank Morris sentenced on one count', *Donegal Democrat*, 13 October 1972.

293 Examples: 'Four men on arms charges', *Dundalk Democrat*, 26 February 1972; '15 Republicans now detained', *The Irish Times*, 25 February 1972; 'Five men on arms charges at Carrickmacross', *The Northern Standard*, 28 April 1972; 'Fourteen remanded in custody', *Dundalk Democrat*, 30 September 1972; 'Local men on arms charges', *Dundalk Democrat* 16 October 1971.

294 'Dundalk trial transferred to Dublin', *The Irish Times*, 7 January 1972.

295 'Seven men free due to lack of evidence', *The Irish Times*, 17 February 1972.

296 'Accused escape bid', *Anglo Celt*, 26 May 1972.

297 'Noisy scenes outside courthouse', *Dundalk Democrat*, 12 February 1972.

298 Military Archive NA 2003/15/17, 'Statement of Lieutenant JJ Gallagher', 14 June 1972.

299 'Peace will never win by terror', *Anglo Celt*, 16 June 1972.

300 Liz Walsh, *The Final Beat: Gardaí Killed in the Line of Duty* (Dublin: Gill and Macmillan, 2001), p. 23.

301 'Rockcorry man killed in Belfast', *Anglo Celt*, 21 July 1972.

302 'Accused of murder of Cavan man', *Anglo Celt*, 5 January 1973.

303 'Hundreds attend soldier's funeral', *Leitrim Observer*, 22 July 1972.

304 'Ex RUC chief from Donegal dies', *Donegal Democrat*, 22 May 2012.

305 'Belturbet RUC Man shot dead in Belfast', *Anglo Celt*, 5 March 1971.

306 '2 members of security forces die', *The Irish Times*, 23 October 1972.

307 'Automatic Arms for the RUC', *The Irish Times*, 12 November 1971.

308 NA (UK) FCO 87/121, 'Cross Border Incidents' in 'Border'.

309 NA (UK) FCO 87/247, 'Border Dossier' in 'Co-operation on Border Security between Defence forces of the UK and ROI'.

310 NA (UK) FCO 87/247, 'Terrorist activity in Clady/Cloughfin' area in 'Co-operation on Border Security between Defence forces of the UK and ROI'.

311 David McKittrick et al., *Lost Lives* (London: Mainstream Publishing, 1999), p. 226–314.

312 'UDR man and wife shot at home', *The Irish Times*, 22 September 1972 (Thomas and Emily Bullock); 'Councillor shot dead at border', *The Irish Times*, 19 December 1972 (William Johnson, member of Police Authority); '2 members of security forces die', *The Irish Times*, 23 October 1972 (Robin Bell, a UDR member, was killed and his brother and father injured in an IRA gun attack near Newtownbutler).

313 Martin Dillon, *The Dirty War* (London: Hutchinson, 1990), p. 124–60.

314 Henry Patterson, 'Border Violence in Eugene McCabe's Victims Trilogy', in *Irish Studies Review*, vol. 19, issue 2 (2011).

315 McKittrick et al., *Lost Lives*, p. 286.
316 Eugene McCabe, *Christ in the Fields* (London: Minerva, 1993).
317 'Tension along the border', *The Northern Standard*, 18 August 1972.
318 'Clones Show cancelled: Northern troubles blamed', *Anglo Celt*, 18 August 1973.
319 McKittrick et al., *Lost Lives*, p. 253.
320 NA 2003/15/18, 'Report on incident at Courtbane', dated 28 August 1972, in 'Incident at Courtbane', Military Archive (Dublin).
321 'O'Malley gives blunt warning to rioters', *The Irish Times*, 25 September 1972.
322 'Men remanded on Dundalk charges', *The Irish Times*, 28 September 1972.
323 'Hooliganism' (editorial), *Dundalk Democrat*, 29 September 1972.
324 'O'Malley gives blunt warning to rioters', *The Irish Times*, 25 September 1972.
325 'Priest warnings to Dundalk rioters', *The Irish Times*, 23 September 1972.
326 Ibid.
327 'Democrat Diary', *Dundalk Democrat*, 23 December 1972.
328 'Shooting Incident in Monaghan Village', *Anglo Celt*, 31 March 1972.
329 'Linked with John Taylor Shooting', *The Northern Standard*, 3 March 1972.
330 'Huge security alert follows UDA bomb attacks', *Donegal Democrat*, 20 October 1972.
331 'Concern over security situation', *Anglo Celt*, 17 November 1972.
332 'UDA bombs Co Donegal Building', *The Irish Times*, 20 November 1972; 'UDA claims Donegal explosion', *The Irish Times*, 6 November 1972; 'Explosion damages Donegal fish port', *The Irish Times*, 2 September 1972.
333 'Belturbet's night of horror', *Anglo Celt*, 5 January 1973.
334 'Commissioners call for greater security', *Anglo Celt*, 5 January 1972.
335 'Editorial', *Anglo Celt*, 5 January 1972.
336 Houses of the Oireachtas sub-committee, *Interim Report on the Report of the Independent Commission of Inquiry into the Dublin Bombings of 1972 and 1973* (2004), p. 118, http://www.dublinmonaghanbombings.org/DubInterim.pdf.
337 Joint Committee on Justice, Equality, Defence and Women's Rights, *Final Report on the Report of the Independent Commission of Inquiry into the Dublin Bombings of 1972 and 1973*, February 2005, http://cain.ulst.ac.uk/events/dublin/barron160205.pdf.
338 Joint Committee on Justice, Equality, Defence and Women's Rights, *Final Report on the Report of the Independent Commission of Inquiry into the Dublin Bombings of 1972 and 1973*, February 2005, http://cain.ulst.ac.uk/events/dublin/barron160205.pdf; Brian Stanley TD in debate on Dublin and Monaghan bombings, Dáil Debates, 17 May 2011, http://debates.oireachtas.ie/Dáil/2011/05/17/00018.asp.
339 Barron Report, *Interim Report on the Report of the Independent Commission of Inquiry into the Dublin Bombings of 1972 and 1973* (2004), http://www.dublinmonaghanbombings.org/DubInterim.pdf.
340 Courtney, *It Was Murder*, p. 133.
341 See Brian Stanley TD in debate on Dublin and Monaghan bombings, Dáil Debates, 17 May 2011, http://debates.oireachtas.ie/Dáil/2011/05/17/00018.asp.
342 'Monaghan's tense week', *The Northern Standard*, 1 December 1972.
343 NA (UK) FCO 87/121, 'Letter from Kelvin White dated December 13, 1972' in file 'Border'.
344 NA (IRL) 2005/7/166, 'Peak holding of refugees in a single day', Interdepartmental Unit on NI.
345 'Exodus from homes continues', *The Irish Times*, 12 August 1971.

346 '4,339 take refuge in Republic', *The Irish Times*, 12 August 1971.

347 'Army says refugee problem easier', *The Irish Times*, 14 August 1972.

348 NA (IRL) 2004/21/494, 'Memorandum for government in dealing with refugees'.

349 'Refugee problem hits Dundalk', *Dundalk Democrat*, 14 August 1971.

350 'Refugees estimated at 6000', *The Irish Times*, 13 August 1971.

351 'Refugees advised to delay return', *The Irish Times*, 16 August 1971.

352 '6,000 have fled South', *The Irish Times*, 13 August 1971.

353 NA (IRL) 2004/21/494, 'Memorandum for government in dealing with refugees'.

354 G2/c/1799/3, 'Refugees from Ni', Military Archives.

355 C/S 111/8/1970, 'Refugees', dated 26 May 1970, Military Archives (Dublin).

356 NA (IRL) 2004/21/494, 'Memorandum for government in dealing with refugees'.

357 Ibid.

358 'Massive Collections for Northern Refugees', *The Sligo Champion*, 20 August 1971; 'Refugees leave with tears', *Leitrim Observer*, 28 August 1971; 'Almost 4,000 refugees in the Republic', *Anglo Celt*, 20 August 1971; 'Refugees pouring into Donegal to escape six county carnage', *Donegal Democrat*, 13 August 1971; 'Refugee problem hits Dundalk', *Dundalk Democrat*, 14 August 1971.

359 NA (IRL) 2004/21/494, 'Memorandum for government in dealing with refugees'.

360 'We couldn't understand the peace', RTÉ Radio, *Documentary on One*, September 2016, http://www.rte.ie/radio1/doconone/2016/0825/811859-we-couldnt-understand-the-peace-glenstal-abbey-a/ (18–20 minutes).

361 '110 in Republic wanted by North', *The Irish Times*, 13 January 1972.

362 '155 on RUC wanted list now in Republic', *The Irish Times*, 5 May 1972.

363 'All Over the Place: People Displaced to and from the Southern Border Counties as a Result of the Conflict 1969–1994', Pobal Research Report (2005), p. 63.

364 'Priest warning to Dundalk Rioters', *The Irish Times*, 23 September 1972.

365 '7 Maidstone escapers cross border to freedom', *The Irish Times*, 24 January 1972.

366 Michael Farrell, *Sheltering the Fugitive?* (Dublin: Mercier, 1985), p. 57.

367 Keogh, *Jack Lynch*, p. 319.

368 NA (UK) FCO 87/41, 'Assistant Commissioner Letter April 1972 to RUC Chief Constable'.

369 NA (IRL) 2005/7/1966, Department of Defence 'Note on refugees', Interdepartmental Unit on Northern Ireland.

370 NA (IRL) 2010/53/889, 'Report from Department of Justice to Department of Taoiseach', in 'NI Security Statistics'.

371 NA (IRL) 2002/8/484, 'Statement to Dáil', 15 December 1971, p. 6.

372 NA (IRL) 2004/7/2675, 'Special Criminal Court' in 'Border Security'.

373 NA (IRL) 2004/7/2675, 'Statistics of Security part II' in 'Border Security'.

374 NA (IRL) 2000/6/159, 'Memorandum for Taoiseach on current security position'.

375 NA (IRL) 2004/7/2675, 'Statistics of Security part II' in 'Border Security'.

376 'IRA Congratulate people of Courtbane', *An Phoblacht*, October 1971; 'Bank Robbery Condemned', *An Phoblacht*, October 1971; 'IRA statements in August', *An Phoblacht*, September 1971.

377 Seán MacStíofáin, *Revolutionary in Ireland* (Edinburgh: Cremonesi, 1975), p. 355.
378 Clarke, *Border Crossing*, p. 11.
379 NA (UK) FCO 33/1468, 'Letter from John Peck to UK representative in Belfast dated May 27, 1971', in 'Co-operation about control of explosives and firearms'.
380 Examples: 'Border town residents urge extra protection', *The Irish Times*, 30 December 1972; NA (IRL) 2002/8/76, 'Letter from Donegal County Council seeking greater security and cross-border police co-operation', 29 January 1971; 'Concern over security in border areas', *The Irish Times*, 18 October 1972; '£10,000 reward on heads of customs wreckers', Donegal Democrat, 29 January 1971.
381 Dunne and Kerrigan, *Round Up the Usual Suspects*, p. 70.
382 'Scare story cost seat-Conlan', *The Northern Standard*, 16 March 1973.

Chapter 4

1 NA (UK) FCO 87/372, 'Letter from British Embassy', 15 October 1974.
2 NA (UK) FCO 87/416, 'GW Harding letter to Arthur Galsworthy', 25 April 1975.
3 'Allegations against Gardaí refuted', *Anglo Celt*, 23 March 1973.
4 'Monaghan ladies had illegal posters', *Anglo Celt*, 29 November 1974.
5 Diarmaid Ferriter, *Ambiguous Republic: Ireland in the 1970s* (London: Profile Books, 2012), p. 343.
6 'Prison Break', *Scannal*, RTÉ One, http://www.rte.ie/tv/scannal/scannalprisonbreak.html.
7 NA 2005/147/310, 'Assistant Commissioner Garvey Report', 2 August 1973.
8 'Text of Taoiseach's statement', *The Irish Times*, 6 February 1973.
9 'We don't want blood, bombs and bullets', *Donegal Democrat*, 23 February 1973.
10 'Blaney topped the poll in NE Donegal', *Donegal Democrat*, 9 March 1973.
11 'Scare story cost seat-Conlan', *The Northern Standard*, 16 March 1973; 'Sectarian Tactics Alleged', *The Northern Standard*, 30 March 1973.
12 John Healy, 'Silence on North except...', *The Irish Times*, 9 February 1973.
13 'General Election Post mortem', *Hibernia*, 16 March 1973, p. 16.
14 Keogh, *Jack Lynch*, p. 375.
15 'Blaney topped the poll in NE Donegal', *Donegal Democrat*, 9 March 1973.
16 'Election Results', *Anglo Celt*, 2 March 1973.
17 Craig, *Crisis of Confidence*, p. 157.
18 Ferriter, *Ambiguous Republic*, p. 75.
19 Garrett FitzGerald, *All in a Life* (London: Gill and Macmillan, 1991), p. 197.
20 Ibid., p. 198.
21 'Paddy Donegan: Promoting the Army', *Hibernia*, 16 November 1973.
22 'Pat Cooney: Great expectations unfulfilled', *Hibernia*, 19 October 1973.
23 'Explosion at pub owned by Minister', *The Irish Times*, 27 March 1975.
24 'Bomb near Minister's platform', *The Irish Times*, 9 July 1973.
25 'Provisionals threat to two Ministers', *The Irish Times*, 6 February 1975.
26 Patterson, *Ireland's Violent Frontier*, p. 67.
27 'Cooney gives warning to parents about IRA', *The Irish Times*, 2 December 1974.
28 Sean Boyne, *Gunrunners: The Covert Arms Trail to Ireland* (Dublin: O'Brien Press, 2006), pp. 150–4.

29   NA (UK) FCO 87/247, 'FCO Telegram from Galsworthy number 207', 13 dated April 1973.

30   'Why was Claudia released O'Malley asks', *The Irish Times*, 5 April 1973.

31   Craig, *Crisis of Confidence*, p. 159.

32   Ibid., p. 160.

33   NA (UK) FCO 87/247, 'FCO Telegram from Galsworthy number 236 Border Security', dated 14 April 1973.

34   Ibid.

35   Craig, *Crisis of Confidence*, p. 164, interview with Dermot Nally, Department of Taoiseach.

36   NA (UK) FCO 87/247, 'FCO Telegram from Galsworthy number 236 Border Security', dated 14 April 1973.

37   NA (UK) FCO 87/247, 'FCO Telegram from Galsworthy number 212', 16 April 1973.

38   Patterson, *Ireland's Violent Frontier*, p. 60.

39   Barron Inquiry into Dublin Monaghan Bombing December 2003, p. 55, http://cain.ulst.ac.uk/events/dublin/barron03.pdf.

40   Patterson, *Ireland's Violent Frontier*, p. 52.

41   NA (UK) FCO 87/371, 'Galsworthy to FCO July 5, 1974'.

42   Patterson, *Ireland's Violent Frontier*, pp. 54–5.

43   NA (UK) FCO 87/248, 'Letter from Kelvin White to RC Cox' June 25, 1973

44   Ibid.

45   FitzGerald, *All in a Life*, p. 198.

46   Ferriter, *Ambiguous Republic*, p. 177.

47   FitzGerald, *All in a Life*, p. 224.

48   'Removal of Whip from Ahern to be discussed', *The Irish Times*, 28 May 1973.

49   NA (UK) CJ4/799, 'Letter to FCO from Brian Major', 23 January 1974.

50   Ferriter, *Ambiguous Republic*, p. 177.

51   'Lynch knew Littlejohns were agents in January', *The Irish Times*, 14 August 1973.

52   FitzGerald, *All in a Life*, p. 226.

53   Craig, *Crisis of Confidence*, p. 169.

54   FitzGerald, *All in a Life*, p. 232.

55   NA (IRL)2005/4/954, 'Minutes of meeting with Northern executive February 1, 1974'.

56   NA (UK) FCO 87/245, 'Terrorist Operations in Border areas', 11 September 1973.

57   NA (UK) CJ4/810, 'Border Security by Army HQ', 30 January 1974.

58   'Finlay to head Security Inquiry', *The Irish Times*, 9 November 1973.

59   'Cooney warns of Closing Buildings used by the IRA', *The Irish Times*, 16 January 1974.

60   'Donegan steps up campaign to raise Army strength by 3000', *The Irish Times*, 5 January 1974.

61   '15 still held after Border raids', *The Irish Times*, 4 January 1974.

62   NA (UK) CJ4/799, 'Cross border Contacts Minutes of Baldonnel meeting', 16 January 1974.

63   NA (IRL) 2005/4/954, 'Minutes of meeting with Northern executive', 1 February 1974.

64   Ibid.

65   NA (IRL) 2005/4/850, 'Special Criminal Court'.

66 FitzGerald, *All in a Life*, p. 224.
67 NA (IRL) 2005/4/834, 'Telegram from Irish Ambassador regarding conversation with Rees'.
68 NA (UK) CJ4 810, 'Notes on Dublin visit February 18, 1974'.
69 NA (UK) FCO 87/371, 'Letter to John Allen in NIO August 6, 1974'.
70 Patterson, *Ireland's Violent Frontier*, p. 74.
71 'Angry Cosgrave blames Britain for NI crisis', *The Irish Times*, 24 May 1974.
72 '28 killed, over 100 injured in four car bomb blasts in Dublin, Monaghan', *The Irish Times*, 18 May 1974.
73 Garret FitzGerald, 'The 1974–1975 Threat of a British Withdrawal from Northern Ireland' in *Irish Studies in International Affairs*, vol. 17 (2006), p. 142.
74 FitzGerald, *All in a Life*, p. 244.
75 FitzGerald, 'The 1974–1975 Threat of a British Withdrawal', p. 143.
76 NA (UK) CJ4/810, Border Security, 'Security Cooperation' by Kenneth Thom, 15 August 1974.
77 Patterson, *Ireland's Violent Frontier*, p. 83.
78 NA (UK) FCO 87/294, 'Security Cooperation'.
79 NA (UK) FCO 87/294, Report by Arthur Galsworthy, 25 September 1974.
80 Ibid.
81 NA (UK) FCO 87/537, 'Minutes of January 8, 1975 between Secretary of State and Cooney'.
82 Albert Reynolds, *Albert Reynolds: My Autobiography* (London: Transworld Ireland, 2009), p. 89.
83 FCO 87/537, 'Minutes of January 8, 1975 between Secretary of State and Cooney'.
84 John Bew et al., *Talking to Terrorists: Making Peace in the Basque Country and Northern Ireland* (London: Hurst and Company, 2009), p. 51.
85 Ibid., pg 58
86 NA (UK) FCO 87/539, 'Discussions at government buildings', 28 May 1975.
87 Ferriter, *Ambiguous Republic*, p. 178.
88 NA (UK) FCO 87/416, 'Republic of Ireland: Annual Review', 18 February 1975.
89 Ibid.
90 NA (UK) FCO 87/537, 'Minutes of January 8, 1975 between Secretary of State and Cooney'.
91 'Cooney drops idea for vote on claim over NI', *The Irish Times*, 23 September 1974.
92 Mícheál Mac Gréil, *Prejudice and Tolerance in Ireland: Based on a Survey of Intergroup Attitudes of Dublin Adults and Other Sources* (Dublin: Research Section, College of Industrial Relations, 1977), p. 415.
93 'Lynch restores Haughey, Gibbons', *The Irish Times*, 31 January 1975.
94 'Disquiet at FF policy change', *The Irish Times*, 31 October 1975.
95 Dermot Keogh, *Jack Lynch: A Biography* (Dublin: Gill and Macmillan, 2008), p. 400.
96 NA (UK) FCO 87/424, 'Galsworthy telegram', 3 November 1975.
97 FitzGerald, *All in a Life*, pp. 270–5.
98 NA (IRL) 2010/53/889, 'Department of Justice report on crime to Department of Taoiseach'.
99 'Donegan steps up campaign to raise Army strength by 3000', *The Irish Times*, 5 January 1974.
100 'Security Bill now about £100 million', *The Irish Times*, 10 September 1975.

101 NA (IRL) 2005/147/310, 'Report by Ned Garvey', 25 July 1973.

102 NA (IRL) 2005/7/606, 'Security in the Republic', p. 3.

103 'Army on border at highest level ever', *The Irish Times*, 14 October 1974.

104 NA (IRL) 2005/7/607, Document entitled 'Security'.

105 'Garrison Town: People's reaction strongly unfavourable', *The Northern Standard*, 14 September 1973.

106 'Refused Service in Local Pub', *The Northern Standard*, 26 October 1973.

107 NA (UK) FCO 87/371, 'Notes on RUC meeting with Garda Commissioner', 2 April 1974.

108 Kieran McCarthy, *Republican Cobh and East Cork Volunteers since 1913* (Dublin: Nonsuch Publishing, 2008), p. 357.

109 NA (IRL) 2005/20/150, 'Aid to civil power monthly analysis', August 1974.

110 NA (IRL) 2004/16/11, 'Operational Commitments', 13 July 1973.

111 'Military involvement', *Hibernia*, 30 August 1974.

112 'Donegan's Mounted Foot', *An Phoblacht*, 25 October 1974.

113 'The Army's first victim', *Hibernia*, 24 August 1973; 'The Second Army Victim', *Hibernia*, 30 August 1974.

114 Kieran McCarthy, *Republican Cobh and East Cork Volunteers since 1913* (Dublin: Nonsuch Publishing, 2008), p. 355.

115 FitzGerald, *All in a Life*, p. 315.

116 Ferriter, *Ambiguous Republic*, p. 342.

117 'The Saturday Interview Edmund Garvey', *The Irish Times*, 13 September 1975.

118 Ferriter, *Ambiguous Republic*, p. 343.

119 Conor Brady, *The Guarding of Ireland: The Garda Síochána and the Irish State 1960–2014* (Dublin: Gill and Macmillan, 2014), p. 94.

120 'Garda Action being considered following disciplinary moves', *The Irish Times*, 18 August 1975; 'Garda to present case to Cooney', *The Irish Times*, 15 August 1975; 'Department denies Garda group's claim', *The Irish Times*, 6 August 1975; 'Garda clerks on work-to-rule; Garda body resigns in pay claim protest', *The Irish Times*, 30 March 1974.

121 Ferriter, *Ambiguous Republic*, p. 345.

122 Gene Kerrigan and Derek Dunne, *Round Up the Usual Suspects* (Dublin: Magill, 1984), p. 100.

123 Ferriter, *Ambiguous Republic*, p. 344.

124 NA (UK) CJ4/833, 'Secretary of state's visit to South Down and South Armagh', 28 October 1975.

125 'FF Protest over Dáil Promotions', *The Irish Times*, 30 June 1975.

126 Joe Dowling TD, 'Army Promotions', Dáil Debates, 8 July 1975.

127 Thomas Meaney, 'Army Promotions', Dáil Debates, 9 July 1975.

128 NA (UK) FCO 87/199, 'British Embassy report', 18 December 1973.

129 John Kelly, Committe on Finance vote 20, Dáil Debates, 14 February 1974.

130 'Cooney warns of closing buildings used by IRA', *The Irish Times*, 16 January 1974.

131 'Patrick Cooney's Blacklist', *Hibernia*, 12 April 1974.

132 'Claudia', *An Phoblacht*, 21 July 2005.

133 'Censorship of speech results in RTE row', *The Irish Times*, 26 June 1974.

134 'Journalist Concerned at jailing of editor', *The Irish Times*, 10 October 1974.

135 'Garda seize 10,000 booklets in Drogheda', *The Irish Times*, 16 July 1973; 'James McElwaine prosecuted', *The Northern Standard*, 4 November 1973.

136 'Convict the lot', *Hibernia*, 25 July 1975.
137 '15 are held after republican funeral', *The Irish Times*, 9 June 1975; 'Seven arrested after shots fired during Saor Eire Funeral', *The Irish Times*, 14 June 1975.
138 Fitzgerald, *All in a Life*, p. 280.
139 NA (IRL) 2004/21/637, 'Policing Common Law Enforcement Area'.
140 'Garda Review gives Sunningdale proposals a cautious welcome', *The Irish Times*, 24 January 1974.
141 NA (IRL) 2005/155/6, 'Letter from Assistant Commissioner Edward Garvey stamped 6/7/1975'.
142 Ibid.
143 NA (IRL) 2008/79/3109, 'Assessment of possibilities of Military intervention in Northern Ireland: Basic Planning assumptions'.
144 Ibid.
145 Craig, *Crisis of Confidence*, p. 186.
146 NA (IRL) CJ4/1289, 'Letter from M Hodge ROI Department', 26 June 1975.
147 NA (UK) CJ4/1055, 'Irish Security Forces', 27 April 1976.
148 NA (IRL) 2004/16/11, 'Operational Commitments', 13 July 1973.
149 NA (IRL) 2004/16/11, 'Threat to Military installations', 7 August 1973.
150 'Assaulted by RUC in Garda Station', *An Phoblacht*, 31 August 1973; 'Dublin Castle Nest of Spies', *An Phoblacht*, 17 August 1973; 'Beatings by Garda', *An Phoblacht*, 17 August 1973.
151 '19 Escape after jail blasts at Portlaoise', *The Irish Times*, 19 August 1974.
152 Walsh, *The Final Beat*, p. 40.
153 'Prisoner Killed as Portlaoise Breakout fails', *The Irish Times*, 18 March 1975.
154 'Violence at IRA Funeral', *Sunday Independent*, 23 March 1975.
155 'Garda Council Official Jailed for Six Months', *The Irish Times*, 10 July 1973.
156 'Six soldiers accused of possessing explosives', *The Irish Times*, 12 November 1974.
157 'Phone men sentenced to penal servitude', *The Irish Times*, 29 June 1973.
158 'Garda Inquiry seeks to bolt doors after Provisional leaks', *The Irish Times*, 3 January 1975.
159 NA (IRL) 2005/155/6, 'Letter from Chief Superintendent to Department of Justice', stamped 20 June 1975.
160 NA (UK) FCO 87/248, 'State of links between security forces in Northern Ireland and Eire at 4 June, 1973'.
161 NA (UK) CJ4/833, 'Staff paper for discussion at D Ops Meeting', 27 November 1975, 'Cooperation with Irish Security Forces in border areas'.
162 NA (IRL) 2008/79/3109, 'Intelligence Assessment', Spring 1977.
163 NA (UK) FCO 87/375 FCO, Telegram 22 British Army–Gardaí incident, 10 May 1974 & 9 May 1974.
164 NA (UK) FCO 87/375, 'Garda account telex no 226', 12 May 1974.
165 NA (UK) FCO 87/375 FCO, Telegram 22 British Army–Gardaí incident, 10 May 1974 & 9 May 1974.
166 NA (UK) FCO 87/537, Letter from SS Bampton to John Hickman in British Embassy, 20 January 1976.
167 NA (UK) FCO 87/248, 'State of links between security forces in Northern Ireland and Eire', 4 June 1973.
168 Barron Inquiry into Dublin Monaghan Bombing, December 2003, p. 84, http://cain.ulst.ac.uk/events/dublin/barron03.pdf.

169 Oireachtas Report into the Bombing of Kay's Tavern, Dundalk, p. 44, http://www.macguill.ie/Kay's-Tavern-Final-Report.pdf.

170 NA (UK) FCO 87/374, Border Cooperation report by Brigadier McMullan on meeting with General O'Carroll, 28 February 1974.

171 NA (UK) CJ4 810, 'Letter from Jamie Flanagan, Chief Constable', 11 March 1974.

172 Burbridge and Holroyd, *War without Honour*, p. 102.

173 NA (UK) CJ4/833, 'Border Cooperation with Gardaí'.

174 NA (UK) FCO 87/371, 'Text from Irish Ambassador to Prime Minister', 9 August 1974.

175 NA (IRL) 2007/116/76, Extract from report on meeting between Minister for Foreign Affairs and UN Secretary General.

176 NA (UK) FCO 87/378, 'Border Incident near Aughrim Cavan', 16 December 1974; Border Incident near Aughnacloy, 1 December 1974.

177 NA (UK) FCO 87/ 376, 'Shooting Incident at Crossmaglen', 1 August 1974.

178 Patterson, *Ireland's Violent Frontier*, p. 87.

179 NA (UK) FCO 87/374, 'The Carrickarnon incident', Telegram 117, 9 March 1974.

180 NA (UK) CJ 4/810, 'Security Cooperation note by KC Thom', 15 August 1974.

181 NA (UK) FCO 87/295, Letter from John Born to GW Harding in FCO December 6, 1974.

182 'An Tanaiste's own version', *The Northern Standard*, 5 January 1973.

183 'UDA man named as victim of car bomb', *The Irish Times*, 19 March 1973.

184 Barron Inquiry into Dublin Monaghan Bombing, December 2003, p. 77, http://www.taoiseach.gov.ie/eng/Work_Of_The_Department/Economic_International_Northern_Ireland/Northern_Ireland/Northern_Ireland_Publications/InterimDubMon.pdf.

185 NA (UK) FCO 87/245, 'Terrorist operations in border areas', 11 September 1973.

186 Garret FitzGerald, Report on visit to Clones, 12 November 1973, Garret FitzGerald papers, p. 215, 566.

187 NA (UK) FCO 87/245, Annex C murder of Private Lilley, 7 September 1973.

188 FitzGerald, *All in a Life*, p. 201.

189 NA (UK) FCO 87/245, Galsworthy letter to Kelvin White, 20 June 1973.

190 'Clones News Townspeople Apprehensive', *Anglo Celt*, 16 February 1973; 'Security on the border', *Anglo Celt*, 27 April 1973.

191 'Clones Football Invasion', *The Northern Standard*, 3 August 1973.

192 'If Garda Collaborate, they share British risk', *The Irish Times*, 1 August 1973.

193 'Raiders kill man in payroll snatch', *The Irish Times*, 4 August 1973.

194 'The Road that motorists avoid', *Anglo Celt*, 28 December 1973.

195 'Clones house bombed-man shot in back', *Anglo Celt*, 16 November 1973.

196 McNulty, *Exiled*, p. 112.

197 John Courtney, *It Was Murder* (Dublin: Blackwater, 1996), p. 63.

198 'Rumours from Monaghan', *Documentary on One*, RTÉ Radio 1, 32 minutes, http://www.rte.ie/radio1/doconone/rumours.html.

199 Ibid., 48 minutes

200 'Five sentenced to life imprisonment', *The Northern Standard*, 14 June 1974.

201 'Easter Parade', *The Northern Standard*, 19 April 1974.

202 'Fugitive Hero', *The Northern Standard*, 28 June 1974.

203 Oireachtas Report into the Bombing of Kay's Tavern, Dundalk, p. 186, http://www.dublinmonaghanbombings.org/KaysInterim.pdf.
204 NA (UK) CJ4/1094, 'Cross Border and Rural PIRA groups'.
205 Barron Inquiry into Dublin Monaghan Bombing, December 2003, p. 328, http://www.taoiseach.gov.ie/eng/Work_Of_The_Department/Economic_International_Northern_Ireland/Northern_Ireland/Northern_Ireland_Publications/InterimDubMon.pdf.
206 Ibid., p. 30.
207 Ibid., p. 354.
208 Ibid., p. 343.
209 Ibid., p. 286.
210 '19 escape after jail blasts at Portlaoise', *The Irish Times*, 19 August 1974.
211 Brian Hanley, 'They Started All This Killing', in *Irish Historical Studies*, May 2013.
212 Barron Inquiry into Dublin Monaghan Bombing, December 2003, p. 84, http://www.taoiseach.gov.ie/eng/Work_Of_The_Department/Economic_International_Northern_Ireland/Northern_Ireland/Northern_Ireland_Publications/InterimDubMon.pdf.
213 NA (UK) FCO 87/247, 'Border Dossier'.
214 NA (UK) CJ4/812, 'Security on the border Telephone conversation White/Thom'.
215 NA (UK) CJ4/810, 'Border incidents in Strabane/Clady', December 1973.
216 NA (UK) FCO 87/248, Letter to FCO dated 15 June 1973.
217 NA (UK) FCO 87/374, 'Rocket attack on Belleek RUC station', 8 January 1974.
218 NA (UK) CJ4/640, Arthur Galsworthy letter, 10 January 1974.
219 'Petigigo was Donegal's Claudy', *Donegal Democrat*, 5 October 1973.
220 'Youth dies in Van attack', *The Irish Times*, 10 August 1973.
221 'Cattle dealer shot dead by RUC', *Donegal Democrat*, 25 May 1973.
222 'Young RUC man's murder strongly condemned', *Donegal Democrat*, 2 November 1973.
223 'Soldier gets away from kidnappers', *The Irish Times*, 26 June 1974.
224 'Ambush in Mayo denounced', *The Irish Times*, 4 September 1973; 'British Officer undeterred by attack', *The Irish Times*, 24 August 1973.
225 'Aughnacloy UDR member abducted and shot', *The Northern Standard*, 25 January 1974.
226 'Gardaí-RUC under Fire', *The Irish Times*, 17 December 1973.
227 'RUC detective killed', *Anglo Celt*, 14 December 1973.
228 'RUC man killed in County Armagh Ambush', *The Irish Times*, 28 February 1973.
229 'Young Cork IRA man's funeral', *The Irish Times*, 14 May 1973.
230 McNulty, *Exiled*, p. 108.
231 'Man fatally wounded in gun battle with RUC', *The Irish Times*, 16 November 1973.
232 'Dead man had been acquitted by Special Court', *The Irish Times*, 13 August 1973.
233 'Gardaí–RUC under Fire', *The Irish Times*, 17 December 1973.
234 Paddy Harte, *Young Tigers and Mongrel Foxes: A Life in Politics* (Dublin: O'Brien Press, 2005), p. 212.
235 'Executed man's body in car–Army Told', *The Irish Times*, 25 August 1973.
236 'McGuinness says he didn't lie over Disappeared but "made a mistake over dates"', *Sunday Life*, 17 June 2014.

237 'Boy was shot in head near border', *The Irish Times*, 5 June 1973.
238 'Woman who fought for 37 years to get the truth to an IRA murder', *Belfast Telegraph*, 25 September 2010.
239 'Church alert after UFF threat', *Irish Press*, 6 September 1973.
240 'Man charged with Galway murder', *The Irish Times*, 17 August 1974.
241 'Raiders kill man in payroll snatch', *The Irish Times*, 4 August 1973.
242 'Former Blayney man shot by British Army', *The Northern Standard*, 30 March 1973.
243 'Smithboro woman murdered', *The Anglo Celt*, 10 August 1973.
244 NA (UK) CJ4/812, 'Cooperation with the south'.
245 Patterson, *Ireland's Violent Frontier*, p. 87.
246 'British post attacked from Lifford', *The Irish Times*, 23 February 1974.
247 Ibid.
248 NA (UK) FCO 87/374, 'Telegram 22 February 1974 on Lifford incident'.
249 NA (UK) FCO 87/374, 'Telegram number 11', 25 February 1974, from Galsworthy.
250 NA (UK) CJ4 812, 'Border Security', 8 November 1973, by Brigadier Garrett.
251 NA (UK) CJ4/810, 'Border Security Visit to HQ 3 Brigade Lurgan', 20 February 1974.
252 'Le Cheile honouree', *An Phoblacht*, 4 February 2010; 'Bedside guard on shot man', *Irish Press*, 23 February 1974; 'Accussed was once a UDR member', *The Irish Times*, 11 January 1974.
253 'Armagh, the blood stained county', *The Irish Times*, 3 September 1975.
254 Patterson, *Ireland's Violent Frontier*, p. 92.
255 Oireachtas Report into the Bombing of Kay's Tavern, Dundalk, p. 139, http://www.dublinmonaghanbombings.org/KaysInterim.pdf.
256 NA (UK) FCO 87/423, Minutes of meeting at Irish embassy, 5 November 1975.
257 Ibid.
258 Richard English, *Armed Struggle: A History of the IRA* (London: Pan, 2003), p. 380.
259 'RUC Question Man about Miami Showband Killings', *The Irish Times*, 1 August 1975.
260 'Loyalist Killers in UDR claims Mallon', *The Irish Times*, 26 August 1975.
261 Oireachtas Report into the Bombing of Kay's Tavern, Dundalk, p. 26, http://www.oireachtas.ie/documents/committees29thDáil/committeereport2006/Kays_Tavern_Final_Rep.pdf.
262 'Seven shot dead in North's violence', *The Irish Times*, 2 September 1975.
263 'Three Shot dead in Killeen', *The Irish Times*, 3 June 1975.
264 NA (UK) CJ4/833, 'Murders attributable to PIRA since February 10, 1975'.
265 'Big Army Inquiry after Ambush deaths', *The Irish Times*, 24 November 1975.
266 Barron Inquiry into Dublin Monaghan Bombing, December 2003, p. 320, http://www.taoiseach.gov.ie/eng/Work_Of_The_Department/Economic_International_Northern_Ireland/Northern_Ireland/Northern_Ireland_Publications/InterimDubMon.pdf.
267 Raymond Murray, *The SAS in Ireland* (Dublin: Irish American Book Company, 1990), p. 128.
268 Barron Inquiry into Dublin Monaghan Bombing, December 2003, p. 246.
269 'IRA man shot', *The Northern Standard*, 17 January 1975.
270 Oireachtas Report into the Bombing of Kay's Tavern, Dundalk, p. 12, http://www.oireachtas.ie/documents/committees29thDáil/committeereport2006/Kays_Tavern_Final_Rep.pdf.

271 'GPO Bookseller undertakes to cease trading', *The Irish Times*, 12 March 1976; 'Fined for illegal collection', *Anglo Celt*, 26 October 1973; '21 Prosecutions for illegal collections', *The Irish Times*, 6 October 1973.

272 'Judge warns against IRA booklet', *Anglo Celt*, 22 March 1974.

273 'Hunger Strike Protesters fined in Ballyshannon', *Donegal Democrat*, 24 October 1975.

274 'Harassment of Provisionals', *The Northern Standard*, 23 May 1975.

275 NA (IRL) 2007/116/742, Letter from Dublin Corporation to Taoiseach dated 6/4/77' and 24 March 1977 circular was issued to all local authority managers to clean up political graffiti.

276 NA (UK) FCO 87/325, 'Castleblaney Riots', 28 October 1974.

277 Patsy McArdle, *The Secret War* (Dublin: Mercier, 1984), p. 41.

278 'Suspended sentences and fines for Ballybofey riot', *Donegal Democrat*, 24 October 1975.

279 Maurice Walshe in interview with Michelle Maloney, 'Green and Blue' Project, http://www.green-and-blue.org/wp-content/uploads/2014/01/Maurice-Walsh-edited-transcript.pdf.

280 Interview with Pat O'Leary, 'Green and Blue' Project, http://accounts.ulster.ac.uk/repo24/files/original/42b1572a586d5f9bd755905b3723c6fa.pdf.

281 Interview with B.J. Kealy, 'Green and Blue' Project, http://www.green-and-blue.org/wp-content/uploads/2014/01/BJ-Kealy-Interview-Transcript-edit.pdf.

282 McNulty, *Exiled*, p. 170.

283 Ibid., p. 74.

284 'Two escape after shots fired at Gardaí', *The Irish Times*, 13 May 1974; 'Men Shoot at Garda Patrol near border', *The Irish Times*, 23 April 1974; 'Garda car halted at gunpoint', *The Irish Times*, 15 August 1973; 'Rifle pointed at Garda', *The Northern Standard*, 19 October 1973; 'Gardaí threatened by gunmen after chase', *The Irish Times*, 21 July 1973; 'Gardaí tackled Armed ex council member', *The Irish Times*, 17 September 1974; 'Shots Fired at Gardaí in Leitrim', *Anglo Celt*, 26 April 1974; 'Lucky escape for Garda', *The Northern Standard*, 19 July 1974; '5 years for hijacking Garda car', *The Northern Standard*, 19 July 1974.

285 'They could not bury their dead in peace', *The Northern Standard*, 13 June 1975.

286 '3 Gardaí robbed of uniforms', *The Irish Times*, 22 April 1974; 'Garda beaten robbed of uniform', 18 April 1974; 'Garda Assaulted and stripped in West Cavan', *Anglo Celt*, 19 April 1974.

287 'Don't cooperate warn Provisionals', *The Irish Times*, 16 September 1974; 'If Gardaí Cooperate they share British Risk', *The Irish Times*, 1 August 1973; 'Warning by Cooney to IRA on border acts', *The Irish Times*, 24 April 1974.

288 'Seven years jail on arms charge', *The Irish Times*, 18 October 1973.

289 NA (IRL) 2004/16/115, 'Protest March Portlaoise', 4 December 1973.

290 'Mallon sentenced to 10 years penal servitude', *The Irish Times*, 16 April 1975.

291 'Garda doing a wonderful job', *The Irish Times*, 1 July 1972.

292 NA (IRL) 2004/16/106, 'Report on Crowley Funeral in Cavan', 28 June 1973.

293 'Warning by Cooney to IRA on border attacks', *The Irish Times*, 24 April 1974.

294 NA (UK) FCO 87/537, 'Blocking of Unapproved Roads'.

295 NA (IRL) 2005/145/2554, 'Road Closures'.

296 NA (UK) FCO 87/538, 'RUC/Garda Joint Coordinating Committee February 24, 1976'.

297　NA (UK) FCO 87/423, 'Meeting between Garret FitzGerald and Secretary of State November 5, 1975'.

298　NA (IRL) 2005/145/2554, 'Superintendent AJ Murtagh letter', 23 September 1975.

299　'Villagers protest on border road closure', *The Irish Times*, 1 July 1974.

300　NA (UK) FCO 87/371, 'Telegram 25', 5 July 1974.

301　NA (IRL) 2005/145/2554, 'Chief Supt JP McMahon letter', 9 September 1975.

302　NA (IRL) 2010/19/1618, 'Letter from D Hamill to Swift', dated 5 May 1977.

303　Patterson, *Ireland's Violent Frontier*, p. 86.

304　NA 2010/19/1618, 'Letter from D Hamill to Swift', dated 5 May 1977.

305　'Kidnap: Provos in disarray', *Hibernia*, 17 October 1975.

306　'Costello wounded in Waterford', *The Irish Times*, 8 May 1975; 'Hoax bombs blown up at Goulding home', *The Irish Times*, 9 May 1975; 'Man shot dead in Cork city', *The Irish Times*, 11 June 1975.

307　Gerard Hogan and Clive Walker, *Political Violence and the Law in Ireland* (Manchester: Manchester University Press, 1989), p. 243.

308　Dunne and Kerrigan, *Round Up the Usual Suspects* (1984), p. 100.

309　Ibid., p. 98–100.

310　NA (IRL) 2010/19/1687, 'Breakdown and location of border incidents'.

311　Henry Patterson, 'War of National Liberation or Ethnic Cleansing: IRA Violence in Fermanagh during the Troubles', in *Terror: From Tyrannicide to Terrorism*, eds Brett Bowden and Michael T. Davis (Brisbane, Australia: University of Queensland Press, 2008), p. 2.

312　NA (UK) FCO 87/248, 'Letter from Kelvin White to RC Cox', 25 June 1973.

313　NA (UK) CJ4/396, 'Cooperation between British and Irish Security Forces'.

314　Barron Inquiry into Dublin and Monaghan bombings, p. 343. http://www.taoiseach.gov.ie/eng/Work_Of_The_Department/Economic_International_Northern_Ireland/Northern_Ireland/Northern_Ireland_Publications/InterimDubMon.pdf.

Chapter 5

1　FCO 87/603, 'Republic of Ireland annual review for 1976', circa December 1976.

2　'Boys Brigade came under fire from retreating bombers', *Donegal Democrat*, 15 December 1978.

3　NA (UK) CJ4 2244, 'Discussion at Glencairn', 20 June 1978.

4　NA(IRL) 2006/133/693, 'IDU on Northern Ireland Agreed report of meeting of January 16, 1976'.

5　NA (UK) FCO 87/603, 'Republic of Ireland Annual Review for 1976'.

6　Ibid., p. 10.

7　NA (UK) CJ4/1049, 'Personal Security', letter from P.J. Goulden, 15 July 1976.

8　NA (UK) FCO 87/491, Garda Investigation, 27 July 1976.

9　Kieran Conway, *Southside Provisional: From Freedom Fighter to Four Courts* (Dublin: Orpen Press, 2014), p. 197.

10　'12 years penal servitude for setting fire to Dublin premises', *The Irish Times*, 11 November 1976.

11　Sean O'Callaghan, *The Informer* (London: Corgi, 1999), p. 240.

12 Joint Oireachtas Committee, *Interim Report on the Report of the Independent Commission of Inquiry into the Bombing of Kay's Tavern, Dundalk* (2006), p. 168, http://www.dublinmonaghanbombings.org/KaysInterim.pdf.
13 'Britannia rules the courts', *An Phoblacht*, 11 June 1976.
14 Darach McDonald, 'Why the hunger strike failed', *Hibernia*, 29 April 1977.
15 Ibid.
16 'Dublin has massive parade backing peace', *The Irish Times*, 30 August 1976.
17 'Marching for Peace', *The Northern Standard*, 26 November 1976.
18 Brian Trench, 'Blaney's machine rolls on', *Hibernia*, 2 July 1976.
19 'Big Anti Blaney Votes at Fianna Fáil Ard Fheis', *Donegal People and Derry News*, 21 February 1976.
20 'Fianna Fáil the main losers', *Donegal People and Derry News*, 19 June 1976.
21 NA (UK) FCO 87/539, 'Meeting between Fianna Fáil and Secretary of state', 29 May 1976.
22 NA (UK) FCO 87/603, 'Republic of Ireland Annual Review for 1976'.
23 'Britain acts swiftly amid fears of loyalist reprisals', *The Irish Times*, 7 January 1976.
24 NA (UK) FCO87/496, 'Background material the security situation in Northern Ireland'.
25 Patterson, *Ireland's Violent Frontier*, p. 97.
26 NA (IRL) 2008/79/3154, 'Note on overflights request and annex of incidents'.
27 Patterson, *Ireland's Violent Frontier*, p. 67.
28 NA (IRL) 2006/133/693, 'IDU on Northern Ireland Agreed report of meeting of January 16, 1976'.
29 'British propaganda hard to take-Fitzgerald', *The Irish Times*, 2 February 1976.
30 'Volleys fired at Stag ceremony; eleven hurt in scuffles', *The Irish Times*, 23 February 1976.
31 'Cabinet bans Provisionals 1916 March', *The Irish Times*, 22 April 1976.
32 'Whip withdrawn from Thornley by 22 votes to 3', *The Irish Times*, 29 April 1976.
33 'Fitzgerald denies SAS men's prosecution is "political"', *The Irish Times*, 17 May 1976.
34 Jimmy Leonard TD, Monaghan, Dáil Debate, 13 May 1976.
35 Raymond Murray, *The SAS in Ireland* (Dublin: Irish American Book Company, 1990), p. 175.
36 Ibid.
37 NA (UK) CJ4/1641, 'Review of SAS article in Guardian', 11 December 1976.
38 Murray, *The SAS in Ireland*, p. 168–9.
39 NA (UK) FC0 87/668, List of nine relevant files on topic removed from file and destroyed. The National Archives denied a Freedom of Information request for material on the incursion on the grounds that the file contained information that could damage UK–Ireland relations. Email to Patrick Mulroe from Keara Donnelly, National Archives, 8 June 2015.
40 'Security Breach', *An Phoblacht*, 23 July 1976.
41 NA (UK) FCO 87/489, 'Press reaction to Ambassador's assassination', circa July 1976.
42 Ibid.
43 NA (IRL) 2006/133/709, 'British press reaction to bombing', circa July 1976.
44 Ibid
45 Ferriter, *Ambiguous Republic*, p. 212.

46   Derek Dunne and Gene Kerrigan, *Round Up the Usual Suspects* (Dublin: Magill, 1984), p. 181.

47   John Bew et al., *Talking to Terrorists: Making Peace in the Basque Country and Northern Ireland* (London: Hurst and Company, 2009), p. 80.

48   NA (UK) FCO 87/493, Hickman letter to Harding in FCO 19 August 1976.

49   Patterson, *Ireland's Violent Frontier*, p. 101.

50   'Heavier jail terms for IRA membership, warns Cooney', *The Irish Times*, 28 February 1976.

51   Patterson, *Ireland's Violent Frontier*, p. 67.

52   FCO 87/603, 'Republic of Ireland annual review for 1976', circa December 1976.

53   Garret FitzGerald, *All in a Life* (London: Gill and Macmillan, 1991), p. 313.

54   'Fianna Fáil's best day in opposition', *The Irish Times*, 10 September 1976.

55   NA (UK) CJ4 1824, 'Meeting at Department of Foreign Affairs', 8 December 1976.

56   Gerard Hogan and Clive Walker, *Political Violence and the Law in Ireland* (Manchester: Manchester University Press, 1989), p. 260.

57   'FF seeks Donegan's dismissal for remark about President', *The Irish Times*, 19 October 1976.

58   'Five votes decide Donegan should not be asked to resign', *The Irish Times*, 22 October 1976.

59   FitzGerald, *All in a Life*, p. 318.

60   Ferriter, *Ambiguous Republic*, p. 343.

61   FCO 87/486, The Irish Internal scene, 26 October 1976.

62   Patterson, *Ireland's Violent Frontier*, p. 104.

63   'Callaghan raps Ireland over terrorism pact', *The Irish Times*, 11 February 1977.

64   'Garda has lost his head', *An Phoblacht*, 25 June 1976; 'Brutalised by Special Branch', *An Phoblacht*, 25 June 1976; 'You live in a Police state', *An Phoblacht*, 15 May 1976.

65   'The Law', *The Irish Times*, 14 February 1977.

66   FitzGerald, *All in a Life*, p. 314.

67   'Cosgrave sets tone for brief and intense election campaign', *The Irish Times*, 23 May 1977.

68   'Cabinet discusses protection after attacks on two TDs', *The Irish Times*, 20 April 1977.

69   'Survey indicates FF lead over Coalition', *The Irish Times*, 2 June 1977.

70   'Election Forecast', *Hibernia*, 27 May 1977.

71   Ferriter, *Ambiguous Republic*, p. 343.

72   '*Irish Times* poll suggest a FF's hard sell is catching', *The Irish Times*, 8 June 1977.

73   Frank Dunlop, *Yes, Taoiseach: Irish Politics from Behind Closed Doors* (Dublin: Penguin, 2004), p. 106.

74   Patsy McArdle, *The Secret War* (Dublin: Mercier, 1984), p. 43.

75   Joe Lee, *Ireland 1912–85: Politics and Society* (Cambridge: Cambridge University Press, 1989), p. 484.

76   'Conor Cruise O'Brien', *The Telegraph*, 19 December 2008.

77   'The Dáil Independents: Promise unfulfilled', *Hibernia*, 10 August 1978.

78   NA (UK) CJ4/1755/1, 'General Election in Republic of Ireland Implications for Northern Ireland', point 12.

79   'Patterson urges Protestant support for Fianna Fáil', *Donegal Democrat*, 10 June 1976.

80   NA (UK) FCO 87/608, 'Discussion with Sean Donlon Department of Foreign Affairs', 9 June 1977.
81   NA (UK) CJ4/1755/1, 'Fianna Fáil Policy towards Northern Ireland', 22 June 1977.
82   NA (UK) FCO 87/610, Robin Haydon, 'Relation with new Irish government', 22 July 1977.
83   'Laissez Faire', *Hibernia*, 30 September 1977.
84   NA (IRL) 2007/116/750, Report of plenary meeting September 1977.
85   Patterson, *Ireland's Violent Frontier*, p. 114.
86   'Little Cabinet talent', *Hibernia*, 24 June 1977.
87   NA (UK) FCO 87/602, 'The Fianna Fáil Cabinet', 14 July 1977.
88   NA (UK) CJ4/1752, 'Charles Haughey Profile', 23 June 1977.
89   Albert Reynolds, *Albert Reynolds: My Autobiography* (London: Transworld Ireland, 2009), p. 82.
90   Bertie Ahern, *Bertie Ahern: The Autobiography* (London: Cornerstone, 2009), p. 42.
91   Ferriter, *Ambiguous Republic*, p. 86.
92   NA (UK) CJ4/1752, 'Charles Haughey Profile', 23 June 1977.
93   NA (UK) FCO 87/602, 'Government popularity', 19 December 1977.
94   'FF "soft" with IRA says Cooney', *The Irish Times*, 11 November 1977.
95   'Collins must show his hand', *Hibernia*, 30 September 1977.
96   'Commission to inquire into treatment of suspects in custody', *The Irish Times*, 7 October 1977.
97   'Fingerprint scandal', *Magill*, November 1977.
98   'Cabinet and Commissioner in dispute on Amnesty report', *The Irish Times*, 7 September 1977.
99   Ferriter, *Ambiguous Republic*, p. 345.
100 CJ4/2249, Goulden, 'Letter re Garda Commissioner', 1 December 1977.
101 Conway, *Policing Twentieth Century Ireland*, p. 150.
102 Conor Brady, *The Guarding of Ireland* (Dublin: Gill and Macmillan, 2014), p. 121.
103 'Summonses dispute angered Gardaí', *The Irish Times*, 26 January 1978.
104 Brady, *The Guarding of Ireland*, p. 121.
105 NA (UK) CJ4 22/47, 'Jane Henderson note on conversation with Ambassador', February 1978.
106 NA (UK) CJ4/2239, 'Telegram 42', 20 January 1978.
107 'Clarification call follows Taoiseach's hint of an amnesty', *The Irish Times*, 9 January 1978.
108 'Lynch "boosting" the IRA', *The Irish Times*, 10 January 1978.
109 Patterson, *Ireland's Violent Frontier*, p. 120.
110 'Mason's comments annoyed cabinet', *The Irish Times*, 11 January 1978.
111 'Lynch stands firm on North and Amnesty statements', *The Irish Times*, 11 January 1978.
112 'Government denies terrorism claim', *The Irish Times*, 21 February 1978.
113 'Mason attacks claim by Taoiseach on cross border violence', *The Irish Times*, 21 February 1978.
114 'Mason's remarks chill relation', *The Irish Times*, 8 March 1978.
115 NA (UK) CJ4/2247, 'Aide Memoire', 16 June 1978.
116 NA (UK) CJ4/2240/2, 'M60 Machine Guns. Did they come through the Republic?', 1978.

117 NA (IRL) 2007/111/2008, 'Media Briefings by British Authorities', 1978.

118 NA (UK) CJ4/2240/1, 'Security Cooperation: Exchange of Information with Irish', 10 March 1978.

119 'Fitzgerald backs Lynch in row with Mason', *The Irish Times*, 11 March 1978.

120 NA (IRL) 2007/111/2008, 'Northern Ireland: Violence and the border', 14 March 1978.

121 NA (IRL) 2007/111/2008, 'Violence in Northern Ireland', 14 March 1978.

122 Ibid.

123 NA (UK) CJ4/2231, 'Prime Ministers meeting with Taoiseach', 7 April 1978.

124 NA (UK) CJ4/2243, 'Full session on politics', 5 May 1978.

125 Patterson, *Ireland's Violent Frontier*, p. 120.

126 NA (UK) CJ4/2247, 'Report on meeting between Frank Dunlop and PJ Goulden', 16 May 1978.

127 NA (UK) CJ4/2243, 'Haydon's note on Anglo Irish relations', 26 April 1978.

128 NA 2008/79/3100, 'Hugh Swift reply to September dossier', 13 October 1978.

129 Ibid.

130 NA (UK) CJ4//2245, Haydon to NIO, 'Cross border Security Cooperation', 8 November 1978.

131 Dermot Keogh, *Jack Lynch: A Biography* (Dublin: Gill and Macmillan, 2008), p. 423–35.

132 NA (UK) CJ4/2751, 'Brief for incoming Secretary of State', 17 April 1979.

133 NA 2010/53/889, 'Report sent from Department of Justice to Department of Taoiseach on crime', 1979.

134 '70% of armed crime has nothing to do with subversives', *The Irish Times*, 4 September 1978.

135 Conor Brady, *The Guarding of Ireland* (Dublin: Gill and Macmillan, 2014), p. 98.

136 'Editorial', *Garda Review*, June 1976.

137 'Disciplinary action for attending Stagg funeral', *The Irish Times*, 7 July 1976.

138 'Ex Garda who sold state papers is released by court', *The Irish Times*, 11 January 1978.

139 'Gardaí and Dublin elite colluded with IRA', *The Irish Times*, 4 December 2014.

140 NA (UK) CJ4/1055, 'RUC/Garda Joint Coordinating Committee Meeting', 23 April 1976.

141 NA (UK) FCO 87/537, 'Anglo Irish Security Cooperation', 20 January 1976.

142 NA (UK) CJ4/2245, 'Cross Border Security Cooperation', 19 September 1978.

143 Conway, *Southside Provisional*, p. 184–5.

144 'RTE got it wrong about the Clerkin case-and I know because I was there', *Evening Herald*, 26 August 2009.

145 Conway, *Policing Twentieth Century Ireland*, p. 118.

146 'Gunman wounds Garda at border', *The Irish Times*, 9 June 1976; 'Shots fired at border', *The Irish Times* 21 January 1976; 'Detective shot in city car chase', *The Irish Times*, 18 December 1976; 'Two Hijack Garda car near Kells', *The Irish Times*, 4 September 1976; 'Monaghan labourer gaoled for five years', *Anglo Celt*, 16 June 1978; 'Garda assaulted on Christmas Eve', *Anglo Celt*, 30 June 1978; 'Shots fired at detective', *Anglo Celt*, 17 August 1979; 'Charged with attempting to murder Garda', *Anglo Celt*, 3 August 1979; 'Incident at Monaghan Garda Station', *Anglo Celt*, 22 June 1979; 'Garda held at Gunpoint', *The Irish Times*, 21 July 1978; 'Growing disquiet at attacks on Gardaí', *Donegal and Derry People*, 3 September 1977; 'Two Gardaí wounded in gun battle', *The Northern Standard*, 6 April 1979.

147 'Freedom of Speech', *The Northern Standard*, 26 April 1979.
148 'A dastardly act', *The Northern Standard*, 5 April 1979.
149 Conway, *Policing Twentieth Century Ireland*, p. 131.
150 'Behind the shields and helmets', *An Phoblacht*, 5 March 1976.
151 'What stirred the conscience of the Judge', *An Phoblacht*, 9 July 1976; 'Obscene torture in Tralee Garda barracks', *An Phoblacht*, 9 July 1976; 'Another Garda torture story', *An Phoblacht*, 14 April 1976; 'Brutalised by Special Branch', *An Phoblacht*, 25 June 1976; 'Emergency Law: behind the headlines', *An Phoblacht*, 19 October 1976; 'Garda Barracks Ill treatment', *An Phoblacht*, 19 October 1976; 'Special Branch Harassment in Drogheda', *An Phoblacht*, 19 March 1976; 'Garda Brutality in Ballyconnell', *An Phoblacht*, 20 September 1976.
152 Conway, *Policing Twentieth Century Ireland*, p. 148.
153 'Special Treatment', *Garda Review*, March 1976.
154 'Gardaí using North style brutality in interrogation techniques', *The Irish Times*, 14 February 1977.
155 'Division in Garda ranks on brutality', *The Irish Times*, 26 February 1977.
156 Conway, *Policing Twentieth Century Ireland*, p. 145.
157 Ibid.
158 'Garda says he heard screams', *The Irish Times*, 27 May 1977.
159 'Garda brutality allegations rejected by Special Court', *The Irish Times*, 21 June 1977.
160 Derek Dunne and Gene Kerrigan, *Round Up the Usual Suspects* (Dublin: Magill, 1984), p. 181.
161 'Fingerprint Scandal', *Magill*, November 1977.
162 Conway, *Policing Twentieth Century Ireland*, p. 183.
163 'Government rejects main proposals on Garda custody', *The Irish Times*, 13 September 1978.
164 'Editorial: The Barra Ó Briain report', *Garda Review*, September 1978.
165 'The seeds of a police state', *Magill*, September 1983.
166 NA (UK) CJ4/3935, 'Allegations of Garda Brutality', 15 September 1978.
167 'Garda Brutality', *Magill*, May 1979.
168 'Inquiry begins into allegations against Monaghan Gardaí', *The Irish Times*, 30 June 1978.
169 Joe McVeigh, *Taking a Stand: Memoir of an Irish Priest* (Dublin: Mercier, 2008), p. 144.
170 Ibid.
171 NA (UK) CJ4/3935, 'Allegations of Garda Brutality: Report of the Ó Briain Committee', 15 September 1978.
172 'Many armed thefts hardly even investigated', *The Irish Times*, 5 September 1978.
173 NA (UK) CJ4/3935, 'Allegations of Garda Brutality', 15 September 1978.
174 'Many armed thefts hardly even investigated', *The Irish Times*, 5 September 1978.
175 NA 2006/133/25, 'Memorandum for Government by Minister for Finance', 1976.
176 NA 2006/133/25, 'Department of Justice reply to Memorandum for Government by Minister for Finance 1976', 20 December 1976.
177 NA (UK) FCO87/934, 'Security Cooperation with Republic of Ireland: Visit of Jack Lynch', 5 September 1979.
178 Patrick McEntee, *Commission of Investigation into Dublin & Monaghan Bombings Final Report* (2007), p. 70–2, http://cain.ulst.ac.uk/events/dublin/macentee040407final.pdf.

179   'They learn by experience-we don't', *The Irish Times*, 6 September 1978.
180   Ibid.
181   NA (IRL) 2006/133/25, Memorandum for Government by Minister for Finance 1976.
182   Conway, *Policing Twentieth Century Ireland*, p. 96.
183   NA (UK) CJ4/2737, 'Command control: current situation', 1979.
184   'RUC and Garda Cooperation is kept very quiet', *The Irish Times*, 18 July 1979.
185   NA (UK) CJ4/2737, 'Cross border communication', 6 August 1979.
186   NA (UK) CJ4/2737, 'Goliath speech security equipment', 1979.
187   NA (UK) FCO 87/536, 'State of security assessment: Republic of Ireland', 28 October 1976.
188   NA (UK) CJ4/2739, 'Border cooperation background note', circa December 1978.
189   NA (UK) CJ4/2244, 'RUC Aughnacloy', 8 September 1978.
190   Ibid.
191   'Army under fire again', *The Northern Standard*, 25 November 1977; 'Vote of confidence in Army', *The Northern Standard*, 21 October 1977; 'Bad blood between Gardaí and soldiers', *Donegal Democrat*, 10 February 1978.
192   'The Visible Army', *Magill*, May 1979.
193   NA (UK) CJ4/2247, 'Border Superintendents', circa 1978.
194   'RUC and Garda Cooperation is kept very quiet', *The Irish Times*, 18 July 1979; 'Playing the UN game on the Irish border', *The Irish Times*, 19 July 1979.
195   NA (UK) CJ4/2737, 'Relations with the Irish government: Security', 2 August 1979.
196   Ibid.
197   Ibid.
198   NA (UK) Defe 24/1916, 'Monthly border report', March 1978.
199   NA (UK) CJ4/1758, 'Border Report on RUC Division N', January 1977.
200   NA (UK) CJ4 2919, 'Examples of cooperation with Gardaí', September 1979.
201   NA (UK) Defe 24/1916, 'Border report on RUC Division N for May 1977-Clady-Strabane', 8 June 1977.
202   NA (UK) CJ4/1758, 'Border Report', October 1976.
203   NA (UK) Defe 24/1916, 'K Division report November 1- December 4, 1976'.
204   Joint Oireachtas Committee, *Interim report into Dublin Monaghan Bombing* (2003), p. 195, http://www.taoiseach.gov.ie/attached_files/Pdf%20files/InterimDubMon.pdf.
205   NA (UK) CJ4/1758, 'Border Report', September 1976.
206   Joint Oireachtas Committee, *Interim report into Dublin Monaghan Bombing* (2003), p. 196, http://www.dublinmonaghanbombings.org/DubMonInterim.pdf. Weir was sergeant in charge in Newtownhamilton from 1 September 1977.
207   NA (UK) CJ4/1758, 'Police Division K Report', June 1976.
208   Joint Oireachtas Committee, *Interim report into Dublin Monaghan Bombing* (2003), p. 55, http://cain.ulst.ac.uk/events/dublin/barron03.pdf.
209   'The soldier who took on the IRA in sortie over the border 37 years ago', *Irish Independent*, 31 October 2011.
210   NA (UK) FCO 87/499, 'Border Incursions', 1976.
211   NA (UK) CJ4/1758, 'Border report on RUC N Division for August', 1976.
212   NA (UK) CJ4/1758, 'Border Report', dated 21 September 1976.
213   NA (IRL) 2008/79/3101, 'Note regarding border incursions', July 1978.

214 NA (IRL) 2008/79/3154, 'Garda/RUC contact', 1976.

215 NA (IRL) 2008/79/3154, 'Letter to Sean Donlon, Department of Foreign Affairs from secretary Department of Justice', 9 September 1976.

216 Interview with John Nulty, 'Green and Blue' Project (2014), http://www.green-and-blue.org/wp-content/uploads/2014/01/John-McNulty-edited-interview-transcript.pdf.

217 NA (UK) CJ4/2247, 'Letter from Kenneth Newman to Brian Cubbon Permanent Undersecretary in Northern Ireland Office', 24 November 1977.

218 NA (UK) CJ4/2247, 'Letter from Paul Burton in Northern Ireland Office to John Goulden in British Embassy', 15 December 1977.

219 NA (UK) CJ4/2999, 'Talks with Irish government officials', 27 September 1979.

220 NA (UK) CJ4/2243, 'Minutes of full session on politics', 5 May 1978.

221 NA 2007/111/2008, 'Violence in Northern Ireland', 14 March 1978.

222 NA 2008/79/3100, 'Cross border security', 20 September 1978.

223 NA 2009/120/2117, 'Garda strength', 1979.

224 'Strengthening of Gardaí in urban areas welcomed', *The Irish Times*, 27 August 1977.

225 NA (UK) CJ4/2999, 'A comparison of British and Irish Security forces assigned to border duties', 18 September 1979.

226 NA (UK) CJ4/2244, 'Cross border cooperation by PWJ Buxton', 19 June 1978.

227 NA (UK) CJ4/2244, 'Numbers attached to file on cross border cooperation by PWJ Buxton', 19 June 1978.

228 NA (UK) DEFE 24/1916, 'Border Report', October 1976.

229 NA (UK) DEFE 24/1916, 'Monthly border report', 2 January 1978.

230 NA (UK) FCO 87/934, 'Contacts and Communication with the South', 3 September 1979.

231 NA (UK) CJ4/2247, 'DFA views on Anglo Irish Security Cooperation', 1 March 1978.

232 Interview with Pat O'Leary, 'Green and Blue' Project (2014), http://accounts.ulster.ac.uk/repo24/files/original/42b1572a586d5f9bd755905b3723c6fa.pdf

233 Joint Oireachtas Committee, *Final Report on the Report of the Independent Commission of Inquiry into the Bombing of Kay's Tavern, Dundalk*, November 2006, Superintendant Courtney evidence to Oireachtas Inquiry, p. 39–42, http://www.macguill.ie/Kay's-Tavern-Final-Report.pdf.

234 David McKittrick et al., *Lost Lives* (London: Mainstream Publishing, 1999), p. 1473.

235 'McMorrow jailed for 10 years on arms charge', *The Irish Times*, 15 July 1977; 'Charged with attempting to murder Garda', *Anglo Celt*, 3 August 1979; 'Monaghan labourer gaoled for five years', *Anglo Celt*, 16 June 1978; 'Shots fired at detective', *Anglo Celt*, 17 August 1979; 'Two hijack Garda car near Kells', *The Irish Times*, 4 September 1976; 'Shots fired at Gardaí', *The Irish Times*, 21 January 1976; 'Two Gardaí wounded in gun battle', *The Northern Standard*, 6 April 1979; 'Assault on Cloone Garda', *Leitrim Observer*, 21 January 1977.

236 'Garda tells of vicious attack', *The Northern Standard*, 14 October 1977; 'Garda assaulted on Christmas Eve', *Anglo Celt*, 30 June 1978; 'Six months for Garda assault', *The Northern Standard*, 9 June 1978; 'Incidents at H Block demo described', *The Northern Standard*, 2 January 1979; 'Assaulted off duty Garda in Butt Hall toilet', *Donegal Democrat*, 20 February 1976.

237 'After 8 years Orangemen march again', *Donegal Democrat*, 14 July 1978.

238 'Gardaí stoned after Orangemen march', *Donegal Democrat*, 18 August 1978.

239 'IRA man still free after 5 escape bombed cell', *The Irish Times*, 16 July 1976.

240 'Three men sought after killing Ambassador', *The Irish Times*, 22 July 1976.

241 'Collaborators warned in Oglach statement', *An Phoblacht*, 11 June 1976.

242 NA (IRL) 2008/79/3109, 'Intelligence Assessment', 15 February 1977.

243 NA (IRL) 2008/79/3109, 'Miscellaneous incidents', July–December 1976.

244 Interview with Joe Lynch, 'Green and Blue' Project (2014), http://accounts. ulster.ac.uk/repo24/files/original/8faf854642c321c7b7205a963b78e646.pdf

245 'Monaghan Garda victim of booby trap', *The Northern Standard*, 22 October 1976.

246 Ibid.

247 Brady, *The Guarding of Ireland*, p. 102.

248 'RTE got it wrong about the Clerkin case-and I know because I was there', *Evening Herald*, 26 August 2009.

249 'Garda Clerkin', *Irish Press*, 18 October 1976.

250 NA (UK) CJ4/1756, 'Terrorist incidents', 1 April 1976–31 October 1977.

251 Ibid.

252 NA (UK) CJ4/1756, 'Brief for Ambassador in Dublin on Cross Border security', circa December 1977.

253 NA (UK) CJ 4/1055, 'Incidents which follow up facilities would have benefitted Gardaí', circa May 1976.

254 NA (IRL) 2008/79/3154, 'Response to over flight request', circa May 1976.

255 NA (IRL) 2010/19/1687, 'Border Incidents the 2% figure and after'.

256 Conway, *Southside Provisional*, p. 99.

257 NA (UK) CJ4/2853, 'RUC GARDA Coordinating committee report on South Armagh', 1976.

258 NA (IRL) 2008/79/3109, 'Intelligence Assessment', Spring 1977, 15 February 1977.

259 NA (UK) CJ4 1307, Letter to Merlyn Rees from Northern Ireland forces headquarters, 31 January 1976.

260 Ibid.

261 NA (IRL) 2007/111/2008, 'Violence in Northern Ireland', March 1978.

262 Joint Oireachtas Committee, *Final Report into the killing of Seamus Ludlow*, 2006, p. 32, http://cain.ulst.ac.uk/issues/violence/docs/ludlowreport06final.pdf.

263 'Patrick Livingstone Conviction for Good Samaritan Murder quashed', *RTÉ News*, 25 June 2013, http://www.rte.ie/news/2013/0625/458796-patrick-livingstone-court/.

264 NA (UK) CJ4/1054, 'Cross Border and Rural PIRA groups', circa March 1976.

265 NA (IRL) 2005/145/2554, 'Letter from Chief Superintendent Richard Cotterell', 24 September 1975.

266 'Seventeen injured in Castleblayney bomb blast', *The Irish Times*, 8 March 1976.

267 'Councillors want more security', *The Northern Standard*, 12 March 1976.

268 NA (IRL) 2005/145/2554, 'Letter from JP McMahon on closure of cross border roads', September 1975.

269 'Uproar as debate on security grows personal', *The Northern Standard*, 26 March 1976.

270 NA (IRL) 2006/145/36, 'Town clerk Castleblayney UDC to Minister for Justice', 9 March 1976.

271 NA (IRL) 2006/145/40, 'Setting up community service corp', 17 March 1976.

272 NA (IRL) 2010/19/1618, 'D Hamill note on border roads', 5 May 1977.

273 Joint Oireachtas Committee, *Interim Report on the Independent Commission of Inquiry into the Bombing of Kay's Tavern, Dundalk* (2006), pp. 152–3, http://www.dublinmonaghanbombings.org/KaysInterim.pdf.

274 Ibid., p. 154.

275 Joint Oireachtas Committee, *Interim Report into Murder of Seamus Ludlow* (2005), p. 33, http://www.dublinmonaghanbombings.org/LudlowInterim.pdf.

276 Ibid., p. 66.

277 Ibid., p. 94.

278 Ibid., p. 98.

279 Interview with Jimmy Fox, nephew of Seamus Ludlow, *Aftermath Project* (2014), http://aftermath-ireland.com/portfolio/jimmy-fox-interview/.

280 'Louth Border sensation: eight SAS men who crossed charged in Dublin', *Dundalk Democrat*, 8 May 1976.

281 'Cross border abduction by SAS', *Dundalk Democrat*, 17 July 1976.

282 NA (UK) CJ4/1640, 'Incident at Dromad', 12 July 1976; 'Draft FCO telegram to Dublin', July 1976.

283 Murray, *The SAS in Ireland*, p. 182.

284 NA (UK) CJ4/1758, 'Area Police Division H', August 1976.

285 NA (UK) CJ4/1640, 'Incursion at Belcoo', 9 June 1976, BM Webster.

286 Tosh Lavery, *Tosh: An Amazing True Story of Life, Death, Danger and Drama in the Garda Sub-Aqua Unit* (Dublin: Penguin, 2015).

287 'Dragged over border by SAS', *An Phoblacht*, 26 March 1976; 'SAS suspected of brutal border beatings', *The Northern Standard*, 31 March 1978.

288 'Court told of shooting incident outside hotel', *The Irish Times*, 29 June 1976.

289 Anthony Bradley, *Requiem for a Spy: The Killing of Robert Nairac* (Dublin: Irish American Book Company, 1993); Joe Tiernan, *The Dublin and Monaghan Bombings and the Murder Triangle* (Dublin: Joe Tiernan, 2002); John Parker, *Secret Hero: The Life and Mysterious Death of Captain Robert Nairac* (London: John Blake, 2004); Martin Dillon, *The Dirty War* (London: Hutchinson, 1990).

290 Joint Oireachtas Committee, *Interim Report on Dublin Monaghan Bombing* (2003), p. 249, http://www.dublinmonaghanbombings.org/DubMonInterim.pdf.

291 Ibid., p. 189.

292 'Provisionals admit killing officer', *The Irish Times*, 17 May 1977.

293 'Provos insist they got their man', *Hibernia*, 20 July 1978; 'British soldier killed in Armagh', *The Irish Times*, 13 July 1978; 'Big search for Keady killers', *The Irish Times*, 21 August 1978; 'Murder victim's body moved', *The Irish Times*, 27 June 1978; 'British Army chief killed in South Armagh', *The Irish Times*, 18 February 1978; 'Three British soldiers shot dead in Crossmaglen', *The Irish Times*, 22 December 1978.

294 McKittrick et al., *Lost Lives*, 742–72.

295 NA (UK) CJ4/1055, 'Cross border and rural groups', 27 April 1976.

296 NA (IRL) 2008/79/3109, 'Intelligence assessment', 15 February 1976.

297 'UDR man shot in Monaghan', *The Irish Times*, 10 March 1977; 'UDR man shot', *The Northern Standard*, 11 March 1977.

298 'Currie condemns RUC man's death', *The Irish Times*, 24 December 1979; 'RUC reservist shot by IRA in Monaghan', *The Northern Standard*, 27 December 1980.

299 'RUC, Garda witnesses give evidence in murder trials', *The Irish Times*, 30 June 1981.

300 McKittrick et al., *Lost Lives*, p. 837.

301   NA (IRL) 2006/132/141, 'Crime statistics Glaslough', 1969–1980.
302   McKittrick et al., *Lost Lives*, p. 849, see Norman and James Strong; Gene Kerrigan *Hard Cases: True Stories of Irish Crime* (Dublin: Gill and Macmillan, 1996), p. 231, see Gay Murphy.
303   'Missing Constable is Monaghan man', *The Northern Standard*, 23 June 1976.
304   NA (IRL) 2006/132/41, 'Letter from Desmond Leslie to Minister for Justice', 14 February 1980.
305   NA (IRL) 2006/132/41, 'Chief Superintendent Broderick to Commissioner B', 28 February 1978.
306   Patterson, *Ireland's Violent Frontier*, p. 129.
307   NA (UK) CJ4/3084, 'Security briefing RUC L Division', circa 1980.
308   NA (UK) CJ4/2244, 'Speaking note on border security', August 1978.
309   Patterson, *Ireland's Violent Frontier*, p. 133.
310   NA (IRL) 2010/53/747, 'Taoiseach's meeting with Lord Brookeborough', Monday 16 June 1980.
311   *Seamus McElwaine IRA Freedom Fighter*, YouTube, https://www.youtube.com/watch?v=NY-GCyOr-Ok, 4 minutes 30 seconds.
312   Patterson, *Ireland's Violent Frontier*, p. 135.
313   Jack Holland and Susan Phoenix, *Phoenix: Policing the Shadows* (London: Hodder and Stoughton, 1997), p. 208.
314   *Loughgall Martyrs*, part 3, YouTube, https://www.youtube.com/watch?v=n_D7h-MbOoI.
315   Kerrigan, *Hard Cases*, p. 245.
316   *Loughgall Martyrs*, part 1, YouTube, https://www.youtube.com/watch?v=MKem Zthpxak.
317   'Councillor takes responsibility for ammunition', *The Irish Times*, 16 July 1982.
318   NA (IRL) 2007/111/2008, 'The use of the border by the Provisional IRA', 6 March 1978.
319   'RUC and Army comb South Derry after murder of policemen', *The Irish Times*, 8 April 1977.
320   NA (IRL) 2007/111/2008, 'The use of the border by the Provisional IRA', 6 March 1978.
321   'Dawn raid on Carrigans Garda station', *Derry People and Donegal News*, 27 August 1977.
322   'Terrorists rake Garda station with gunfire', *Donegal Democrat*, 2 September 1977.
323   'Gardaí fired on in 100mph Sligo–Leitrim chase', *Leitrim Observer*, 17 February 1977.
324   'Garda believe the Provisionals', *The Irish Times*, 9 September 1977.
325   'Donegal Gardaí get firearms training in gang search', *The Irish Times*, 30 August 1977.
326   'Sinn Féin statement "utter fabrication" say Gardaí', *Derry People and Donegal News*, 3 September 1977.
327   'Time the kid gloves were off', *Donegal Democrat*, 11 September 1977; 'Growing disquiet at attacks on Gardaí', *Derry People and Donegal News*, 3 September 1977.
328   NA (UK) CJ4/2240/1, 'Speaking note on extra territorial jurisdiction', 20 March 1978.
329   'Wanted man captured at border', *The Northern Standard*, 16 September 1977.
330   'Man who hijacked Garda car jailed', *The Irish Times*, 21 June 1978; 'County Antrim Man jailed for seizing Garda car', *The Irish Times*, 20 June 1978.

331 'Murder squad appeals for public cooperation', *Derry People and Donegal News*, 11 February 1978.

332 'Man gets life for murder', *The Irish Times*, 1 March 1979.

333 'Found dead on farm', *Derry People and Donegal News*, 15 February 1979.

334 'IRA victims Donegal connection', *Donegal Democrat*, 9 June 1978.

335 'Donegal 7 being tortured', *Donegal Democrat*, 7 April 1978.

336 'Gardaí capture M60 machine gun', *Donegal Democrat*, 28 April 1978; 'Garda swoop unearths weapons cache', *Donegal Democrat*, 17 November 1978; 'IRA training camp found', *Donegal Democrat*, 28 October 1977; 'Court story of bomb factory in rented house', 20 January 1978.

337 Patterson, *Ireland's Violent Frontier*, p. 129.

338 NA (UK) CJ4/3084, 'Security briefing RUC L Division', circa 1980.

339 *Donegal Democrat*, 'Authorities worried by renewed border activity', 25 August 1978.

340 NA (IRL) 2008/79/3100, 'Cross Border Security', 20 September 1978.

341 NA (UK) CJ4/2999, 'Notes on talks with Irish officials', 23 October 1978.

342 NA (UK) FCO 87/934, 'Contacts and Communication with the south', 3 September 1979.

343 'Gardaí provoke trouble in Portlaoise', *An Phoblacht*, 18 March 1976; 'Two still in hospital following clashes', *The Irish Times*, 5 April 1977; 'Monaghan airs protest', *An Phoblacht*, 7 May 1976.

344 NA (IRL) 2008/79/3109, 'Intelligence Assessment', Spring 1977.

345 'Inquiry begins into allegations against Monaghan Gardaí', *The Irish Times*, 30 June 1978.

346 'Brits Out slogan', *Donegal Democrat*, 1 April 1977; 'Row over Sinn Féin Slogans', *The Northern Standard*, 29 November 1979; 'Troubles the major obstacle', *Derry People & Donegal News North*, 16 April 1977.

347 'Sinn Féin Statement on road painting', *Donegal Democrat*, 19 May 1978; 'Row over Sinn Féin slogans', *The Northern Standard*, 29 November 1979.

348 'Sinn Féin Statement on poster campaign', *Derry People and Donegal News*, 23 March 1977.

349 'Brothers charged with painting wall slogans', *Donegal Democrat*, 13 October 1978; 'Slogans painted on bridge', *Anglo Celt*, 9 September 1977.

350 'Unemployed electrician gaoled for painting slogans', *The Northern Standard*, 16 February 1979; 'Three months for painting slogans', 26 January 1979.

351 'Northerners get six months for assault on Garda', *Dundalk Democrat*, 21 February 1976.

352 Peter Pringle, *About Time: Surviving Ireland's Death Row* (Dublin: The History Press, 2012), p. 126.

353 McNulty, *Exiled*, p. 219.

354 'Churchyard riot. 11 go to criminal court', *The Northern Standard*, 28 May 1976.

355 'Councillors protest', *Dundalk Democrat*, 3 January 1976.

356 'Dead Volunteer honoured', *An Phoblacht*, 30 July 1976.

357 'Two jail terms for attempted murder of Scotland yard official', *The Irish Times*, 30 July 1976.

358 'Bishop condemns attack on Cavan wedding party', *The Irish Times*, 24 May 1976.

359 'Brutalised by Special Branch', *An Phoblacht*, 25 June 1976; 'Cavan allegations refuted', *Anglo Celt*, 4 March 1977; 'What stirred the conscience of the Judge', *An Phoblacht*, 9 July 1976.

360 'Shotgun wrecks society wedding', *Hibernia*, 31 August 1978; 'Evidence on Trim shooting builds up', *The Irish Times*, 29 August 1978.

361 'Gaoled for 6 months at Monaghan Garda station', *Anglo Celt*, 22 June 1979.

362 'University of crime and subversion', *Irish Independent*, 22 July 1977.

363 NA (UK) CJ4/2999, 'Examples of Cooperation with Garda', circa September 1979.

364 NA (IRL) 2010/53/929, 'Criminal Law Jurisdiction Act', DFA, October 1980.

365 Kerrigan, *Hard Cases*, p. 6.

366 NA (IRL) 2010/53/929, 'Criminal Law Jurisdiction Act', DFA, October 1980.

367 NA (UK) FCO 87/539, 'Meeting between Secretary of State and Fianna Fáil leadership', 29 May 1976.

368 NA (UK) FCO 87/539, 'Meeting between Secretary of State and Patrick Cooney and Garret Fitzgerald', 28 May 1976.

369 NA (UK) CJ4/3303, 'Security Coordinating committee meeting', 29 September 1977.

370 NA (IRL) 2010/19/1687, 'Border incident reports: the 2% figure and after', circa 1978.

371 NA (UK) CJ4/2744, 'PVCP-Londonderry enclave', 1978.

372 Ibid.

373 'Army watched policeman's killers cross border', *The Irish Times*, 12 July 1977.

374 Examples include: 'Bus Passengers ordeal', *Donegal Democrat*, 22 February 1976; 'Hijacking of Donegal bus', *Donegal People*, 21 February 1976; 'Car Hijacked on Clones–Cavan Road', *The Northern Standard*, 27 February 1976; 'Car hijacked in Castleshane', *The Northern Standard*, 2 April 1976.

375 'Dead man found with throat cut', *The Irish Times*, 23 February 1976.

376 'Two die in blasts three shot dead', *The Irish Times*, 26 January 1976.

377 'Woman dies in hijack crash', *The Irish Times*, 22 December 1976.

378 'Clones man killed near Belfast', *Anglo Celt*, 1 April 1977.

379 'Dublin woman dies as bomb explodes in Enterprise train', *The Irish Times*, 13 October 1978.

380 NA (UK) CJ4/2244, 'Border Security: the Republics case', 8 September 1978.

381 NA (UK) FCO 87/121, 'Cross Border Incidents', in 'Border', 1972.

382 NA (IRL) 2010/19/1687, 'Border Incidents the 2% figure and after'.

383 'Cooney puts challenge out to clergy', *The Irish Times*, 15 January 1977.

384 Patrick McEntee, *The Commission of Investigation into Dublin and Monaghan Bombings Final Report* (2007), p. 110, http://www.dublinmonaghanbombings.org/CommissionOfInvestigationFinalReport.pdf.

385 NA (UK) CJ4/2751, 'Draft brief on Relations with Irish Republic', 17 April 1979.

386 NA (UK) FCO 87/934, 'Contacts and Communication with the South', 3 September 1979.

387 NA (UK) CJ 4/2999, 'RUC/Garda Cooperation: the chief Constable's four points', 1979.

388 NA (UK) CJ4/2245, 'Cross Border security cooperation', PJ Goulden, British embassy, 19 September 1978.

Chapter 6

1 Ministry of Defence, *Operation Banner* (2006), p. 28, http://www.vilaweb.cat/media/attach/vwedts/docs/op_banner_analysis_released.pdf.

2   David McKittrick et al., *Lost Lives* (London: Mainstream Publishing, 1999), pp. 793–8.

3   Peter Smithwick, *Report of the Tribunal of Inquiry into Suggestions that Members of An Garda Síochána or Other Employees of the State Colluded in the Fatal Shootings of RUC Chief Superintendent Harry Breen and RUC Superintendent Robert Buchanan on the 20th March 1989* (2013), p. 330, http://static.rasset.ie/documents/news/smithwick-tribunal-final.pdf.

4   Ibid., p. 517.

5   John Walsh, *Patrick Hillery: The Official Biography* (Dublin: New Island, 2008), p. 247.

6   'O'Malley supported in tough line against IRA', *The Irish Times*, 21 February 1972.

7   'Protests likely over border battle', *Irish Press*, 28 January 1972.

8   Craig, *Crisis of Confidence*, p. 186.

9   Ibid., p. 188.

10 Buzan, *People, States and Fear*, p. 115.

11 Ibid., p. 131.

12 Brady, *The Guarding of Ireland*, p. 161.

13 Craig, *Crisis of Confidence*, p. 164, interview with Dermot Nally, Department of Taoiseach.

14 NA (UK) CJ4/2247, 'Letter from Paul Burton in Northern Ireland Office to John Goulden in British Embassy', 15 December 1977.

15 Patterson, *Ireland's Violent Frontier*, p. 193.

16 NA (UK) FCO 87/603, 'Republic of Ireland annual review for 1976', circa December 1976; NA (UK) CJ4/810, Kenneth Thom, 'Security Cooperation', in 'Border Security', 15 August 1974; NA (UK) FCO 87/42, 'Telegram no 306', 28 April 1972.

17 O'Halpin, *Defending Ireland*, p. 332.

18 'The GUBU Diary: Inside the grotesque, unbelievable, bizarre, unprecedented events of 1982', *The Irish Times*, 29 September 2012; 'GUBU response: My memory of events in 1982 gives a very different picture', *The Irish Times*, 10 October 2012.

19 Conway, *Policing Twentieth Century Ireland*, p. 102.

20 Ibid., p. 102.

21 Ibid., p. 110.

22 Ibid., p. 133.

23 Craig, *Crisis of Confidence*, p. 186.

24 'Orders from the Captain', *The Irish Times*, 4 March 1977.

25 http://www.borderroadmemories.com/.

26 Harte, *Young Tigers and Mongrel Foxes*, p. 204.

27 'Warning by Cooney to IRA on border attacks', *The Irish Times*, 24 April 1974.

28 Thomas McNulty, *Exiled: 40 Years an Exile* (Dublin: O'Brien Press, 2013), p. 125.

29 O'Halpin, *Defending Ireland*, p. 326.

30 McNulty, *Exiled*, p. 78.

31 O'Halpin, *Defending Ireland*, p. 333.

32 Conway, *Southside Provisional*, p. 178.

Bibliography

Archives

Military Archives of Ireland (Military Archives Dublin).
National Archives of Ireland (NA IRL).
National Archives of UK (NA UK).

Official Publications

Final Report on the Report of the Independent Commission of Inquiry into the Bombing of Kay's Tavern, Dundalk, Joint Committee on Justice, Equality, Defence and Women's Rights, Houses of the Oireachtas (November 2006).

Interim Report on the Report of the Independent Commission of Inquiry into the Dublin and Monaghan Bombings of 1974, Joint Committee on Justice, Equality, Defence and Women's Rights, Houses of the Oireachtas (December 2003).

Final Report on the Report of the Independent Commission of Inquiry into the Dublin Bombings of 1972 and 1973, Joint Committee on Justice, Equality, Defence and Women's Rights, Houses of the Oireachtas (February 2005).

Final Report on the Report of the Independent Commission of Inquiry into the Murder of Seamus Ludlow, Joint Committee on Justice, Equality, Defence and Women's Rights, Houses of the Oireachtas (March 2006).

The McEntee Commission Report into Dublin and Monaghan Bombings (2007).

Minutes of Public Accounts Committee Hearing of Arms Trial.

Official reports of Dáil Debates, 1968–78.

Public Hearings by Dáil Subcommittee on the Barron Report (2005).

Report of the Tribunal of Inquiry into Suggestions that Members of An Garda Síochána or Other Employees of the State Colluded in the Fatal Shootings of RUC Chief Superintendent Harry Breen and RUC Superintendent Robert Buchanan on the 20th March 1989 (2013).

Newspapers and Periodicals

An Phoblacht
Anglo Celt
Belfast Telegraph
Belfast Newsletter

Evening Herald
Garda Review
Hibernia
Magill
Meath Chronicle
Donegal News & Derry People
Dundalk Democrat
The Guardian
Irish Independent
Irish Press
The Irish Times
Leitrim Observer
The Northern Standard
The Sligo Champion
Sunday World
The Telegraph
United Irishman
Cedar Lounge Revolution [blog]

Television Programmes/Documentaries/Radio/Oral Histories

Aftermath Project, Interview with Jimmy Fox, nephew of Seamus Ludlow, 2004, http://aftermath-ireland.com/portfolio/jimmy-fox-interview/.
Green & Blue, oral history project, http://www.green-and-blue.org/stories/.
If Lynch Had Invaded, RTÉ, http://www.rte.ie/tv/programmes/if_lynch_had_invaded.html.
Loughgall Martyrs, parts 1 and 3, Youtube [video series].
Rumours from Monaghan, RTÉ Radio Documentary.
Seamus McElwaine IRA Freedom Fighter, YouTube, https://www.youtube.com/watch?v=NY-GCyOr-Ok.

Books and Journal Articles

Ahern, Bertie, *Bertie Ahern: The Autobiography* (London: Cornerstone, 2009).
Allen, Gregory, *The Garda Síochána: Policing Independent Ireland 1922–82* (Dublin: Gill and Macmillan, 1999).
Alonso, Rogelio, *The IRA and Armed Struggle* (London: Routledge, 2007).
Anderson, Malcom and Eberhard Bort, *The Irish Border: History, Politics, Culture* (Liverpool: Liverpool University, 1999).
Arthur, Paul, *Special Relationships: Britain, Ireland and the Northern Ireland Problem* (Belfast: Blackstaff, 2000).
Barker, Alan, *Shadows: Inside Northern Ireland's Special Branch* (London: Mainstream, 2004).

Baylis, John and Steve Smith, *The Globalization of World Politics* (Oxford: Oxford University Press, 2005).

Bew, John, Martyn Frampton and Inigo Gurruchaga, *Talking to Terrorists: Making Peace in Northern Ireland and the Basque Country* (London: Hurst and Company, 2009).

Bishop, Patrick and Eamonn Mallie, *The Provisional IRA* (London: Corgi, 1987).

Boland, Kevin, *We Won't Stand Idly By* (Dublin: Kelly Kane, 1973).

Bowyer Bell, J., *In Dubious Battle: The Dublin and Monaghan Bombings 1972–74* (Dublin: Poolbeg, 1996).

Boyne, Sean, *Gunrunners: The Covert Arms Trail to Ireland* (Dublin: O'Brien Press, 2006).

Bradley, Anthony, *Requiem for a Spy: The Killing of Robert Nairac* (Dublin: Irish American Book Company, 1993).

Brady, Conor, *Guardians of the Peace* (Dublin: Prenderville, 2000).

— *The Guarding of Ireland: The Garda Síochána and the Irish State 1960–2014* (Dublin: Gill and Macmillan, 2014).

Burbridge, Nick and Fred Holroyd, *War without Honour* (Hull: Medium, 1989).

Buzan, Barry, *People, States and Fear: An Agenda for International Security Studies in the Post-Cold War Era* (Colchester: ECPR Classics, 2009).

Buzan, Barry, Ole Waever and Jaap de Wilde, *Security: A New Framework for Analysis* (London: Lynne Riennar, 1998).

Cadwallader, Anne, *Lethal Allies: British Collusion in Ireland* (Mercier: Cork, 2013).

Clarke, George, *Border Crossing: True Stories of the RUC Special Branch, the Garda Special Branch and IRA Moles* (Dublin: Gill and Macmillan, 2009).

Clarke, Liam and Kathryn Johnston, *Martin McGuinness: From Guns to Government* (London: Mainstream Publishing, 2001).

Coakley, John and Liam O'Dowd, *The Irish Border and North–South Co-Operation: An Overview* (Dublin: Irish Academic Press, 2005).

Conway, Kieran, *Southside Provisional: From Freedom Fighter to Four Courts* (Dublin: Orpen Press, 2014).

Conway, Vicky, *The Blue Wall of Silence: The Morris Tribunal and Police Accountability in Ireland* (Dublin: Irish Academic Press, 2010).

— *Policing Twentieth Century Ireland: A History of An Garda Síochána* (London: Routledge, 2014).

Courtney, John, *It Was Murder: Murders and Kidnapping in Ireland* (Dublin: Blackwater, 1996).

Craig, Anthony, *Crisis of Confidence: Anglo-Irish Relations in the Early Troubles 1966–1974* (Dublin: Irish Academic Press, 2010).

Crawford, Colin, *Inside the UDA: Volunteers and Violence* (London: Pluto, 2003).

Cruise O'Brien, Conor, *States of Ireland* (London: Panther, 1972).

Delaney, Eamonn, *An Accidental Diplomat: My Years in the Irish Foreign Service* (Dublin: New Island Books, 2001).

Devlin, Paddy, *Straight Left: An Autobiography* (Belfast: Blackstaff, 1993).

Dillon, Martin, *The Dirty War* (London: Hutchinson, 1990).

Doyle, Colman, *People at War* (Dublin: F.D.R. Teoranta, 1975).

Drogheda Community Forum, *Dispelling the Myths* (Drogheda: Drogheda Community Forum, 2004).

Duggan, John, *The Irish Army* (Dublin: Gill and Macmillan, 1991).

Dunlop, Frank, *Yes, Taoiseach: Irish Politics from Behind Closed Doors* (Dublin: Penguin, 2004).

Dunne, Derek and Gene Kerrigan, *Round Up the Usual Suspects* (Dublin: Magill, 1984).

English, Richard, *Armed Struggle: A History of the IRA* (London: Pan, 2003).

— *Irish Freedom: The History of Nationalism in Ireland* (London: Pan Macmillan, 2006).

Fanning, Ronan, 'Playing It Cool: The response of the British and Irish government to the crisis in NI 1968–69' in *Irish Studies in International Affairs*, vol. 12 (2001).

Farrell, Michael, *Sheltering the Fugitive? The Extradition of Irish Political Offenders* (Dublin: Mercier, 1985).

Faulkner, Pádraig, *As I Saw It* (Dublin: Wolfhound, 2005).

Ferriter, Diarmaid, *Ambiguous Republic: Ireland in the 1970s* (London: Profile Books, 2012).

FitzGerald, Garret, 'The 1974–75 Threat of a British withdrawal from Northern Ireland' in *Irish Studies in International Affairs*, vol. 17 (2006).

FitzGerald, Garret, *All in a Life: An Autobiography* (London: Gill and Macmillan, 1991).

Guelke Adrian, *Northern Ireland: The International Perspective* (Dublin: Palgrave, 1988).

Hanley, Brian, '"I ran away"? The I.R.A. and 1969: the evolution of a myth' in *Irish Historical Studies*, November 2013.

— 'Internment 1970', *The Cedar Lounge Revolution*, website (2015).

— 'Then they started all this killing: attitudes to the IRA in the Irish Republic since 1969' in *Irish Historical Studies*, vol. 38, issue 151 (May 2013).

Hanley, Brian and Scott Millar, *The Lost Revolution: The Story of the Official IRA and Workers Party* (Dublin: Penguin, 2009).

Harris, Clodagh, 'Anglo-Irish Elite Co-operation and the Peace Process: The impact of EEC/EU' in *Irish Studies in International Affairs*, vol. 12 (2001).

Harte, Paddy, *Young Tigers and Mongrel Foxes: A Life in Politics* (Dublin: O'Brien Press, 2005).

Hogan, Gerard and Clive Walker, *Political Violence and the Law in Ireland* (Manchester: Manchester University Press, 1989).

Holland, Jack and Susan Phoenix, *Phoenix: Policing the Shadows* (London: Hodder and Stoughton, 1997).

Kelly, James, *Orders for the Captain* (Dublin: Kelly Kane, 1971).

— *Thimbleriggers: The Dublin Arms Trials of 1970* (Dublin: James Kelly, 1999).

Kennedy, Michael, *Divisions and Consensus: The Politics of Cross-Border Relations in Ireland 1925–1969* (Dublin: IPA, 2000).

Keogh, Dermot, *Jack Lynch: A Biography* (Dublin: Gill and Macmillan, 2008).

Kerrigan, Gene, *Hard Cases: True Stories of Irish Crime* (Dublin: Gill and Macmillan, 1996).

Lavery, Tosh, *Tosh: An Amazing True Story of Life, Death, Danger and Drama in the Garda Sub-Aqua Unit* (Dublin: Penguin, 2015).

Lee, Joe, *Ireland 1912–85: Politics and Society* (Cambridge: Cambridge University Press, 1989).

Mac Ginty, Roger, 'Almost Like Talking Dirty: Irish Security Policy in Post-Cold War Europe', in *Irish Studies in International Affairs*, vol. 6 (1995).

Mac Gréil, Mícheál, *Prejudice and Tolerance in Ireland: Based on a Survey of Intergroup Attitudes of Dublin Adults and Other Sources* (Dublin: Research Section, College of Industrial Relations, 1977).

McArdle, Patsy, *The Secret War: An Account of the Sinister Activities along the Border involving Gardaí, RUC, British Army and the SAS* (Dublin: Mercier, 1984).

McCabe, Eugene, *Christ in the Fields* (London: Minerva, 1993).

McCarthy, Kieran, *Republican Cobh and East Cork Volunteers since 1913* (Dublin: Nonsuch Publishing, 2008).

McGuire, Charles, 'Defenders of the state: the Irish Labour Party, coalitionism and revisionism, 1969–77', in *Irish Studies Review* (2015), DOI: 10.1080/09670882.2015.1054123.

McGuire, Maria, *To Take Up Arms: My Year with the IRA Provisionals* (New York: Viking, 1973).

McKittrick, David, Chris Thornton and Seamus Kelters, *Lost Lives: The Stories of Men, Women and Children Who Died as a Result of the Northern Ireland Troubles* (London: Mainstream Publishing, 1999).

McNiffe, Liam, *A History of the Garda Síochána: A Social History of the Force 1922–52, with an Overview of the Years 1952–1997* (Dublin: Wolfhound, 1997).

McNulty, Thomas, *Exiled: 40 Years an Exile* (Dublin: TMN Publications, 2013).

MacStíofáin, Seán, *Revolutionary in Ireland* (Edinburgh: Cremonesi, 1975).

McVeigh, Joe, *Taking a Stand: Memoir of an Irish Priest* (Dublin: Mercier, 2008).

Maguire, John, *IRA Internments and the Irish Government: Subversives and the State 1939–1962* (Dublin: Irish Academic Press, 2008).

Maloney, Ed, *A Secret History of the IRA* (London: WW Norton, 2002).

— *Voices from the Grave: Two Men's War in Ireland* (London: Public Affairs, 2010).

Mansergh, Martin, 'The Background to the Irish Peace Process' in A *Farewell to Arms? Beyond the Good Friday Agreement*, edited by Michael Cox, Adrian Guelke and Fiona Stephen (Manchester: Manchester University Press, 2006).

Ministry of Defence (UK), *Operation Banner: An Analysis of Military Operations in Northern Ireland* (London: Minstry of Defence, 2006).

Mullan, Don, *The Dublin and Monaghan Bombings: The Truth, the Questions and the Victims' Stories* (Dublin: Wolfhound, 2000).

Mulqueen, Michael, *Re-evaluating Irish National Security: Affordable Threats* (Manchester: Manchester University Press, 2009).

Murray, Raymond, *The SAS in Ireland* (Dublin: Irish American Book Company, 1990).

Ó Beacháin, Donnacha, *Destiny of the Soldiers: Fianna Fáil, Irish Republicanism and the IRA 1926–1973* (Dublin: Gill and Macmillan, 2010).

O'Brien, Justin, *The Arms Trial* (Dublin: Newleaf, 2000).

O'Callaghan, Sean, *The Informer* (London: Corgi, 1999).

Ó Cuinneaghain, Míchéal, *Monaghan, County of Intrigue: An Insight into the Political, Legal, and Religious Intrigues in this Border Area during the Period 1968–1979* (Monaghan: publisher unknown, 1979).

O'Donnell, Catherine, *Fianna Fáil, Irish Republicanism and the Northern Ireland Troubles 1968–2005* (Dublin: Irish Academic Press, 2007).

O'Donnell, Ruan, *Special Category: The IRA in English Prisons 1968–1978* (Dublin: Irish Academic Press, 2012).

O'Dowd, Liam and James Corrigan, 'Securing the Irish Border in a Europe without Frontier', in *Borders, Nations and States: Frontiers of Sovereignty in the New Europe*, edited by Liam O'Dowd and Thomas M. Wilson (Aldershot, Hants, England: Avebury, 2006).

O'Duffy, Brendan, *British–Irish Relations and Northern Ireland: From Violent Politics to Conflict Regulation* (Dublin: Irish Academic Press, 2007).

O'Halpin, Eunan *Defending Ireland: The Irish State and its Enemies Since 1922* (Oxford: Oxford University Press, 1999).

— '"A Greek Authoritarian phase"? The Irish Army and the Irish Crisis 1969–1970', in *Irish Political Studies*, vol. 23, no. 4, December 2008.

Official Sinn Féin Publication *Fianna Fáil and the IRA* (Dublin: Sinn Féin, 1972).

O'Malley, Desmond, *Conduct Unbecoming: A Memoir* (Dublin: Gill and Macmillan, 2014).

O'Sullivan, Michael P., *Patriot Graves: Resistance in Ireland* (Chicago: Follet, 1972).

Parker, John, *Secret Hero: The Life and Mysterious Death of Captain Robert Nairac* (London: John Blake, 2004).

Parker, Tom, 'The Fateful Triangle: Identity Politics, Security Policy and Anglo-Irish Relation', in *National Counter Terrorism Strategies*, edited by Robert Orttung and Andrey Makarychev (Amsterdam: IOS Press, 2006).

Patterson, Henry, *Ireland's Violent Frontier: The Border and Anglo-Irish Relations During the Troubles* (London: Palgrave, 2013).

— *The Politics of Illusion: A Political History of the IRA* (London: Serif, 1989).

— 'Sectarianism Revisited: The Provisional IRA campaign in a border region of Northern Ireland', *Terrorism and Political Violence*, vol. 22, no. 3 (2010).

— 'War of National Liberation or Ethnic Cleansing: IRA Violence in Fermanagh During the Troubles', *Terror: From Tyrannicide to Terrorism*, eds Brett Bowden, and Michael T. Davis (Brisbane, Australia: University of Queensland Press, 2008), pp. 230–42.

Pobal Research Report, *All Over the Place: People Displaced to and from the Southern Border Counties as a Result of the Conflict 1969–1994* (Dublin: Pobal, 2005).

Pringle, Peter, *About Time: Surviving Ireland's Death Row* (Dublin: The History Press, 2012).

Reynolds, Albert, *Albert Reynolds: My Autobiography* (London: Transworld Ireland, 2009).

Ruane, Joseph and Jennifer Todd, *The dynamics of conflict in Northern Ireland Power, conflict and emancipation* (Cambridge: Cambridge University Press, 1996).

Savage, Robert, *A Loss of Innocence? Television and Irish Society 1960–72* (Manchester University Press: Manchester, 2015).

Smith, M.L.R., *Fighting for Ireland? The Military Strategy of the Irish Republican Movement* (London: Routledge, 1995).

— 'The Intellectual Internment of a Conflict: The Forgotten War in Northern Ireland', in *International Affairs*, vol. 1, issue 75 (1999).

Tiernan, Joe, *The Dublin and Monaghan Bombings and the Murder Triangle* (Dublin: Joe Tiernan, 2002).

Walsh, Dick, *Des O'Malley: A Political Profile* (Kerry: Brandon, 1986).

Walsh, John, *Patrick Hillery: The Official Biography* (Dublin: New Island, 2008).

Walsh, Liz, *The Final Beat: Gardaí Killed in the Line of Duty* (Dublin: Gill and Macmillan, 2001).

Walsh, Maurice, *G2: In Defence of Ireland: Irish Military Intelligence 1918–45* (Cork: Collins, 2010).

Walshe, Dermot J., *The Irish Police* (Dublin: Roundhall, 1998).

Index